THE BAIZHANG ZEN
MONASTIC REGULATIONS

BDK English Tripiṭaka Series

THE BAIZHANG ZEN MONASTIC REGULATIONS

(Taishō Volume 48, Number 2025)

Translated from the Chinese

by

Shohei Ichimura

Numata Center
for Buddhist Translation and Research
2006

First Printing, 2006
ISBN: 1-886439-25-7
Extended ISBN: 978-1-886439-25-2
Library of Congress Catalog Card Number: 2006921497

Published by
Numata Center for Buddhist Translation and Research
2620 Warring Street
Berkeley, California 94704

Printed in the United States of America

A Message on the Publication of the English Tripiṭaka

The Buddhist canon is said to contain eighty-four thousand different teachings. I believe that this is because the Buddha's basic approach was to prescribe a different treatment for every spiritual ailment, much as a doctor prescribes a different medicine for every medical ailment. Thus his teachings were always appropriate for the particular suffering individual and for the time at which the teaching was given, and over the ages not one of his prescriptions has failed to relieve the suffering to which it was addressed.

Ever since the Buddha's Great Demise over twenty-five hundred years ago, his message of wisdom and compassion has spread throughout the world. Yet no one has ever attempted to translate the entire Buddhist canon into English throughout the history of Japan. It is my greatest wish to see this done and to make the translations available to the many English-speaking people who have never had the opportunity to learn about the Buddha's teachings.

Of course, it would be impossible to translate all of the Buddha's eighty-four thousand teachings in a few years. I have, therefore, had one hundred thirty-nine of the scriptural texts in the prodigious Taishō edition of the Chinese Buddhist canon selected for inclusion in the First Series of this translation project.

It is in the nature of this undertaking that the results are bound to be criticized. Nonetheless, I am convinced that unless someone takes it upon himself or herself to initiate this project, it will never be done. At the same time, I hope that an improved, revised edition will appear in the future.

It is most gratifying that, thanks to the efforts of more than a hundred Buddhist scholars from the East and the West, this monumental project has finally gotten off the ground. May the rays of the Wisdom of the Compassionate One reach each and every person in the world.

NUMATA Yehan
Founder of the English
Tripiṭaka Project

August 7, 1991

Editorial Foreword

In January 1982, Dr. NUMATA Yehan, the founder of the Bukkyō Dendō Kyōkai (Society for the Promotion of Buddhism), decided to begin the monumental task of translating the complete Taishō edition of the Chinese Tripiṭaka (Buddhist canon) into the English language. Under his leadership, a special preparatory committee was organized in April 1982. By July of the same year, the Translation Committee of the English Tripiṭaka was officially convened.

The initial Committee consisted of the following members: (late) HANAYAMA Shōyū (Chairperson), (late) BANDŌ Shōjun, ISHIGAMI Zennō, (late) KAMATA Shigeo, KANAOKA Shūyū, MAYEDA Sengaku, NARA Yasuaki, (late) SAYEKI Shinkō, (late) SHIOIRI Ryōtatsu, TAMARU Noriyoshi, (late) TAMURA Kwansei, URYŪZU Ryūshin, and YUYAMA Akira. Assistant members of the Committee were as follows: KANAZAWA Atsushi, WATANABE Shōgo, Rolf Giebel of New Zealand, and Rudy Smet of Belgium.

After holding planning meetings on a monthly basis, the Committee selected one hundred thirty-nine texts for the First Series of translations, an estimated one hundred printed volumes in all. The texts selected are not necessarily limited to those originally written in India but also include works written or composed in China and Japan. While the publication of the First Series proceeds, the texts for the Second Series will be selected from among the remaining works; this process will continue until all the texts, in Japanese as well as in Chinese, have been published.

Frankly speaking, it will take perhaps one hundred years or more to accomplish the English translation of the complete Chinese and Japanese texts, for they consist of thousands of works. Nevertheless, as Dr. NUMATA wished, it is the sincere hope of the Committee that this project will continue unto completion, even after all its present members have passed away.

It must be mentioned here that the final object of this project is not academic fulfillment but the transmission of the teaching of the Buddha to the whole world in order to create harmony and peace among humankind. To that end, the translators have been asked to minimize the use of explanatory notes of the kind that are indispensable in academic texts, so that the attention of general readers will not be unduly distracted from the primary text. Also, a glossary of selected terms is appended to aid in understanding the text.

To my great regret, however, Dr. NUMATA passed away on May 5, 1994, at the age of ninety-seven, entrusting his son, Mr. NUMATA Toshihide, with the continuation and completion of the Translation Project. The Committee also lost its able and devoted Chairperson, Professor HANAYAMA Shōyū, on June 16, 1995, at the age of sixty-three. After these severe blows, the Committee elected me, Vice President of Musashino Women's College, to be the Chair in October 1995. The Committee has renewed its determination to carry out the noble intention of Dr. NUMATA, under the leadership of Mr. NUMATA Toshihide.

The present members of the Committee are MAYEDA Sengaku (Chairperson), ISHIGAMI Zennō, ICHISHIMA Shōshin, KANAOKA Shūyū, NARA Yasuaki, TAMARU Noriyoshi, Kenneth K. Tanaka, URYŪZU Ryūshin, YUYAMA Akira, WATANABE Shōgo, and assistant member YONEZAWA Yoshiyasu.

The Numata Center for Buddhist Translation and Research was established in November 1984, in Berkeley, California, U.S.A., to assist in the publication of the BDK English Tripiṭaka First Series. The Publication Committee was organized at the Numata Center in December 1991. Since then the publication of all the volumes has been and will continue to be conducted under the supervision of this Committee in close cooperation with the Editorial Committee in Tokyo.

MAYEDA Sengaku
Chairperson
Editorial Committee of
the BDK English Tripiṭaka

Publisher's Foreword

On behalf of the members of the Publication Committee, I am happy to present this volume as the latest contribution to the BDK English Tripiṭaka Series. The Publication Committee members have worked to ensure that each volume in the series has gone through a rigorous succession of editorial and bookmaking efforts.

The initial translation and editing of the Buddhist scriptures found in this and other BDK English Tripiṭaka volumes are performed under the direction of the Editorial Committee in Tokyo, Japan. Both the Editorial Committee in Tokyo and the Publication Committee, headquartered in Berkeley, California, are dedicated to the production of clear, readable English texts of the Buddhist canon. In doing so, the members of both committees and associated staff work to honor the deep faith, spirit, and concern of the late Reverend Dr. Yehan Numata, who founded the BDK English Tripiṭaka Series in order to disseminate the Buddhist teachings throughout the world.

The long-term goal of our project is the translation and publication of the texts in the one hundred-volume Taishō edition of the Chinese Buddhist canon, along with a few influential extracanonical Japanese Buddhist texts. The list of texts selected for the First Series of this translation project may be found at the end of each volume in the series.

As Chair of the Publication Committee, I am deeply honored to serve in the post formerly held by the late Dr. Philip B. Yampolsky, who was so good to me during his lifetime; the esteemed Dr. Kenneth K. Inada, who has had such a great impact on Buddhist studies in the United States; and the beloved late Dr. Francis H. Cook, a dear friend and colleague.

In conclusion, I wish to thank the members of the Publication Committee for the extraordinary efforts they have undertaken in the course of preparing this volume for publication: Senior Editor Marianne Dresser, Hudaya Kandahjaya, Eisho Nasu, Reverend Kiyoshi Yamashita, and Reverend Brian Nagata, President of the Numata Center for Buddhist Translation and Research.

John R. McRae
Chairperson
Publication Committee

Contents

Contents

Translator's Introduction

The Nature and Function of the
Zen Monastic Regulations

To function efficiently, people gathered together with a common goal, whether secular or religious, must have a set of rules and disciplines that regulate daily life and the proceedings of the community as a whole. The community of Chan (Zen) practitioners that began to evolve in mid–sixth-century China gradually formalized its own definitive set of monastic regulations during the eighth century. The original Zen monastic regulations, referred to throughout this text as the *Ancient Regulations,* are known to have been innovated by Zen Master Baizhang Huaihai (720–814 C.E.).

Baizhang was the third holder of the Zen lineage extending from the Sixth Patriarch Huineng (638–713), and thus he was the eighth patriarchal descendant of the legendary Dhyāna Master Bodhidharma (Puti Damo). Bodhidharma is believed to have first transmitted the Zen tradition to China during the first half of the sixth century. The seven or eight generations of Zen patriarchs preceding Baizhang lived and practiced in the temples of other schools, such as the Vinaya school, as they had no established monastic institution of their own. For this reason, the *Baizhang Zen Monastic Regulations* served as the institutional framework that clearly defined the community of Zen practitioners as an independent school of Buddhism.

"*Qinggui,*" rendered as "monastic regulations" in this translation, is an abbreviation of "*qingjinghaizhongqinggui,*" meaning "the regulations of the pure oceanlike community." These monastic regulations bear the fundamental features of the Vinaya, the monastic rules and disciplines of the early Buddhist community (sangha) in India. The earliest Buddhist sangha spontaneously evolved around

Śākyamuni Buddha as a professional brotherhood of celibate mendicants who were exclusively engaged in seeking religious liberation. Upon conversion, members of the Buddhist sangha committed themselves by taking an oath to a set of precepts (*śīla*) conferred by the Buddha, and voluntarily subjected themselves to the body of Vinaya rules and disciplines held in common by the community.

To be precise, *śīla* (*jie*) and *vinaya* (*lü*) are not to be taken as synonymous. The *śīla*s are fundamentally moral principles, the substance of spirituality immanent in all human beings. The *vinaya*s, on the other hand, are formal regulatory codes of conduct, relating only to the community of Buddhist disciples and ordained monastics. Understood metaphorically, *vinaya* is like the raft that one may use to cross the river but which must be left behind on reaching the other shore. In Chinese Buddhist usage, however, these terms are almost always compounded as *jielü*, which accordingly gives two distinct meanings to the Zen monastic regulations formalized by Baizhang.

The Chinese monastic regulations were thus in part founded on morality and in part comprised of moral commandments. In their evolution, the technical and legalistic nature of the Vinaya gave way to greater moral and spiritual significance. Hence, in the merging of substance and form, the original *Baizhang Zen Monastic Regulations* represented a viable Chinese adaptation of the Indian Buddhist formalism of the Vinaya.

The Textual Origin of the
Baizhang Zen Monastic Regulations

The original version of the *Baizhang Zen Monastic Regulations* (*Baizhangqinggui*), referred to throughout this text as the *Ancient Regulations,* is known only through a limited number of passages quoted in works of later periods. For instance, Yangyi (974–1020), a Zen layman, quoted the original in his "Preface to the Original Monastic Regulations," which is part of the *Jingde Era Records of the Transmission of the Flame of Dharma (Jingdechuandenglü,* thirty fascicles, 1004), attributed to Yongan Daoyuan.

By the time of the *Monastic Regulations of the Zen Garden* (*Chanyuanqinggui*), more commonly known as the *Chongning Monastic Regulations,* compiled by Zhanglu Zongze in 1103, near the end of the Northern Song dynasty (960–1126), the original text of the *Baizhang Zen Monastic Regulations* is assumed to have been totally lost. The *Chongning Monastic Regulations* is therefore the only extant early text available to us today. Although its contents are believed to be far from identical to Baizhang's original *Ancient Regulations,* this text has been upheld in the tradition as the most authentic standard of the original spirit.

During the Southern Song dynasty (1127–1280) and the period of Mongol invasion and rule during the Yuan dynasty (1260–1368), the Chinese felt their world to be in a time of degeneration. As a result, perhaps, of this unstable and tumultuous period, a series of attempts at reform were made to compile an authentic edition of Zen monastic regulations. During this time the following texts came into existence:

1. *Daily Monastic Regulations for Entering the Zen Community* (*Ruzhongzhiyongqinggui*), 1209, by Chongshou.

2. *Monastic Regulations Indispensable for Entering the Zen Community* (*Ruzhongxujiqinggui*), 1263, author unknown.

3. *Collected Essentials of the Revised Zen Monastic Regulations* (*Conglinjiaotingqingguizongyao*), 1274, by Weimian (also known as the *Xianshun Regulations* after the name of the era).

4. *Zen Monastic Regulations Ready for Use* (*Chanlinbeiyunqinggui*), 1311, by Yixian (also known as the *Zhida Regulations* after the name of the era).

5. *Huanzhuan Monastic Regulations,* 1317, by Mingben.

It is not unreasonable to assume that the revised *Baizhang Zen Monastic Regulations* came into existence as the culmination of these reform attempts.

In a parallel to this trend in China, a similar movement in Japan produced many works in succession, as follows:

1. *Eihei Zen Monastic Regulations* (*Eiheishingi*), 1237–1249, by Eihei Dōgen, founder of the Japanese Sōtō school of Zen.

2. *Enichisan Monastic Regulations* (*Tōfukujishingi*), 1318, attributed to Enni (1202–1280), known as the national master Shōichi.

3. *Keizan Monastic Regulations* (*Keizanshingi*), 1324, by Jōkin Keizan (1268–1325), fourth patriarchal descendant of Eihei Dōgen.

4. *Daikan Monastic Regulations* (*Dajianqinggui*), 1332, attributed to Qingzhuo Zhengdeng (1274–1339) of the Yanyi sect of the Linji (Rinzai) school, who emigrated from China to Japan.

5. *Ōbaku Monastic Regulations* (*Huangpiqinggui*), 1654, attributed to Yinyuan Longqi (1592–1673), also a Chinese emigrant to Japan.

The *Enichisan, Keizan,* and *Daikan Monastic Regulations,* in particular, were works contemporary to the *Baizchang Zen Monastic Regulations* (*Revised under the Yuan Imperial Edict*), and interactions between the texts are well attested to.

At the time of these reform movements, Dongyang Dehui was the abbot of the monastic temple, Master Sage of Great Wisdom and Long Life (Dazhishoushengchansi), founded by Baizhang Huaihai himself more than five centuries earlier. In his memorialization in 1333, Dehui proposed to the Yuan imperial court his intention to compile a comprehensive text of Zen monastic regulations. He requested the court to grant authorization for the publication of the completed text and sanction its effective enforcement in all Zen monastic temples in the land. The primary goal Dehui set forth in his petition was the creation of a unified code of monastic regulations, so that all hitherto unreconciled discrepancies among existing practices could be settled once and for all. The court appointed Dehui to lead the project, and additionally appointed Xiaowen Dasu, then abbot of the Great Dragons Flying to Assemble for Celebration Temple (Dailongxiangjiqingsi), to head the editorial work.

Among the many available sources, Dehui chose as his major sources for this compilation three works: Zongze's *Chongning Monastic Regulations,* Weimian's *Xianshun Regulations,* and Yixian's *Zhida Regulations.* In his epilogue to the text, Dehui explained his criteria and methods for finalizing his text by means of "matching differences, collecting identities, cutting redundancies short, correcting passages expressed in dialect or colloquialism, filling in missing passages, retaining both those that are mutually complementary in one place and conflicting in another, giving footnotes wherever an attempt was made to reconcile differences." Dehui, however, emphatically asserted that nothing was deleted or added arbitrarily according to his individual interpretation. His reform intent seems to have accomplished its goal by introducing secular authority into the affairs of a religious institution. Yet it is suspected that this may have gradually set the stage for the growth of extreme formalism within the tradition, thereby stifling spontaneous spiritual expression.

Textual Editions and Influences
in Subsequent Periods

The completed text had far-reaching effects in the subsequent periods of the Ming (1368–1644) and Qing (1644–1912) dynasties. Following the precedent set in the Yuan, the Ming imperial court repeatedly decreed, in 1382, 1417, and again in 1424, that Dehui's *Baizhang Zen Monastic Regulations (Revised under the Yuan Imperial Edict)* should be the standard for all Zen monastic institutions and should be strictly complied with by every Zen practitioner. In 1442, the seventh year of Zhengtong, nearly a century after the initial edition, the Ming imperial court authorized the reprint edition of the text in response to the petition memorialized by Zhongzhi, then abbot of the temple of Mount Baizhang. This was the edition the Taishō Tripiṭaka edition mainly relied upon, with corroboration with the Japanese reprint of the Five Monasteries Edition (*Gozanban*) published in 1356. The present English translation is based on the Taishō edition, which was based on Ming Zhengtong reprint and the Five Monasteries Edition.

The text continued to enjoy influence under the Qing imperial court. Textual authority was reasserted in 1823 by Yirun's commentary, the *Record of Testimony and Meaning of the Baizhang Monastic Regulations (Baizhangqingguizhengyiji)*, and the text was reprinted in 1871. The text also retained influence in the Japanese

Zen community. The *Baizhang Zen Monastic Regulations* was reprinted in Japan in 1356, just two decades after the initial publication of the text in China, as the Five Monasteries Edition (*Gozanban*), and again in 1720 under the editorial guidance of Zen Master Mujaku Dōchū (1653–1745). This Japanese reprint is called the Kyōho Edition after the name of the era, and a detailed commentary on it was written by editor Dōchū himself, entitled the *Commentary on the Baizhang Monastic Regulations with Left-side Notes* (*Hyakujōshingisakei*).

Besides the main text, the Zhengtong edition comprises the preface to the edition composed by the government official Huyong and others, and an addenda of ten articles. Briefly, these are:

1. The "Preface to the Commemorative Tower of the Late Zen Master Baizhang Huaihai."

2. The "Record of the Pavilion of the Model Master Baizhang Huaihai Enshrined at the Temple."

3. The "Preface to the Original Monastic Regulations" by Yangyi.

4. Zongze's Preface to the *Chongning Monastic Regulations*.

5. Weimian's Preface to the *Xianshun Regulations*.

6. Yixian's Preface to the *Zhida Regulations*.

7. The *Preface to the Baizhang Zen Monastic Regulations* (*Revised under the Yuan Imperial Edict*) by the Hanlin academician Ouyangxuan.

8. Dehui's Epilogue to the *Baizhang Zen Monastic Regulations* (*Revised Under the Yuan Imperial Edict*).

9. Ouyangxuan's Epilogue to the *New Entitlement of the Patriarch Baizhang*.

10. Letters of Correspondence by Zen Masters Yishan and Yuanxi, and Duben's Note of Tribute to their endeavor.

Huyong's preface and these ten addenda are important from the point of view of historical and hagiographic studies, but since they are not directly related to the subject matter of monastic regulations per se, they were not included in this translation. It is hoped, however, that a detailed study of these works will be published along with the notes of the main text sometime in the future.

Problems of Translation and Future Research

In this translation, the term "practitioner" is used throughout to designate those who committed themselves to a professional career in Zen, because it is a closer equivalent to the Sanskrit term *bhikṣu,* Buddhist mendicant, monk, priest, or clergy (public or government religious officials). The Chinese text specifies chapter divisions and sub-chapter topics, but provides no further specifications for textual and topical breakdown. Hence, numerical ordering, sub-topic specifications, and paragraph indentations are provided in this translation as an aid to readers. One of the reasons why research and translation of Zen monastic regulations lags behind translation work on other types of Buddhist materials is that mere linguistic knowledge or academic training is insufficient to analyze and decipher the cryptic shorthand of such texts. There are many cases that present difficulties to even an experienced translator. In the case of this text, I have fully availed myself of Dōchū's detailed *Commentary on the Baizhang Monastic Regulations with Left-side Notes* during the translation process.

In future studies on monastic regulations, I believe that it is imperative to bring to the public an English version of the twelfth-century *Chongning Monastic Regulations* in order to foster comparative study between texts and encourage further research into the original spirit of the *Baizhang Zen Monastic Regulations.*

Finally, I would like to express my gratitude to the Ven. Dōnin Minamizawa, Kannin of Eiheiji, for his invaluable support of this project, and my deep appreciation to the Numata Center for Buddhist Translation and Research for the opportunity to include this translation in its English Tripiṭaka series.

THE BAIZHANG ZEN MONASTIC REGULATIONS
(Revised under the Yuan Imperial Edict)

Compiled by Dehui, Abbot of the Master Sage
of Great Wisdom and Long Life Temple

Edited by Dasu, Abbot of the Great Dragons
Flying to Assemble for Celebration Temple

Fascicle One

Chapter I

Festivities and the
Observance of Rites

I. Preface to the Chapter

What people value most is found in the realization of the Way 1112c20
(Dao). Hence, from ancient times, the sublime rulers of this land
have continued to revere the teachings of our Western Sage (the
Buddha) and have never failed to treat Buddhists in a manner well
beyond conventional propriety. This is because they revere the
Way. With respectful consideration, the Yuan imperial court has
treated Buddhists most honorably; we are exempted from taxes
and levies of service and are permitted to remain in our place (i.e.,
monasteries and temples) in order to fully devote ourselves to the
realization of the Way.

Our indebtedness to imperial favor is as vast as heaven and
earth, beyond measurement. We are obliged to realize the insight
of Buddha-nature and return to the abode of highest good. We
will give full play to the wondrous faculty of insight to transcend
[the world] to the height of spirituality, lead the populace toward
spontaneous conversion, and thereby promote benevolence and
long life in this world. This is the way we pay our indebtedness
to the throne. It is the goal for which we Buddhists strive whole-
heartedly. With respect to everyday life, we have a rule to pray

for imperial well-being every morning and evening and at each mealtime so as not to become unmindful of it.

II. Festivity of the Imperial Birthday

1. Inauguration of the Rite
of the Imperial Birthday

When the day of celebrating the imperial birthday arrives, the first step is to set up the place for the rite of prayer for the Adamantine Immeasurable Life Buddha (Vajrāmitāyus; Jingangwuliang-shou). For the sake of proper expression of reverence, no one should be allowed to be absent for the duration of the entire month [in which the imperial birthday occurs]. One day before the inauguration of the rite, the practice hall official (this position is also referred to as director of the practice hall and director of practitioners' affairs) prepares the signboards, writes the announcement of the rite on two separate sheets of paper, and attaches one sheet to the board to be posted on the right side of the temple's main gate and the other to the tablet of sutra titles, which is hung higher in the Buddha hall. (Format given below.) The announcement is written on yellow paper. [The director of the practice hall] is obliged to prepare the name list for rotating shifts according to ordination seniority. Each name must be listed together with the status [as regards the schedule].

Five days in advance, the director of the practice hall, accompanied by a novice attendant, visits the official of the scribes' quarters, carrying a sheet of paper in his sleeve. (Having been notified beforehand, the head scribe awaits the director's arrival. The director greets the scribe with an informal prostration with unopened sitting cloth.) After a single prostration, the director of the practice hall says:

May I request you to compose the word of tribute for the inauguration of the rite of the imperial birthday.

4

(If the official is not available at the time, the scribe's assistant performs this role, and if neither is available, any previous composition may be substituted. Format of the word of tribute given below.)

Upon completing the composition, the scribe official presents it to the abbot for inspection and then takes it to the practice hall director himself in order to pay a return courtesy visit. After an informal prostration, he thanks the director for his prior visit. The latter copies the composition onto two sheets of yellow paper, and proceeds to the abbot's office accompanied by his novice attendant, who carries a crepe-wrapped tray, equipped with candles and an incense burner. After burning incense and performing an informal prostration, the director asks the abbot for his approval:

> This is the word of tribute prepared for the inauguration of the rite for the imperial birthday, sir. Your inspection is requested.

Upon approval [of the tribute by the abbot], the novice attendant notifies the abbot by announcing:

> The sutra chanting to inaugurate the rite of the imperial birthday is scheduled for tomorrow morning at the Buddha hall, sir.

The [practitioners in the] various quarters are immediately notified, and the wooden tablet announcing the sutra chanting is hung at the entrance to the practice hall. The abbot's incense offering assistant notifies the abbot: "The ascent to the Dharma hall is scheduled for tomorrow, sir."

2. The Ascent to the Dharma Hall

At 3:00 A.M. (i.e., the fifth watch of the night), when the abbot makes his rounds, burning incense through the aisles of the practice hall, the incense offering assistant reminds the abbot of the scheduled event once again, saying:

> Following the breakfast of rice gruel (*shuifan*), the ascent to
> the Dharma hall is scheduled, sir.

The assistant instructs the guest master to post in the practice hall a wooden tablet inscribed with [the words] "Ascent to the Dharma hall." At breakfast, the practice hall director strikes the octagonal wooden post with its mallet to signal the moment when the first serving of rice gruel is completed, then immediately strikes it again and makes the following announcement:

> I announce to you, fellow practitioners, that when we hear
> the bell ring after breakfast, each of us, properly attired, will
> proceed to the Buddha hall and inaugurate the prayer rite
> for the imperial birthday. Respectfully announced.

After striking [the octagonal wooden post again] to signal the end of the announcement, the director goes and stands before the abbot, bows with palms together, and then makes a single round through the aisles of the hall, starting from the raised sitting platform of the primary seat official, going out to the lower outer hall, then to the upper outer hall, and finally returning to the center of the inner hall to bow before the altar of the guardian bodhisattva (usually Mañjuśrī) before leaving the hall.

After a short recess after breakfast, the practice hall novice attendant reports to the abbot's guest master when the Buddha hall is ready, [that is, when] incense, candles, tea and sweet hot water, the cymbals, and a portable incense burner [have been prepared]. The guest master in turn conveys this message to the abbot, then to his chief assistant. The abbot's attendant strikes the wooden sounding board at the abbot's office and begins a series of drumbeats to signal [commencement of the rite]. Before all this takes place, the wooden sounding board at the practitioners' quarters is struck three times to call them to return to the practice hall, where they wait in their places in sitting meditation (zazen), facing the wall as usual. At the sound of the drum, the practitioners turn to face each other across the aisles. Also upon hearing the drum, the training faculty officials, who have previously assembled outside, enter the hall and take their respective places. The primary seat official follows. The west hall official, the retired officials and retired subfunctionary officials of the temple, and the functionaries of various offices take their seats in the outer hall.

As the drumming begins, the abbot comes to his reception hall, and when he takes his seat, his chief assistant greets him with a bow and stands on the east side of the hall, while the novice attendants salute him likewise and stand on the west side. When the drumming changes pitch, the chief assistant proceeds to the Dharma hall, stands by the left side of the main rostrum seat, and waits for the practitioners to assemble. At the practice hall the training faculty officials descend to the floor, bow before the altar of the guardian bodhisattva, and lead the practitioners toward the Dharma hall. Approaching the rostrum seat, they line up facing it and bow, then move back to form the west-order column, slightly away from the center, and stand facing east. The practitioners take parallel positions behind their column. It is inappropriate for practitioners to go to their places before the officials arrive and take their places.

When the drumming commences, an official at the novice attendant's hall also strikes the wooden sounding board three times, and the ceremonial leader leads the group of novice attendants toward the kitchen hall. They line up in two columns in front of the hall, facing each other, and wait for the change of drum pitch. The administrative officials come out of the hall at the moment the drum changes pitch; the novices greet them with a bow and then follow them to the Dharma hall. When the training faculty officials take their positions in the west-order column, the administrative officials proceed to line up in front of the rostrum, and, after a bow, move back to take their positions in the east-order column, led by the head administrative official, where they stand facing west. The novice attendants then take parallel positions behind the administrative officials at a slight distance from them.

The chief assistant returns to the abbot and escorts him to the main rostrum seat. All novice attendants salute the abbot with a bow. When the abbot reaches the rostrum, the novice attendants close in behind the administrative officials. During the winter months, everyone is required at this moment to take off his cap to bow. With a gesture of greeting, the abbot ascends the rostrum seat, followed by his chief assistant, and receives from him [powdered] incense proffered on the lid of an incense case. The abbot reverently raises it with a word of blessing, and completes the word of tribute for imperial longevity. Thereupon, receiving the [blessed] incense back, the chief assistant pours it into the burner with his left hand, simultaneously placing next to it a stick of incense with his right hand while giving a word of prayer. After a slight bow, the chief assistant descends the rostrum and returns to his place.

After the abbot sits down cross-legged and adjusts his robe, the incense offering assistant and colleagues go before the rostrum, turn toward the abbot, bow in unison, and return to their places, led by the chief assistant. Next, the primary seat official leads the west-order members in similar manner. They bow toward the abbot in unison, in tandem with the practitioners [behind the west-order column]. Third, the administrative officials bow in the same manner toward the abbot, in tandem with the novice attendants [behind the east-order column]. The ranking west hall resident and east hall resident likewise go before the rostrum and bow. Thereupon, the chief assistant ascends the rostrum, offers incense with his left hand, turns to the abbot, and bows toward him with a gesture of offering his unopened sitting cloth. (This is called "the request for a Dharma session on behalf of the practitioners.")

Thereupon the chief assistant descends the rostrum and stands to the side. When the question-and-answer session is over, the abbot explains the meaning of the assembly:

> On such-and-such day, we respectfully perform the commemoration of the imperial birthday. On this day in such-and-such month, this temple shall inaugurate the continual session of prayer for the Adamantine Immeasurable Life Tathāgata for the duration of an entire month. From today, practitioners

of this temple shall continuously recite the sacred scriptures at the Buddha hall in rotating shifts. Your subject So-and-so, abbot of this temple, has ascended this high seat this morning and has expounded the sublime truth and primary meaning of the Dharma. We dedicate the great merit thereby accrued toward everlasting imperial well-being.

When the abbot has finished preaching, he addresses the assembly:

Now, descending from this hall, let us proceed, with proper attire and dignity, to the hall of the great Buddha and inaugurate the commemorative rite of the imperial birthday. Respectfully stated.

On this day, if government officials are present at the morning session it is customary not to give any words of appreciation for their participation, in regard to the primary respect [being shown] the imperial throne.

3. The Rite of the Imperial Birthday

When the large bell begins to toll, preceded by three strikes of the practice hall bell, the practitioners assemble at the Buddha hall and take their positions facing the altar. The abbot commences offering tea and sweet hot water before the Buddha image. As the head administrative official hands over these offering items to the abbot one by one, the abbot censes each offering and hands it to his chief assistant who, standing near the pedestal of the image, places each item before the Buddha image. When this is done, the abbot returns and stands at his position. As the novice attendants begin to play the cymbals, the practice hall director steps forward toward the central incense burner and, with a salutation to the abbot, offers incense, assisted by the abbot's assistant who carries an incense case. Next, the ranking east and west hall residents simultaneously step forward in pairs to offer incense. (If any abbots of other temples happen to be present, the chief assistant of the host temple invites them to the altar to offer incense in a similar manner, prior to the offering of incense by the host temple's dual order officials, i.e., of the east and west orders.)

Next, a pair of officials from the dual orders proceed together to the incense burner, bow toward the Buddha image with palms together, and, after offering incense, turn toward the abbot, salute him in unison, and return to their respective positions. The whole assembly of practitioners performs three prostrations with half-opened sitting cloth.

Thereupon, the dual order officials turn to face each other, and the abbot kneels in the center before the altar. The guest reception official approaches on his knees, carrying a portable incense burner; simultaneously the abbot's incense offering assistant also approaches on his knees, carrying an incense case. In the meantime, the director of practitioners' affairs reads the word of tribute addressing the Buddha, and the guest reception official pours incense into the burner. Thereupon, the abbot stands and folds his sitting cloth. The director then leads the entire assembly in a recitation of the *Śūraṃgama-dhāraṇī*s and, when the recitation is completed, he proclaims the following invocation of merit transference:

> We solemnly dedicate the great merit accrued from reciting the sacred chapter of the *Śūraṃgama-dhāraṇī*s to the present imperial highness for this day of festivity, well-being, and longevity. Veneration to Adamantine Immeasurable Life Tathāgata, Benevolent King (Kāruṇikārāja; Renwangpusa) Bodhisattva Mahāsattva (*mohesa;* "great being"), and Mahā-prajñāpāramitā (Mohebanruoboluomi; Great Perfection of Wisdom).

Thereupon, all leave the hall.

4. Sutra Chanting in Rotating Shifts

Each day, the novice attendants of the director of the practice hall are required to present a list of the names for the rotating shifts

to the abbot, the training faculty officials, and the other practitioners and obtain their approval, at least one day before the date   1113c
of [the shift] assignment. The list consists of the name and status
[of each assignee] and their affixed signatures. By carefully con-
sidering the number of practitioners, they should produce copies
of [the shift] assignments based on ordination seniority and
arranged in proper order of the particular days, and upon completion of one rotation proceed to the next, and so on. The tablets
listing the sutra titles that are to be recited during the period are
hung over the rear pillars of the Buddha hall.

    Each day of [the rotating shift], the assignees conduct them-
selves with utmost seriousness, entering the hall after the large
bell tolls. They are obliged to maintain proper attire and dignity,
carry an incense case for venerating the Buddha, and recite the
sutras at their assigned position. Every day the administrative
official must prepare incense and candles without fail, and also a
simple meal for the assignees. The director offers incense and sweet
hot water and cleans the altar every day. When evening comes,
the assignees toll the large bell and retire from the hall. The practice hall novice attendants as well as those of the Buddha hall
must always be ready to serve the assignees so as to enable them
to carry out the sutra chanting without slackening.

    If government officials should happen to visit the temple to
offer incense in commemoration of the imperial birthday, the bell
should be tolled to assemble the practitioners to recite the sacred
verses of Immeasurable Life Tathāgata (Amitābha; Wuliang-
shourulai) and invoke the name of the Great Medicine Buddha
(Bhaiṣajyaguru; Yaoshirulai). The service is concluded with the
following invocation of merit transference:

> Such-and-such government official of such-and-such locality
> has visited the temple to offer incense and prayer. The prac-
> titioners have completed the recitation of the sacred chap-
> ter of verses. We solemnly dedicate the merit thereby accrued
> to the present imperial highness for this day of festivity,

well-being, and longevity. Veneration to Adamantine Immeasurable Life Buddha, and so on.

5. The Prayer Service on the Days
Ending in Three and Eight
of the Month of Festivity

On the days ending in three and eight (i.e., the third, eighth, thirteenth, eighteenth, twenty-third, and twenty-eighth) during the month of the rite of the imperial birthday, regular prayer services must be conducted in the Buddha hall [instead of the practice hall]. On these days, after the noon meal the practice hall attendants notify the abbot, as well as the offices of both the training faculty and the administration, of the time of the prayer service and post the tablet announcing the prayer service at the entrance of the practice hall to inform the practitioners. Before the evening session, the wooden sounding boards located in the various corridors of the temple are struck three times to assemble the practitioners at the Buddha hall, where they take their positions facing the Buddha's altar. The abbot's arrival is signaled by three strikes of the metal gong located at the kitchen hall. Next, at the sound of the large bell, the abbot offers incense and returns to his position. Immediately, the director steps forward from his east-order position and reads the prayer:

> The imperial wind forever sends fresh air, and the imperial way forever flourishes, while the Buddha's sun shines ever more brightly and the wheel of the Dharma perpetually turns.
>
> For the sake of assisting the aforementioned causes, let us pray by calling the [ten sacred names of the Buddhas]: Luminous Pure Dharma Body Vairocana Buddha (Pariśuddha-dharmakāyavairocanabuddha; Qingjingfashenpilushenafo), and so on.

(Upon completion of the prayer of the ten sacred names of the Tathāgatas, the following invocation of merit transference is given:)

We solemnly dedicate the merit hereby accrued to the present imperial highness for this day of festivity, well-being, and longevity. Veneration to Adamantine Immeasurable Life Buddha, and so on.

After the practice hall bell is tolled three times the practitioners bow and leave the hall.

6. The Propriety for Welcoming
the Abbot's Return

When the abbot returns from visiting temples in other districts, prefectures, cities, or provinces, it is customary for the resident practitioners to toll the large bell and assemble at the main gate to receive him and follow him to the abbot's office, where all greet him with a bow.

7. Inauguration and Fulfillment of the Rite
of the Imperial Birthday Recorded
in the *Ancient Regulations*

The *Ancient Regulations* (i.e., the original *Baizhang Zen Monastic Regulations*) record that the practitioners who participated in the rite of the imperial birthday were given a certificate [commemorating their participation] from the director of the practice hall, while temporary visitors or recent arrivals were given a similar certificate from the guest reception official, in order to verify their status and career. This is because in olden days, Buddhist as well as Taoist practitioners were required to pay a tax for their exemption [on religious grounds] from levies of service. Upon payment, each received a government certificate verifying his status of exemption from physical labor. In those days, therefore, besides the required items [a practitioner takes with him when traveling] (see Chapter VII, part IV) and the certificate of ordination, an annual certificate was required to verify one's status as exempt from government levies, to verify one's participation in a particular temple's summer retreat, and to verify one's participation in a particular temple's rite of the imperial birthday from inauguration through fulfillment. These certificates were a necessary precaution for avoiding any sort of criminal charge [for dereliction of civic duties]. Though such certificates are not in use today, mention is made here to show such bygone regulations.

III. Various Formats [for Signs]

1. Format of the Signboard with Yellow Paper

For the Festivity and Rite of the Imperial Birthday:

>Respectfully meeting at Such-and-such Temple in such-and-such district and province on such-and-such day and month

>For the Day of Festivity of the Imperial Birthday

This temple will conduct the commemoration rite on such-and-such day and month.

The inauguration of the rite is scheduled at the Buddha hall, in the place set up for the prayer rite to Adamantine Immeasurable Life Buddha, and practitioners are assigned to recite the sacred mantras and the sacred names of the Buddhas continually every day for the duration of a month.

We dedicate the great merit thereby accrued to the festivity of the imperial birthday and the promotion of imperial well-being for the sake of

1114a

>The Everlasting Life of the Present Emperor

May the Buddha's supernatural vision clearly illuminate and the Dragon God of Heaven witness the sincerity of the foregoing statement.

>Day, month, and year

14

Respectfully stated by the imperial subject,
Head Administrative Official So-and-so
The imperial subject, Abbot Priest So-and-so

2. Format for the Tablet of Sutra Titles

The sutra titles are given here:

Flower Ornament Sutra (Avataṃsaka-sūtra; Huayanjing)

Śūraṃgama-sūtra (Dafodingwanxingshoulengyenjing; Sutra on the Buddha's Omnipotent Valiant March)

Lotus Sutra (Saddharmapuṇḍarīka-sūtra; Dachengmiaofa-lianhuajing)

Sutra of Golden Splendor (Suvarṇaprabhāsottama-sūtra; Dachengjinguangmingjing)

Sutra of Perfect Enlightenment (Yuanjuejing)

Diamond Sutra (Vajracchedikāprajñāpāramitā-sūtra; Dachengjingangbanruoboluomijing)

Sutra of the Benevolent King (Renwangbanruoboluomijing)

Day and month

Respectfully placed as indicated above
Director, imperial subject,
Priest So-and-so

3. Format of the List of Names for Assignment According to Seniority

The names of each day's duty assignment at the Buddha hall are respectfully given below (to be written on a sheet of white paper):

Day and month

Imperial subject, Abbot So-and-so; So-and-so Primary Seat Official; So-and-so Secretarial Official; So-and-so Tripiṭaka Hall Official; So-and-so Guest Reception Official; So-and-so West Hall Official

Day and month

So-and-so practitioners; So-and-so senior practitioner; So-and-so Head Administrative Official

[continued below as above]

> Day and month
> Prepared by Practice Hall Official So-and-so

IV. Words of Tribute for Various Occasions

1. The Word of Tribute for the Inauguration of the Rite of the Imperial Birthday

It is reverently thought by the foregoing participants that there is no partiality whatsoever under the heavenly canopy, nor is there any measurement by which to fathom which is higher and wider between heaven and earth. The descending illumination is so dazzling that its brightness cannot be compared even with that of the sun and moon. One only knows that it is futile to look up to praise it; nor is there any limit to it even when one tries to make a tribute to it. One can only entrust oneself to the care of the imperial realm, and thereby faithfully weigh the four kinds of indebtedness (i.e., indebtedness toward parents, people, kings, and the Three Treasures). Thus, one is obliged to exert one's mind in loyalty and love, respectfully wishing the throne to be filled with the three kinds of blessing (i.e., longevity, wealth, and male offspring).

The axis of the north star winds around like lightning, and the dragon's appearance spreads a banquet on the ground.

The imperial network covers myriads of rivers and mountains, thereby bringing all of them to imperial deliberation, while the three thousand worlds of the lotus storehouse [manifested by Vairocana Buddha] make the great dominion of the empire ever more spacious (i.e., prosperous). There is no drop of water wasted, nor is there any idle person morning or evening. May the imperial couple rise, the auspicious star shine, the exalted seat be ever in peace, the unicorn and phoenix bring good fortune, and the wise lead, making myriads appear as they are. Respectfully presented.

2. The Word of Tribute for the Fulfillment of the Rite of the Imperial Birthday

The blooming of the lotus flower is an auspicious sign in this world, just as it was auspicious that the Buddha was born into this world. The enlightenment he realized under the *bodhi* tree has continued in succession in this world of humans for as long as the age of heaven. By nature, the divine quality accumulated through previous lives was cultivated in order to inherit the great and splendid plans of the Sage (i.e, Śākyamuni Buddha). How vast is the Yuan! How supreme is the Yuan! It embodies the origin and abides in the very heart of it. It meets with the utmost zenith and returns to it, and thereby erects the utmost and establishes its center of the universe.

1114b

The harmonious way of our tradition has, indeed, received an advantage at the time of the best governance, comparable to that of the ancient Sage. The bells and drums of this forest (i.e., monastic temple) enjoy times of peace, their sound expanding and increasing. Grasses, trees, and insects receive the permeating benefit of such advantage. Good omens inaugurate the dawn and hymns celebrate the flowery hill. While the robes (i.e., hands) fall and do nothing, yet may heaven and earth take their positions, myriads of things be nourished and grow, forms be created, the principles of *yin* and *yang* be harmonized, the four seasons be in proper order, longevity be enjoyed for ten thousand years, and the root and branches be extended for one hundred generations.

3. The Word of Praise on Coronation Day and the Four Monthly Days of Festivity

On the commemorative day of the imperial coronation, at the beginning of the month and mid-month, and on the eighth and twenty-third days of each month, the practice hall novice attendants are obliged, the night before, to notify the practitioners of the ceremonial rite [to be conducted the next day], and post the tablet indicating the schedule of sutra chanting. The following morning, when the sound of the large bell ceases, the practice hall bell is tolled to assemble the practitioners and all proceed to the Buddha hall. The director leads the recitation of the *Śūraṃgama-dhāraṇīs* and invokes the name of Medicine Buddha. When this rite is completed, the director concludes with the following invocation of merit transference:

> On the morning of such-and-such day and month, Abbot So-and-so, who has been entrusted with the Dharma, at Such-and-such Temple of such-and-such district and province, has respectfully assembled all the members of this temple at the Buddha hall, and they have recited in unison the [*dhāraṇīs*] of the *Śūraṃgama-sūtra* and praised the sacred names of the Buddhas. The merit thereby accrued is dedicated to the festivity and promotion of everlasting imperial well-being and longevity. Veneration to Adamantine Immeasurable Life Buddha, Benevolent King Bodhisattva, and so on.

4. The Word of Praise for the First and Mid-month Days in the Tripiṭaka Hall

From ancient times, it has been customary on these days to read the sutras and conduct the prayer for imperial longevity. Today it is regarded as a norm, a most suitable expression of reverence for the throne, to rise early in the morning and assemble at the Tripiṭaka hall to conduct the prayer rite for the sake of imperial longevity before the altar. As an alternative, the practice has been that after breakfast and after the morning session is over, the bell is tolled to assemble the practitioners and they proceed to the Tripiṭaka hall for the same purpose. The director recites the title of the *Great Perfection of Wisdom Sutra (Mahāprajñāpāramitā-sūtra; Banruoboluomiduojing)* while the practitioners silently pray. The abbot then leads the procession, each member holding his palms together, in three circumambulations around the building, or a single circumambulation if the number of participants is too large. They then return to their former positions and remain standing. Thereupon, the director calls for the chanting of the *Mahā-kāruṇikacitta-dhāraṇīs (Dabeixintuoloni; Esoteric Prayer Verses Praising Great Compassion)* and concludes with the following invocation of merit transference:

> The Lotus-store ocean in the Huayan ("Flower Ornament") universe is filled with vast perfect illumination. Its artfulness in creating effects is beyond the creation of nature, and its path totally transcends names and words. The light of the sun, moon, and stars winds down like lightning, submerging in the absolute state of existence-as-it-is. Although light rushes back and forth in all six directions (i.e., north, east, south, west, zenith, and nadir), this ocean is profoundly quiescent. The mystery of this ocean is indeed inexhaustible no matter how much and how far it is praised and exalted.
>
> On the felicitous morning of the first day of the month (or mid-month day), the abbot of this temple of such-and-such province, entrusted with the Buddha-Dharma, the imperial subject, priest So-and-so, has respectfully called for this assembly of all the practitioners of this temple. Having completed three circumambulations of the Tripiṭaka hall, we recited the title of the *Great Perfection of Wisdom Sutra,* with mindfulness and continued to turn the wheel of the Dharma treasure

of the heavenly palace and intoned in unison the sacred *Mahā-kāruṇikacitta-dhāraṇī*s. The merit thereby accrued is dedicated to the festivity and promotion of everlasting imperial well-being and longevity. Veneration to Adamantine Immeasurable Life Buddha, Benevolent King Bodhisattva Mahāsattva, and Mahāprajñāpāramitā.

5. The Word of Praise
for Daily Ritual Services

Twice a day, at breakfast and the noon meal, the practitioners leave the practice hall and are obliged to assemble at the Buddha hall. The director intones the *Amitābha-dhāraṇī* (*Wuliangshouzhou; Immeasurable Life Dhāraṇī*) three times and concludes with the following invocation of merit transference:

> Having intoned the sacred verses of the esoteric chapter, we respectfully dedicate the merit accrued thereby to the festivity and promotion of the well-being and longevity of the present emperor. Veneration to Adamantine Immeasurable Life Buddha, and so on.

6. The Festivity for the Birthday
of the Crown Prince

1114c

On the evening before the appointed day, the practice hall novice attendants should notify the practitioners of the scheduled sutra chanting by posting a tablet. Next morning, they toll the practice hall bell to assemble the practitioners at the Buddha hall. The director recites the *Śūraṃgama-dhāraṇī*s and invokes the name of Medicine Buddha. (This is identical to the rite of the four monthly commemorative days.) The director concludes the service with the following invocation of merit transference:

> Such-and-such Temple in such-and-such district and province respectfully acknowledges the felicitous birthday of the Crown Prince. All the practitioners of this temple have assembled at

20

the Buddha hall and reverently chanted the *Śūraṃgama-dhāraṇī*s and praised the sacred name of Medicine Buddha. The merit accrued thereby is dedicated to the festivity of the birthday of the Crown Prince, divine heir-apparent. Before the Buddha's shrine we humbly pray: May the wheel of the sun be turned many more times and the brightness of the moon be increased manyfold, so that they will be able to illuminate the whole ocean under heaven. May the mountain be like sandstone and the river like a girdle so that the foundation of the nation can be strengthened. Veneration to Adamantine Immeasurable Life Buddha, and so on.

7. The Prayer Invocation for the Months of Benevolence

The first, the fifth, and ninth months are called "months of benevolence." The day before the first day of each of these months, the director of the practice hall instructs his novice attendants to notify the abbot and the head administrative official, post the signboard at the entrance of the Buddha hall, and prepare the tablets of sutra titles and the list of names with assignments for rotating shifts. Each day, the large bell is tolled before sutra chanting begins, and the scheduled sutras are recited in the Buddha hall. The end of the day is concluded with a word of praise. This continues for the duration of the month.

The origin of this practice can be traced to the third year of Kaihuang of the Sui dynasty, when a decree was issued throughout the land that during the designated months (i.e., the first, fifth, and ninth) as well as on the six specific days of religious austerity, each temple was required to set up a place of practice for prayer and invocation and no life should be taken or injured. According to a sutra, the deity Vaiśravaṇa (Pishamentian), who is said to have conducted inspection tours every year over the four great continents, happened to regulate the southern continent and prohibited the slaughter of animals during the first, fifth, and ninth months. When Tang provincial governors received their appointments to their respective territories, they customarily used to [celebrate the occasion] by sponsoring a feast for their victorious soldiers, whose number was never less than several ten-thousands, thus increasing the slaughter of animals for food. Since animal slaughter was prohibited in those months, a system was developed to the effect that new governors were not appointed during the first, fifth, or ninth months. Popular belief, however, wrongly attributed this custom to superstitious fear.

End of Chapter I: Festivities and the Observance of Rites

Chapter II

Discharging Indebtedness
to the State

I. Preface to the Chapter

The state has the duty of conducting the sacrificial rite for the supreme, for the imperial ancestors, and the rite for the four seasons. This is to clarify the merits of these rites, to promote the original spirit, and thereby ensure the continuity of successive rulers. The present dynastic court reveres the Buddha, and from the founding Emperor Shizu onward each reign has erected temples. Each emperor is said to govern the realm of heaven and earth as an incarnate Buddha body (*nirmāṇakāya*), and upon completing his task of transforming the realm returns to the state of Buddhahood. Thus, in those temples in the capital that are supported by the government, the imperial portrait is placed in the Buddha's altar. Five times a month, the portrait is enshrined with offerings and words of reverence as though for a living person and is venerated with a kind of nurturing protective thought.

We can observe generally that wherever the imperial power of spiritual transformation flows, it has spread along with the teachings of the Buddha with no obstruction. Thus, Buddhist followers have been bathed in the benevolent waves and marshlands. Shouldn't we find a way to repay our debt for that to which we are indebted?

II. State Memorial Days

As the memorial day of the emperor's demise approaches, the head administrative official is obliged, the evening before, to

notify the practice hall official of the coming event, have his
novice attendants inform the abbot and the dual order officials,
and post the signboard for the sutra chanting. Finally, [he should]
set up the imperial seat on the rostrum in the Dharma hall and
place the imperial tablet, with the sacred name (i.e., that of the
deceased emperor) solemnly inscribed on a sheet of yellow paper,
enshrining it with incense, a flower vase, candle stand, table, and
floor sheet. On the appointed day, the practitioners assemble at
the Dharma hall at the signal of the practice hall bell. When the
abbot enters and finishes offering incense, tea, and sweet hot
water, the director of the practice hall calls for the chanting of
the *Śūraṃgama-dhāraṇī*s. After [the chanting] is over, he concludes the service with the following invocation of merit transference:

> So-and-so, abbot of Such-and-such Temple, entrusted with
> the Buddha-Dharma, in such-and-such district and province,
> acknowledges the memorial day of the late Emperor So-and-
> so, and has respectfully assembled all the practitioners of
> this temple, chanted in unison the *Śūraṃgama-dhāraṇī*s,
> praising the Buddha's omnipotent power, and invoked the
> sacred name [of the Great Medicine Buddha]. We (respect-
> fully) dedicate the merit thereby accrued to the enshrine-
> ment of the imperial carriage with further assistance. It is
> humbly wished that the imperial spirit may enjoy all the cor-
> ners of the universe, assume a visit on the chariot formed of
> clouds and winds, receive the delight of his abode in the cen-
> ter of the sky and of his palace inlaid with precious gems and
> his pavilion adorned with colorful gems. Veneration to all the
> Buddhas of the ten directions (the four cardinal directions,
> the four intermediate directions, zenith, and nadir, i.e., every-
> where) and the three periods of time (past, present, and
> future, i.e., in all times), [to all the arhats, bodhisattvas, and
> *mahāsattva*s, and to Mahāprajñāpāramitā].

III. Various Prayer Services

Whenever an occasion for prayer arises, the place of its performance must be prepared in strict accordance with the rules, and must be furnished with food and other offerings. The abbot is obliged to maintain a state of mental concentration (*samādhi*) and to become more attentive. The practitioners must carry out their duties in a tidy and austere manner, while the administrative officials are obliged to supervise the outer and inner temple operations and make their rounds through various quarters and buildings in order to keep them clean. If any government official happens to visit the temple to offer incense, he must be extended both a respectful welcome and farewell. Prior to the appointed day of prayer, the head administrative official is obliged to notify the abbot of the need for the particular prayer invocation, and the director of the practice hall is also invited for consultation. His novice attendants are then instructed to inform the practitioners of the coming event and to post the signboard announcing the prayer service.

Twice a day, at morning and noon mealtimes, the practitioners assemble at the signal of the bell to chant sutras. Either the reading of the three Tripiṭaka scriptures or the four major groups of scriptures (i.e., the *Perfection of Wisdom Sutra* [*Prajñāpāramitā-sūtra; Banruojing*]; the *Sutra of the Heap of Jewels* [*Mahāratnakūṭa-sūtra; Dabaojijing*]; the *Flower Ornament Sutra;* and the *Nirvana Sutra* [*Niepanjing*]) is to be carried out for three, five, or seven consecutive days, according to the particular situation. In the cases of prayers for sunshine or rain, practitioners are grouped in teams of ten, twenty, thirty, or fifty members, led by the first member of each team, so that the sutra chanting can be carried out without interruption from one team to another. Each team of practitioners chants the *Mahākāruṇikacitta-dhāraṇīs*, the *Dhāraṇī for Changing Disaster to Fortune (Xiaozaijixiangtuoluoni)*, and the *Dhāraṇī for Inviting Great Rain (Dayunzhou)* thirty-seven times each. This is called the "uninterrupted wheel of chanting." After a whole day of chanting, there should be a rite of fulfillment and a word of invocation, with earnest wishes for a favorable response. The format of each invocation is given below.

1. The Prayer Invocation for Sunshine

It is anxiously observed that vicious rain has caused much damage by preventing things from realizing their function. Hundreds of rivers have swept away all things, leaving no place of refuge. This is a result of the karma shared in common by all people. Since heaven and earth are equally impartial, we have respectfully prepared the ceremonial place of prayer to invite fair weather and teams of practitioners have with utmost sincerity conducted uninterrupted prayer through chanting sacred scriptures (sutras) and esoteric verses (*dhāraṇī*s) each day in order to appeal to the Buddhas. The objective of this prayer is fair weather. May a prompt response be granted, so that the persistent clouds may be swept away from all fields in the four directions, the gloomy disharmony be dispersed, the bright sun may appear in the center of the sky and its glorious rays illuminate, enabling all human activities to occur in proper order and enabling myriads of things to realize the fulfillment of their lives.

2. The Prayer Invocation for Rain

It is anxiously observed that the sun's overbearing rays precipitate disasters for all kinds of crops. This is not a punishment heaven sends from above but a result of the mounting transgressions of people below. Thus, it is hoped that the various Buddhas, by extending their compassion, will respond to the chanting of the sacred esoteric verses and the words of invocation. We have respectfully prepared the ceremonial place of prayer for inviting rain and teams of practitioners have with utmost sincerity conducted uninterrupted prayer through chanting sacred scriptures and esoteric verses in

order to appeal to the Buddhas. The objective of this prayer
is abundant rainfall. May a prompt response be granted, so
that the people may be rescued from the difficulty of such
oppressive situations. This is indeed most difficult and dan-
gerous. May the cloud dragon rise over the mountains and
rivers, bringing about abundant rain, so that farm work may
be done and the harvest season may be completed once again.

3. The Prayer Invocation for Snowfall

It is anxiously observed that whenever the winter is unusu-
ally warm, living things are always harmed. Snowfall purifies
the noxious atmosphere of the land below. We thus offer
incense with utmost sincerity, wishing for the good omen of
snowflakes amassed on the ground. We have respectfully prepared the ceremonial place of prayer for invoking snowfall
and teams of practitioners have with utmost sincerity conducted uninterrupted prayer through chanting sacred scriptures and esoteric verses each day in order to appeal to the
Buddhas. The objective of this prayer is snowfall. May a
prompt response be granted, so that snowclouds may spread
equally over thousands of miles and there may be abundant
rain and snowfall in the eight regions of the universe, the six
agencies of nature (i.e., heat, water, metal, wood, soil, and
crops) may operate through the threefold processes (i.e., essential, efficient, and self-regenerating), grasses and trees may
grow thick, the two principles of *yin* and *yang* may be harmonized, and the five primary elements of nature (i.e., fire,
water, wind, metal, and earth) may be in good order, and,
thereby, gods and humans may be in harmony.

4. The Prayer Invocation for the
Dispersion of Locusts

It is anxiously observed that flying locusts fill the entire sky.
This is a bad omen to be feared, for after they disappear by

entering the ground, no one knows where they may stir up calamities again. Unless supernatural efficacy is rendered, no matter how many human hands may attempt it, the dispersion [of these locusts] cannot be accomplished. Thus, we have respectfully prepared the ceremonial place of prayer for the banishment of locusts, and teams of practitioners have with utmost sincerity conducted uninterrupted prayer through chanting the sacred scriptures and esoteric verses each day in order to appeal to the Buddhas. The objective of this prayer is the expulsion and dispersion of locusts. May a prompt dispersal be granted, so that rains and winds wash and blow all the locusts away, into the rivers where they may take the course of their own karma, the people may regain a sense of safety, and a normal way of life may resume.

5. The Prayer Invocation
for a Day of Eclipse

It is predicted that an eclipse will take place today, and that the five regulatory agencies of time (i.e., year, day, month, constellation, and calendrical numeration) are slightly out of proper order. Because of such disorder, it is feared that the mighty force of heaven might cause the six kinds of evil celestial phenomena (i.e., periods of continuous cloud cover, drought, wind, rain, darkening, and gloaming) to occur. Thus, in order to rescue the people from their fear and protect them from confusion, we rely on the power of the Buddhas. Teams of practitioners have respectfully conducted uninterrupted prayer through chanting the sacred scriptures and esoteric verses in order to extend our help and protection. May the spirit of the sun promptly regain its light so that its five variegated rays spread wide, illuminating the earth's surface below and causing shadows to disappear, and the sun shines brightly throughout the sky.

6. The Prayer Invocation for a
Day of Lunar Eclipse

The moon is the master of the night through its shining nature of *yin*. The faintness of its illumination during an eclipse reveals heaven's inauspicious omen to the people. Humans rely on the moon's illumination, and heaven demonstrates its power of punishment to the people for their transgressions by inducing a lunar eclipse. Because they have subjected themselves to the rules of restraint by avowing their past transgressions, the practitioners of the sangha are deemed able to generate utmost sincerity and attempt to restore the illumination from this inauspicious phenomenon through chanting the sacred scriptures and esoteric verses in order to proffer their assistance. May the flowery moon promptly return to its brightness, so that evil darkness extinguishes its trace and the clear light may once again manifest itself over the earth's land, hills, and rivers. May the moon maintain long life so as to include myriads of phenomena in its vast and cool palace.

End of Chapter II: Discharging Indebtedness to the State

End of Fascicle One

Fascicle Two

Chapter III

Discharging Religious Indebtedness

I. Preface to the Chapter

Buddha-nature is the fundamental basis of humanity. It is neither possible to know its origin even if one were to shake heaven and earth, nor to know its fulfillment by exhausting myriads of years. Buddhas and sentient beings are equally endowed with this nature. By acquiring insight into this nature, one reaches the summit of wondrous enlightenment; by straying from it, one is washed away by the waves of life and death. From one *kalpa* to the next, one goes through different births in the sixfold cycle of rebirth in accordance with one's karmic retribution, and finds no end to this process. The sacred teaching of the Buddha, upon which we rely, is vast and open to anyone to follow for refuge.

We Zen practitioners have reverently inherited the formality of the (Buddha's) attire and the lineage of his Dharma transmission. What we advocate as his principle of practice are the codes of discipline and morality (*vinaya*); what we propagate as his word of truth is the body of teachings (*śāsana*); and what we transmit as his mind of transcendence is the state of meditation (*dhyāna*). Moreover, our compliance with the so-called Great Origin is to identify ourselves with the totality of the Buddha's wondrous faculty, alone through which, for the first time, we are called the Buddha's disciples and transmit the life of his insight. Is it then [merely] worldly convention to conduct services on the memorial days of the patriarchs?

II. The Buddha's Birthday Commemoration

1. The Ascent to the Dharma Hall

Prior to the day, the practice hall official collects contributions from the practitioners and entrusts the collection to the head administrative official in order to obtain various offerings. He is also obliged to have the word of tribute composed and approved. (The procedure is identical to that of the imperial birthday rite.) When the appointed day comes, the head administrative official respectfully sets up a small pavilion decorated with flowers in the Buddha hall and places in it a statue of the infant Buddha with a tray of scented water, and provides a pair of small dippers and various offerings in front of the pavilion. When everything is ready, the abbot ascends the main rostrum seat [of the Dharma hall], and after offering incense, says:

> On the felicitous morning of the Buddha's birthday, disciple So-and-so, abbot of Such-and-such Temple in charge of the Buddha's teaching, reverently offers fragrant incense to express care and devotion for the sake of the Original Patriarch, Śākyamuni Tathāgata, the Great Preceptor (*mahopādhyāya; daheshang*). In response to his great compassion, I earnestly pray: May all the Buddhas manifest themselves in this world within every successive moment of our consciousness so as to rescue all beings of this Dharma world (*dharmadhātu*).

Next, the abbot sits down cross-legged and says:

> On this eighth day of the fourth month, we greet the commemorative morning of the birth of the Original Patriarch Śākyamuni Tathāgata, the Great Preceptor. By assembling

all the disciples of this temple, and also by offering incense, flowers, candles, sweet water, and tea, as well as fruit and delicacies, we hereby express our care and devotion for him. Disciple So-and-so, abbot of this temple, a remote descendant in charge of the Buddha's teaching, has ascended this main rostrum seat to offer the teaching of [the Buddha's] vehicle of religious salvation. With the special merit thereby accrued, we wish, in part, to discharge our indebtedness to the refuge bestowed upon us by his compassion and, in part, along with all sentient beings of the Dharma world, to express our celebration for the event of the Buddha's birth that was indeed of rare occurrence.

2. The Celebration of the Buddha's Birth

Next, after preaching, the abbot addresses the assembly once again:

> I respectfully announce that after leaving here we shall proceed to the Buddha hall with proper attire and dignity and commemorate the day by bathing the [statue of the infant] Buddha and chanting sutras.

The abbot descends the rostrum seat and leads the practitioners toward the Buddha hall. When the practitioners have taken their respective positions, facing the Buddha image, the abbot burns incense and performs three prostrations with half-opened sitting cloth before the altar. Without folding his sitting cloth, he proceeds to the altar and conducts the offering of sweet hot water and food. His guest reception assistant hands him the offerings, while the incense offering assistant places them on the altar. The abbot returns to his position and again performs three full prostrations, and once again proceeds to the altar to offer incense, a monetary gift, and tea. Once again he returns to his position, performs three prostrations, and stands, folding his sitting cloth.

With a bow, the director of practitioners' affairs signals the dual order officials to step forward for incense offering, in pairs, while the rest of the practitioners perform three prostrations with opened sitting cloth. In the meantime, the abbot kneels to offer incense at a portable incense burner, while the director begins to read the word of tribute, addressing the Buddha:

> The single moon, abiding in the sky, magnanimously
>   imprints its image into the multiple waves of water,
1116a
> The single Buddha, coming into this world, has made
>   multiple Buddhas appear and sit on a lotus flower,
> The single light issuing from the Buddha's forehead
>   illuminates all three worlds,
> The single flow of nectar benefits all sentient beings born
>   through the four different modes at once.

Completing the word of tribute, he immediately calls for chanting the verse of bathing the [image of the infant] Buddha:

> Now I respectfully bathe the Tathāgatas,
> The merit body (sambhogakāya) that embellishes their
>   pure insight,
> I wish all sentient beings to be freed from the five kinds
>   of defilement,
> And equally realize the pure Dharma body (dharmakāya)
>   of the Tathāgata.

When all the practitioners complete their circuit around [the hall] and bathing of the statue, [using the dippers to pour sweet water from the tray over the figure,] the director calls for the chanting of the Śūraṃgama-dhāraṇīs and concludes with the following invocation of merit transference:

> We dedicate the merit accrued from this chanting to the
> absolute truth and ultimate reality for the sake of adorning
> the bodhi that is the fruit of Buddhahood. We wish thereby
> to discharge the four kinds of indebtedness and help those
> who abide in the three worlds to equally realize enlighten-
> ment and, together with all sentient beings of the Dharma

world, we wish to perfectly realize omniscient knowledge (*sarvajñāna*). Veneration to the Buddhas of the ten directions and the three times, and so on.

3. The Word of Tribute

The Great Ocean is profoundly quiescent, and we hear nothing but the rumbling vibration of its current. The Great Void is totally transparent, and we see nothing but the latitudinal movement of its respective weft and warp. Due to the greatness of the Dharma body, it manifests itself within phenomenal traces by having sentient beings respond to an appointed time, helping them all to realize perfect enlightenment. In the time of moral and social degeneration, it manifests itself as Śākyamuni's birth. [The Śākya prince] abandoned his luxurious garments and took up filthy clothes in order to wander [in pursuit of enlightenment]. He abandoned the illusory treasure city and ascended the summit of the treasure mountain. Yet he returned [to this world] to lead others, hand in hand. Though his initial birthday has been honored repeatedly ever since, we can never fully repay our indebtedness. We earnestly wish and implore: May the winds of truth be fanned into this latter-day world, and the shining sun of insight be raised in the center of the sky. Though there is neither Buddha nor [Māra], may each of all *dharma*s proclaim the precious verses of bathing the Buddha. Though there is neither filth nor purity, may particle after particle of dust cleanse the golden body.

III. The Buddha's Enlightenment and Nirvana

1. The Buddha's Enlightenment Day

Prior to the day marking the Buddha's enlightenment, the practice hall official collects contributions from the practitioners and entrusts the collection to the head administrative official in order to obtain various offerings. He is also obliged to have the word of tribute composed and approved. (This process is identical to that of the Buddha's birthday commemoration.) [On the day commemorating the Buddha's enlightenment,] the abbot ascends the rostrum seat of the Dharma hall and celebrates the day by offering incense and addressing [the assembly] as follows:

> On the day of the Buddha's enlightenment, So-and-so Bhikṣu, abbot of Such-and-such Temple, remote descendant of the Buddha's teaching, respectfully offers precious incense for the Great Teacher and Original Patriarch Śākyamuni Tathāgata, to express our care and devotion on behalf of all the sentient beings of the Dharma world. We wish, in part, to discharge our indebtedness to the compassion bestowed upon us and, in part, to wish that all sentient beings of the Dharma world will equally realize perfect enlightenment.

Next, the abbot sits cross-legged on the rostrum seat and says:

> On the eighth day of the twelfth month, we reverently greet the commemorative day on which the Original Patriarch Śākyamuni Tathāgata, the Great Teacher, realized enlightenment. Assembling all the practitioners of this temple and offering incense, flowers, candles, and tea, as well as fruit and delicacies, we have expressed our care and devotion to the original master of our religion. From now, I, So-and-so Bhikṣu, abbot of Such-and-such Temple, remote descendant of the Buddha's teaching, shall preach the vehicle of his religious salvation from this rostrum seat. With the special merit thereby accrued, we wish in part to discharge our indebtedness to the compassion bestowed upon us and, in part, along with all sentient beings of the Dharma world, wish for them to discover their own insight and turn the great wheel of the Dharma by entering into each infinitesimal particle.

Next, the abbot preaches and afterward addresses the assembly again, as follows:

I respectfully announce that we shall leave this hall and, with proper dignity and decorum, proceed to the hall of the great Buddha to chant sutras.

The abbot then descends the rostrum seat and leads the assembly. Entering the Buddha hall, he offers incense, performs three prostrations with opened sitting cloth, and conducts the rite of offerings. When he kneels to burn incense on a portable incense burner, the director of practitioners' affairs begins to read the word of tribute for the Buddha:

Perceiving the morning star over Mount Perfect Enlightenment (Zhengjueshan), the Buddha realized the path. Lifting the sun of insight in the great universe composed of a thousand universes, he thereby let its illumination flow forth [from generation to generation].

When the word of tribute is completed, the director immediately calls for chanting the sutras and concludes with the same invocation of merit transference as before.

2. The Buddha's Nirvana Day

On the day of commemoration for the Buddha's nirvana, initially the abbot offers incense at the Buddha hall to conduct the mid-month prayer chanting for imperial well-being, and following that he ascends the rostrum seat at the Dharma hall for preaching as usual. At the moment of incense offering, he addresses the assembly:

On this day of the Buddha's nirvana, So-and-so Bhikṣu, abbot of Such-and-such Temple, remote descendant of the Buddha's teaching, respectfully offers precious incense to express our care and devotion for the Great Teacher and Original Patriarch Śākyamuni Tathāgata. We wish, in part, to discharge our indebtedness for his compassion in bestowing refuge on us and, in part, to express, along with all sentient beings of the Dharma world, our dear remembrance of him. May his Dharma body be ever present, may his Dharma wheel turn once again, and may all sentient beings attain insight into the nature of true existence as neither origination nor cessation (*anutpattikadharmakṣānti; wushengren*).

Next, the abbot sits cross-legged on the rostrum seat and says:

On the fifteenth day of the second month, we reverently honor the commemorative day of *parinirvāṇa* on which the Original Patriarch, Great Teacher Śākyamuni Tathāgata, entered total cessation. Assembling the practitioners and reverently offering incense, flowers, candles, tea, fruit, and delicacies, we express our care and devotion to the master. I, So-and-so Bhikṣu, abbot of this temple, remote descendant of the Buddha's teaching, have ascended this rostrum seat in the Dharma hall and now preach the wondrous mind of nirvana. With the special merit accrued thereby, we wish, in part, to discharge our indebtedness to the compassion bestowed on us, and in part, along with all sentient beings of the Dharma world, to perfectly realize omniscient knowledge.

Next, the abbot preaches, and afterward addresses the assembly again:

I respectfully speak to you. Upon descending from our seats, we shall leave this hall and proceed to the Buddha hall with dignity and decorum and chant sutras for this Nirvana Day.

The abbot descends the rostrum seat and leads the practitioners. Entering the Buddha hall, he offers incense, performs three prostrations with opened sitting cloth, and kneels to burn incense on a portable incense burner. Meanwhile the director of practitioners' affairs begins to read the word of tribute for the Buddha:

The pure Dharma body essentially has neither phenomenal appearance nor disappearance but, through the power of the vow of great compassion, it shows [its traces] as phenomenal appearance or nonappearance.

When the word of tribute is completed, he immediately calls for chanting the sutras and concludes with the same invocation of merit transference as before.   1116b

3. The Word of Tribute for Enlightenment Day

Since enlightenment has originally been accomplished in the immemorial past, how should one rely on one's experience and practice for becoming a Buddha? People use it in daily life, they are not aware of it, only attributing it to the enlightened [beings] of the past. It is only when one realizes insight oneself, and helps others realize the same insight, that the ultimate path of enlightenment is accomplished. The Buddha is called the World-honored One because he knows both the world of convention and its transcendence. He initiated the path of conversion through his entire career by following the standard tradition of the past Buddhas. When he sat under the *bodhi* tree, the Evil One's (Māra's) palace darkened the entire world, but the Buddha made the lotus flower (*utpala*) bloom and the wheel of the Dharma forever turn brightly. Thus, enlightenment is compared to the initial moment of brilliant illumination and only later, upon reflection, did he demonstrate the authentic transmission of that enlightenment to his disciples by [silently] lifting a flower by its stalk. At the moment when one fully realizes what is truly eternal, both existence and nonexistence disappear, enlightened and unenlightened become equally a dream or illusion. While myriad phenomena continue to change, past and present become one moment in which heaven and earth are lost in a dazzling ray of light. Indeed, what do any of the remote descendants really know? They only chant the words that have been left by the Original Teacher and are anxious about [their lack of real insight]. It is earnestly wished: May form and non-form, light and darkness, all equally express the miraculous sound of the Dharma, and may squirming worms and living creatures equally realize ultimate insight and meritorious virtue.

4. The Word of Tribute for Nirvana Day

When the Buddha preached his teachings to people, he did so in accordance with their respective individual capacities. The *Lotus Sutra* informs us that he entrusted to his disciples the future task of religious propagation and granted them the certificate of authentication of their future realization. To encourage and restrain his disciples, the Buddha instructed in his last teaching the strict observance of Vinaya rules and disciplines and spoke of what is permanent. How much more authentic could a transmission be when the realization of Buddhahood was directly transmitted to [the second patriarch, Kāśyapa,] who understood the meaning that Śākyamuni imparted by [silently] lifting a flower by its stalk. Thus, at the moment when the fallen leaves (i.e., the sensory faculties) returned to their source, he was gratified with the completion of the tasks he was given.

Whoever is trapped in the world of illusion is bound to reach its end according to the universal fact of impermanence. Abiding in multiple illusions, one is obliged to return to what they really are; this is called "ultimate quiescence." Yet, the mysterious gem (i.e., the mind) always illuminates turbidity and filth without discrimination, and the precious moon does not avoid casting its reflection onto polluted water. Great concentration has no limit in space and always abides through myriads of *kalpas* as many as the sands of the Ganges River. The one who is perfectly endowed is able to respond anywhere and at any time, manifesting myriads and myriads of forms of his body. Nevertheless, we cannot forget the historical aspect of the Buddha and we feel that his memory is ever more dear to us on this memorial day. We earnestly wish: May the Buddha rectify wrong views entertained by those of us who are remote descendants of his teaching, reverse the trend of this degenerate period to that of Right Dharma in which both [supreme] concentration and insight are equally practiced, and convert the Evil One (Māra) and his entire clan to be leading protectors of the religion.

5. A Brief Biography of the Buddha

The Buddha was born on the continent of India. His family belonged to the noble class (*kṣatriya*), and his family name was Gautama. This Sanskrit name is translated as "Sweet Beet" in Chinese. The first ancestor, a royal sage, was shot with a hunter's arrow. At his death, his blood flowed into the ground, from which two sugarcane stalks sprouted. One grew into a male child called King Gautama, and the other a female child called Queen Sumatī. Together they bore a child who then became a universal ruler (*cakravartin*), turning the wheel of governance over his realm. Because the king came from a descendant of the sun, his race was also called "the sun's race." From that time, after seven hundred generations, the lineage reached the time of King Śuddhodana. Because [during his previous lifetimes] the Buddha had fulfilled meritorious deeds for myriads of *kalpa*s, he entered the womb of Queen Māyā by descending from the Tuṣita Heaven. He was born on the eighth day of the fourth month in the twenty-sixth regnal year, Jia and Yin of King Shao (r. 1052–1001 B.C.E.) of the Zhou dynasty. He was named Sarvasiddhārtha ("One Whose Every Goal Has Been Accomplished"). On the seventh day after his birth, his mother died and he was raised by his mother's younger sister, Mahāprajāpatī.

At the age of twenty-five, Prince Siddhārtha left the palace and went to the forest of the sage Bhārgava. He cut off his hair and became a mendicant. He exchanged his luxurious garments for a hunter's clothing, crossed the Ganges River to the south, and reached the hills of Gayā, where he practiced meditation and austerities. For six years, Siddhārtha toiled hard, maintaining his endurance with only a single grain of hemp and rice [a day]. He thought to himself that if he continued the ascetic way, heretics would claim that self-abnegation is the way to reach nirvana. So, instead he bathed in the Nairañjaṇā River and accepted a meal of milk-rice gruel from the cowherd maiden Sujātā. The god Indra made a seat out of *kuśa* grass and bade him sit on it cross-legged. [Māra,] the king of the evil ones, mobilized his army to try to disrupt Siddhārtha's meditation, but none of Māra's attempts could prevail in disrupting his determination. Thus, [Māra] departed after saluting the Buddha with apologies and repentance. On the morning of the eighth day of the second month, when he saw the morning star, Siddhārtha suddenly attained a great intuitive understanding and realized the highest path, highest, perfect enlightenment (*anuttarā samyaksaṃbodhi*). (Some traditions hold that this occurred on the eighth day of the twelfth month, the first year of Zhengjian of Zhou; there are different interpretations in other traditions.) He was then thirty years old.

Immediately, the Buddha is said to have preached the *Flower Ornament Sutra* at the seat of enlightenment (*bodhimaṇḍa*) in the forest of Magadha. The listeners, [whose understanding] had not yet ripened, were unable to comprehend the teaching as if they were deaf and dumb. For three weeks, the Buddha meditated under various trees and thought of entering nirvana. Meanwhile Brahmā and Indra respectfully requested the Buddha three times to remain and teach what he had realized. Thus, the Buddha traveled to the Deer Park where he conducted the First Turning of the Great Wheel and taught the three vehicles (i.e., the *śrāvakayāna,* the *pratyekabuddhayāna,* and the *bodhisattvayāna*) initially to his five disciples, including Kauṇḍinya. Here he taught the Four Noble Truths, the twelve links of the chain of causation (*pratītyasamut-pāda*), the six principles (*pāramitā*s) of practice, and so forth.

Twelve years later, at the age of forty-two, the Buddha introduced a more advanced teaching, recorded in the general Mahayana texts (the Vaipulya sutras), and thereby was able to educate more disciples and consolidate a firm basis of his sangha. It was during this period that he criticized the shortcomings of the Hinayana and praised the perfect teaching of the Mahayana. From this time on, for thirty years, the Buddha taught the general Mahayana teachings in such texts as the *Vimalakīrtinirdeśa-sūtra,* the *Śūraṃgama-dhāraṇī*s, the *Perfection of Wisdom Sutra,* and so forth. By then, having reached his seventy-second year, he began to teach the *Lotus Sutra* and thereby entrusted his [evangelical] task to his disciples and assured their future realization of Buddhahood. Yet, in the following eight years, he continued to detail his original intent.

In the fifty-third regnal year of King Mu, year of Ren and Shen, at the age of seventy-nine, the Buddha for the first time visited the Tuṣita Heaven to preach for his mother. In his absence, King Udayana, who yearned for his master, ordered a golden image to be cast, and when the Buddha descended from heaven the golden statue is said to have welcomed his return. The Buddha's aunt Mahāprajāpatī and her five hundred female followers, as well as such saintly disciples as Śāriputra, Maudgalyāyana, seventy thousand arhats, and so forth, felt unable to bear the passing of their master and hence passed away at the same time. The bodhisattvas, the four groups of followers (i.e., monks [*bhikṣu*s], nuns [*bhikṣuṇī*s], laymen [*upāsaka*s], and laywomen [*upāsikā*s]), the eight groups of demigods, and the kings of the birds and animals all assembled, while the Buddha allowed Cunda, a smith, to make the last food offering. For the sake of his disciples, the Buddha preached the principles of impermanence (*anitya*), suffering (*duḥkha*), and emptiness (*śūnyatā*).

The Buddha also announced that the supreme Right Dharma had already been entrusted to his primary disciple Mahākāśyapa, and that Mahākāśyapa would become a great refuge for the rest of the disciples in the same way as the Tathāgata himself had been. He also knew that Ānanda had been waylaid by the Evil One (Māra) outside the *śāla* forest, and he summoned Mañjuśrī to call him back, saying that Ānanda was his brother who had served him well for over twenty years, that he learned the Dharma as seamlessly as water poured into a vessel of any form [takes the shape of that vessel], and hence he wanted Ānanda to record his last teaching in the *Nirvana Sutra.* Mañjuśrī conveyed the Buddha's wish to Ānanda and brought him back to the place.

1117a

Furthermore, the Buddha told Ānanda that the brahman Subhadra, who was one hundred and twenty years old and who had not yet discarded his attachment to self, must be brought to listen to the Tathāgata's last teaching by being informed that the Buddha would enter nirvana that night. At once, Subhadra came to listen to the Buddha's teaching and immediately attained the state of arhatship. Thus, the Buddha announced: "Immediately after I realized the path, I converted Kauṇḍinya, and now I have converted Subhadra at last. I have thus completed my task. What ought to be done has been done." At midnight of the fifteenth day of the second month, he once again addressed his disciples: "O disciples, after my death, you must pay respect to the *prātimokṣa* rules and disciplines. [The *prātimokṣa*] is your master regardless of whether I am or am not in this world. There is no lessening of its importance." He lay his right side on a cloth decorated with seven kinds of precious gems. There was not a single voice heard anywhere, and the Buddha passed away.

Aniruddha immediately went to the Tuṣita Heaven to tell Queen Māyā that the Buddha had entered *parinirvāṇa*. As she came down from heaven, the Buddha once again raised himself to preach, in order to console his mother, and then said to Ānanda, "You must know that because I fear there might appear some unfilial people in the future, I have exemplified filial piety by coming out of the golden coffin to greet my mother." At that moment, Mahākāśyapa, leading the group of five hundred disciples, arrived running from the hills of Mount Gṛdhrakūṭa (Vulture Peak) and greeted him with lamentation. Once again the Buddha miraculously revealed the mark of the sacred symbol of the "Wheel of One Thousand Spokes" on the soles of his feet. Heavenly beings brought aromatic woods to the cremation site, and the cremation fire continued to burn by itself for seven days.

Lay followers deposited the Buddha's relics in eight golden vases. King Ajātaśatru as well as the kings of eight countries, the god Indra, and other gods as well as the *nāga* kings, all vied for acquisition of the relics. Minister Upakitta remonstrated with them to stop fighting [over the relics] and advised them to divide and distribute them among themselves. Thus, they divided the relics into three portions, one for the heavenly gods, a second for the *nāga* kings, and the third was further divided among the eight kings. King Ajātaśatru obtained eighty-four thousand pieces, placed each within a purple and gold case, and enshrined them in stupas he had built in the regions of the five major rivers that flow into the Ganges River.

IV. Nirvana Day of the Emperor's Religious Counselor

1. The Memorial Rite for the Master

When the memorial day comes, the tablet of the master's name must be respectfully placed on the altar and properly enshrined. Offerings of incense, flowers, candles, tea, fruit, and delicacies should be carefully prepared. The director of practitioners' affairs is obliged to have the word of tribute composed and approved. (The procedure is identical to that of the Buddha's Memorial Day.) In the evening before the day [of the memorial], the attendants of the practice hall official are instructed to inform the practitioners of the following day's event and post the signboard indicating the sutra chanting. On the appointed day, the bell is tolled to assemble the practitioners, and they line up facing the rostrum seat. Notified of their readiness, the abbot comes out to offer incense, sweet hot water, food, a monetary gift, and tea, and then performs three prostrations with opened sitting cloth. When he picks up incense and utters the word of insight, the director of practitioners' affairs with a bow signals the dual order officials to step forward, in pairs, to offer incense, while the practitioners perform prostrations with opened sitting cloth in unison. The abbot kneels to offer incense at a portable incense burner, while at the same time the director [of practitioners' affairs] reads the word of tribute. He then subsequently calls for the chanting of the prayer verses and concludes with the following invocation of merit transference:

> The merit accrued from the foregoing deed of chanting shall be dedicated to the one [designated] "Above the Emperor" under the imperial heaven (i.e., the emperor), the great sage who assisted imperial governance by introducing religion and propagating letters, the spiritual ruler who, endowed with supreme virtue, universal enlightenment, and true illumination, unfailingly assisted the throne in ruling the nation, the Buddhist disciple from the Western Heaven (i.e., Tibet) and the imperial counsel of the great Yuan. We wish to discharge our indebtedness to him for the compassionate refuge bestowed upon us. Veneration to the Buddhas of the ten directions and the three times, and so on.

2. The Word of Tribute

1117b

Heaven inaugurated the nation of Yuan and magnanimously created the great sage as its counselor. The path he followed was honorable and supreme, and he indeed became a spiritual ruler by creating the Mongol script. He quietly helped the foundation of cultural conversion and privately assisted the imperial rule. When he spoke, his speech became a religious text. When he lifted his foot, his act became rule. His rank was among a thousand Buddhas, the generosity he extended matched that of earth, and his supreme intelligence matched that of heaven. The highest honor was shown him by the posthumous title, "Above the Emperor." Honoring his memorial day today, we look upon his gracious illumination more admiringly than ever. We earnestly pray that his holiness may once again ride on the carriage of vows and help the governance and transformation of the populace with the universal language of all seas, and, taking pity in the present age of spiritual decline, rekindle the principle of religion unchanged for a thousand years.

3. A Brief Biography of the Religious Counselor

The imperial counselor of religion, Baheshiba ('Phags-pa), whose ordained name was Huichuangxianjixiang, was a man of Tibet. He was born on the thirteenth day of the fourth month in the year of the "sixth stem and boar." His father was called Suonangancang. During the beginning of Tibet, there was a national master of Buddhism, Śāntarakṣita (Chanhengluojida) by name. He realized the supreme insight and acquired the supernatural powers, and his descendants equally excelled in spiritual matters and religious practice through successive transmission. The rulers of that country honored them as their religious counselors. The man of the seventeenth generation, Sasijiawa (Sakya-pa) by name, was the paternal uncle of the master. As he was by birth well endowed [in intelligence], he studied under his uncle and was able to chant from memory a thousand or two of the sacred *gāthā*s and secret verses just by silently reading through them. At the age of seven, he gave his first lecture and demonstrated his speech, showing himself to be well versed and totally commanding.

At the age of fifteen, in the year of the "tenth stem and ox," he came to know that the heavenly mandate would fall to Emperor Shizu, Longdeyuanqian (Kublai Khan). He traveled swiftly on horseback to reach the capital in order to officiate for him at the ordination ceremony of the Buddhist laity for Xianzong, his queen Zhongwei, and the Crown Prince (i.e., Shizu), imparting special meaning to the event of their conversion. After six years had passed, in the year of the "seventh stem and monkey," Shizu ascended the throne and established the Yuan dynasty in the Zhongtong era. Thereupon, the master was appointed "national master" and granted the imperial seal to administer Buddhist religious affairs throughout the country, separating, for the first time, religious matters from secular affairs. Four years later, bidding farewell to the emperor, he returned west. However, he was called back before a year had passed. In the seventh year of Zhiyuan, the "seventh stem and horse," he was entrusted with the task of creating a new set of scripts as standard for the great Yuan empire. Singlehandedly he carried out the task, and before even a day had passed he successfully formulated patterns and strokes into a system of letters. Since his accomplishment was profoundly satisfactory to imperial expectation, a decree was immediately issued for the prompt enactment of its usage throughout the respective divisions of capitals, provinces, prefectures, and districts. The system of the new scripts became the greatest law of the age. The master was appointed religious counselor to the throne, the spiritual ruler embodying the great treasure of the Buddha-Dharma, and was granted the imperial seal.

Once again the master returned to the west. Eleven years later, the emperor sent a special envoy to officially invite him back to the capital. During his visit to the capital, he refused the emperor's request to stay there and returned to his temple [in Tibet]. Despite imperial efforts, he could not be persuaded to remain in the capital. On the twenty-second day of the eleventh month in the seventeenth year of Jiyuan, the master passed away. Upon learning of his death, the emperor could hardly bear his dear memory and ordered a great stupa built in the capital in order to enshrine the ashes of the master. The circular structure of this stupa was beautifully decorated in gold and dark blue, and indeed the building had no equal, past or present. (The foregoing biography is found in the epigraphy composed by Hanlin scholars such as Wangpan and others, under imperial edict.) In later years, the master was given the following posthumous title:

1117c

> The one [designated] "Above the Emperor" under the imperial heaven, the great sage who assisted imperial governance by introducing religion and propagating letters, the spiritual ruler who, endowed with supreme virtue, universal enlightenment, and true illumination, unfailingly assisted the throne in ruling the nation, the Buddhist disciple from the Western Heaven (Tibet) and the imperial counselor of the great Yuan.

End of Chapter III: Discharging Religious Indebtedness

Chapter IV

Honoring the Patriarchs
of the Zen Tradition

I. Preface to the Chapter

The reason that each person should enshrine his ancestors is to regard the beginning of his form and life as important. Form and life begin with love, and yet forms change in time, and so does love exhaust itself in time. Yet the spiritual aspect of the essential nature (i.e., Buddha-nature) is never obscured, because it neither depends on life nor does it disappear when life ends. Therefore, the Buddha taught that humans must acquire clear insight into this nature. And yet, misguided by words and statements, scholars of later periods cannot grasp the true meaning, as if a doctor were to adhere to the medical textbook too well and forsake actual treatment with medicine and acupuncture. What value is there in this? Only when the patriarch of our school, Bodhidharma (Puti Damo), came to China and taught the path of direct experience for the first time were people awakened clearly to neither search for the miraculous nature of the self through the use of words nor through its total rejection but to see why [the essential nature] must be realized beyond sounds of the voice and forms of expression. Thus, any one of us who succeeds in the lineage and hands it on to another must accomplish this just as fire naturally burns fuel or water takes the form of the vessel [into which it is poured].

There is no difference, not even as slight as a single hair, between past and present. Doesn't this tradition emphasize the meaning of original form and life? In later days, Zen Master Baizhang Dazhi instituted the Zen monastic regulations so that the practitioners of our tradition could abide by their own standards, and this was, indeed, the origin of the Zen monastic community. The Venerable Shouduan of Haihuiyuan Temple advised that it is our duty to enshrine [a figure of] Bodhidharma in the center, Baizhang to his right, and the founder of each temple to his left. Look for this information in the introductory chapter of the *Regulatory Rules of the Patriarchal Hall (Zutanggangji)*.

II. The Memorial Day of Bodhidharma

1. The Memorial Rite for the Patriarch Bodhidharma

Prior to the appointed day, the practice hall official is obliged to organize the memorial service by collecting contributions and see that word of tribute is composed and approved. (The procedure is identical to that of the Buddha's nirvana day.) In the evening before the day [of the rite], the ceremonial place should be prepared in due manner in the Dharma hall, by enshrining solemnly the patriarch's portrait on the rostrum seat, and arranging an incense burner, flower vases, and an incense table in front of it. At the right-hand side of the rear of the hall a meditation couch, a brush duster, and a clothes rack with robes hung upon it (it is not correct to set up a bed couch and fan) should be set up, and at the left-hand side of the rear of the hall a chair, desk, incense burner, vases, incense, and candles should be set up and some scriptures placed on the desk. The practice hall novice attendants notify the practitioners of the coming event and post the signboard indicating sutra chanting, and also announce to them:

> There will be the memorial service with sutra chanting this evening, and also another for fulfillment chanting tomorrow mid-morning. Please be reminded of proper attire.

Before the evening Zen session, the practice hall bell is tolled to assemble the practitioners at the Dharma hall. Meanwhile, notified of the assembly, the abbot arrives at the hall. Drumming signals the special rite of offering sweet hot water. The abbot burns incense and performs three prostrations [with opened sitting cloth]. Without folding his sitting cloth, he proceeds to the altar to offer hot water, and, returning to his place, performs another three prostrations. Once again he proceeds toward the altar and salutes it with a gesture of offering the hot water. Then he returns to his seat, performs two prostrations, and folds up his sitting cloth. A signal of three drumbeats is given, and immediately after the hand bell is struck by the novice attendant, the director of practitioners' affairs steps forward from his east-order column and leads the prayer service, saying:

> Ernestly reflecting upon the tradition, our religion transmits Zen experience in the manner of direct finger-pointing [by the patriarch Bodhidharma] and gratefully depends on the reverberation of the subsequent waves of descendants who transmit it. The ultimate Way is vast and difficult to name; we hesitate to enjoin this brilliant luster of the Way to any of those remote future generations. May the practitioners pray for the gracious assistance of the Buddhas by intoning their ten sacred names: the Luminous Pure Dharma Body Vairocana Buddha, and so on.

1118a

The prayer concludes with the director intoning the following invocation of merit transference:

> We respectfully dedicate the merit accrued from the foregoing prayer to the First Patriarch Bodhidharma, perfectly enlightened Great Master. We wish to discharge our indebtedness to the compassion bestowed upon us as our refuge. Veneration to the Buddhas of the ten directions and the three times, and so on.

After the practice hall bell tolls three times, the practitioners leave the hall, or they may be invited to take their seats for an evening meal.

While the evening bell tolls, the practice hall bell signals the practitioners to assemble and proceed toward the Dharma hall once again. The abbot offers incense, and the director of practitioners' affairs leads the chanting of the *Śūraṃgama-dhāraṇīs* and concludes by intoning the following invocation of merit transference:

> The pure Dharma body has essentially neither phenomenal appearance nor disappearance, but because of the great compassion and power of its vow, it shows, as it were, phenomenal appearance as well as disappearance. We implore: May compassion shine its bright mirror reflection upon us. On the fifth day of this month, the memorial day has arrived on which the First Patriarch Bodhidharma, the perfectly enlightened Great Master and Great Priest, entered absolute quiescence. Assembling all the disciples and offering incense and provisions, we thereby express our care and devotion for the master. We humbly dedicate the merit accrued from chanting the [*dhāraṇīs* of the] *Śūraṃgama-sūtra* for the sake of discharging our indebtedness to the compassion which has bestowed refuge upon us. We humbly pray: May unerring practitioners endeavor to promulgate the tradition of Bodhidharma and thereby realize the wondrous insight that is limitless, and become a worthy receptacle of Mahayana Buddhism. Veneration to the Buddhas of the ten directions and the three times, and so on.

Next, the ceremonial leader leads the novice attendants to line up before the [image of the] patriarch, and in unison they say, "We are here, sir," perform prostrations, and chant the sutras. Lastly, lay devotees line up to worship the patriarch.

Early the next morning, the abbot burns incense, performs prostrations, offers sweet hot water and rice gruel, and participates in the rice gruel breakfast, sitting to the side of the [image of the] patriarch. After breakfast, he once again burns incense and offers tea, while the director of practitioners' affairs leads the chanting of the *Mahākāruṇikacitta-dhāraṇīs*, concluding with the following invocation of merit transference:

> The merit accrued by the foregoing chanting shall be respect-
> fully dedicated for the sake of the First Patriarch Bodhi-
> dharma, perfectly enlightened Great Master and Great Priest.
> May this help us discharge our indebtedness to the compas-
> sionate refuge he bestowed on us. Veneration to the Buddhas
> of the ten directions and the three times, and so on.

Between breakfast and the noon meal, the practice hall bell is
rung to assemble the practitioners at the Dharma hall, where they
line up facing the altar. The abbot offers incense, performs three
prostrations with opened sitting cloth, and proceeds toward the
incense burner, leaving his sitting cloth open, to offer sweet hot
water and food. He is aided by the guest reception assistant, who
hands the offerings [one by one] from the abbot to the incense
offering assistant, who respectfully sets them on the table beside
the patriarch's tablet. When this is completed, the abbot returns
to his position and performs three prostrations as before, then once
again immediately goes forward to burn incense and offer a monetary gift. Upon returning [to his position, the abbot] peforms
another three prostrations, then stands, folding his sitting cloth.
Thereupon, drumbeats signal the special serving of tea. (This procedure is identical to that of the special serving of sweet hot water.)

After the special serving of tea, the abbot offers incense with
prayer and utters a word of tribute. When his address is over, the
attendants play cymbals to create musical sounds; simultaneously,
the director of practitioners' affairs steps forward from the east-
order column and, bowing with palms together, invites the abbot
to offer incense. The latter's assistant, carrying a portable incense
case, hands him incense before the burner. Next, the director invites
the ranking practitioners of the east and west halls, followed by
the dual order officials, to proceed in pairs to offer incense at the
incense burner. When this is over, the entire assembly performs in
unison three prostrations with opened sitting cloth, and facing the
altar the director says:

The pure Dharma body has in essence neither phenomenal appearance nor disappearance. Only because of great compassion and the power of its vow, it manifests, as it were, phenomenal appearance as well as nonappearance.

The director continues to read the word of tribute as the abbot kneels to burn incense at a portable incense burner. Next, the director calls for the chanting of the *Śūraṃgama-dhāraṇīs* and concludes with the following invocation of merit transference:

The merit accrued by the foregoing chanting shall be respectfully dedicated for the sake of the First Patriarch Bodhidharma, perfectly enlightened Great Master and Great Priest. May this help us discharge our indebtedness to the compassionate refuge he bestowed upon us. Veneration to the Buddhas of the ten directions and the three times, and so on.

Next follows sutra chanting by the novice attendants.

2. The Word of Tribute

How great was the authentic transmission of the Dharma to China by the distinguished descendant of the enlightened spiritual ruler. His insight, "vast, limitless openness and nothing especially holy," indeed broke the vital point of the pedantic scholasticism then prevalent. When hundreds of rivers reach the vast ocean they all lose their singularity. When the bright sun shines in mid-sky there is no shadow to follow anything on the ground. Pointing to the mind of humans, he enabled us to see that "to become a Buddha" means to become mind itself. Experiencing the wondrous path, one forgets words; while, having lost words, one [directly] sees the path. As this is a greatly beneficial teaching in the world, it should widely flourish in terms of its tradition. Making a rare appearance in this turbid world by becoming the First Patriarch, he found a Mahayana receptacle [in Huike, the Second Patriarch] in the country of China and totally immersed him in the grain.

Today, we honor the day when he left the single sandal behind (i.e., the memorial day) and we have prepared in our best manner an exquisite vegetarian dish. The robe of faith symbolizes the weightiness of the Buddhas and patriarchs and the strength capable of bearing a thousand weights. May a single flower once again bloom in the spring of heaven and earth, so that its fragrance may be transmitted through tens of thousands of generations.

3. A Brief Biography of Bodhidharma

The patriarch was born the third son of the king of Xiangshi in South India. His family belonged to the noble class, and his own name was originally Bodhitāra. Later, along with his two brothers he happened to meet the twenty-seventh patriarch Prajñātāra. Because the master saw the innate capacity of the patriarch, he tested him and his brothers in debate on the meaning of his gift of a gem to them. [After years of study and practice under Prajñātāra,] the patriarch had already discovered and cultivated the essential nature of the mind. Prajñātāra told him, "You have acquired the whole inclusive principle and since 'Dharma' conveys the entire inclusive meaning of the Mahayana, your name should be changed to 'Dharma.'" Thus, the patriarch's name became Bodhidharma.

The patriarch asked his master, "As I have accomplished the essentials of the religion, in which country should I propagate Buddhism? Please, give me a suggestion, sir."

Prajñātāra replied, "Although you have obtained the essential of my religion, you shall not go anywhere far distant. Just stay in South India and wait for an opportunity sixty-seven years after my death. Then you should go to China where you can set up a great Dharma session to teach the best qualified, but do not leave India immediately lest you become quickly exhausted by the troublesome environment of China's capital city."

On the twenty-first day of the ninth month in the eighth year of Putong of Liang, in the year of the "fourth stem and sheep,"

1118b

Bodhidharma arrived in Southern China. Suang, the prefect of Guangzhou, sent an official report to Emperor Wu of Liang (r. 464–549). The emperor dispatched his envoy with a decree inviting the patriarch to his imperial court. Bodhidharma arrived in Jinling on the first day of the tenth month and spoke with the ruler, but they did not reach an accord in their meeting. Thereupon Bodhidharma crossed the Yangzi River to the north on the nineteenth day and reached Luoyang on the twenty-third day of the eleventh month, which was the tenth year of Taihe under the reign of Emperor Xiaoming of the Wei dynasty. He stayed in Shaolinsi, the temple of Mount Songshan, and spent years facing the wall in silent meditation. No one was able to fathom his purpose; he was called the "wall-facing brahman." On the fifth day of the tenth month in the nineteenth year of Taihe ("fourth stem and dragon"), he passed away while sitting upright in meditation. He was buried on Mount Xiongershan on the twenty-eighth day of the twelfth month of the year, and a memorial stupa was erected within Dinglinsi. During the Tang dynasty, Bodhidharma was honored by the title Yuangue Dashi ("Fully Enlightened"), and the stupa is called Kongguan ("Contemplation of Emptiness").

III. The Memorial Day for Baizhang

1. The Memorial Rite for Baizhang

Prior to the appointed day, the practice hall official collects contributions to obtain various offerings. On the evening before the day, the ceremonial place should be set up properly in the Dharma hall. The portrait of the master is placed on the rostrum seat and various vessels for the rite of offerings are solemnly set up on the central altar as well as on tables on the right and left sides at the rear of the hall. There will be a memorial service with sutra chanting in the evening, and also another for the fulfillment of the memorial service on the following day, including a special serving of tea, the word of insight and prayer with incense offering, and the word of tribute, as well as incense offering by the dual order officials and three prostrations with opened sitting cloth performed by all the practitioners in unison (so far, the proceedings are identical with those of the memorial rite for Bodhidharma), but excluding the prayer chanting. The invocation of merit transference for the evening rite is as follows:

> The pure Dharma body has essentially neither phenomenal appearance nor disappearance, but because of great compassion and the power of its vow, it shows, as it were, phenomenal appearance as well as nonappearance. We implore: May compassion shine its bright mirror reflection upon us. On the seventeenth day of the first month, we have respectfully honored the memorial day on which Baizhang Dazhi, Jiaming Huangcong Miaoxiang Changshi, entered absolute quiescence. Assembling all the disciples and offering incense and provisions, we thereby express our care and devotion for the master. We humbly dedicate the merit accrued from chanting the [*dhāraṇīs*] of the *Śūraṃgama-sūtra* for the sake of discharging our indebtedness for the compassion which has bestowed refuge upon us. We humbly pray: May the rare flower of the *uḍumbara* tree once again appear to herald springtime in the garden of enlightenment, and the insight of the sun extend daylight to forever illuminate the night of dark delusion. Veneration to the Buddhas of the ten directions and the three times, and so on.

2. The Word of Tribute

He spoke, it became the law of the land. It exactly marks the norm and establishes the standard. Through tens of thousands of generations, the Way he established has been known as worthy of reverence. It contains principles and precedences, on the basis of which the harmonious life of the Zen monastic institution has flourished, creating many notable personalities. The Chinese expressions in the *Book of Regulations* (*Qingguai*) exactly correspond to those of the Sanskrit Vinaya. The richness of the content is comparable with that of the literary works of Shiqu and Tianlu. In content, the discourses of teaching (sutras) and the rules of restraint (Vinaya) are combined in a mutually complementary form, and the precision represents a specimen of golden sentences and gemlike phrases combined. The rules of regulation are ceremonial forms that display footprints inside the building; they do not represent the manner of footsteps by which men collect silk floss outside in the field. Whether one should follow a certain norm or leave it, the words avoid the weight and subtlety of thought. Whether one should depart from an occasion or enter into it, the principle permeates every wonder. He ought to be enshrined along with every Zen patriarch. Why should he be enshrined only on his memorial day? May the victorious flags of Indra in his strife overcome all evil ones and heretics, and may great trees of shady coolness such as Linji fill the Buddhist world.

3. A Brief Biography of Baizhang

The master was a native of Changle of Fuzhou province, son of the Wang family. He renounced the world in childhood and was broadly trained in the three areas of Buddhist study (*śīla, samādhi,* and *prajñā*). He sought out Mazu for instruction and training in Jiangxi province and joined his flourishing Zen community. Among Mazu's able young disciples, Dazhu, Nanquan, Guizong, and so forth were called great figures, yet the master was appointed primary seat official. When Mazu passed away in Letan, Baizhang succeeded to his position, but due to the increase in the number of practitioners the place became overcrowded with little extra space, and he decided to leave.

While traveling, he passed Xinwu and took a rest below Chelun Peak. A man called Ganzhenyuochang donated land and requested him to stay. In the meantime many more practitioners had gathered around him, and finally he decided to build a temple, naming it Datuoti ("Great Development and Improvement"). He passed away on the seventeenth day of the first month in the ninth year of Yuanhe. It is said that the forest of fir trees appeared to look fiery, as if burned, and the beautiful gorge dried up by springtime. The four groups of followers mournfully buried his ashes on Daxiong Peak ("Great Virility"). Prior to this event, a foreign ascetic monk, Sima (Dhutadhara; Toutuozhe) by name, had chosen this place as the burial site, saying, "Since this peak is linked to three other peaks but has not been fully appreciated for its wonderful beauty, if his holiness [were buried] on this mountain, it would enhance his stature as a spiritual ruler and command reverence throughout the land." It is said that the people of that period all agreed with him.

The Tang imperial court granted Baizhang the title Dazhi Chanshi ("Chan Master Great Wisdom") in the first year of Changqing. The stupa erected at the burial site was called Dabaoshenglun ("Great, Precious, Victorious Wheel"). The Song imperial court further added the title Juezhao ("Mirror of Enlightenment") in the first year of Daguan, and the commemorative tower built was called Huiju ("Assembly of Wisdom"). In the third year of Yuantong the great Yuan court further added another title, Zen Master Hongzongmiaoxing ("Grand Master Wonderful Practice").

IV. The Memorial Rites for the Founder and the Patriarchs

The founder's memorial day and the successive patriarchs' religious deeds should be properly honored. Whoever contributed to the temple must be enshrined in the Dharma hall the evening before each memorial day. (The procedure is identical to that of the memorial service for Baizhang.) The word of tribute may be exempted. The head administrative official should prepare various offerings. If the word of tribute is omitted for the memorial days of the successive patriarchs, it is not necessary to conduct the special serving of tea and sweet hot water.

Prior to the appointed day, the practice hall official notifies the head administrative official to prepare a set of offerings to be placed on the altar. The tablet of the patriarch in question must be placed at the western end of the rostrum seat. In the morning, after breakfast, the abbot and the dual order officials stand in a single horizontal line facing the altar. The director of practitioners' affairs steps forward and salutes the officials, inviting them to offer incense in pairs. When this is completed and the officials have returned to their positions, the entire assembly performs in unison three prostrations with [opened sitting cloth.] The abbot's assistant does the same at the end of the east-order column. (The *Zhida Regulations* suggest that though the memorial rite of chanting is directed to a particular patriarch, it is not appropriate to prepare only a single set of meal offering.) The director calls for the chanting of the *Mahākāruṇikacitta-dhāraṇī*s and concludes with the following invocation of merit transference:

> The vast ocean of illumination of the Tathāgata's insight comprises the waves of whirlpools like the cycle of birth and death (samsara). The teaching of great concentration (*samādhi*) dissolves the distinctions of coming and going, past and present. We implore: May compassion shine its bright mirror reflection upon us.
>
> On this day of such-and-such month, the temple respectfully honors the memorial day of So-and-so, Patriarch and Zen Master, of such-and-such generation in the succession of this temple. By offering various delicacies, we express our care and devotion for him, and the assembly of practitioners has chanted the *Mahākāruṇikacitta-dhāraṇī*s. The merit thereby accrued shall be dedicated to enhance the enshrinement of the patriarch with ever more reverence. We respectfully implore: May the sun of insight once again shine, illuminating the luminous seed in the patriarchal room, reviving the springtime of trees and flowers [that flourished] in Shaolinsi, and so on.

1119a

Alternatively, the same sacred verses may be chanted by those [who come from the same region as the honored patriarch] or by those who have gathered for an annual retreat for the sake of a particular patriarch. It concludes with the following invocation of merit transference:

> The merit accrued by the foregoing chanting shall be dedicated for the sake of the great master and teacher So-and-so to enhance his enshrinement with ever more reverence. Veneration to the Buddhas of the ten directions and the three times, and so on.

If monetary alms are again distributed, the *Śūraṃgama-dhāraṇī*s may be chanted and [the ceremony] concludes with the same invocation of merit transference as before.

V. The Memorial Rite for the Master of the Dharma Succession

1. Sutra Chanting

Virtuous patriarchs of the past devoted themselves sincerely to the task of promulgating the Zen vehicle of Buddhist spirituality, to the discovery and cultivation of the essential nature of one's self, and to the instruction of junior practitioners in order to teach them what one should receive from one's predecessor and what one should transmit to one's successor. This was the way they paid their debt, just as citing the three crucial passages uttered by Haojian of Baling became the honorable act to discharge indebtedness at the memorial service of Yunmen. The predecessors had profound thoughts, and honoring them is the path of grave importance that should not be abandoned.

Prior to the appointed day, the abbot requests the head administrative official to prepare a set of offerings and provisions with his own money. The evening before the day [of the memorial], the altar should be set up in the Dharma hall in due manner. The

attendants of the practice hall official are obliged to notify the practitioners about the coming event and post the signboard indicating the sutra chanting. That evening, the *Śūraṃgama-dhāraṇīs*
are chanted; those who are from the same province [as the honored master] and those who are related in his Dharma lineage may
chant the *Mahākāruṇikacitta-dhāraṇī*s. This is followed by the
novice attendants' chanting; the invocation of merit transference
is the same as before.

Early the next morning, the abbot offers rice gruel at the altar
and participates in the breakfast meal, and upon completion of
this rite, the practitioners chant the *Mahākāruṇikacitta-dhāraṇī*s,
while those who come from the same province and who are related
in Dharma lineage intone the *Śūraṃgama-dhāraṇī*s. At mid-morning, there should be the sutra chanting for the rite of fulfillment.
The abbot offers food, conducts a special serving of tea, and utters
the word of insight and the prayer for offering incense. (The proceeding is identical to that of Bodhidharma's memorial service.)
The officials of the dual orders jointly offer incense, while the entire
assembly performs three prostrations with opened sitting cloth.
(Since all practitioners, from the senior onward, have originally
gathered to receive the abbot's instruction, they are obliged to pay
their respects to the abbot's master as well.)

At the time of the midday meal, the abbot enters the practice
hall, burns incense, and performs prostrations with opened sitting
cloth [before the altar of the sacred guardian image], and returns
to his position. The abbot's personal assistant presents a monetary
gift to the altar. (If he happens to be at the Dharma hall to conduct the same rite, it is not appropriate to present a monetary gift
during the sutra chanting, because to do so would be impolite.)

After the noon meal, the abbot serves tea and the incense
offering assistant carries out the proceeding.

2. The Special Serving of Tea for the Portrait

After the noon meal is over, the abbot's guest reception assistant
delivers to the west hall guest resident and the dual order officials

an invitation to participate in a special serving of tea to be conducted before the patriarch's portrait that evening. As the participants move their respective seat markers to the right side of their seats, the abbot makes a gesture of greeting to request them to take their seats. He then proceeds to offer incense and sweet hot water at the altar, and then serves sweet hot water to the participants. Returning to his position, the abbot again burns incense, performs three prostrations with opened sitting cloth, and stands up to bow toward the invitees, thanking them for their presence. Three drumbeats signal the end of the serving of sweet hot water, and the participants leave the hall. If there are three or five guests of the west hall, their seats must be assigned symmetrically opposite the dual order officials. The abbot himself serves sweet hot water to the west hall residents of the first seat section, whereas his assistant serves the dual order officials of the second seat section.

If there is no west hall guest in attendance, the first serving is exempted, and fruit or cake are served when the sutra chanting is over. The retired dual order officials must be invited beforehand, and senior or junior practitioners related in the Dharma lineage or colleagues trained under the same master must be also invited. Novices and those who are indirectly related are not entitled to participate in the event. When all participants are seated, the abbot stands to offer incense and sweet hot water. Thereupon, his assistant burns incense and proceeds to serve sweet hot water and fruit or cake.

End of Chapter IV: Honoring the Patriarchs
of the Zen Tradition

Chapter V

The Abbot, Resident Bearer of the Dharma

I. Preface to the Chapter

Four hundred years after the initial introduction of Buddhism to China, Bodhidharma arrived in this country. Further, the Buddhist Way transmitted by the First Patriarch reached Master Baizhang through eight patriarchal successions. The ultimate truth of the Way was the sole concern of the succession [of patriarchs], who received it from one and passed it on to the next. Some of the patriarchs resided in caves, while others sojourned in Vinaya school temples.

During this period, there was no official called "abbot" (*zhuchi*, "upholder or bearer of the Dharma"). By the time of Baizhang, however, the Zen school had begun to flourish. This was because, following the prevailing fashion of the day, not only princes and ministers, rulers, and public officials who dominated the highest strata of society, but also Confucian and Taoist scholars and common people from all walks of life in the lowest stratum of society visited Zen practitioners to enquire about the Way. When the number of practitioners of Zen rapidly increase, unless they deeply respect their teacher's authority, the rules and disciplines transmitted by the latter may not be rigorously maintained. Thus, for the first time, teachers and masters were given a position of authority under the title "abbot" and were called by the honorable title "senior or head priest" (*zhanglao*), just as in the Indian Buddhist tradition, Śāriputra, Subhūti, and so on were addressed honorably as "elder" or "head monk" (*thera*), on account of both their ordination seniority and their excellent qualities and virtues.

[In order to accommodate the growing numbers of Zen practitioners,] larger buildings were constructed to house them, and the two sets of official positions (i.e., the dual orders of east and west) were created to divide responsibilities. As a result, the monastic system was made to work splendidly. In the matter of labor, even the abbot was obliged to take equal part in the work along with the practitioners. Baizhang always said, "A day of no work, a day of no eating." How could this principle represent a life of wealth and riches, amassing heaps of rice or stores of grain! How could it embody a life of comfort that depends on the toil of slaves? In early days, therefore, the monastic leader was elected by his fellow practitioners and the appointment was reported to the government. In some cases, an invitation [to become abbot] was even declined. Later, however, the position of abbot became a position of high status to be purchased at great price or forcefully seized as if it were a rare commodity.

If, indeed, one is unworthy of the office of abbot, one's temple is bound to decline and [eventually] cease to exist. If, again, [after the death of an abbot,] a group of unreformed cohorts is left behind, no one knows how they might increase in number within a few decades. We sometimes hear about the tragic retributions that people receive in the next life [as the result of such an offense]. Indeed, such sufferings are unbearable to hear about. Shouldn't we take heed not to repeat a similar offense, and should we not fear its retribution?

II. The Abbot's Daily Schedule

1. The Ascent to the Dharma Hall

i. First Day of the Month and Mid-month Day

In general, on the evening before the first and fifteenth (i.e., mid-month) days of each month, the abbot's incense offering assistant notifies him:

Tomorrow morning, the first day of the month (or mid-month day), prayer for imperial well-being is scheduled and the ascent to the Dharma hall is in order, sir.

In the morning, [the incense offering assistant] once again reminds the abbot about the proceeding and instructs the guest reception attendant to post the signboard indicating the ascent to the Dharma hall and informing practitioners of the day's event. The usual three tolls of the practice hall bell after the rice gruel breakfast should not be made on this day. As soon as the rostrum seat is set in the Dharma hall, the practice hall novice attendant reports to the primary seat official that it is ready, and strikes the wooden sounding board located outside the practitioners' quarters. The practitioners then return to the practice hall and sit cross-legged. The abbot's novice attendant first notifies the abbot of this, then his assistant official, and then begins to drum. The dual order officials, leading the practitioners and novice attendants, enter the Dharma hall, proceed to the rostrum seat, salute with a bow, separate themselves into their respective east- and west-order positions, and stand facing each other.

Ushered by his assistant official, the abbot ascends the rostrum seat, offers incense, addresses the assembly with the word of celebration (for details, see Chapter I, part IV, section 4), and, after taking his seat cross-legged, encourages those practitioners who are motivated to learn to open their minds and thereby promulgate the path. If any guests are present, the abbot thanks them for their participation at this time. If the audience is so large that he might fail to mention some of their names, the assistant official keeps notes of the names [of guests] and presents them to the abbot when necessary. If the abbot of another temple or a renowned guest of the west hall are present, their seats should be placed on the right-hand side of the rostrum seat, while the guest seats for government officials are placed at the left-hand side, opposite each other. (If these participants know the proper form and honor the Dharma, they will not take their seats but remain standing.)

ii. Ascent to the Dharma Hall on the
Every-fifth-day Dharma Session

On occasions of the every-fifth-day Dharma session, the dual order officials first reach the base of the rostrum seat, go around to their respective order's position, and remain standing there. The abbot ascends the high seat but does not burn incense nor utter the word of insight or blessing. (The rest of this procedure is identical to the former.) If a renowned senior practitioner happens to be visiting the temple, a special ascent to the Dharma hall may be scheduled in honor of his visit, or the host abbot may invite the guest to ascend the rostrum seat to preach. If requested by lay donors, the abbot is obliged to ascend the rostrum seat to preach for them at any time.

iii. Ascent to the Dharma Seat for the
Question-and-Answer Session

In olden days, whenever studious practitioners were troubled by a religious matter they resorted to a question-and-answer dialogue among themselves. Thus developed a session called "question-and-answer dialogue." In the early days, participants were not hindered by words and expressions. Nowadays, those who call themselves "Zen experts" or who say they are "conversant in Zen" obliterate the moral retribution of cause and effect, augment bad habits, and act as if they were in a theatrical performance, even bursting into boisterous laughter, which is very disappointing to any observer. How, indeed, could these people promote our teaching or deliver blessings for imperial well-being? If [such people] happen to be near government officials or renowned persons, a brief explanatory excuse [about them] must be made. Today, contemporary practitioners, without exception, seek excessive words of praise and appreciation. This is especially contrary to the Buddhist tradition. If they want to talk about the practical affairs of the temple, they may do so on the occasion of tea at the abbot's hall. One must refrain from engaging in frivolous discussion and annoying others.

2. The Evening Dharma Session

In general, preaching on Zen to an assembly of practitioners is called a "session." In the past, to assist students, Zen masters held 1119c such an assembly in the morning as well as in the evening [during which] their students could consult [the abbot with their questions] and improve [their insight]. There is hardly any occasion when this type of session would fail to arouse the Way of Zen among students. Hence, it has been made compulsory to conduct a Dharma session around dusk every day. Till today, the Zen monastic institution has upheld the rule of practicing zazen prior to the evening session, just as in the first day of the month and mid-month day prayer [sessions], the every-fifth-day Dharma session, and the ascent to the high rostrum seat. Accordingly, prior to their attendance at the Dharma session, practitioners take their seats and sit cross-legged in the main hall.

If the abbot does not call for an assembly for the session by the onset of dusk, the practice hall novice attendant, receiving his instruction, notifies the primary seat official and rings the hall bell three times. This is called the "call-off bell." Such a call-off occurs when the abbot has just begun his tenure at the temple, when the temple receives a visit from government officials or patron donors, or when the abbot is away from the temple on a special invitation or is engaged in preaching at a funeral rite. On occasions other than these, for instance, on the four annual festivity days (i.e., the opening and closing days of the summer retreat, the day of the winter solstice, and New Year's Day), the regular evening session is converted into a "night session," which is signaled by the evening bell. This is called a "small or supplemental session." In this way, the abbot can also meet the requirements of convention. The supplemental session may also be called a "family session" or "home teaching," and it must be noted that the absence of the call-off bell means that a session will be held still later in the day.

3. The Small or Supplementary Session

From its inception, the supplemental session has no determined place of meeting. According to the size of the audience, it is held either in the abbot's reception hall or in the Dharma hall. In the afternoon, the assistant official notifies the abbot, "The supplemental session is in order this evening, sir," and instructs the guest reception attendant to inform the practitioners and post the signboard announcing the session. There is no call-off bell this evening. When the evening bell begins to toll, the attendant reports the time of the supplementary session to the abbot and starts a series of drumbeats. When the practitioners have assembled and the dual order officials have taken their respective places, the abbot ascends the rostrum seat. (The subsequent proceeding is identical with that of the every-fifth-day session.) The abbot preaches on the doctrine, thanks any special participants, mentioning them all by name, and then closes the session with some instructive words of past Zen masters. He then sits cross-legged.

If it is one of the four festivity days, the abbot may ask the primary seat official to conduct the discourse as his proxy. Also he may announce to the practitioners that the propriety of their morning visit to greet the abbot may be excused [to avoid congestion at his quarters]. When the abbot descends the rostrum seat, the guest novice attendant announces as follows:

> The abbot, Venerable Temple Master, respectfully invites the ranking west hall official, the dual order officials, the retired officials, and visiting Zen practitioners to share a serving of sweet hot water at the reception hall immediately hereafter.

The head administrative official prepares sweet hot water and fruit or cake in advance and has them delivered to the reception hall.

In the past, when Zen Master Chuangzhao of Fenyang stayed in Taiziyuan Temple, he hesitated to conduct night sessions because the region of Fen was extremely cold in winter. A foreign monk arrived one day, and, shaking his staff toward him, said: "You have six capable practitioners among your students. Why don't you conduct a night session?" Then he flew up into the air and disappeared. The master secretly wrote about this event in a verse:

> A foreign *bhikṣu,* holding a shining golden staff,
> Came to Fenyang for the sake of the Dharma.
> He said that I have six students who may become
>   great masters
> And thus, persuaded me to intensify my preaching
>   of the Dharma.

At that time, Chuyuan, the predecessor of Ciming, made Shouzhi the head practitioner. Ciming lived in Shishuang in later years and used to make it a rule for himself to practice zazen in the mountains after the noon meal. At that time, the honorable Hui (Fanghui of Yangqi), was made the head administrative official, and one afternoon, after Ciming went out to practice again, he assembled the practitioners by drumming. Ciming at once hurriedly returned and angrily criticized Fanghui: "To have an evening session at dusk! Where did you get this kind of regulation?" Fanghui gently replied, "What can you tell me about the evening session at Fenzhou? Wasn't it a norm there?" Ciming understood.

4. The Rite of Incense Offering at the Request for General Exhortation

i. Incense offering for Exhortation before the Summer Retreat

Before the inauguration of the summer retreat, the rite of incense offering for exhortation must be conducted. For this event, a senior practitioner who has just returned for a second residency may be appointed ceremonial leader. The director of practitioners' affairs 1120a consults with the practitioners, and together they visit the office of the abbot's assistants to convey their selection. The official of the assistants' quarters replies:

> Allow me sir, to convey your request to the abbot. I shall return to you with his reply.

When the request is accepted, the official assistant reports this to the practice hall official and requests him to hand in the ceremonial position chart. (Format of the chart given below.)

Taking into account the number of practitioners, the practice hall director assigns their positions by arranging them in several columns, distributing these columns into the east and west sections of the hall, and having them stand facing the rostrum seat. The order of the positions must be determined according to ordination seniority, and rehearsals must be held prior to the appointed day. The attendants of the practice hall office collect monetary contributions to purchase three packs of large- and small-grain incense and some sheets of paper to prepare the ceremonial position chart, and they give the collected fees to the ceremonial leader. When the appointed day arrives, the practitioner assistant requests the guest master to set up a screen and a chair, either in the abbot's reception hall or in the Dharma hall, and three incense tables are aligned, with some space between them, before the chair, each set with a pair of candle stands. A small area sufficient for performing prostrations should be cleared in front of each incense table. The practice hall attendants are required to inform the practitioners individually about the proceedings and to post the signboard announcing the incense offering for exhortation. Prior to the ceremony, the assistant official places over the pillar of the Dharma hall a small wooden tablet with the following notice:

> In accordance with the abbot's wish, I hereby give notice that both the distinguished and virtuous officials of the west hall and the primary seat official shall be exempted from participation in the rite of incense offering for general exhortation. Respectfully stated by assistant official So-and-so.

ii. Incense Offering to Request General Preaching

On the appointed day, when the morning meal of rice gruel is over, [the members of] all quarters strike the wooden sounding boards three times. The practitioners assemble in the Dharma hall and stand at their positions as designated by the chart, each carrying an incense case and sitting cloth. The ceremonial leader and the assistant of the director of practitioners' affairs together escort the abbot to the central position. Returning to his place, the ceremonial leader joins the practitioners in saluting the abbot with a bow, and then steps forward, saying: "May your reverence, honorable master, be seated." When [the abbot] has seated himself, the ceremonial assistant hands a piece of large-grain incense to the ceremonial leader and bows in unison with the practitioners. The two in turn burn incense and perform three prostrations with fully opened sitting cloth. Then, after standing and folding their sitting cloths, they bow in unison. The ceremonial leader steps forward to the side of the abbot's chair and says:

> I, So-and-so, and others are deeply concerned with the matter of life and death and with the swiftness of impermanence. We earnestly wish that in your compassion you preach to us   1120b the causality of dependent origination (*hetu-pratyayatā*).

[In his discussion,] the abbot should raise three *kōan* cases, referring to the experiences of some eminent masters of the past, and then give his own comments on these topics.

The ceremonial leader then returns to the former position and bows. Offering another piece of incense, he returns to his position among the other practitioners, where he remains standing with his hands folded over his chest. [At that moment] two groups of three practitioners each from the east and west sections step forward to burn incense. The first two of the east group go to the eastern table's incense burner, while the third one [from this group] goes to the middle table's burner. The first two of the west group go to the western table's burner, while the third group goes to the middle table's burner. [The members of] both groups in turn burn incense and bow. Subsequently, three east group members return by way of the eastern side of the hall, while three west group members return by way of the western side of the hall. Each group as before slowly proceeds to the very end of their respective sections. In similar manner, the next two groups of three, moving up in their respective lines, step forward with their hands folded over their chests, but while returning to their former positions [they] hold both palms together. When all members of both sections have offered incense in this way and have returned to their places, they then perform in unison three prostrations with opened sitting cloth and [stand] without folding their sitting cloths. The ceremonial leader proceeds to express thanks:

> We are extremely gratified with the compassion and preaching granted to us by So-and-so, abbot of Such-and-such Temple, and we are most grateful to the master.

Returning to the central position, the ceremonial leader performs in unison with the other practitioners three prostrations as before, and then once again steps forward, saying:

> At this time and in this temple, we all wish for the abbot, the Venerable Master of this Zen temple, good health and a felicitous life each day.

Returning to his place, [the ceremonial leader] once again performs three prostrations [in unison with the practioners] as before and then stands, folding his sitting cloth.

Thereupon the novice attendant strikes the drum five times, and the dual order officials turn from their positions to line up before the abbot's seat, while the ceremonial leader takes his place at the lower end of the [column of] west order officials. When these officials have each completed offering incense, they return to their positions and turn to face to each other. The retired officials and subfunctionaries, having burned incense, stand behind the line of those officials who have completed offering incense. When the abbot has finished preaching, all the participants turn toward the rostrum seat while standing. The ceremonial leader burns incense and performs three prostrations with fully opened sitting cloth in unison with the other practitioners. If this formality is excused by the abbot, [the cermonial leader simply] performs a single prostration with unopened siting cloth and steps forward, saying:

> Due to a fortunate past life, I, So-and-so, and others have been able to receive your compassion and preaching. We are extremely gratified and grateful.

All the participants bow in unison along with [the ceremonial leader]. Then, leading the participants, he thanks the assistant of the director of practitioner's affairs with a prostration with unopened sitting cloth at the left front section of the Dharma hall. Next, the practitioners in unison thank the ceremonial leader with a prostration with unopened sitting cloth.

iii. The Special Serving of Tea and Other Servings after the Ceremony

1120c

The guest reception assistant, setting up a crepe-covered desk and a brush and inkslab, prepares beforehand a letter of invitation for tea reception on the basis of seniority. When the ceremony is over, the guest reception assistant invites each of the participants to line up in the lower section of the Dharma hall, requests them to confirm if their names are duly listed in the book, and obtains permission from the primary seat official to be present as an honorary participant. After the noon meal, a series of drumbeats signals the practitioners to return to their places. The guest reception assistant and the [assistant of the] director of practitioners' affairs jointly conduct the serving of tea. (The procedure is identical with that of the special tea serving.)

That evening, the abbot invites the ceremonial leader and the assistant of the director of practitioner's affairs to an evening meal; the primary seat official is also invited as an honorary participant. Next morning, the abbot once again invites the ceremonial leader for tea, and at mid-morning invites both the ceremonial leader and the director's assistant for a light refreshment. If all members equally participate in the ceremonial offering of incense, the primary seat official takes the role of the ceremonial leader, and for the special serving of tea, the official of the west hall is also invited as an honorary participant. When a new abbot has been inaugurated and appoints his officials, the administrative official prepares the incense, and the primary seat official, leading the rest of the practitioners, earnestly requests the abbot to give them an opportunity to conduct the rite of incense offering. The abbot may open his office for individual visitation for the sake of the member practitioners. (According to the ancient rule, no one was permitted to visit the abbot for individual instruction in his room before the incense offering rite had been completed.)

Ceremonial Position Chart for Incense Offering

				Abbot					
	incense burner			incense burner			incense burner		
	First	Second		Third		Third		Second	First
		4 3 2 1	A		B	1 2 3 4		
		5 6 7 8		C		D	8 7 6 5		
		12 11 10 9				9 10 11 12		
		13 14 15 16	E	Q	F	16 15 14 13		
return path (palms joined)		20 19 18 17		G		H	17 18 19 20	return path (palms joined)
		21 22 23 24		path to make	24 23 22 21		
		28 27 26 25	I	offering (hands	J	25 26 27 28		
		29 30 31 32		folded at	32 31 30 29		
		36 35 34 33	K	chest)	L	33 34 35 36		
		37 38 39 40	M		N	40 39 38 37		
		44 43 42 41		Q		41 42 43 44		
		45 46 47 48	O		P	48 47 46 45		
	West Section					East Section			

A. Primary Seat Official   B. Head Administrative Official
C. Primary Seat Official   D. Administrative Associate
E. Secretarial Official   F. Treasury Official
G. Tripiṭaka Hall Official H. Director of the Practice Hall
I. Tripiṭaka Hall Official J. Treasury Official
K. Guest Reception Official L. Treasury Official
M. Bath Hall Master   N. Kitchen Hall Official
O. Shrine Hall Master   P. Maintenance Official
Q. Ceremonial Leader

5. General Preaching

When practitioners conduct the rite of incense offering in a request for general preaching, the abbot is required to take his seat wherever it is set up. When patron donors request a special preaching, or when the abbot takes the initiative to give a discourse for the sake of the practitioners, he at once ascends the rostrum seat. In general, when regular preaching is scheduled, the assistant official instructs the guest reception attendant to post the signboard informing the practitioners. The place must be set either in the Dharma hall or the abbot's reception hall, and after the morning meal the abbot's attendant notifies him of its beginning time and then strikes the drum with an interval in between to signal the beginning. After the practitioners have assembled, the assistant official escorts the abbot into the hall. The remaining proceedings are identical with those of the supplementary Dharma session.

6. Individual Instruction through Visitation

[Allowing students to visit the master for private instruction] (*rushi*, "entering into the master's room") is the way a Zen master examines his students. He urges them on when their understanding is insufficient, strikes at their unguarded throat, and presses them with regard to their imbalances. In order for the furnace to produce gold, no admixture of lead or mercury should be found, nor should any faulty elements remain when cutting a jewel.

Whether it is in the twilight of evening or early dawn, at any place or any time, this standard must be maintained. Therefore, in the past practitioners always carried a small incense case with them at all times. Whenever they heard three drumbeats, they promptly went to [the master's room to] receive instruction.

(The practice we have today sets forth six such occasions during each month, namely, the days ending in three and eight [i.e., the third, eighth, thirteenth, eighteenth, twenty-third, and twenty-eighth days of each month], and [this system] is intended to provide opportunities similar to those of former days.)

When the abbot opens his room for individual visitation, the assistant official instructs the guest reception novice attendant to post the signboard before the morning meal in front of the practice hall as well as in all the quarters to inform the practitioners of the schedule. An image of Bodhidharma should be placed in the reception hall and incense, candles, and a place for prostrations should be set up on the left side, facing the image. When the practitioners leave the practice hall after breakfast, the guest reception attendant strikes the drum three times with an interval in between the drumbeats. The abbot offers incense to the image of Bodhidharma and performs three prostrations in unison with his assistant. He then returns to the next room where he takes his seat, while his assistant, after bowing, goes to stand on the left side of the room and the attendant stands on the right side.

The primary seat official, followed by the practitioners, burns incense and performs three prostrations before the image of Bodhidharma, and in a close line they reach the master's room. The practitioners follow, one after another, waiting their turn to burn incense and perform prostrations with opened sitting cloth. No disturbance should ever be allowed to occur. The abbot's assistant burns incense and, after bowing, goes out to usher in the primary seat official, who enters the room with a salute. When entering the room, the practitioner is obliged to step into the room with his left foot first and use his left hand to burn incense, step forward and bow toward the master, and go to the right-hand side of [the abbot's] chair.

While standing there, he listens to the master or speaks to him if he so wishes. [To withdraw,] he steps to the left of the chair, makes a bow, and [steps backward] to perform a prostration with unopened sitting cloth. He then leaves the room, again leading with his left foot, and salutes the next practitioner, thus signaling him to enter the room in the same manner. As one practitioner comes out another goes in with a bow, one after another, with no pause in between.

If the primary seat official is himself an established master, due to having once been the west hall official of a superior temple, or if a renowned practitioner happens to visit the room and burns incense, the abbot leaves his seat to salute him and respectfully sees him out of the room. In the case of a regular ascent to the rostrum seat of the Dharma hall, such personalities may be excused from participation [in this rite] by public announcement. (This custom was also developed in recent times. In the past, real practitioners did not hesitate to encounter the Buddhas and patriarchs at any time. Why should anyone follow convention? The point is that [the manner of this ritual] depends on the kind of master.)

The rear hall primary seat official usually leads the practitioners. New residents of the temple should make a visit [to the abbot] for direct instruction. The assistant brings up the end of the line, enters the room last, similarly receives instruction, offers incense, and performs three prostrations with opened sitting cloth. The novice attendant also burns incense and performs three prostrations with opened sitting cloth. Thereupon, the abbot burns incense before the image of Bodhidharma, performs three prostrations with opened sitting cloth, and leaves the room.

7. Prayer Chanting on the Days of the Month Ending in Three and Eight

In the *Ancient Regulations,* prayer chanting was observed on the third, eighth, thirteenth, eighteenth, twenty-third, and twenty-eighth days of each month. Today, [however,] it is observed only on three days: the eighth, eighteenth, and twenty-eighth of each month. The practice hall official is obliged to make a chart of the ceremonial positions in the practice hall based on ordination seniority. (Format of the chart given below.) When the appointed day comes, the entrance area of the practice hall must be swept and cleaned, and in the afternoon the practice hall office attendant informs the practitioners of the schedule for prayer chanting and posts the signboard announcing the event. Before the evening Dharma session, [around four o'clock in the afternoon,] after confirming that incense and candles are prepared and ready for use in the practice hall as well as in all other buildings, the abbot notifies the dual order officials and instructs the attendants to strike, first, the wooden sounding board located by his office; next, the one located at the skylit hall adjacent to the practice hall, and then all the wooden sounding boards located in the various corridors connecting the buildings. When the abbot comes out from his hall, signaled by three strikes of the metal gong located at the kitchen hall with an interval between strikes, the practitioners take their positions as designated in the chart and remain standing. New arrivals are required to stay behind the abbot's assistant.

Followed by his assistant, the abbot makes a round from the patriarch's shrine hall to the local spirit shrine, then to the Buddha hall, burning incense and performing prostrations at each place. When he reaches the Buddha hall, the large bell is tolled [to signal his arrival]. The dual order officials gather beforehand at the entrance of the practice hall, and upon hearing the sound of the metal gong, enter the hall and take their respective positions. The alms master signals the abbot's entrance into the practice hall with seven tolls of the practice hall bell. The abbot proceeds to offer incense at the altar of the guardian bodhisattva, receiving the incense from his assistant who carries the incense case. Meanwhile the abbot's secretarial assistant goes directly to his designated position. The guest reception assistant proceeds to the front of the [column of] the west order officials and, with a bow, invites them to the serving of sweet hot water; he then goes around to the front of the [column of] the east order officials and invites them. The abbot then comes out into the outer hall and stands in the center, followed by his incense offering assistant. The latter then takes his designated position in the outer hall.

The director of practitioners' affairs leaves his place, comes to the hall entrance and stands facing the abbot and, with his palms together, begins the prayer chanting. The following is the word of prayer to be read on the eighth and eighteenth days:

> May the imperial wind forever send fresh air and the imperial way forever flourish, while the Buddha's sun shines ever more brightly and the wheel of the Dharma perpetually turns. The temple building and the earth protect the Dharma and people, and all the benefactors increase ever more in merit and wisdom. For the sake of the foregoing causes, we shall intone the ten sacred names of the Buddhas: the Luminous Pure Dharma Body Vairocana Buddha, and so on.

[While this is being intoned] the practitioners remain in silent prayer. As each name of the Buddha is intoned, the hall bell is lightly tolled; at the end, to signal the conclusion of the prayer, the bell is immediately tolled again. The word of prayer for the twenty-eighth day is as follows:

> I respectfully address the practitioners. According to the first regnal year of Zhiyuan of the great Yuan dynastic calendar, it has been twenty-two hundred and eighty-four years since the time the Tathāgata, the Great Teacher, entered *parinirvāṇa*. Just as this day is about to pass, so is our lifespan diminishing, like fish in a shrinking pond. What kind of happiness is there in this state of existence? May you exert yourselves in your endeavors as if to extinguish a fire burning on your head. With constant awareness of impermanence, may you strive and refrain from becoming negligent. May the temple building and the earth protect the Dharma and the people, and all the benefactors of the ten directions ever increase merit and wisdom. For the sake of the foregoing causes, we

shall intone the ten sacred names of the Buddhas: the Luminous Pure Dharma Body Vairocana Buddha, and so on.

Having completed the prayer invocation, the director of practitioners' affairs returns to his place. The abbot and the primary seat official enter the hall, one after the other. Next, the distinguished guest official of the west hall enters the hall, burns incense, and upon reaching the board head stands facing the altar of the guardian bodhisattva. Three at a time, the training officials, leading the practitioners, approach the altar of the guardian bodhisattva and bow before it. Turning toward the abbot, they bow before him, and moving to their left they make a round [through the aisles in procession] with their palms together. Upon reaching their respective positions as designated in the chart, each stands in place. Recent arrivals follow the practitioners behind the abbot's assistant, but proceed only up to the rear half of the hall. When the [abbot's] assistant stops behind the altar facing the rear exit, they also stop there and face him.

1121b

Next, the administrative officials enter the hall, bow toward the altar, turn toward the abbot with a bow, and proceed to make a round in similar manner with their palms together, then go out of the hall. The recent arrivals follow the abbot's assistant and leave the hall by the rear exit. The attendant of the practice hall office goes before the primary seat official and says: "The evening session is called off, sir." He departs the hall, passing behind the guardian bodhisattva's altar. Thereupon, the alms serving attendant rings the hall bell three times, and all the practitioners bow in unison and leave their positions in orderly fashion. The altar attendant leaves the hall by passing around behind the altar.

(When the abbot goes out, the dual order officials also follow him and begin to express their thanks to him outside the hall for the invitation to the reception of sweet hot water, though this formality may be excused by the abbot himself. On the twenty-eighth day, after prayer chanting, the serving of sweet hot water is conducted at the abbot's reception hall. The wooden sounding board located by the office is struck to signal this. The abbot's assistant burns incense; the manner of serving sweet hot water is the same as on the usual occasion but is followed by an evening meal. In the *Ancient Regulations*, the serving of sweet hot water was a norm on the days ending in three and eight but there was no evening meal on the eighth and eighteenth days. On those days, no zazen is scheduled prior to the evening session, but the evening session of zazen occurs as usual.)

The Position Chart for Prayer Chanting and Practice Hall Rounds

(The chart below reflects corrections made in reference to Mujaku Dōchū's *Commentary on the Baizhang Monastic Regulations with Left-side Notes*)

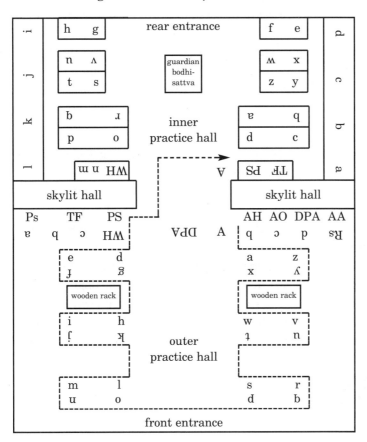

Key

A	Abbot
PS	Primary Seat Official
WH	West Hall Official
AH	Administrative Head
AO	Administrative Officials
DPA	Director of Practitioners' Affairs
TF	Training Faculty Officials
AA	Abbot's Assistants
Ps	Practitioners
Rs	Recent Arrivals

The dotted line shows the initial movement of the three people in the practice hall rounds. The letters a–z show the progression through the hall and final seat positions.

8. Inspection Rounds of the Quarters

The *Ancient Regulations* stipulated that a signboard announcing "inspection round" was to be posted in front of the practice hall to inform the practitioners when the abbot was going to make rounds through the various quarters. In each quarter a seat for the abbot is set up and incense, tea, and sweet hot water are prepared in advance of his arrival. In each quarter the wooden sounding board is struck to assemble the practitioners. When the abbot arrives, they greet him outside the gate of their quarters and follow him into the quarters. The head practitioner of the quarters burns incense and bows to him in unison with the others, and all sit down. The abbot enquires after the practitioners' age and health, and so on, inspects to see if anything is lacking or in short supply, and engages in dialogue with them. When he stands up, the practitioners perform a prostration with opened sitting cloth to thank him. If the formality is excused, they may simply bow instead when seeing him off. When the abbot makes rounds on the first day of the month and mid-month, there is no need to post the signboard.

Nowadays, the inspection rounds of the practitioners' quarters are conducted only on the four annual festivity days and at no other time. If anyone is capable of reviving the *Ancient Regulations,* he should be encouraged to do so.

It is said in the *Mahāsaṃghika-vinaya* (*Mohesengqilü*) that the World-honored One visited the *bhikṣus*' quarters once every five days for five major reasons: first, he was concerned that disciples might be trapped in worldly affairs; second, that they might be attached to conventional doctrines; third, that they might be idly asleep; fourth, to see if anyone might be sick; and fifth, to encourage junior disciples through having them directly witness the dignity of the Buddha.

1121c

9. Reprimanding Measures

The eminent Hanlin scholar Yangyi of the Song dynasty tried to trace the original ideas of the *Baizhang Zen Monastic Regulations* in the great Tripiṭaka scriptural collection in order to fathom the meaning of their creation. Yangyi explained his findings generally as follows: Suppose someone assumes an ordained name or [adopts the form of an ordained person (i.e., wears robes)], and mixes with real practitioners. When such a person, most especially, starts quarrels, the director of practitioners' affairs is obliged to apprehend him and expel him from the temple, nullifying his residency for the sake of relieving the minds of the other practitioners. If a person commits a certain transgression, he may be punished by [being beaten with] sticks. His robes, almsbowl, and requisites may be burned in front of the assembly of practitioners. He should be expelled through the side gate of the temple. All this is to show the disgrace of his transgression. This single rule is seen to bring about four benefits. First, it prevents bad influences that might affect good practitioners on the one hand, and on the other hand creates a sense of reverence and respect for the rules and regulations in the minds of the practitioners. Second, it does not destroy the physical body of an imposter and is in accordance with the Buddha's Vinaya rule. Third, it does not involve public officials and avoids possible legal prosecution or imprisonment. Fourth, it does not create a scandal outside the temple and protects the Zen religious institution.

Thus, the regulations that Baizhang formulated were a reorganization of the Buddhist Vinaya rules and disciplines, which were organized under the fivefold categories of offenses or the sevenfold classifications of transgressions, as the broadest standards acceptable to the whole world. The codes of punishment, such as "exclusion to silence" (*brahmadaṇḍa*), "expulsion from the sangha" (*bahiṣkṛta*), "confession" (*pravāraṇa*), and "formal charge with the penalty of suspension" (*utkṣepaṇīya*), have helped practitioners discipline themselves.

The successive rulers of the imperial courts granted Buddhist ordination to those men of aspiration and strictly obliged them to follow the Buddhist rules and regulations. For instance, regarding an offense committed by a practitioner, insofar as it does not necessarily involve the civil authorities, the temple community is authorized to deal with the offender in accordance with the rules of the monastic regulations. Should a monk fight with someone of higher status than an ordained practitioner, or behave shamelessly and unrestrainedly, or abuse the temple's properties, or steal from the temple's public funds, the temple is authorized to deal with him in accordance with the monastic regulations, and [the matter] need not [become a scandal] in the outside world. Since the title of "Śākya" (i.e., the Buddha's clan name) can be understood to carry ancestral authority over whoever bears that title as a Buddhist, similar to secular convention one is obliged to maintain the ancestral rules and regulations and punish transgressors in accordance with those rules and regulations. When one's conduct is grave, the offender may be whipped and expelled in front of the assembly of practitioners; if the offense is light, a monetary fine, or a fine of incense or oil may be levied and [the punishment] announced on the temple's bulletin board. If one's conduct involves money and goods, his responsibility is pressed with a written record by a consensus of jurors. Through just and

1122a

confidential [action], the offender may be brought to repent and
rectify his wrongdoing by himself.

It is said in the *Ancient Regulations:*

> When any practitioner steals another's possessions, or fights
> with others, or transgresses by drinking alcohol or engaging
> in sexual intercourse, he must be quickly separated from
> other practitioners and expelled from the temple community,
> because if he were allowed instead to stay on the community
> would eventually become corrupt.

Another verse states:

> If an offense is grave, the offender's robe and almsbowl must
> be burned. His shame must be exposed to his fellow practi-
> tioners, and he must be expelled from the temple's side gate.

Zen Master Dahui, while serving as abbot of Ayuwangsi, put
up an announcement to instruct his director of practitioners' affairs
that anyone who argued with others in an unenlightened way
would not be welcome and would be dismissed from the temple,
regardless of whether he may be right or wrong. In some cases,
even if a person is right [in an argument or discussion], he should
be shunned. Even if such a person may feel not quite satisfied,
insofar as he is a practitioner he must bear it with perseverance.
If instead he continues to argue and insists upon being right, this
is an unenlightened attitude. Hence, rejecting both [parties to an
argument, regardless of who is right and who is wrong,] is intended
to preempt the source of argument before it arises.

10. Instructing Young Novices

In general, when the ascent to the Dharma hall is completed on
the first day, mid-month day, and every-fifth-day of each month,
the ceremonial leader's attendant requests the attendant in charge
of the meal proceeding to notify the novice attendants of the various offices of the schedule of the master's lecture, and to post a
signboard in front of the attendants' hall. When the evening bell

is tolled, the wooden sounding board at their attendent novices' hall is struck three times to call them to assemble. The ceremonial leader leads the assembly of novice attendants first to visit the Buddha hall, then the patriarch's hall, practice hall, and practitioners' quarters. At each location, they announce in unison, "We are here, sir." Thereafter, they go to the abbot's reception hall and line up to wait for him.

Escorted by the ceremonial leader, the abbot comes into the reception hall and takes his seat. The ceremonial leader burns incense and, returning to his place, says in a low voice, "We are here, sir." This is repeated by all the novice attendants in unison, and then [they say] softly, "How are you, sir?" The [group] performs three prostrations in unison and then listen attentively to the abbot's disciplinary [admonitions] and instructions. When it is over, the novice attendants again perform three prostrations, and the ceremonial leader announces, "Goodbye, sir," repeated in unison by the novices in lower voices. After a bow, they leave the hall.

If the abbot happens to be occupied with some other engagement [when the assembly arrives], the meal proceeding attendant says, "We come for the evening session, thanking the abbot for his compassion." All greet him, saying in unison, "How are you, sir?" The same attendant next announces, extending his voice, "The session is called off." All say together, "Goodbye, sir," bow in unison, and leave.

11. General Preaching for Novice Attendants

The ceremonial leader visits the office of the abbot's assistants in advance, and after burning incense and performing prostrations, requests the assistant in charge to request the abbot to preach. When the request is granted, the ceremonial leader strikes the wooden sounding board located at the novice attendants' hall to assemble them and thereupon proceeds to the reception hall to wait for the abbot. Following the assistant in charge, the ceremonial leader goes in to escort the abbot. When the abbot takes his seat, the ceremonial leader bows to him, in unison with the novice attendants, burns incense, and, returning to his place, greets him in a low voice, "How are you, sir?" repeated in unison by the novices in a lower voice. All in unison perform nine prostrations. The ceremonial leader steps forward and says:

> I, So-and-so, and others have wished to receive your preaching for some time. We implore you, in your compassion, to grant us the opportunity to hear your preaching on the teaching of the causality of dependent origination.

With a bow, he returns to his former position.

Next day, the signboard of "general preaching" should be posted at the novice attendants' hall. A seat for the abbot, an incense table, and candle stands are placed in the hall. After notifying the novices, the ceremonial leader goes to invite the dual order officials to participate, while the ceremonial assistant, leading the novices, receives the officials at the hall entrance. The ceremonial leader and the hall master go to the office of the practitioner assistants and escort the abbot to the attendants' hall. All the novice attendants welcome him at the hall entrance. When [the abbot] takes his seat, the [abbot's] assistant bows and stands at his side. After the dual order officials complete their greetings, the assistant in charge burns incense and requests the abbot to preach. The ceremonial leader, leading the novices, burns incense, offers greetings, and performs three prostrations. Then, dividing the novice attendants, he has them take their respective positions behind the east and west order officials. After the preaching has been attentively heard, the ceremonial leader, once again leading the novice attendants, has them line up and perform three prostrations. They then all leave the hall and stand to the right of the entrance. After seeing off the abbot and the dual order officials with a bow, the ceremonial leader follows the abbot to the reception hall. He burns a [piece of] large-grain incense and performs nine prostrations before withdrawing. Next, he goes to the office of the [abbot's] assistants and again offers incense and performs three prostrations. Finally both the ceremonial leader and his assistant go round to each of the officials to express their gratitude.

1122b

12. Receiving the Robe of Dharma Transmission

When a special official delegate arrives at the temple, transporting the robe of Dharma transmission to the abbot, the delegate is obliged to meet with the guest reception official to explain the purpose of his visit and also to convey the same to the abbot through his assistant in charge. He may either see the abbot immediately, or the next morning. The assistant in charge instructs the guest master to request the presence of the temple officials. The delegate burns incense and then drinks tea with them. After giving thanks for the tea, he once again burns incense and performs the formal propriety of two prostrations with opened sitting cloth and three prostrations with unopened sitting cloth. If this formality is excused, he performs only a single prostration with unopened sitting cloth and says:

> This is the robe of Master So-and-so, which embodies his faith in the Dharma transmission. I hereby present it to your reverence on his behalf.

Thereupon he leaves the robe and other items wrapped in crepe and withdraws to the next room. The dual order officials participate in the serving of tea, followed by the serving of sweet hot water, and when all this is over, they accompany the delegate to the guest house. The abbot's assistant, moreover, escorts him on a courtesy round of the practitioners' quarters.

On a different day, at the time of his ascent to the Dharma hall, the abbot takes the seat that has been placed at the left side of the rostrum seat. The official delegate performs three prostrations with fully opened sitting cloth and respectfully presents the robe to him. Upon receiving it, the abbot utters a word of insight on the Dharma, and, wearing [the robe] himself, ascends the rostrum seat. If the master of Dharma transmission [from whom he has received the robe has] already passed away, a casket table should be set up at the right rear side of the hall with the deceased master's name tablet on it. After descending the high seat, [the

abbot] makes offerings and chants sutras. The manner in which
[he should] receive the written will is given below.

13. Receiving a Renowned
Virtuous Guest Practitioner

When a renowned practitioner visits the temple, a signboard indicating "senior guest reception" should be posted, and the large bell
tolled to assemble the practitioners to greet the distinguished guest
at the gate. If the visitor prefers a simpler approach, he may just
arrive without prior announcement to the temple. It is the norm
for the abbot to prepare incense and candles in the reception hall
and meet such a guest there. The guest master reports the visit
to the primary seat official by ringing the practice hall bell. Leading the practitioners, the primary seat official reaches the reception hall, burns incense, and greets the guest with a bow. The practitioners withdraw after saluting the guest with a bow, but the
dual order officials and the retired officials remain in the presence
of the honorable guest. After these officials burn incense and drink
tea, the abbot's assistant burns incense and performs prostrations.
Following him, the guest's assistants, novice attendants, serving
men, and sedan chair bearers perform prostrations, all in due order.
Once again the assistant burns incense and serves sweet hot water
to the guest and the temple officials. After this is completed, both
the incumbent and retired officials together escort the guest to the
guest house. The guest reception attendant signals the sedan chair
bearers to be ready. The abbot, accompanied by his assistant,
escorts the guest on a courtesy round of the practitioners' quarters. If the guest is from a monastic temple of lower status, the
[abbot's] assistant takes the role of escorting the guest.

The guest reception assistant, carrying a written invitation,
visits the guest and, after burning incense, invites him to a special serving of sweet hot water:

> The abbot requests your honorable presence at the special
> service of sweet hot water to be held at the reception hall.

May you in your compassion accept this invitation.

Thereupon he hands the written invitation to the guest. (Format given below.) The guest reception assistant further says:

After the serving of sweet hot water, you are invited to partake of an evening meal, sir.

At the reception hall, the abbot's office assistants are obliged to hang curtains and arrange the seat markers designating the special guest seat as well as those of the other participants. The drum signals commencement of the ceremony. The guest is escorted to his seat, incense is offered, and he is invited to drink. After this an evening meal is served, all following a similar format as that of the special serving. When the appointed time comes, the guest reception attendant goes to the guest and escorts him, saying:

The abbot requests your presence for a serving of sweet hot water and fruit this evening.

[The guest reception attendant] also invites the dual order officials to participate in the serving. The abbot's assistant notifies the participants that the abbot is scheduled to go to the Dharma hall the next morning to express his gratitude. In the morning, the guest is invited to a serving of sweet hot water; the [abbot's] assistant burns incense, the attendants bow, and the serving men respectfully greet him verbally. The abbot shares rice gruel with the guest and then invites him to tea. His assistant once again announces, "The ascent to the Dharma hall is in order, sir." A seat has been prepared to the right of the rostrum seat. At mid-morning, a light refreshment is served.

If the guest delegate is of especially great distinction, the primary seat official and other training officials speak to the abbot, enquiring if the guest may be invited to preach the Dharma for the sake of the practitioners. The abbot first makes a visit to the guest delegate to convey their wish to him. When it is granted, the primary seat official, carrying a written invitation, the dual order officials, and the practitioners all visit the guest delegate together

1122c

to burn incense and express their wish [that he preach to them]. Next, they visit the abbot to request him to perform the role of introducing the guest. Thereupon, the signboard notifying the practitioners is posted. Two chairs should be placed in front of the two chairs to the left and right of the rostrum. When the time comes, at the drum signal the abbot and the eminent guest proceed together to their respective places and remain standing there. The abbot introduces the guest to the practitioners and, as usual, takes his seat. The dual order officials proceed forward to salute the guest with a bow. Thereupon the guest goes before the abbot and bows, and at mid-hall he turns toward the assembly and bows in all directions before ascending the rostrum seat. The [abbot's] assistants and the dual order officials, in pairs, step forward from their respective orders and bow toward the rostrum seat; the abbot does the same. After preaching, the guest delegate descends, bows to the abbot, and, as before, bows to the entire assembly. The abbot, the dual order officials, and the practitioners accompany the delegate to the guest house, burn incense, and express their gratitude. The abbot's guest reception assistant prepares a written invitation and escorts the guest to a special dinner reception. The temple prepares food and a gift of money, and the abbot also prepares a monetary gift. The procedure and decorum are the same as those of the usual special serving. If the guest delegate is equal in rank to the abbot, they may deliberate to determine the proper courtesy.

If the guest is senior to the abbot in Dharma succession, the intermonastic reception propriety should be observed, as mentioned previously. [The guest] is escorted to the guest house and offered the main seat. The abbot burns incense and performs prostrations. If it is a matter of the propriety for a person of the same Dharma lineage [as the abbot], the guest must be escorted to the abbot's office and offered the main seat. The manner of receiving and seeing off [the guest] is the same as before, and in the serving of tea and so on the abbot is obliged to conduct the proceedings himself. If the guest strongly declines, [the abbot] may let his assistant conduct the proceedings.

If the visiting practitioner is one of the abbot's disciples in Dharma transmission, or a former temple official under him, or is related in Dharma succession, he must come directly to the abbot's office. The abbot then has the practice hall bell rung to assemble the practitioners there so that he can carry out the interpersonal propriety. The abbot is first invited to take the central seat, and the guest performs an interpersonal disciple-to-master propriety.

Next, the propriety of an intermonastic reception must be explained. The manner of receiving or seeing off [a guest from another temple or monastery] is the same as before. The only difference is that a written invitation for the special serving of sweet hot water is not required. The abbot's guest reception assistant burns incense and verbally invites the guest. Of course, expedient change may be required in accordance with the degree of ordination seniority.

(The different formats for the written invitations for the serving of sweet hot water, special dinner reception, and ascent to the Dharma hall are given below.)

i. Format of the Invitation to a Special Reception of Sweet Hot Water

The abbot of this temple, So-and-so, unceremoniously invites the above titled Venerable So-and-so to a special serving of sweet hot water this evening at the reception hall. May you in your compassion especially grant your presence.

> Respectfully written and presented on
> Date, month, year

ii. Invitation to a Special Dinner Reception

The abbot of this temple, So-and-so, unceremoniously invites the above titled Venerable So-and-so to a special serving of rice gruel tomorrow at the reception hall. May you in your compassion especially grant your presence.

Respectfully written and presented on
Date, month, year

iii. Request for a Special Dharma Preaching

The abbot of this temple, So-and-so, unceremoniously requests
the above titled Venerable So-and-so to preach the Dharma
and teach the practitioners. May you in your compassion especially grant your preaching.   1123a

Respectfully written and presented on
Date, month, year

iv. Format of the Envelope

Invitation to
Zen Master, Venerable So-and-so
Abbot of Such-and-such Temple

14. Donor's Request for Preaching and
Almsgiving for Practitioners

When a patron donor arrives, the guest reception official receives
him and escorts him to the abbot's hall, and, after serving him tea
and sweet hot water, escorts him to the guest house. If the guest
is a great magnanimous benefactor, such as a high-ranking government official, the large bell should be tolled to assemble the practitioners to welcome him at the main gate of the temple. After he
is settled in the guest house, the benefactor invites the guest reception official for consultation, and then accompanies him to the abbot's
hall to burn incense and request the abbot to conduct the ascent to
the Dharma hall [for preaching]. On the appointed day, a seat for
the patron should be set up in front of the rostrum seat and a signboard [announcing the event] to the practitioners should be posted.
The drum signals the [practitioners] to assemble. The guest reception official, together with the patron donor, escorts the abbot. A
hand incense burner, candles, flags, and cymbals must be prepared

beforehand as required for this occasion On reaching the rostrum seat, the abbot ascends it and sits cross-legged while the donor stands before the high seat. The guest reception official, saluting, returns to his place. The patron remains standing during the preaching. (It is not appropriate to sit down during the preaching of the Dharma.)

When the abbot descends from the seat, the patron donor expresses his gratitude.

If the guest wishes to give alms to the practitioners, the abbot must consult with the administrative officials to determine the amount of money required. Counting the number of practitioners and novice attendants, the director of practitioners' affairs calculates the total amount based on the average cost of a meal. A seat for the donor should be prepared in the practice hall next to the abbot. After the meal is over, the donor, accompanied by the administrative official, waits for the primary seat official to come out of the hall, leading the practitioners, and then thanks him and those behind him. Next, the abbot and the primary seat official visit the donor at the guest house to thank him for his benefaction. If the guest donates money for the practitioners, the abbot must hand it over to the administrative official and let him carefully distribute it to the practitioners. Such donations must never be used for any other purpose than that designated [by the donor]. One must remember how clear and evident moral retribution is.

In the *Precious Mirror of Human and Heavenly Worlds (Rentianbaojian)*, the following story is related: Zen Master Shouzhi of Mount Yungai, in Hunan province, was meditating one night in his abbot's office. He suddenly felt scorching heat and heard the noise of dragging chains. He then saw someone wearing a fiery wooden collar, flames still burning up and down. The collar was attached by a chain to the gate's threshold. Astonished, Shouzhi asked, "Who are you? That must cause unbearable suffering!"

The man wearing the burning yoke replied that he was the former abbot, Shouyu, and said, "I never thought I would suffer such pain just because I diverted funds offered by donors for the practitioners to help defray the cost of building their practice hall."

Shouzhi asked, "Is there any way to be relieved from [your suffering]?"

Shouyu replied, "This can be accomplished only by calculating the cost of the building and distributing an equivalent amount to the practitioners." Thereupon, Shouzhi, using his own money, rectified his predecessor's misuse of the funds. One night, Shouyu appeared in a dream to thank Shouzhi, saying that due to the abbot's help he would escape from his hellish suffering, would be able to be reborn in the world of heaven as well as that of human beings, and would again be able to become a Buddhist practitioner after three transmigrations. Scorch marks can still be seen on the gate's threshold.

Despite the fact that Venerable [Shou]yu only used the money donated to the practitioners for building the practice hall, which was, after all, for their use, he nonetheless suffered clear and evident retribution for using donated money for purposes other than that designated. Nowadays, the practice of ignoring moral retribution seems rampant in Zen temples. Not only are [funds and 1123b temple property] diverted for alternative purposes, but also, in extreme cases, temple possessions are stolen for personal use. What can be done about such people?

15. Receiving the Serving of Tea from a Disciple in the Dharma Succession

If a disciple of the abbot in his Dharma lineage visits the temple and wishes to serve tea at the practice hall on behalf of his master, his accompanying administrative official must first meet with his counterpart at the host temple. After the amount of the expense to be shared is determined, the guest disciple must pay that amount to the host temple. The evening before the day of the serving of tea, the guest disciple visits the office of the abbot's assistants to convey his wish and then pays homage at the abbot's office by offering incense and performing a prostration with opened sitting cloth. If this formality is excused, he performs a single prostration with unopened sitting cloth. He then says:

> Tomorrow morning, I wish to humbly conduct a serving of tea at the practice hall. May your reverence in your compassion grant your presence.

The guest master conveys this request to the dual order officials as well as to the retirees of the individual quarters, and posts a signboard announcing the occasion. On the appointed day, a crepe-covered table is solemnly set at the abbot's position in the practice hall. The kitchen hall metal gong is struck to call the practitioners to return to the practice hall. The guest disciple enters the hall behind the abbot in order to help him take his seat. He then turns toward the altar of the guardian bodhisattva and burns incense before it, then proceeds toward the abbot with his hands clasped at his chest and bows before him. He goes around the back of the altar, and [at the moment] he reappears, the abbot signals him to take his seat. The guest takes the head seat on the raised platform of the guest reception official [in the outer hall].

The meal serving attendant announces: "Request to take the bowl down." When the first serving has been completed, the guest disciple leaves his seat, bows before the altar of the guardian bodhisattva, places a monetary gift on the altar, and then proceeds to bow before the abbot and present him with a monetary gift for the practitioners. Thereupon, the kitchen office signals the beginning of the noon meal by striking the wooden sounding board. When the noon meal is over, the practitioners clean and put their almsbowls back in proper order and the table is removed from the abbot's place.

The guest disciple burns incense at the altar, proceeds before the abbot, and bows. Once again, after going around behind the altar, he bows before the incense burner toward the guardian bodhisattva. A bell signals the serving of tea and when [the serving] is nearing completion, the guest disciple proceeds to the abbot and presents tea. Once more he goes around behind the altar, comes before the abbot, and first opening his sitting cloth, says:

It is my greatest joy that you have granted me the privilege of your special presence on this day for this humble propriety and meager offering.

After opening his sitting cloth again, he makes a cordial greeting and then performs three prostrations without reopening the sitting cloth. He follows the abbot [out of the hall] to see him off, then returns to the hall to offer incense. He thanks the officials in the outer hall for their participation, and once again returns to the altar to offer incense and, after ringing the bell, retrieves the tea bowl from the altar. Next he goes to the abbot's office to thank him for his presence. Thereupon, to return his appreciation, the abbot accompanies the disciple back to the guest house.

In the case of an abbot of another temple conducting the propriety of serving tea at the practice hall, noting the time of the noon meal, he makes his request to the abbot of the host temple, accompanies him to the hall, and helps him take his seat. The abbot of the host temple must excuse the guest abbot from the formalities described above, and requests him immediately to take his seat. At the moment when the serving of food is completed, the guest proceeds to burn incense before the altar of the guardian bodhisattva and then bows before the abbot, presents monetary gifts to the altar as well as to the practitioners, burns incense to thank all participants, and returns to his seat to finish the noon meal. Whether he is obliged to conduct the propriety of the serving of tea is contingent on the given situation.

16. Arrival of the Written Will of the
Master in the Dharma Lineage

When an official delegate arrives at the temple with a written will, (the formality of the proceeding is detailed below in part VI, section 17, "Sending Written Wills"), the abbot opens the will and the dual order officials console him. A ritual altar should be set up in the center of the Dharma hall, before which the abbot offers incense and utters a word of insight. With three utterances of grief, he performs three prostrations and offers sweet hot water, and once again performs three prostrations before placing food and monetary gifts on the altar. At the drum signal, following the propriety of the special serving, he performs three prostrations and offers tea. At the signal of three drumbeats, he leaves his seat and folds his sitting cloth. The director of practitioners' affairs calls for chanting the *Śūraṃgama-dhāraṇī*s and concludes with an invocation [of merit transference]. (This is similar to the memorial rite for the master of the Dharma transmission, Chapter IV, part V.) The retirees, those who come from the same native province [as the deceased master], [those who are in the deceased master's] lineage of Dharma transmission, the junior disciples, and the serving practitioners all conduct their rites, while the abbot stands to the left of the table on which the memorial tablet is set.

1123c

(When the abbots of other temples or the ranking west hall official or his Dharma relations of equal rank conduct the rite, the abbot is obliged, along with the official delegate, to perform a prostration in return. In other situations, he is not obliged to do so.)

After all the rites are completed, the director of practitioners' affairs calls for the chanting of the *Mahākāruṇikacitta-dhāraṇī*s and concludes with the following invocation of merit transference:

> We dedicate the merit accrued by this chanting to Great Master So-and-so, abbot of Such-and-such Temple, in order to enhance the enshrinement of his dignity and reverence. Veneration to the Buddhas of the ten directions, and so on.

The primary seat official, representing all the practitioners, consoles the abbot, saying:

> It is unfortunate for the tradition that the master of your Dharma transmission has passed away. We junior practitioners feel extreme sadness because we have lost a support. Nevertheless, may you endure it for our sake and endeavor ever more assiduously on the path.

End of Fascicle Two

Fascicle Three

Chapter V (*continued*)

III. Inviting a New Abbot
for Appointment

1. Sending a Special Official Delegate

In general, when the position of abbot is vacated it is necessary to notify the district government official. Upon receiving official permission, the head administrative official, the dual order officials, and the retired officials meet at tea to decide the matter of sending a delegate [to invite the new abbot]. For this purpose, they draw up the official letters representing: the officials of the training faculty, the administrative officials, the retired officials and retired subfunctionaries, the retired administrative subfunctionaries, and the practitioners. They compose drafts of the letters addressed to the temple community itself, as well as to nearby monastic temples and the entire Zen world throughout the land.

They request the head secretarial official to prepare the signboard announcing the serving of tea and sweet hot water, with the signature of the special delegate. If the head secretarial official is absent or is not available, these tasks may be accomplished by assigning a skilled calligrapher to prepare the two signboards. For this purpose, silk cloth is to be used.

As for the official delegate referred to before, either the head administrative official, one of the retired officials, the primary seat official of the west hall, or a training official of lesser rank may be appointed. Unless a head administrative official is appointed, someone of lower administrative rank must accompany the delegate in order to handle financial matters and act as a consultant. A record book should be prepared in which pertinent facts about the temple are concisely presented, such as the quantity of rice fields and their productivity, other assets and their operations, and the conditions of the new abbot's appointment and the travel arrangements to the temple of his appointment. The party that is to accompany the official delegate representing the temple should be seen to, and on the day of departure the party as a whole visits the various quarters of the temple to bid farewell before departure.

The practice hall bell is rung to assemble the practitioners at the gate to see off the official delegate and his party. A curtain should be hung below the temple gate and seats prepared behind it for the serving of tea and sweet hot water. The dual order officials and the retired officials are invited to participate in the occasion. If the head administrative official is serving as the temple delegate, the administrative member next in rank should conduct the ceremonial serving; if the primary seat official or a retired official is chosen as the delegate, the head administrative official is obliged to conduct it. The ceremonial host respectfully requests the official delegate to take his seat, and burns incense to invite him to drink tea. [The ceremonial official] then returns to his seat, and, along with the official delegate, drinks tea. Once again, the host rises from his seat, burns incense, and returns to his seat to drink sweet hot water together with the delegate. When the tea bowl is retrieved, the official delegate rises, thanks the host, and climbs into the sedan chair.

2. Acceptance of the New Appointment by an Incumbent Abbot

1124a   When the official delegate arrives at the designated temple, he meets first with the guest reception official and together they meet with the head administrative official. After this, the official delegate is escorted to the guest house. Then he visits the primary seat official as well as the various quarters, and finally arrives at the office of the abbot's assistants where he explains the purpose of his visit. The official assistant reports the matter to the abbot and waits for his reply as to whether the invitation is accepted. If [the abbot] accepts, a crepe-wrapped table for the official documents must be prepared. The dual order officials are called to the abbot's office, and when they arrive they escort the abbot to meet with the official delegate. The latter bows and says:

> May the Venerable Abbot be seated in the cross-legged meditation posture.

The abbot sits in the center. The official delegate burns incense and performs three full prostrations with opened sitting cloth. He then steps forward and says:

> As I have been entrusted to be the delegate of Such-and-such Temple, it is my supreme joy to see your countenance filled with compassion.

Thereupon [the delegate] performs another set of three prostrations, saying:

> I respectfully wish at this moment on this day that all is well and felicitous with the newly appointed abbot, great teacher.

He then once again performs three prostrations and folds his sitting cloth. Having responded to each set of prostrations with a single greeting, the abbot then says:

> Though I am hesitant, I have accepted this invitation. I fear that I may not be faultless in the Zen tradition. I am, however, concerned with your traveling a long distance and am most grateful for it.

Thereupon, the official delegate presents the official documents for the prospective appointee. The newly appointed abbot receives them, places them on the table, and opens the letters to read through them, while his assistant respectfully requests the guest to take his seat.

The official delegate is obliged to take his seat opposite the prospective abbot. The west hall ranking official of the host temple sits at a lower position below the guest on this occasion, in order to show his respect for the official delegate who has traveled a long distance.)

When they finish drinking tea, the two officials escort the delegate to the guest house.

The practice hall attendant rings the hall bell to summon the practitioners to the abbot's office to express their congratulations. The head administrative official prepares incense, and the primary seat official and administrative officials burn incense. Upon the first opening of the sitting cloth, they say:

> Our religion is fortunate, and, as we have observed, this community has been made joyous by your transfer and promotion. We are most delighted with this event.

On the second opening of the sitting cloth they say:

> At this time and on this day, we all wish that everything is well and felicitous with the newly appointed master and great teacher.

They complete their formal greeting with three prostrations with unopened sitting cloth. The abbot performs a single prostration and replies:

> I have been chosen for the new position due to good fortune. Yet, I fear I may not warrant this level of praise and congratulation. I am humble about this opportunity.

When the practitioners depart, the guest reception official escorts the official delegate on a round through the practitioners' quarters. The [guest reception official] then receives the record of the temple's assets and the gift items brought from the temple for which the new appointment has been made. That evening a special serving of sweet hot water and evening meal should be made, and later there should be another serving of sweet hot water and fruit. The dual order officials as well as the retired officials participate in these events. The head administrative official bears the responsibility for fulfilling these activities.

3. The Ascent to the Dharma Hall
to Announce the New Appointment

The day after the invitation has been accepted, the abbot ascends
to the Dharma hall to make the announcement [of his new appoint-
ment]. His assistant has made arrangements beforehand, assigning the novice attendants to place the official documents brought
by the guest delegate on the right side below the rostrum seat and
to set up a seat for an official who will read the documents on behalf
of the delegate. This role is likely performed by the host temple's
director of practitioners' affairs, whom the delegate has previously
requested. The proceeding of the event is identical with an ordinary ascent to the Dharma hall, beginning with the assistant's notifying the abbot and the drum signaling his entrance into the hall.
When the abbot reaches the rostrum seat he remains standing
there. An incense table is placed before him. The official delegate
burns incense and presents the documents one by one. He burns
incense and then passes the documents to the abbot, and each time
the abbot says a prayer before burning incense and uttering the
word of insight. When all the documents have been read in this
manner, the delegate burns incense and performs the propriety of
two prostrations with opened sitting cloth and three prostrations
with unopened sitting cloth. If this formality is excused by the abbot
at his discretion, [the delegate] performs only a single prostration
with unopened sitting cloth. When the table is removed, the master ascends the high seat, preaches the Dharma, and thanks the
participants before concluding his discourse.

4. The Delegate's Special Serving of Tea
and a Meal for the New Appointee

The delegate meets with the new appointee beforehand to determine the cost of the noon meal for the practitioners and they agree
on the appropriate ratios of their [respective temple's] financial
responsibility. They add to the funds for gifts for the incumbent
and retired dual order officials and to those practitioners from the

same native province as the abbot-appointee or those who are
related in his Dharma lineage, and to those who have long been
engaged in assisting and serving the abbot. The funds for the noon
meal and so on must be transferred beforehand by the official delegate to the treasury official.

When the appointed day comes, the guest delegate visits the
abbot's office, burns incense, and makes a formal request by performing the propricty of two prostrations with opened sitting cloth
and three prostrations with unopened sitting cloth. At the first
opening of the sitting cloth, he says:

> I have made preparations for a special serving in the prac-
> tice hall at noon today. May you in your compassion grant
> me the honor of your presence at this occasion, though I am
> gravely ashamed of the humble offering.

On opening the sitting cloth the second time, he says:

> At this time and on this day, I wish that all is well and felic-
> itous with the newly appointed abbot and great master.

[The delegate] concludes his formal request by performing
three prostrations with unopened sitting cloth. The abbot replies
with a single prostration. Thereupon, the abbot's guest master
notifies the dual order officials and the retired officials (of the individual quarters), while the official delegate's attendant visits the
various quarters to notify the members of the temple community
about the schedule of the special serving to be conducted by the
guest delegate. A signboard announcing the special serving should
also be posted in the practice hall. The abbot's main seat should
be placed in the practice hall; the guest delegate's seat is prepared
at the first place on the raised sitting platform on the west hall
official's side [of the practice hall]. Signboards announcing the serving of tea and sweet hot water must be posted on each side of the
practice hall entrance.

At the time of the noon meal, the guest delegate waits for the
abbot outside the hall. They enter the hall and the abbot reaches

1124b

his place. The delegate requests him to take his seat, returns to mid-hall to bow, and after requesting the practitioners to take their seats he offers incense to the altar of the guardian bodhisattva. Next he burns incense facing the higher [right] and lower [left] positions on the raised platform of the inner hall, and then does the same in the outer hall. When he returns to the inner hall to bow, the serving of food begins, and when this is completed, he again offers incense and places monetary gifts on the altar, one for the abbot and another for the practitioners. He then returns to his seat for the meal.

At the time when the water left over from washing the bowls is collected from each practitioner, a drum signals the guest delegate to rise from his seat and proceed to burn incense for the serving of tea. The procedure is identical to that of the meal serving. When the serving of tea is completed and the attendants have left the hall, he bows as before [when requesting the abbot and the practitioners to drink tea]. When the abbot puts his cup down, [the guest delegate] performs the formal propriety of two prostrations with opened sitting cloth and three prostrations with unopened sitting cloth. At the first opening of his sitting cloth, he says:

> I, So-and-so, have humbly offered this meal and have received your compassionate presence. This is my greatest joy.

As he opens his sitting cloth for the second time, he makes polite enquiries [into the abbot's health, the weather, and the like], and finishes with three prostrations with unopened sitting cloth. He accompanies the abbot as far as the hall entrance, returns to the inner hall to burn incense, performs three prostrations with fully opened sitting cloth toward the altar of the guardian bodhisattva, and makes a round through the aisles of the practice hall, ending with bows in the outer hall as well as in the inner hall. When he retrieves the tea bowl from the altar, three drum rolls signal his departure from the practice hall. The guest delegate at once proceeds to the abbot's office to express his gratitude. Next, he goes to the head administrative official to thank him for his management of the almsgiving. Once again he returns to the abbot to invite him to the evening meal. Later that evening, after the dinner, there should be a serving of sweet hot water and cake, for which the dual order officials and the retired officials are invited as participants.

5. The Host Temple's Special Dinner Reception for the New Appointee and Guest Delegate

The head administrative official convenes a meeting to prepare for a special dinner reception and discuss matters of offering monetary gifts, as is regularly done on such occasions. The day before the event, the head administrative official goes to the newly appointed abbot to formally invite him by burning incense and performing prostrations. Then he goes to the guest house to invite the official delegate to the reception. Monetary gifts must be made in appropriate amounts, and are not to be contemptuously meager. The wording [of invitations] and decorum to be used are identical to those of ordinary special servings.

The abbot's high seat should be placed in the reception hall, with the seat of the guest delegate to its right. The seats of the dual order officials are at their usual places, facing each other from each side of the hall; the seats of the retired officials are across the hall, facing the high seat; and those of the [abbot's] assistants are behind the administrative officials. The retinue of servants who accompanied the guest official should be provided with a monetary bonus along with the special reception.

It has happened practically everywhere that when an abbot is appointed to serve at another temple, there are always some practitioners and attendants [of his old temple] who tend to take vengeance upon him for past grudges, spreading rumors to government officials and patrons and among ordinary people. Simply because of a single ignorant person, a temple can fall into infamy. Well-established senior practitioners or lay protectors [of the temple], or those of neighboring temples, must take heed of the possibility of such occurrences. Whenever someone progresses to become the abbot of another temple, it would be better to leave behind a feeling of love and respect.

6. Farewell Ascent to the Dharma Hall and Reception of Tea and Sweet Hot Water

On the day of departure, the guest delegate visits all the quarters to bid farewell. The newly appointed abbot ascends the rostrum seat of the Dharma hall and expresses his thanks to the dual order officials, retired officials, and practitioners. When [the abbot] descends from the high seat, he turns toward the high seat at the signal of three drumrolls and performs three prostrations with unopened sitting cloth in unison with the practitioners. He then 1124c departs from the western corridor of the Dharma hall. The practitioners see him off at the temple gate, tolling the large bell and making various sounds with the ritual instruments, while the attendants and workmen line up outside the gate.

The area surrounded by hanging curtains for the farewell serving should be set up beforehand at the gate, and a high seat should be placed within the space, facing the temple buildings. The primary seat official takes the main seat facing outside, while the west hall ranking official and the retired officials take their seats symmetrical to the main seat. The east and west order officials are seated on both lines facing the high seat. The head administrative official conducts the ceremonial serving. He requests the new appointee to take his seat, respectfully burns incense, and returns to his own seat for serving tea. When the tea bowls are collected, he once again stands up to burn incense and returns to his seat for the serving of sweet hot water. When the serving is over, the newly appointed abbot climbs into the sedan chair. Should the dual order officials and the retired officials start to walk alongside the sedan chair, the new appointee should thank them but stop them from doing so. The large bell is tolled until the party is assumed to have [traveled out of earshot].

7. Inviting the West Hall Official
to Become Abbot

The guest delegate meets with the guest reception official upon his arrival, and together they visit the office of abbot's assistants. Through proper introduction by the assistants, he meets with the abbot, burns incense, and performs prostrations with opened sitting cloth. When the meeting and serving of tea are concluded, the guest official is escorted to the guest house. Next, he visits the various official quarters to complete the formal greetings. Thereupon, through the abbot's assistant, he states the purpose [of his visit to the abbot], saying:

> Such-and-such Temple has commissioned me to invite Venerable So-and-so to become its abbot.

The host abbot notifies the dual order officials and the retired officials of the matter, and together they visit the quarters of the invited west hall official. The documents and letters brought by the guest delegate are presented. The ceremonial procedure followed in the latter situation for burning incense and so forth is exactly identical to that of inviting an incumbent [abbot]. Should the [west hall official politely] decline the invitation, his close associates should encourage him to accept it. Upon his acceptance, the abbot invites the new appointee, the dual order officials, and the retired officials to a serving of tea. Thereupon, the new appointee is escorted to the guest house to receive congratulations from various officials and the practitioners in due order. After making rounds of the various quarters and exchanging formal greetings, the new appointee and the guest delegate are invited to a special serving of sweet hot water, an evening meal, and a later serving of sweet hot water and fruit at the abbot's reception hall. The dual order officials are obliged to participate in these special servings.

8. Ascent to the Dharma Hall
by the New Appointee

(If the new appointee is a renowned ranking west hall official or the primary seat official, he is rightly recommended to conduct such an occasion.)

The evening before the day [of the ascent to the Dharma hall], the guest official should visit the host abbot with incense in his sleeve, perform three prostrations with unopened sitting cloth, and say:

> I request you to invite the new appointee to have the opportunity of ascending to the Dharma hall tomorrow.

The next day, after the morning meal, a table for the official documents and a chair should be placed to the right of the rostrum seat in the Dharma hall. The abbot's seat is placed to the left of the high seat. The practitioners are called to assemble by the drum signal. The abbot, entering into the hall, ascends the rostrum seat in similar manner as that of the every-fifth-day ascent to the Dharma hall.

The abbot signals his guest reception assistant to direct the new appointee to sit cross-legged. [The abbot] then eulogizes the opportunity for the new appointee who has accepted the appointment from the point of view of the Dharma, expresses his full support for the appointee's acceptance, and offers the practitioners some words of explanation and consolation. Regardless of whether he relates any instructive Zen insight episode, the abbot descends from the high seat and then stands before the left-side chair, facing the practitioners.

(Songyuan invited Yanshi to take the opportunity to ascend the rostrum seat; Xiaoan likewise invited Songyuan to take such opportunity, but in neither case was a Zen insight episode given. On the other hand, Shiqiao invited Jianchang to [ascend the Dharma seat] and Xian also invited Fuan [to do so], but in both these cases Zen insight episodes were given.)

The official delegate together with the guest reception assistant go before the appointee and bow toward him. The appointee goes before the abbot and bows to him. Next, the dual order officials and the practitioners bow toward him in unison.

If the new appointee is the host abbot's disciple in the Dharma lineage, the abbot grants him a robe and utters a word of insight. The appointed disciple, having donned [the robe], requests [the abbot] to sit cross-legged and performs three prostrations with opened sitting cloth. Without folding his sitting cloth, he greets [the abbot] with the following words:

> So quickly trained as I have been, I am hesitant before my predecessors. Yet, having been encouraged to accept the invitation, I feel it is difficult to decline this public imperative. I cannot help feeling extremely uneasy about it.

He once again performs three prostrations and says:

> I wish on this day and at this time that all is well and felicitous with your reverence, my original master and great teacher.

1125a After another three prostrations, he folds his sitting cloth and steps forward to bow. The abbot replies:

> That to which this path is entrusted is but a single thread which may lead to a great flourishing. Whether one is suitable or not is only of relative importance. I wish you the best in maintaining it.

The new appointee then returns to stand to the right of the high chair.

The guest delegate hands over the documents to the new appointee, and the latter in turn expresses a word of insight for each [document] that he receives. If the appointee is not the abbot's disciple, he comes before the high seat and bows toward the host abbot. Next he bows toward the west order official and the practitioners, and immediately moves to the right of the high seat, where he offers incense over the robe of Dharma transmission and the documents of his appointed temple, each time giving a word of insight. The guest delegate first requests the director of practitioners' affairs to invite the official to read the documents. When the documents have been read, the new appointee utters a word of insight, pointing at the rostrum seat, and then, ascending the high seat, gives instructive words, conducts a question-and-answer session, instructs on doctrinal teachings, and expresses words of appreciation before completing the occasion.

When the new appointee completes the session, he descends the seat, comes before the abbot and formally greets him with the propriety of two prostrations with opened sitting cloth and three prostrations with unopened sitting cloth. At the first opening of the sitting cloth, he says:

> Although I have just been appointed abbot, I may not be faultless with the Zen tradition. I am greatly indebted to you and grateful for your effort in polishing my training.

The abbot replies:

> I rejoice and congratulate you in your appointment as the guide in the human and heavenly worlds. It increases the illumination of the Buddha like that of the sun. This is my greatest delight.

At the second opening [of the sitting cloth], the appointee says:

> On this day and at this time, I together with others wish that all is well and felicitous with your reverence, temple master and great teacher.

He completes the greeting with three prostrations with unopened sitting cloth. This formality may be excused at the abbot's discretion.

Next, [the appointee] bows toward the dual order officials and the practitioners. The guest reception assistant escorts the new appointee on a round through the practitioners' quarters to express appreciation. If the appointee is the abbot's disciple, immediately after his descent from the high seat he performs three prostrations with fully opened sitting cloth before the abbot, and, stepping back, bows toward the officials and practitioners. The rest of

the proceedings, such as making a round through the practitioners' quarters, are just as before. If the appointee holds the status
of a secondary rank in the west hall, there might be some variation in matters of formality at the discretion of the abbot.

9. The Guest Delegate's Special Serving
of Tea for the New Appointee

The official delegate discusses with the new appointee the matter
of the various monetary gifts to be made and determines the
amounts for the abbot's invitation for the new appointee to the
Dharma hall, the practitioners, the official who reads the documents, as well as for the dual order officials, the retired officials,
and those who come from the same native province and nearby
native locality of the new appointee. After breakfast on the
appointed day, the guest delegate visits the abbot with incense in
his sleeve, performs a prostration with unopened sitting cloth, and
requests:

> This morning at noon, I shall offer a humble provision at the
> practice hall for the new appointee. May you in your com-
> passion grant us the honor of your presence on this occasion.

He then visits the new appointee and makes the same request.
The guest reception attendant at the abbot's office and the official
delegate's attendant together visit each quarter to convey the invitation and post the signboard. The new appointee's seat should be
placed in the practice hall opposite the abbot's, and the official delegate's seat should be placed at the first position of the raised sitting platform of the guest reception official in the outer hall. Signboards announcing the serving of tea and sweet hot water must
be posted on each side of the hall entrance.

At the time of the noon meal, the new appointee is directed to
wait for the abbot in front of the practice hall and together they
enter the hall and bow toward the shrine. The guest delegate follows and respectfully requests first the host abbot and then the new

appointee to take their respective seats. Thereupon, [the guest delegate] burns incense and conducts his ceremonial role as described previously. At the conclusion of the meal, the monetary gifts are made, tea is served, and the tea bowl is first collected from the new appointee. Then the official delegate goes before [the appointee], performs the formal propriety of two prostrations with opened sitting cloth and three prostrations with unopened sitting cloth, and then escorts him out through the rear entrance. The official delegate once again returns to the inner hall, performs the same formal greeting toward the abbot, and escorts him out through the front entrance. Once again he returns to the inner hall, burns incense, performs the propriety of three prostrations with fully opened sitting cloth, makes a round through the hall, and bows in the mid-outer hall. When the tea bowl is collected from the altar of the guardian bodhisattva, signaled by three drumbeats, [the delegate offical] leaves the hall. That evening, the new appointee is obliged to invite the guest delegate and others, as described previously, for a serving of sweet hot water, tea, and an evening meal.

10. The Host Temple's Special Dinner Reception for the New Appointee and the Delegate

The abbot's seat should be placed in the main position in the reception hall and the new appointee's seat is placed opposite it in the center, with the official delegate's seat to the left of the abbot and those of the dual order officials and the retired officials on each   1125b
side. The presentation of monetary gifts and ceremonial serving are as described previously.

11. The New Appointee's Farewell Ascent to the Dharma Hall and the Serving of Tea and Sweet Hot Water

The new appointee and the official delegate visit the office of the abbot's assistants to secure the abbot's permission for using the rostrum seat for conducting [the appointee's] farewell ascent. The abbot's seat should be placed to the left of the high seat. At the drum signal the practitioners assemble in the hall. When the abbot enters the hall and reaches his seat, the new appointee immediately goes before him and bows, then turns and bows toward the practitioners. He ascends the high seat, preaches, and descends. Thereupon, he greets the abbot with three prostrations with unopened sitting cloth. Next he faces the rostrum seat, makes a farewell greeting to the practitioners, and in unison with them performs three prostrations with unopened sitting cloth.

At the temple gate, a special seat is placed facing the temple buildings for the new appointee to receive a special serving of tea and sweet hot water. The dual order officials and the retired officials participate in the serving; the head administrative official is in charge of ceremonial conduct. It is the norm to see off the new appointee by tolling the large bell. If the appointee is second in rank after the west hall official, there should be no farewell ascent to the high seat. Before his departure, he visits the abbot together with the official delegate to burn incense and, after three prostrations with unopened sitting cloth, offers a farewell greeting. Next, he makes a round of the practitioners' quarters to express farewell greetings to them. The farewell serving of tea and sweet hot water at the temple gate is as described previously.

IV. Inauguration of the New Abbot

1. Establishment of the Newly Appointed Abbot's Residency at the Temple

In ancient times, the new appointee, upon reaching the gate [of his new temple] in his traveling attire and hat, would remove his hat, pass through the gate, burn incense, and utter a word of insight. In front of the practice hall, he took off his traveling pack, washed his feet, donned a robe taken from his pack, and entered the hall. He then offered incense to the guardian bodhisattva and performed the formal worship through three prostrations with fully opened sitting cloth, followed by his accompanying practitioners. He completed the formality of establishing residency by placing the sack containing his robe and almsbowl at the abbot's designated position in the practice hall, and then proceeded to the Buddha hall to burn incense, express a word of insight, and complete his worship with the formality of three prostrations with fully opened sitting cloth. Next, he offered incense at the shrine of the local deities and the patriarchal shrine hall, giving a word of insight at each place, and finally entered the abbot's office, where once again he gave a word of insight. In appropriate order, he would then perform the initial ascent to the Dharma hall and intone the prayer for imperial longevity.

Nowadays, it is customary for a new appointee to arrive first at the guest house. If it is near the temple, the primary seat official is obliged to lead the practitioners to welcome the new abbot there. But if it is too far, only the dual order officials and the retired officials come to meet him. The official delegate must consult with him beforehand so as to dispatch a note excusing the practitioners from traveling a long distance to present themselves. If the guest house is near, the visiting practitioners must be served tea and sweet hot water, participated in by the dual order officials and the retired officials. The day the new appointee is to enter the temple must be decided upon, and the head administrative official is in charge of all arrangements for that day. The evening before, a signboard informing the practitioners about the schedule for the "reception of the abbot" is posted.

At the appointed time, the practitioners assemble at the temple gate, lining up [on both sides of the path]. The large bell is tolled and other ceremonial instruments are played to celebrate the arrival of the new appointee. The attendants and workmen stand behind the lines of practitioners. When the new appointee reaches the gate, he burns incense and gives a word of insight. At the Buddha hall, he again offers incense and gives a word of insight, and completes his worship with three prostrations with fully opened sitting cloth. When the practice hall bell is rung, the practitioners return there to take their places for the meal. The new appointee enters the hall and offers incense, while the accompanying practitioners perform in unison three prostrations with opened sitting cloth. The director of practitioners' affairs faces the new abbot, bows to him, and escorts him on a round through the hall. The accompanying practitioners then leave the hall. The dual order officials escort the new appointee to the abbot's designated seat and perform three prostrations with unopened sitting cloth.

1125c   Next, the new appointee visits the shrine of the local divinities and the patriarchal shrine hall to offer incense and give a word of insight at each place. When he enters the abbot's office and takes his seat, the abbot's assistant steps forward, burns incense, and stands by his side. As he completes the word of insight, the attendant places by him a table equipped with a brush and inkslab, while the head administrative official presents an official document (format given below). The temple's official seal is also placed on the crepe-wrapped board. The new appointee examines the seal and asks the head administrative official to open it. After examining the seal characters, he stamps the seal over the letters on the envelope. Next he writes the date and stamps over it as well. The head administrative official takes the document, and the abbot's personal assistant (who manages the abbot's personal possessions, such as his robe and almsbowl) puts the seal and table away. When the abbot stands, all the officials line up as their leader burns incense on their behalf, and perform in unison the propriety of two prostrations with opened sitting cloth and three prostrations with unopened sitting cloth. At the first opening of the sitting cloth, the head official says:

> It is most gratifying to us that you have accepted the position here.

At the second opening of the sitting cloth, he says:

We wish that all is well and felicitous with the newly
appointed abbot and great teacher.

They complete the greeting with three prostrations with
unopened sitting cloth.

The neighboring temple representatives, the officials, and the
retired officials step forward to burn incense. When this informal
congratulation is over, the guest reception attendant announces:

There will be a serving of sweet hot water for the neighboring temple representatives, the dual order officials, and the
retired officials at their designated seats.

There follows the serving of some food provisions for the government officials and the representatives of neighboring temples.
If the former abbot, though already having accepted a new position elsewhere, has not yet departed, or if he is staying on in the
east hall as a retiree, the new appointee is obliged to conduct the
propriety of the transfer ceremony before occupying the main rostrum seat as abbot. Only after this ceremony does he receive informal congratulations. Ringing the practice hall bell and leading
the practitioners, he personally escorts his predecessor to his quarters and peforms a prostration with unopened sitting cloth to [the
former abbot]. Thereafter the new abbot receives congratulatory
greetings from the primary seat official and the resident practitioners. Attendants and serving men are all obliged to pay their
respects to the new abbot.

The Document for Presenting the Temple Seal

Bhikṣu So-and-so, head administrative official of this temple,
respectfully presents the single piece of the temple seal to
the newly appointed temple master and great teacher. Awaiting his compassionate acceptance.

Solemnly written and presented,
Date and year

2. The Temple's Invitation to the New Appointee for the Noon Meal

After the new appointee has settled in his official seat at the abbot's office, the head administrative official waits for the moment when the congratulatory proprieties are finished, then comes to the abbot to invite him to the noon meal reception. Beforehand he has prepared a letter of invitation along with an incense burner and a candle, which are carried by an attendant on a crepe-wrapped board. The head administrative official, carrying incense in his sleeve, performs the formality of two prostrations with opened sitting cloth and three prostrations with unopened sitting cloth. At the first opening of the sitting cloth, he says:

> At noon, a humble meal reception will be offered at the practice hall to respectfully welcome your reverence. We earnestly wish that in your compassion you will grant us the honor of your presence on this occasion, though we feel hesitant because of its meagerness.

At the second opening [of the sitting cloth], he enquires about the abbot's well-being, and then completes the formal greeting with three prostrations with unopened sitting cloth. The abbot replies with a prostration. The invitation presented by the administrative official is received by the abbot's guest master or the guest reception assistant, while the preparations must be made at the abbot's place in the practice hall by the guest master of the administrative office. The proceeding is identical with that of the special dinner reception.

The Letter of Invitation to the Noon Meal

> Bhikṣu So-and-so, head administrative official of this temple, respectfully invites the newly appointed temple master to a humble meal reception at the practice hall at noon. We earnestly wish that in your compassion you will grant us the honor of your presence on this occasion.

Written by So-and-so on
Date, month, year

Format of the Envelope

Solemnly sealed for the Honorable Seat
New Appointee, Venerable So-and-so

3. Inaugural Ascent to the Dharma Hall
and Invocation for Imperial Longevity

In ancient times, the inaugural ascent to the Dharma hall was conducted under imperial decree or under the request of a deputy official
of the imperial court, and hence such an event was called for with
magnanimity. Either the provincial judges or the district and prefectural officials requested the new appointee with gifts of silk and
so on, which were presented at the welcoming meal reception, to conduct the inaugural ascent to the Dharma hall at a certain temple or
at its mother temple by providing funds from the government treasury for the meal reception and inaugural events. It is mentioned in
various records written by renowned public officials that each official
himself prepared a signboard announcing such an event, or a signboard indicating the serving of tea and sweet hot water.

Nowadays, the inaugural ascent to the Dharma hall is generally conducted at each temple's expense. The new appointee can
conduct the ceremony of inauguration at any determined time in
order to preside in the temple. The abbot's assistant assigns the
attendants to set up the rostrum seat at the Dharma hall, notify   1126a
the practitioners, and post the signboard indicating the ascent to
the Dharma hall. He copies out the names of government officials
and the representatives of neighboring temples beforehand, and
presents this list to the abbot. A crepe-wrapped table with an incense
burner and a candle stand are placed to the left of the rostrum seat,
and the official documents are displayed on it. [The abbot's assis-
tant] is also obliged beforehand to request the director of practitioners' affairs and the primary seat official to prepare the public

announcement and to compose the word of tribute on behalf of the temple community. The training official next in rank or renowned practitioners who have gathered from neighboring temples or from the Zen world in general compose the rest of the tributes. Moreover, one of the neighboring temple representatives must be chosen and requested beforehand to conduct the commencement of the event by striking the octagonal woooden block with its mallet. The seats of the government officials should be placed opposite the rostrum seat.

The abbot's assistant notifies the master of the beginning of the event and instructs an attendant to begin drumming to assemble the practitioners. When all have assembled, [the assistant] and the official delegate together escort the abbot into the Dharma hall. Crimson lanterns have been placed in the hall, cymbals are sounded, and flowers are scattered. The abbot reaches his designated place and stands. If he is not wearing the robe of Dharma transmission, he must raise up the word of insight on the Dharma [that he has written] before donning the robe. After this, the official delegate steps forward, burns incense, and performs the formal propriety of two prostrations with opened sitting cloth and three prostrations with unopened sitting cloth. At the first opening of the sitting cloth, he says:

> Today, you have accepted the responsibility of this Zen institution for the sake of our benefit. This is most gratifying to us.

At the second opening, [the official delegate] enquires politely about the master's well-being, and then completes his greeting with three prostrations with unopened sitting cloth. The abbot responds with a single prostration.

First, the abbot presents the public announcement. After he raises the word of insight, he gives the written proclamation to the director of practitioners' affairs to read. Next, he gives a word of insight for each congratulatory message one by one as presented by the temple community, the neighboring temples, and the Zen world in general, and returns each respectively to its originator who then reads it. If a government official who originally sponsored the new appointee's conduct of the inaugural ascent to the Dharma hall is present, and if he has prepared a word of congratulation, he presents it to the abbot himself. The abbot is obliged to give a word of insight also before [the congratulatory message] is read by the official. After all the messages have been read, the abbot points toward the rostrum seat and raises the word of insight regarding the high seat that he is about to ascend. Immediately afterward he ascends the high seat and offers incense for the invocation of imperial longevity. Next, he offers incense for the sake of the imperial religious councilor, the offices of the imperial chamberlain and the censorate, the district and prefectural government offices, and also for civil and military bureaucrats. For each offering, the assistant hands incense to the abbot. Finally, and only when offering incense for his own teacher in the Dharma transmission, the abbot takes out his own incense from his sleeve and burns it.

The abbot now sits cross-legged and arranges his robe. His assistant burns incense, descends the high rostrum, and bows. The dual order officials then step forward to bow toward the abbot. The abbot's assistant once again ascends the rostrum, burns incense, and bows. The proceeding is the same as that of the ascent to the Dharma hall on the first day and mid-month day. The abbots of neighboring temples who escorted the new appointee to the temple are also obliged to come forward and bow. Through his assistant, the abbot requests the government officials to take their seats. Thereupon the lead official, selected from among the representatives from the neighboring temples, strikes the octagonal wooden post with its mallet and announces:

> May the honorable colleagues, endowed with superior insight and understanding, concentrate upon the absolute transcendent truth (*paramārtha*).

The abbot gives some words of instruction, participates in question-and-answer exchanges, preaches the essence of doctrine, and finally expresses thanks to the representatives of neighboring temples and the government officials with the following words:

I have conducted the inaugural session solely for the sake of celebrating imperial longevity; hence, I refrain from uttering many words and statements.

The official delegate, the dual order officials, and the retired officials abbreviate their words of appreciation. Details are given below, in section 5. The inaugural session is then completed. The senior practitioner once again strikes the octagonal wooden post with the mallet and announces:

May the honorable colleagues see directly the Dharma of the King of the Dharma (i.e., the Buddha), that this is the Buddha-Dharma.

Thereupon, the abbot descends from the high seat.

The government officials congratulate the abbot first, and are then escorted by the guest reception official to the guest house. The guest master attendant brings forward the incense burners and candle stands and places them in a horizontal line before the abbot's seat. After the official delegate offers incense and performs the formal propriety of two prostrations with opened sitting cloth and three prostrations with unopened sitting cloth, the attendant of the practice hall office announces:

The greetings of the representatives of the neighboring temples are in order.

Next, he announces:

The greeting by the west hall official is in order.

After the official performs a prostration with opened sitting cloth, the [practice hall attendant] once again announces:

The greetings of the administrative officials are in order.

The officials also perform the formal propriety of two prostrations with opened sitting cloth and three prostrations with unopened sitting cloth. Next, with these announcements, the primary seat official and the practitioners, including the retired officials, the retired subfunctionary officials, the retired subfunctionary assistants, and the retired officials of various quarters, are ushered in. All burn incense and together with the practitioners perform the same formal propriety as before. When this is completed, further congratulatory greetings are made by the managerial officers of the temple estate and storage, hermitages, and tower buildings; those who are related [to the abbot] in Dharma lineage; those who come from [his] native province; and recent arrivals. The abbot now takes his seat, and his assistant and his own disciples burn incense and perform the formality of three prostrations with fully opened sitting cloth. Next, the attendants of the official functionaries burn incense and perform prostrations, followed by the 1126b other attendants led by the ceremonial leader; they likewise burn incense and perform prostrations. Finally, the business affairs workers, the transportation workers, the estate foremen, the carpenters, the skilled workers, and the laborers all come to pay their respects and perform prostrations.

After receiving all these congratulatory greetings, the abbot pays a visit to the guest positions to thank the government officials and the representatives of the neighboring temples. He then proceeds on rounds through various quarters in due order. The resident practitioners of each quarter must prepare a table with incense, an incense burner, and candle stands, as well as a special seat. They are also obliged to wait for the abbot's visit in proper dignity and decorum outside the entrance of each quarter. The master of the quarters waits at the lower end of the entrance, escorts the abbot into the quarters, and requests him to take a seat. The master of the quarters burns incense, reciprocated by the abbot's offering of incense. [The abbot] makes a polite enquiry into the well-being of the practitioners and expresses his appreciation, and is then escorted out. The practitioners of the retirees' quarters, such as officials and assistants, and the members of the practitioners' quarters are all required to line up at the entrance gates of their buildings to both greet and see off the abbot.

4. The Temple Community's Special Serving of Tea and Sweet Hot Water for the New Abbot

Signboards announcing the special serving of tea and sweet hot water must be posted on each side of the outer practice hall. The head administrative official prepares the written invitation (format given below). He then visits the abbot's office, accompanied by an attendant carrying a crepe-wrapped board with incense, a burner, and a candle stand, and burns incense to request the master's presence on the occasion of the special serving. If full formality is excused, [the head administrative official] may simply greet the abbot with a prostration with unopened sitting cloth and say:

> After the noon meal, a special serving of tea is scheduled at the practice hall in honor of your reverence. May you in your compassion grant us the honor of your presence at that time.

He then presents the written invitation and asks the guest master to notify the dual order officials, the retired officials, and the practitioners to participate in the special serving of tea. The signboard announcing the serving of tea and sweet hot water should be posted to inform the practitioners. The abbot's seat must be specially set up in the practice hall for this occasion.

(In recent times, it has become customary that when the metal gong located in the kitchen hall is struck at the time of the noon meal, the head administrative official enters the practice hall, burns incense, performs three prostrations with opened sitting cloth, and makes a round through the hall in order to invite the practitioners to such special proprieties. However, this occasion is exclusively for the sake of expressing congratulatory greetings to the abbot on the part of the temple community as a whole. In the *Ancient Regulations,* there was no rule about making a round in order to invite the practitioners to the occasion, and it is more appropriate to dismiss this custom, which was only recently created.)

Sometime after the noon meal, the drumming commences to assemble the practitioners at the practice hall. The administrative official escorts the abbot into the hall, requests him to take a seat, burns incense at the altar of the guardian bodhisattva, and then burns incense before the master. Going around behind the altar, he returns to the center of the hall and stands. When the serving of tea is completed throughout the hall, and as soon as the tea jars have been carried out, the administrative official once again goes to the abbot and invites him to drink tea. Returning to his former position, again going around behind the altar, he burns incense before the altar and performs three prostrations with opened sitting cloth. Thereupon, he and all the dual order officials go before the abbot to perform the formal propriety of two prostrations with opened sitting cloth and three prostrations with unopened sitting cloth. They then escort the abbot from the hall. The administrative official once again returns to the hall, burns incense, bows toward both sections of the hall, and retrieves the tea bowl from the altar of the guardian bodhisattva before leaving. The serving of sweet hot water is to be conducted in the same manner. However, there is no rule that the host official should leave the hall to escort the abbot, as it is customary to serve the evening meal after the sweet hot water has been served.

Format of the Written Invitation

Bhikṣu So-and-so, head administrative official of this temple, respectfully extends an invitation to the abbot for a special serving of tea (and sweet hot water) today, after the noon meal and toward the evening. It is to be held at the practice hall in order to express our greetings and congratulations. We earnestly wish that in your compassion you will grant us the honor of your presence for this occasion.

Respectfully written on
Date, month, year

Format of the Envelope

The format for the envelope is identical to that of the previous invitation.

5. The Supplementary Session on the
First Evening of the Inauguration

After the noon meal, the abbot's assistant reports to him, saying, "The supplementary session is scheduled for this evening, sir."

The guest master must inform the practitioners and post the signboard indicating the session. He is obliged to note down the following names: the official delegate, the dual order officials, and the retired subfunctionary assistants, as well as the retired officials of various quarters; the managerial officers of the temple estates, storages, hermitages, and tower buildings; newly arrived practitioners; the new abbot's assistants who accompanied him; and guests such as Zen experts and their associates. In addition, [the guest master] must record in detail the names of those government officials and representatives of neighboring temples who remain at the host temple, including their whereabouts, on the basis of which he makes a list to present to the abbot.

When the evening bell sounds, the abbot's assistant notifies the master and has the attendants strike the wooden sounding board and drum for one session. The practitioners assemble and the dual order officials take their respective places. The abbot then enters the hall, ascends the high seat, gives instruction, answers questions, preaches the essential doctrine, and finally thanks all participants in the session. The attendant carries a candle and the assistant presents the name list. It is desirable that all the names should be intoned without omission. Thereupon, the abbot descends, and the guest reception official's attendant announces:

> The temple master invites the officials representing the neighboring temples, the dual order officials, the west hall ranking official, the retired officials, the retired subfunctionaries, official assistants, and Zen experts to a serving of sweet hot water at the reception hall immediately after this session.

The head administrative official escorts the government officials to the guest house where sweet hot water and fruit are served.

1126c

6. The Ascent to the Dharma Hall for
Patron Donors of the Temple Buildings

The evening before the day [of this event], the head administrative official should notify the abbot. The next morning, the abbot's assistant requests the guest reception attendant to post the signboard informing the practitioners of the abbot's forthcoming ascent to the hall. The head administrative official orders the patriarchal shrine hall to be enshrined and various offerings to be prepared. After the morning rice gruel, the abbot conducts a special ascent to the Dharma hall. There he explains the meaning of his ascent and preaches the Dharma. After descending from the high seat, he leads the assembly to the patriarchal shrine hall, burns incense, serves tea and sweet hot water to the altar, and offers food. The director of practitioners' affairs calls for sutra chanting and concludes the event with the proper invocation of merit transference.

7. The Special Meal Reception
for the Official Delegate

The head administrative official reports to the abbot [prior to the event] to consult with him on the amount to be remunerated to the official delegate and the reader of the official documents. The abbot prepares monetary gifts, properly following the norms. On the appointed day, curtains are placed in the reception hall and seats are designated according to rank. The dual order officials and the retired officials should be invited to participate. After setting up the special seats, the guest reception assistant himself escorts the main guest, while the guest reception attendant invites the remaining participants. The propriety of this serving is the same as that of an ordinary special serving.

8. Extending the Terms of the
Dual Order Officials

After conducting the special reception for the official delegate, the dual order officials visit the abbot and express their intention to resign from their offices. The abbot, however, must not immediately accept their resignations. He instructs his assistant and the guest reception attendant to prepare sweet hot water and a crepe-wrapped board equipped with an incense burner and candle stand. Accompanied by his assistant, the abbot visits the head administrative official's quarters, and so on, and tries to persuade him and the other officials to stay on in their offices. The guest reception attendant notifies each quarter and escorts the abbot to each of them. The abbot takes his seat and the guest reception attendant and assistant respectively sit on either side of him. The practitioner assistant must burn incense and serve sweet hot water with utmost cordiality so as to persuade [the officials who have tendered their resignations] to stay on. Even if some officials have already stayed beyond their regular terms, this should be tolerated. The officials, however, may once again express their intent to resign to the abbot at another appropriate time.

9. Remunerations for Those Who Assisted the Abbot's Departure and Arrival

In general, the government officials, lay patrons, and the abbots of neighboring temples who assisted the new abbot at his inauguration into office at the temple must be rewarded with due remuneration. The abbot should visit the district and prefectural government offices. If he has to travel a great distance from his mountain temple, he should dispatch his attendant to inform the head administrative official, the primary seat official, and the director of practitioners' affairs of his whereabouts. In the event that he must be away from the temple for some length of time, the head administrative official enquires about the time of his return and requests the director of the practice hall to post the signboard informing the practitioners about "meeting the abbot." The abbot's return is announced by tolling the large bell. The abbot may send a message beforehand to excuse this formality and upon his arrival proceed directly to offer incense at the Buddha hall and at the shrine of local divinities. The primary seat official, leading the practitioners, then visits the abbot's office to welcome him back. After a bow, the practitioners withdraw but the abbot requests the dual order officials to remain and serves them sweet hot water before they leave. The abbot's assistant and attendant on duty in the office burn incense and perform prostrations. Next, the ceremonial leader together with the novice attendants perform prostrations. Thereupon the abbot is obliged to make rounds through the various quarters in order to thank the temple community.

If the temple is within a town or city, and if there is no specific morning or evening time [for the abbot's] departure and arrival, there is no need for such procedures. The abbot may return to the hall incognito, in which case the dual order officials and the retired officials are obliged to visit him and enquire about his well-being.

Master Wuzhun, at the time of his residence in Jingshan (Xingshengwanshousi), had a busy schedule of religious activities and arrived and departed frequently. Each time he returned to the practice hall in time to partake of the morning gruel and the noon meal along with the practitioners. He then requested his guest reception attendant get permission from the assistant of the guardian bodhisattva to strike the octagonal wooden post located at the back of the hall at the moment the practitioners were about to step down [from the raised sitting platform]. The assistant then announced: 1127a

> May the practitioners remain a moment where they stand. The abbot is going to make a round of the hall.

[Wuzhun] then burned incense and walked the aisles of the hall. This announcement was then made:

> The master asks that the practitioners should not take the trouble to visit his office.

However, the dual order officials and the retired officials are nonetheless obliged to visit the abbot [upon his return] to welcome him.

10. Keeping the Accounts of the Original
Temple Plan and Material Resources

After the new abbot has been installed, he should meet with the dual order officials and the retired officials over tea to enquire in detail about the temple's business affairs, the original temple plan, various contract documents, and the temple's material resources in order to itemize them and differentiate between public and private items. The abbot must prevent fraud or corruption by keeping clear accounts of the temple's possessions, such as grain and other material goods. This requires detailed inspection.

11. Receiving the Invitation from the
Dual Order Officials and Retired Officials
for a Special Serving of Tea

On the appointed day, the primary seat official, the head administrative official, and the head retired official, representing their colleagues, visit the abbot's office and burn incense to invite the abbot to the reception. Next, they invite the abbot's assistants and disciples. The abbot's seat should be placed at the main position of the reception hall, while the dual order officials and the retired officials are assigned their usual positions [facing each other]. The abbot's assistants and his accompanying disciples bow toward the abbot and then take their respective seats at the end of the row of the officials' seats. When the time comes, the primary seat official escorts the abbot into the reception hall, respectfully requests him to take his seat, and performs the formal propriety. If excused [from the formal propriety], he simply burns incense, steps forward to bow, and presents a monetary gift. Representing all the officials, the primary seat official, the head administrative official, and the senior retired officials together greet the abbot with a bow and return to their seats. After the meal is over, the primary seat official stands to burn incense. If this formality is excused, he remains seated, drinking tea. The proceedings are identical to that of inviting the respresentatives of neighboring temples, old colleagues, minor functionaries, those related in the Dharma lineage, one's own disciples, and so on to such similar receptions. In serving, the host officials must consider sometimes changing the order of the seating arrangments depending upon the participants' higher or lower rank.

V. Retirement from the Office of Abbot

If the abbot is aged and suffers from illness, or if his mental agility declines, or if things do not go well with him, he himself should know when it is time to retire. He is obliged to clearly account for all public and private monetary expenditures and property in his records. As to those material goods that belong to the office of the abbot, it is necessary to clearly distinguish them as public belongings and itemize them; duplicate copies of this account should be signed by the abbot, the dual order officials, and the retired officials and imprinted with the official seal of the temple. The abbot and the head administrative officials keep duplicates for future reference, and the abbot's office must be guarded by an official of public standing. On the day of his retirement, the abbot ascends to the Dharma hall, expresses his thanks, says farewell, descends from the high seat, and, at the signal of three drumbeats, departs. If the retired abbot chooses to stay on in the east hall of the temple, his successor is obliged to look after his well-being with the utmost care and decorum.

There is an example of this present matter. When Emperor Lizong of the Song decided to build a temple for his deceased empress on the farmyard that belonged to Lingyinsi, the temple's honorable abbot, Chijueh Chonggong, retired that very day and went to Lushan, carrying his own travel pack and wearing a hat. The emperor sent messengers to try to persuade the former abbot to return, but his effort was in vain. Chijueh's noblemindedness shines throughout the millennium. Who could ever surpass his deed?

VI. Death of the Abbot and the Written Will

1. Death [of the Abbot]

1127b   In the event that the abbot should begin to fall seriously ill, he beforehand invites the dual order officials and the retired officials to examine all his possessions, which will then be collected in a package and
sealed; the articles are to be kept at the office under a reliable official's
guard up to the time of their auction. If the abbot has goods to distribute to specific residents and in general, he is required to do so
impartially. Since a feeling of indebtedness and a grudge are not
identical, one should not create cause for later dispute. If one's possessions are meager everything must be arranged as simply and fru-
gally as possible. The abbot should also instruct his disciples who
wear hemp cloth [in mourning] to refrain from loudly weeping.

The abbot must request the primary seat official to conduct
the funeral rite. Excusing all ritual performances, he orders the
rite to be conducted only with the chanting of the verse of "impermanence," just as with any other practitioner's passing away. No
temple funds should be expended, nor should too much of the practitioners' time be required. If the abbot has contributed to the temple, the members of the temple community may remember him
with a sense of love. If he has more than a usual amount in his
possession, the funeral service may be conducted in accordance
with this amount. Written wills addressed to government officials,
patrons, or neighboring temples and [the abbot's] relations in
Dharma lineage must be delivered.

2. The Written Will

The Letter of Request Concerning One's Funeral

So-and-so, abbot of the Such-and-such Temple, thanks the
assisting causes of the world. Yet wind and the flame of a

candle do not stand still. Whatever I possess are gifts from donors and are not part of the temple's public property. I, therefore, ask the dual order officials to take all my possessions and request Venerable So-and-so to be in charge of my funeral rite. The remaining materials must be distributed to the practitioners for their service in chanting sutras. Do not extend the performance of the rite to the point at which an expenditure from the temple's public fund becomes necessary. May this be kindly understood, and everything be done in the way here described.

Date and year
Abbot, Venerable So-and-so

Format of the Written Will

I. Addressed to the ranking officials:

I have enjoyed your association for some time. I cannot help but recall occasions of meeting and parting [in life]. Succeeding to my present position, pushing and pulling, I have carried it out by a toad's effort from an insignificant basis. Lightning and dew abruptly disappear. A cloudy mountaintop becomes more and more remote. I dare pray, take care of yourself. Please accept this letter. Omitting the formality.

II. Addressed to the abbots of neighboring temples:

There is no abbot in action. Hence, this temple relies on the light of the neighboring wall for everything. The external world seen in a dream is originally nonexistent. However, I am thankful for the illusion of this world which has been an assisting cause. There is no particular word at the time of departure, except that my mind runs fast. May the sun of the Buddha increase in its brightness and thereby make the tradition ever more vibrant. Please take good care of yourself.

III. Addressed to [the abbot's] relations in the Dharma lineage:

Because of my insatiable desire I have occupied my present position and have sometimes happened to ignore many friends who share the same instruction in Dharma training, and I regret this matter. Now my lifespan is coming to an end. With respect, I send this letter to convey my wish at my departure: May you brighten the honorable virtue of our common teacher. As to the religious goal, one must exert one's own strength and not let his efforts decline. Please take good care of yourself.

IV. Envelope:

Addressed to

Venerable So-and-so
Title, with Veneration

Respectfully sealed by

Venerable Bhikṣu So-and-so
Such-and-such Temple

3. Laying the Deceased in the Portable Shrine

When the abbot has passed away, his practitioner assistant immediately asks the guest reception attendant to go to the practice hall and inform the practitioners. Striking the octagonal wooden post once, the attendant announces:

The Venerable Master, abbot of this temple, left this message to the practitioners: "Wind and fire are separated and can no longer reach one another."

He once again strikes the octagonal wooden post. Next, he informs the members of the various quarters about the event. The attendant of the practice hall official rings the practice hall bell to assemble the practitioners. They visit the abbot's office and, after expressing their condolences, the primary seat official, the dual order officials, and the retired officials consult together about writing the obituary notice (format given below) and delivering it to the neighboring temples. As for the master of the funeral rite, a request must be made to a renowned senior official of a neighboring temple, to the abbot of the nearest temple, or to the primary seat official of the home temple. If a particular person is designated in the will, that person must be invited in accordance with the will.

The disciples of the deceased and his close followers cleanse the body, drape it in new cloth, shave the head, and lay the body in the portable shrine. The verse left by the deceased is posted on the left side of the shrine. The director of practitioners' affairs, leading the disciples of the deceased, burns incense, invites the primary seat official to conduct the rite of laying the body in the shrine, and places the shrine in the reception hall along with a table holding an incense burner and candles, and a carpet. He then conducts offerings.

1127c

At the appointed time, the practice hall bell is tolled to assemble the practitioners for the funeral rite. Toward the end of this rite, the director of practitioners' affairs steps forward and intones the following prayer:

> The relationship of the transcendent and its phenomenal embodiment is mysterious in having shown its phenomenal trace in the world of humans and heavenly beings. The master's sincere nature is perfect and clear, and his intuitive capacity well accorded with that of the Buddhas and patriarchs. It is respectfully reflected that the Venerable Master, abbot of this temple, his dazzling insight like a moon, shed his light over thousands and thousands of miles of waves. Our grief is sincere indeed, and accords with the feeling of the Buddhas of the ten directions. Though we look up reverently we find no ground, and our determination does not go afar but returns. We have assembled here with sincerity to intone our prayer by praising the [ten sacred] names of the Buddhas: the Luminous Pure Dharma Body Vairocana Buddha, and so on.

Next, he calls for the chanting of the *Mahākāruṇikacitta-dhāraṇī*s, and concludes with the following invocation of merit transference:

> The merit accrued by chanting the foregoing esoteric verses is intended to enshrine the indescribable rewarding state of non-arising, which the Venerable Master, abbot of this temple, has realized. Veneration to the Buddhas of the ten directions and the three times, and so on.

Once again, he calls for the chanting of the *Śūraṃgama-dhāraṇī*s and concludes with the following invocation of merit transference:

> The merit accrued by chanting the *Śūraṃgama-dhāraṇī*s is intended to promote and honor the head of the temple, the Venerable Master's rank and state of realization. Veneration to the Buddhas of three times and the ten directions, and so on.

That evening, when the practitioners have assembled and after the prayer chanting is over, the director of practitioners' affairs says:

> I speak to the practitioners. The Venerable Master, abbot of this temple, has already returned to the true state of quiescence. We have all lost our support. Remind yourselves earnestly of the sole truth of impermanence and guard against falling into a state of unrestrainedness. For the sake of this intention, let us intone the [ten sacred] names of the Buddhas: the Luminous Pure Dharma Body Vairocana Buddha, and so on.

The invocation of merit transference is identical to the above. Twice a day, at morning and noon respectively, rice gruel and rice must be served, and three times a day (morning, noon, and evening), tea and sweet hot water must be served. At each serving, the practitioners should perform the service of chanting sutras, which is concluded by the director of practitioners' affairs with the same invocation of merit transference as before.

Nowadays, popular manners and customs have become corrupted. Some practitioners want to be assigned to the management posts of estates, storage, and manpower but do not obtain them, while some steal temple property. When the abbot [duly] punishes such acts according to the monastic regulations, these evil ones not only do not repent their wrongdoing but also harbor grudges against the abbot. Informed of his passing, they make all sorts of derogatory remarks about him as if such behavior gives them great pleasure. In extreme cases, they may even vandalize the enshrined coffin, openly taking the clothing and goods by force to demonstrate their brutality. The senior official in charge of the funeral rite, the representatives of the neighboring temples, patron donors, government officials, general participants, and the associates in Zen practice must protect the postmortem affairs. For who [among us] ever escapes death? How much more should those wicked people who have come for training under the deceased master and yet commit such transgressions be expelled, punished, and reformed! If the master of the funeral rite can ahead of time set up guidelines of discipline and reform the regulations so as to prevent such crimes before their occurrence, this would contribute greatly to the outward beauty of all the proceedings of the funeral rite.

Format of the Obituary Note

Bhikṣu So-and-so in charge of the funeral rite of Such-and-such Temple, respectfully notifies you that a bereavement has befallen the above temple, whose abbot, Venerable So-and-so, suddenly returned to the transcendent on such-and-such day of this month.

> Date and year
> Written by Bhikṣu So-and-so, in charge of
> Such-and-such Temple's funeral rite

Format of the Envelope

Obituary Notice Addressed to

Zen Master, Venerable So-and-so
Such-and-such Temple

Respectfully sealed

4. Inviting the Director of the Funeral Rite (Chief Mourner)

When the invited director of the funeral rite arrives, it is customary to toll the large bell to assemble the practitioners at the temple gate to receive him. When he reaches the front of the shrine, he burns incense. The primary seat official and the practitioners bow toward him and withdraw. The dual order officials and the retired officials escort him to the guest house, and, after burning incense, perform prostrations with opened sitting cloth. The director of the funeral rite sits on the main seat, while the primary seat official sits beside him. The latter stands up to burn incense and, after returning to his seat, serves tea to the guest.

The disciples of the deceased master then line up in front, burn incense, and perform the formal propriety of three prostrations with fully opened sitting cloth. The practitioner assistants and novice attendants of the abbot's office and the ceremonial leader, leading all the attendants, burn incense and perform prostrations in succession. After them, the workers of the abbot's office pay their respects. When all this is over, sweet hot water should be served, and the guest then sees off the dual order officials as they withdraw. The treasury official prepares food for the guest and the dual order officials who are participating in the rite. Next, the guest is escorted on rounds of the various quarters in due order.

In general, the position of director of the funeral rite must be assigned to a very distinguished, virtuous practitioner. For instance, Yuanwu Keqin conducted funeral rites for Zen Master

1128a

Kaifu Daoning and helped Venerable Dawei Shangao inherit the Dharma transmission from Kaifu Daoning. Such is the paradigm.

5. Appointment of the Directors of the Funeral Rite

After the senior practitioner who has been designated director of the funeral rite completes his rounds through the various quarters, he is accompanied to the guest house by the dual order officials, the retired officials, and the disciples of the deceased master. There he is shown the record of the abbot's personal possessions, the written wills, and so on left by the deceased. Over tea, he discusses the practical matters of the funeral rite with the officials and requests them to take charge of the roles of the secretarial duty, the directors of various affairs, guest reception duty, patriarchal office duty, and the various assistant functions. He is in turn deemed to oversee the entire matter of the funeral proceedings (details given below), except for two ceremonies that he himself should conduct, namely, leading the three utterances of grief "ai" and conducting the supplementary session to be held before the deceased master.

The funeral garments (types listed below) must be distributed. If there is no silk or other kind of cloth available, respective amounts of money equivalent to the cost of each garment may be distributed under the circumstances. By consulting the primary seat official, the director of the funeral rite divides all the possessions of the deceased into three portions. The first portion is to be used for the purchase of the funeral garment for the director of the funeral rite, on sutra chanting, candles, and lighting; the second portion is for the temple's expenditure for preparing additional provisions above the regular food offerings; and the third portion is for practitioners' ritual services in chanting sutras, ceremonial acts, and the costs of various signboards. The director of the funeral rite must be impartial and fair-minded and must not seek personal gain. The accompanying practitioners and attendants cannot interfere in the proceedings once the director takes up his role as required.

Every day, sutra chanting, offerings of monetary gifts, and servings of tea and sweet hot water must take place. One representative of each group of the dual order officials and the retired officials is requested to be in charge of the treasury. In general, frivolous talk should be avoided. The practitioner assistant of the guardian bodhisattva keeps accounts. The director of the funeral rite publicly appoints either the guest master or the tea master to be in charge of his secretariat. For this matter he should consult with the director of practitioners' affairs. The guest reception official receives the incoming guests for the funeral services, while the director of the funeral rite assigns workers to various tasks by announcing their names and assignments on signboards.

6. Ceremonial Garments for the Funeral Rite

[1] Assistants and disciples of the deceased: hemp-cloth patched garment.

[2] Dual order officials: hemp-cloth patched garment.

[3] Director of the funeral rite and the eldest practitioner of those related in the Dharma lineage: raw silk-cloth patched garment.

[4] Retired officials, subfunctionary secretaries, practitioners from the same native province, relations in Dharma lineage, and representatives of various temples: raw silk waist sash.

[5] Lay patrons: raw silk waist sash.

[6] Abbot's office attendants: hemp-cloth hood and patched garment.

[7] All other attendants: hemp-cloth hood.

[8] Foremen of workers attached to the abbot's office: hemp-cloth hood and trousers.

[9] Foremen of the temple estate, undertakers, and workers: hemp-cloth hood.

7. Kinds of Buddhist Funeral Rites

[1] Laying the deceased's body in the portable shrine at the reception hall.

[2] Moving the place of the shrine at the Dharma hall. (Items 2–9 take place at the Dharma hall.)

[3] Closing the door of the shrine.

[4] Placing the portrait of the deceased in the Dharma hall.

[5] Uttering the word of grief "*ai.*"

[6] Serving tea and sweet hot water to the deceased.

[7] Conducting a supplementary Dharma session before the deceased spirit.

[8] Serving tea and sweet hot water to the deceased.

[9] Lifting the shrine.

[10] Placing the portrait of the deceased in the portable pavilion at the temple gate.

[11] Serving tea and sweet hot water to the deceased.

[12] Making fire for cremation.

[13] Collecting and enshrining the remains.

[14] Auctioning the possessions of the deceased.

[15] Lifting the remains.

[16] Depositing the remains.

[17] Enshrining the portrait and tablet in the patriarchal shrine hall.

[18] Depositing the remains or interring the entire body in the tower.

[19] Casting earth.

(If the deceased left many possessions, tea and sweet hot water should be served every day and the rites of "turning the shrine around backward toward the rear," "turning the remains around backward toward the rear," and so on should be performed.)

8. Moving the Shrine to the Dharma Hall

After the body has lain in the shrine for three days, it must be covered with a curtain. An area surrounded by curtains in the upper rear section of the Dharma hall should be set up, in which a meditation couch, a clothes rack, and a variety of objects that the deceased master used everyday are arranged so as to resemble his room as if he were still alive. The portrait and tablet with his name should be placed on the rostrum seat in the central part of the hall, 1128b and a platform surrounded by a raw silk screen is made into an altar for ritual offerings.

In the lower rear section of the hall, the shrine surrounded by hemp-cloth curtains should be set up, in front of which a table equipped with an incense burner and candle stands is placed. Incense should be kept burning constantly and the candles are kept lit at all times. There should also be flower vases holding artificial paper flowers [representing *śāla* tree flowers].

Rice gruel and rice are offered every day at breakfast and noon respectively, and mealtimes are accompanied by sutra chanting. Crimson lanterns, cymbals, and funeral flags are prepared, and the practice hall bell is rung to assemble the practitioners for the ritual conduct of "moving the shrine" from the reception hall to the Dharma hall. Once the portable shrine is carried to the Dharma hall and placed in the designated lefthand side of the hall, the rite of closing the door of the shrine should be performed.

9. Placing the Portrait, Uttering the Expression of Grief, and Serving Tea and Sweet Hot Water

After the funeral shrine has been moved to the Dharma hall and the door closed, the rite of placing the portrait is performed. When this is over, and if there is any written will, the practitioner assistant, the director of the funeral rite, and the primary seat official together present it to the practitioners, saying:

> This is the word of the Venerable Master, abbot of the temple, at the time of his departure, which the primary seat official is ready to present to you.

The director of the funeral rite himself gives the will to the primary seat official, who passes it through incense smoke over the burner and in turn hands it to the director of practitioners' affairs to read. The attendant of the director of the funeral rite is

144

obliged to attach the written will to the right-side curtain that hangs in the central rear section of the hall.

The director of the funeral rite says:

> The Venerable Master, abbot of this temple, has returned to the state of total quiescence. It is appropriate [for us] to utter the expression of grief together.

After completing the ritual act, he repeats *"ai"* three times together with the practitioners. The disciples of the deceased abbot, who have lined up under the curtain, weep. When the serving of tea and sweet hot water is completed, they line up in front of the portrait and perform prostrations before returning to their former places under the curtain. The director of the funeral rite burns incense and performs prostrations toward the portrait. The dual order officials, the retired officials, and the practitioners then burn incense in turn and perform prostrations one after another, while the disciples of the deceased master also perform prostrations at the left side of the portrait. The director of the funeral rite comes to the curtain and consoles the disciples of the deceased, and they express their thanks by performing three prostrations. Next, the director of the funeral rite offers condolences to the dual order officials and the practitioners, saying:

> Although unfortunately we have lost our abbot who suddenly passed away, we earnestly wish that everyone keep up their efforts with diligence.

The primary seat official replies:

> We still rely on the late master for our strength.

The dual order officials and the practitioners console the disciples of the deceased master, saying:

> Unfortunately the temple has lost the Venerable Master, abbot of the temple, who has returned to the transcendent. We wish, however, that you fulfill your task through restraining your grief.

The disciples must guard the shrine during the night.

The director of the funeral rite makes a list and order of assignments for the rite of offerings (format given below) and attaches it to the curtain in the left-hand side of the hall. In general, the funeral addresses are composed by the head secretarial official appointed by the director of the funeral rite. Two or three times each day rites of offering are conducted, and no one should hesitate to participate in them. It is most likely, however, that lay patrons and the representatives of various temples may arrive at various times, and so the order of the proceedings must be expedient. In cases when the deceased abbot's relations in Dharma lineage or his former students approach the gate, the guest reception official meets them, reports their arrival to the director of the proceedings, and only after funeral garments are delivered to them do they conduct the rite of offering.

Whatever monetary donations are left after purchasing all the offerings must be returned to the temple public fund so as to finance the hosting of all the accompanying members of the various temples' representatives. The director of the funeral rite, the dual order officials, and the retired officials meet to discuss the matter of the deceased master's possessions, and except for those that must be handled in accordance with the written will, the monetary value of each remaining item must be estimated according to its qualities of new or old, short or long, and so on. This is intended to avoid disputes at the time of auctioning.

10. Conducting the Supplementary Session, the Serving of Tea and Sweet Hot Water, Prayer Chanting, and the Funeral Offering

On the evening before cremation, the director of the proceedings, carrying incense in his sleeve, along with the director of practitioners' affairs and the disciples of the deceased abbot, visits the guest house to request the person designated as the director of the funeral rite to conduct the supplementary session in honor of the deceased. The high seat in the Dharma hall should be set up before-hand and immediately after the first toll of the evening bell, drum-ming commences to signal the beginning of the session, calling the practitioners to assemble and the dual order officials to bow before the high seat. (This is identical to the procedure of an ordinary session.) The director of the funeral rite, accompanied by his prac-titioner assistant, ascends the seat and burns incense. If no prac-titioner assistant accompanies him, the practitioner assistant of the guardian bodhisattva of the practice hall performs the role of assisting in the rite.

After the session, the director of the funeral rite descends from the high seat and receives thanks from the disciples of the deceased master, who line up before him to perform prostrations.

The primary seat official, leading the practitioners, burns incense in front of the funeral shrine, and, remaining there, con-ducts the ritual offering of tea and sweet hot water. When this is   1128c over, the director of practitioners' affairs of the temple calls for prayer chanting, stating as follows:

> I address the practitioners. The Venerable Master, abbot of
> this temple, has entered nirvana. This day has already passed
> by, and so has our lifespan been diminished, just as a fish liv-
> ing in a shrinking pond. What kind of happiness is there in
> this state of affairs? All of us must exert ourselves as if to
> extinguish a fire burning on our heads. May you be reminded
> of the truth of impermanence and refrain from falling into
> unrestrainedness. By assembling the practitioners, we have
> solemnly paid our respects to the shrine at the side of its cur-
> tain and are about to intone the names of the Tathāgatas
> endowed with myriad virtues for the sake of the deceased
> master to promote his rank of honor and reverence. Now I
> respectfully call the practitioners to intone the ten sacred
> names of the Buddhas. Veneration to the Luminous Pure
> Dharma Body Vairocana Buddha, and so on.

Next, the director of practitioners' affairs calls for chanting the *Mahākāruṇikacitta-dhāraṇī*s, and gives the invocation of merit transference:

> The merit accrued by this chanting is intended solely for the sake of the late Venerable Master, abbot of this temple, who has just passed away. We earnestly wish that due to his retention of the power of vow, he will manifest an apearance as rare as the *uḍumbara* flower once again, guide the wheel [of the ship] of compassion to sail through the waves of life and death, and help the strayed multitudes reach the far shore of enlightenment. I once again request the practitioners to offer prayer. Veneration to the Buddhas of the ten directions and the three times, and so on.

When this is over, the guest reception official of the temple calls for the chanting of the *Śūraṃgama-dhāraṇī*s, and concludes with the following invocation of merit transference:

> The merit hereby accrued is intended on this evening before the day of cremation to promote the status of honor and reverence for the sake of the Venerable Master, abbot of this temple, who has just passed away. Veneration to the Buddhas of the ten directions and the three times, and so on.

Thereupon, offerings are made one after another, in due order. At the end the *Mahākāruṇikacitta-dhāraṇī*s are chanted and the rite concludes with the same invocation of merit transference as before.

Attendants and workers pay respects to the shrine, and when the chanting is over, the attendant of the director of the proceedings announces:

> The primary seat official invites the practitioners to a serving of sweet hot water and fruit at their designated seats.

Thereupon, the practitioners leave the Dharma hall, while the disciples of the deceased master as well as the attendants and workers of the abbot's office are obliged to attend the spirit of the deceased [abbot] through the night.

11. Order of the Funeral Rites of Offerings

[1] Administrative officials.

[2] Training faculty officials.

[3] Director of the funeral rite (*zhusang*, literally, "chief mourner").

[4] West hall official.

[5] Retired officials.

[6] Retired subfunctionary officials.

[7] Representatives of various Zen temples.

[8] Retired administrative subfunctionaries.

[9] Renowned senior practitioners.

[10] Head of practitioners' quarters.

[11] Secretarial functionaries.

[12] Former practitioner assistants of the deceased master.

[13] Practitioners from the same native province.

[14] Practitioners related in the Dharma lineage.

[15] Practitioners in charge of various hermitages and towers.

[16] Disciples of the deceased master.

[17] Grand-disciples.

[18] Attendants of the abbot's office.

[19] Attendants of the six major offices.

[20] Head of the attendants' hall.

[21] Workers of the abbot's office.

[22] Bearers of the master's sedan chair.

[23] Foremen of the workers.

[24] Foremen of the estate workers.

[25] Workers in charge of lights and fire.

[26] Building maintenance workers.

[27] Construction workers, [carpenters, and so on].

12. Funeral Procession for the Cremation and Placing the Portrait at the Temple Gate

Serving Tea and Sweet Hot Water

The head administrative official and the director of the funeral rite together manage the performance of funeral rites, and see to the preparation of a portable portrait pavilion decorated with flowers, funeral flags and banners, musical instruments, umbrellas, chairs to be set before the shrine, sweet hot water, incense burners, crimson lanterns, bamboo spatulas, canes, Zen dusting brushes, incense cases, robes and garments, and so on. The disciples of the deceased master follow behind the shrine to escort the procession, which is announced by tolling the large bell and all other instrumental sounds. The prayer for lifting the shrine is:

> The golden casket of the Buddha rose by itself and went through the town of Kuśinagara. While flags and banners waved in the sky, it proceeded to the glorious rite of cremation. I request the practitioners to intone the [ten sacred] names of the Buddhas so as to clarify the distance to be climbed and to assist in the path of enlightenment. Veneration to the Luminous Pure Dharma Body Vairocana Buddha, and so on.

(In case the body is to be interred in the tower instead of being cremated, the statement must be changed from "proceeded to the glorious rite of cremation" to "proceeded to the glorious rite of interment.")

The special director of the funeral rite in charge of practitioners' affairs, who undertakes the proceeding, steps forward to burn incense, and, escorting the disciples of the deceased master, conducts the rite of lifting the funeral shrine.

When the shrine reaches the temple gate, the rite of placing the portrait in a portable pavilion and serving tea and sweet hot water should be conducted. Both require the chanting of sutras. The dual order officials and the practitioners line up at the gate to await the shrine. The director of practitioners' affairs of the temple stands under the gate, facing toward the temple buildings with palms together, and intones the sacred verses devoted to Amitābha Buddha or the four sacred names of the Buddhas and bodhisattvas; the practitioners also intone them in unison.

The director of the funeral rite, leading the practitioners in two columns, proceeds on foot, scattering pieces of artificial paper flowers (called "snow-willow leaves") to the right and left along the way. No one is allowed to touch another's shoulders or exchange words; all should feel a sense of sadness. The head administrative official and the director of practitioners' affairs specially appointed for the funeral proceeding walk at the end of the line, and the guest reception official and the assistant of the guardian bodhisattva pass out monetary gifts along the way.

13. Cremation

When the procession reaches the cremation pyre, the director of practitioners' affairs specially appointed for the funeral rite waits for the moment when the head administrative official finishes offering incense and tea, then steps forward to burn incense and, leading the disciples of the deceased master, conducts the rite of touching flame to the pyre. The director of practitioners' affairs of 1129a the temple calls for prayer:

> On this day, the Venerable Master, abbot of this temple, terminating all conditions for conversion, swiftly returned to true eternity. [The casket of the Buddha went through the town of Kuśinagara, and] it is said that fire flamed up spontaneously to cremate his body. I request the practitioners to intone prayer for the sake of assisting the path of enlightenment. Homage to the Pure Land of the Western World, Amitābha Buddha of great compassion and commiseration, and so on up to the ten names of prayer.

When all participants have chanted the prayer in unison, the director of practitioners' affairs continues:

We have respectfully intoned the sacred names to help the rite of conversion.

The essential nature (of the deceased) is equal to that of his predecessors; his excellent capacity does not falter even before the Buddhas and patriarchs; he helped the junior practitioners, and his compassionate mind permeates the world of humans and heavenly beings. With his body comprising hundreds of illusory and phenomenal elements, he is now entering the state of fiery concentration (*tejodhātu samādhi*). Having offered three servings of tea and having burned incense over a single burner, we shall receive this deed and carry out the task earnestly. Salutation to the holy community of disciples (sangha).

Next, the director of practitioners' affairs calls for the chanting of the *Mahākāruṇikacitta-dhāraṇi*s, and states the following invocation of merit transference:

The merit accrued from intoning prayer and chanting is intended to promote the status of honor and reverence for the sake of the late Venerable Master, abbot of this temple, on the occasion of cremation. Veneration to the Buddhas of the ten directions and the three times, and so on.

The guest reception official then calls for the chanting of the *Śūraṃgama-dhāraṇi*s, and concludes with the same invocation of merit transference as before. Next, the practitioners from the same native province [as the deceased abbot] chant sutras in unison with all the practitioners. When this is over, the primary seat official leads the practitioners back to the temple and the noon meal is served. In the meantime, the deceased master's disciples, practitioners from the same native province, and relations in the Dharma lineage remain behind to wait for the fire to be extinguished and to collect the remains.

When the noon meal is over, the practice hall bell is rung to assemble the practitioners. They proceed to receive the remains, with a few workmen carrying the funeral banners at the front of the procession, and return to the reception hall to conduct the rite of enshrining the remains and placing the portrait. Sutras should be chanted and funeral offerings presented before the portrait. Twice a day, morning and noon, rice gruel and rice, respectively, should be served, and three times a day tea and sweet hot water should be served. This may be continued for ten days or half a month, with the practitioners in attendance chanting sutras. These practices cease once the remains are deposited in the tower.

14. Interment of the Body in the Tower

When the funeral shrine reaches the tower, the head administrative official offers incense and flowers, and then the director of practitioners' affairs specially appointed for the funeral rite steps forward to burn incense and, leading the disciples of the deceased master, conducts the rite of burial of the body. When this is over, the director of practitioners' affairs calls for prayer, saying:

> I urgently remind you of the occasion [when Śākyamuni Buddha miraculously revealed to Mahākāśyapa (second in the Dharma succession) the sacred mark of the Dharma wheel on the soles of both his feet,] and also of the Zen tradition of the single sandal left behind by the First Patriarch [in China] (Bodhidharma), which revealed the essence of Zen. Whether it is hidden or manifest, the intuitive faculty in its entirety supports the beginning and the ending of each *dharma*. I request the practitioners to intone the ten sacred names of prayer for the sake of assisting the path of enlightenment. Veneration to the Pure Land of the Western World, Amitābha Buddha of great compassion and commiseration, and so on.

(After this is completed, he continues.)

> By intoning the ten sacred names, we have intended to assist [the deceased] in entering the Pure Land of Amitābha Buddha. We wish that the limitless insight and compassion

of the wide-spreading cloud reveal the truth that in the world of the four modes of birth, there is neither birth nor death (i.e., from the transcendental point of view), and also preach the doctrine that within the six migratory passages of rebirth there is no recipient such as "self" nor is there any agent such as "person" who undergoes rebirth. Having made three servings of tea and burned incense over a single burner, we shall receive this deed and carry out the task earnestly. Salutation to the holy community of disciples.

The procedures of calling for sutra chanting and recitation of the sacred names are identical with that of the rite of cremation, but in the invocation of merit transference, the phrase "at the occasion of cremation" must be changed to "at the occasion of interment." When the grave is covered, and all are waiting for everything to be readied, the rite of "casting earth" should be performed.

After placing the portrait in the reception hall and making offerings before it, the director of the funeral rite burns incense and performs prostrations before the portrait. Next, the representatives of the neighboring temples, the dual order officials, the practitioners, and the disciples of the deceased master all perform prostrations before the portrait. Thereupon, the disciples burn incense and express their thanks to the director of the funeral rite by performing three prostrations with fully opened sitting cloth. Next, the dual order officials and the practitioners also thank the director of the funeral rite, saying:

> The temple has had an unfortunate loss with the abbot's passing away. We are indebted to you for overseeing the funeral rite.

The director of the funeral rite replies:

> Thanks to your cooperation, I was able to avoid negligence and failure [in my duties].

Along with the director of funeral proceedings and others, the director of practitioners' affairs specially appointed for the funeral rite makes rounds of the various quarters to express his thanks. Next, the disciples of the deceased master also make rounds through the quarters to express their gratitude, while the director of practitioners' affairs escorts the practitioner assistants of the late master and of the practice hall shrine back to the practitioners' quarters. Tea and sweet hot water should be served three times a day, accompanied by sutra chanting by the practitioners on each occasion. This is continued until the portrait and the name tablet are enshrined in the patriarchal shrine hall. Enshrining the deceased master in that hall may be accomplished when the new abbot is inaugurated, with due ritual conduct, of course.

15. Auctioning the Possessions of the Deceased

On an appointed day, a long table equipped with brushes, inkslabs, and a bell should be set up either in the outer practice hall or in the upper and lower front sections of the Dharma hall. The practice hall bell is tolled to assemble the practitioners. The primary seat official and the director of the funeral rite take their seats symmetrically to the rear left and right sides, while the dual order officials and the practitioners sit according to the form for regular occasions. The director of practitioners' affairs specially appointed for the funeral rite, the guest reception official, and the assistant in charge of the altar of the guardian bodhisattva sit directly opposite the director of the funeral rite. The director of practitioners' affairs [of the temple] calls for prayer, saying: 1129b

> Leaving the robe behind to express one's faith in Dharma transmission is the normative rule of every patriarch. Breaking human greed through the insight of the Dharma is the traditional practice handed down by our predecessors. Placing human possessions into auction now is intended to express the truth of impermanence. I request the practitioners to intone the [ten sacred] names of the Tathāgatas. Veneration to the Luminous Pure Dharma Body Vairocana Buddha, and so on.

After [the assembly] has intoned the names of the Buddhas, [the director of practitioners' affairs] opens the package containing the deceased master's possessions and sets them out according to the order of numbering on the table to conduct the rite of presenting items for auction. After all items are displayed, he rings the bell once and states:

> The method of auction is based on the existing practice, and everyone is required to examine the qualities of each item for himself as to whether it is new or old, short or long, so that he should not regret when no contesting voice comes forth. Respectfully stated.

If there are many possessions to be handled, all items except those designated in the written will are auctioned in the order of their display by the director of practitioners' affairs. The director of funeral proceedings and his helpers who manage the rite of auction must carry out their task impartially. The director of practitioners' affairs calls out the price of an item and rings the bell, while the attendants look around to confirm the name of the person who has responded to the call. The guest reception official copies the name on the bulletin board and the assistant in charge of the guardian bodhisattva prepares a card with that person's name on it. After the auction is completed, the number of items and amounts of money recorded on paper must be accounted for jointly and recorded on the bulletin board by the director of the funeral rite. Mixing up the papers that record prices and arbitrarily reducing the set price of each item is not allowed. It is the responsibility of the director of the funeral rite to supervise the entire process and maintain the principle [of impartiality] underlying the rite.

Nowadays, however, the lottery is the method used in most cases, as it can greatly reduce the possibility of dispute. This method consists of using small pieces of paper on which one thousand characters are inscribed serially, representing a serial order of numbers. Each numbered paper is copied in triplicate or has three divisions marked by an official stamp. According to the number of practitioners who may possibly participate in the event, the director of the proceedings and his assistant jointly seal these lottery tickets in an envelope. At the appointed time, the dircector of the funeral rite delivers the envelope to the dual order officials to check the seal, and then it is opened by the primary seat official. The guest reception official distributes the tickets, each consisting of one-third portion, to the participating practitioners. The attendant of the practice hall official follows after the practitioner assistant, carrying a tray. The practitioner assistant cuts the remaining tickets into halves and places one half on the tray. The tray is placed next to the primary seat official along with another tray filled with water.

The director of practitioners' affairs presents an item and reads out its price. At that moment the primary seat official asks a young novice to pick up one half-piece of a lottery ticket from the tray and give it to him. The latter opens it, examines the number, and passes it to the attendant of the practice hall to announce. The practitioners now open their half-pieces for identification. The person who holds the matching number responds at once. If he does not want the item, he should not respond, and if there is no response after three calls, the primary seat official places that particular ticket into the tray of water. Next, the young novice is asked to pick another half-ticket from the tray, and the number of the item is called in the same manner. If someone responds, the attendant of the practice hall collects the corresponding ticket from that person. The primary seat official examines the two pieces to confirm that they match, then reports this to the director of practitioners' affairs and gives him the two half-tickets. Thereupon, the director of practioners' affairs declares that the item in question will go to the practitioner who held the matching ticket. The bell is rung once, and the guest reception official records the name of the person and the item on the bulletin board. The practitioner assistant then issues a card to the alms-serving master who delivers it to the practitioner.

As soon as their sale has been determined, items such as robes and so forth should be put back into the basket one by one, until the last item has been auctioned. Thereupon the director of practitioners' affairs rings the bell once and recites the following invocation of merit transference:

> The foregoing activity of auction and prayer is intended to promote the rank of honor and reverence for the late Venerable Master, abbot of the temple, who passed away. Veneration to the Buddhas of the ten directions and the three periods, and so on.

When the practitioners leave the hall, those who have acquired an item in the auction turn in the card they have received, pay the amount of money specified on the bulletin board, and receive the item. If any items are not picked up after three days, they are again put on auction with adjusted prices. The accounts of all transactions must be recorded in a document. The ancient method of auction is also detailed in [Chapter VII,] "The Practitioners of the Zen Community," [part X, section 7].

Format of the Account Book

> Since the abbot passed away, his possessions were respectfully put up for auction, and they have yielded the amount of money recorded below. The balance of revenue and expenditure is given at the end.

1129c

Revenue amount	Auction held of such-and-such items
Revenue amount	Payment collected for such-and-such items
Expenditure amount	Already paid for such-and-such items
Expenditure amount	To be paid for such-and-such items (itemized in detail)
Total revenue amount	

Total expenditure amount

Balance   Such-and-such amount used for the initial seventh-
           day memorial service and for the cost of sutras pur-
           chased for practitioners and attendants

Date and year
Recorded by So-and-so,
Attendant of the Director of the Funeral Rite

Presented to

The person in charge of the account books,
the dual order officials, and the officials
of the funeral rite (to be audited and signed)

16. Depositing the Remains in the Tower

The evening before the appointed day, funeral banners should be
prepared for the men who will carry them at the forefront of the
procession. On the appointed day, the bell is rung to assemble the
practitioners. The head administrative official offers incense and
then conducts the rite of raising the remains. On reaching the
memorial tower, the rite of depositing the remains into the tower
should be carried out. The call for sutra chanting, the recitation
of the sacred names of the Buddhas, and the concluding invocation are all identical to the rite of interring the body. After returning to the reception hall, offerings should be made before the portrait and the proceedings for thanking the director of the funeral
rite and so on are as before.

17. Sending Written Wills

When all the funeral affairs are completed, the director of the
funeral rite requests the practitioner assistants [of the secretariat]
to deliver the written wills as special official delegates to the various temples, the deceased abbot's relations in Dharma lineage,
lay patrons, and government officials. It is desirable to choose only

very capable persons for this purpose since the official delegates are obliged to engage in conversation when they meet with the high-ranking officials of various temples.

When the official delegate reaches the designated temple, he first meets with the guest reception official, who then escorts him to the office of the abbot's assistant. A crepe-wrapped table has been set up beforehand, and the written will is placed there. The assistant announces to the abbot the arrival of the official delegate, and the abbot then meets the delegate and requests the dual order officials to join him for opening the delivered letter. The official delegate steps forward, bows, and says: "May your reverence sit cross-legged."

If the abbot gives some word, the official delegate must immediately reply and, after burning incense, perform a prostration with opened sitting cloth. If this formality is excused, the official delegate may perform prostrations with unopened sitting cloth in the usual manner.

After burning incense, drinking tea, and waiting for the arrival of the dual order officials, the official delegate stands and expresses his thanks for the tea, offers a piece of large-grain incense before the burner, and performs a prostration with opened sitting cloth, saying:

> Venerable So-and-so of such-and-such locality passed away on such-and such day and month. I have been entrusted with delivering his written will as well as his gift to your reverence.

Thereupon, the official delegate presents the letter and the item. The abbot replies:

> Our tradition has lost an important person, and I cannot help but feel sorrow.

As the dual order officials step forward to bow, the primary seat official moves to the side of the abbot, some distance apart. The official delegate sits across from the abbot and one rank space away from the dual order officials. When tea is over, the official delegate straightens his posture, and the abbot addresses him:

> It is unfortunate for the tradition that Venerable So-and-so passed away. I cannot help but feel sorrow.

The attendant prepares a paper-cutting knife, the letter, and the item, which the assistant hands to the master, who passes them [through the smoke from] the incense burner and returns them to the assistant. He, in turn, passes them to the director of practitioners' affairs. Receiving the paper-cutting knife from the attendant, the director of practitioners' affairs opens the envelope and reads the letter, whereupon the assistant invites the official delegate to sit directly in front of the abbot.

1130a

(The west hall ranking official withdraws a little behind the seat in order to show his respect to the official delegate.)

The abbot's assistant, after burning incense, serves sweet hot water and then escorts the official delegate to the guest house. The abbot visits the latter to bow, followed by his assistant and the dual order officials. Then the guest reception official escorts the official delegate on rounds through the various quarters, beginning with the four quarters such as the administrative office quarters, the training faculty quarters, the retired officials' individual quarters, and the retired administrative officials' hall. Thereupon, the abbot's assistant notifies the official delegate that he is invited to a special serving of sweet hot water. The evening meal follows the serving of sweet hot water, and later that night a serving of sweet hot water and cake is given.

If the written letter is delivered from any of the large monastic establishments, the dual order officials participate in the reception; if it is delivered from any lesser temple, only an official representative, the director of practitioners' affairs, and the abbot's assistant participate. The head secretarial official is requested to compose a notice of the funeral rite on behalf of the temple but the notice of the funeral rite from the abbot's office may be composed by the abbot himself. The monks of the Zen world, [the deceased abbot's] relations in Dharma lineage, and the serving practitioners are all obliged to carry incense in their sleeves and conduct the rites of offering. The abbot's assistant must attend to their conduct at each occasion.

Next morning, the abbot serves tea in honor of the deceased. A table holding the deceased's name tablet, with various offerings displayed before it, should be set up in the left rear part of the Dharma hall. The practitioner assistant announces the event of an ascent to the Dharma hall, while the attendants inform the practitioners and post the signboard at the practice hall to announce the event. A crepe-wrapped table, on which the letter and material items are placed, should be set before the high seat and the abbot's seat to the left of the high seat. The drum signals the practitioners to assemble in the hall. The abbot enters the hall, proceeds to the high seat, and stands before it. When the drumming ends, he steps forward to the incense table, while the official delegate escorted by the guest reception official go before him, across the table. [The official delegate] performs the formal propriety of two prostrations with opened sitting cloth and three prostrations with unopened sitting cloth. Burning incense and opening his sitting cloth for the first time, he says:

> I have rushed to deliver the will to your reverence, and cannot help feeling apprehensive of my manner in meeting with your reverence.

Opening his sitting cloth the second time, he says:

> On this day and at this time, I respectfully wish that all is well and felicitous with the master abbot of this temple.

He then completes his greeting with three prostrations with unopened sitting cloth and hands the letter to the abbot. Thereupon the abbot censes the letter and gives it to his assistant who, in turn, hands it to the director of practitioners' affairs to read.

The official delegate bows toward him and withdraws behind the guest reception official of the east order. The abbot then ascends to the rostrum seat and preaches.

After descending from the high seat, the abbot goes before the funeral name-tablet set on the desk, burns incense, serves sweet hot water, makes offerings, serves tea, and performs prostrations with opened sitting cloth. The official delegate returns to the right side of the high seat and bows toward him. The director of practitioners' affairs steps forward from the east order, bows to the abbot, and burns incense while his assistant presents to him an incense case. When the dual order officials complete the incense offering, the abbot and all the officials in unison perform prostrations with opened sitting cloth. Thereupon the director of practitioners' affairs reads the notice of the funeral rite. The abbot again performs prostrations with opened sitting cloth, and the official delegate returns his prostrations. The director of practitioners' affairs calls for the chanting of the *Śūraṃgama-dhāraṇī*s and concludes with the following invocation of merit transference:

> With the merit hereby accrued we intended to promote the rank of honor and reverence for the sake of Venerable So-and-so of Such-and-such temple. Veneration to the Buddhas of the ten directions and the three times, and so on.

The dual order officials, the residents of the four quarters, the practitioners from all regions, those of various temple functionaries, and those who come from the same native province all make funeral offerings, to which the official delegate returns prostrations respectively. He should not, however, return prostrations to lower-ranking practitioners related in the Dharma lineage, the deceased's disciples, or serving subfunctionaries.

When the funeral rite has been completed, the service of chanting the *Mahākāruṇikacitta-dhāraṇī*s and its concluding invocation of merit transference is conducted. Thereupon, the official delegate steps forward and performs two prostrations with opened sitting cloth and three prostrations with unopened sitting cloth to thank the abbot. If this formality is excused, he performs only the three prostrations with unopened sitting cloth. Next, the official delegate makes rounds through the various quarters to thank the practitioners. Afterward the temple prepares a special dinner reception for the official delegate, in which the dual order officials are invited to participate. If the deceased master had previously held the position of abbot at this temple, he may be enshrined in the patriarchal shrine hall on the same day. If so, after the chanting is completed, the name tablet is carried to the shrine hall and the current abbot offers incense and places it in the shrine with a due word of tribute. The official delegate then expresses a word of thanks to the master.

If the deceased was the incumbent abbot of the temple, his enshrinement in the patriarchal hall occurs after three days of services conducted before the remains at the reception hall, during which time the new abbot has arrived. The latter then conducts services for transfering the deceased abbot's name tablet to the patriarchal shrine hall. If there is no written will or material items left for the new abbot, the deceased abbot's disciples and relations in the Dharma lineage, who are obliged to make the request, first visit the temple to meet the abbot's assistant and then meet the abbot with the due formality of offering incense and

1130b performing prostrations with opened sitting cloth. After burning incense and drinking tea, the representing official sits properly upright and states the purpose of his visit. After that, he or the group is escorted to the guest house. Next he visits the primary seat official, the administrative official, the retirees' individual quarters, and the retired officials to consult and determine the date of enshrinement. He is obliged to arrange offerings and prepare monetary gifts. After the rite of offerings and the service of sutra chanting at the Dharma hall, where the abbot conducts the proceedings with the proper word of tribute, the remainder of the proceeding is identical to that described above.

18. Special Dinner Reception for the Director of the Funeral Rite, the Director of the Proceedings, and the Manager of Funeral Affairs

The temple is obliged to prepare meals and monetary gifts in accordance with differences in rank. Both the dual order officials and the retired officials are invited to participate in these occasions. The primary seat official takes the main seat at the abbot's office, the seat markers are set up to indicate the seating arrangement, and the head administrative official oversees the proceedings just as on any occasion of special reception. After tea, the practice hall bell is rung to assemble the practitioners, and the large bell is tolled to send off the master of the funeral rite at the temple gate.

VII. Appointing the New Abbot

The incumbent and retired dual order officials meet for tea at the office of the head administrative official to discuss the matter of selecting a prospective candidate for the position of abbot. They name every renowned virtuous person from all parts of the Zen world for the position; they must include the practitioners in the process of selecting finalists. It is customary to select a person who is well qualified by his authentic insight, virtue, seniority, integrity, and, most importantly, by his ability to fulfill the practitioners' trust and expectations. It is also the norm to consider the consensus opinion of the abbots of the various temples. After reviewing all these qualifications, the officials list their names for petition, place their signatures on the letter of petition, and, after notifying the government agency, send an invitation to the candidate.

If an excellent master assumes the rank of abbot of the temple, it is most beneficial for the temple community, not only because more attention is given to the Dharma and Way but also because the temple's prominence as a religious institution increases. Therefore, care must be taken to avoid corrupting influences from officials who sometimes organize as a cabal in order to retain their status by appointing someone who is from the same native province or is related in the Dharma lineage, rather that selecting a person of authentic insight and virtue. These people seek to monopolize the position of abbot through insidious methods of influence, bribery, and scheming. Such cases set a temple on the path of decline by further corrupting its system. It cannot be emphasized strongly enough that one must refrain from this kind of activity. To repeat, one must refrain from this kind of activity.

Zen Master Mingjiao said:

> What does the term *"zhuchi"* (literally, "resident bearer of the Dharma," or abbot) in the Buddhist teaching mean? *Zhuchi* means "the person through whom the Dharma is maintained and will not perish for a long time." The three divisions of practice, moral discipline (*śīla*), concentration (*samādhi*), and transcendental insight (*prajñā*), are the instruments for the maintenance of the Dharma. The monastic order and its institutional structures are the material basis for maintaining the Dharma. The Dharma means the path of the Great Sage (the Buddha). The material basis and the instrument become meaningful only when practitioners begin to put them to good use. It is inevitable that by improving the instrument one improves the material basis; and that by improving the material basis, one may improve the instrument. When both factors are improved and become good, one is obliged to maintain their excellence and abide in them.
>
> In ancient times, the resident bearer of the Dharma at Vulture Peak was Mahākāśyapa, while that of the Bamboo Forest was Śāriputra. Due to the greatness of these masters, the Dharma of the Sage continued to exist for a long time. Since the Sage entered nirvana so many generations have passed that we have long since become unable to trace them. By fortunate coincidence, we in the Zen tradition have the name of *zhuchi* and its authority and benefit. Throughout the

land, however, everything has become conventional, crowded, and confused. The institution of *zhuchi* appears little different from worldly convention. Unless the Sage were to reappear, who could rectify this state of affairs? Unless those of us in the position of guarding the institution are watchful and selective, it will be impossible to prevent the original spirit of the Sage and his Dharma from declining, no matter how earnestly we wish to maintain and uphold it. This would be most lamentable. What else can I wish for? 1130c

End of Chapter V: The Abbot,
Resident Bearer of the Dharma

End of Fascicle Three

Fascicle Four

Chapter VI

The Dual Order Offices

I. Preface to the Chapter

The dual order offices (*liangxuzhang*) were established [for the abbot] to manage various things for the sake of the member practitioners [of his monastic community], so that he may [freely] engage himself in teaching the essentials of the [Buddhist] religion, promulgating the path of practice, and embellishing the patriarchal tradition. Insofar as the handling of money and rice storage and experiencing various duties are concerned, no one fails to acquire good training through worldly matters as well as nonworldly religious matters. Thereafter, when he reaches an official position, takes the title of "master," teaches students, and deals with things, he is able to realize the transcendent truth, execute worldly operations, and become a so-called [perfected] person who fulfills himself and helps others fulfill themselves.

In the past, the east and the west order offices exchanged their positions and reciprocated their functions. Accordingly, neither officials felt pleasure or displeasure regarding the respective orders and ranks, whether superior or inferior. It is, therefore, wrong that today the officials are divided into the two orders. In extreme cases, the two groups compete against each other, allowing no compatibility if either one's influence tilts to the stronger or weaker side. Therefore, whoever oversees them as their head should assert the ancestral warning that cautions against falling into such discord, and should wish to prevent its occurrence. All that is needed is to be cautious and selective regarding one's appointees, encourage them to devote themselves to their respective tasks, and refrain from speaking divisive words.

II. The Training Faculty of the West Order

1. The Primary Seat Official of the Front Part of the Practice Hall

The primary seat official (*shouzuo*) is the model standard of the monastic institution, comparable to the visual organ of humans and gods. He [sometimes] takes the seat as proxy of the abbot to preach the Dharma in order to penetrate and open up the [doctrinal] understanding in the minds of junior practitioners, and leads the practitioners in the practice of zazen, respectfully committing himself to adhering to the monastic rules and regulations. He is obliged to advise the treasury as to whether or not each meal (i.e., rice gruel in the morning and rice at noon) is prepared well. When the community ceases to comply with normative propriety, he may have to show what punishment is mandated by the regulations. Compassionate toward the aged, the sick, and the dying, he should take care of them up to their funeral rites. As a whole, he must be ready to act practically in all matters that concern the practitioners, like a collar attached to all clothes or a controlling rope attached to an entire net.

Even a well-established senior practitioner or the abbot of a large monastery, if asked with proper honor and reverence, should accept and serve in the role of primary seat official. This is called "acting for the sake of others by forsaking one's own." Mañjuśrī Bodhisattva, though he was the teacher of the seven past Buddhas, agreed to become the primary seat official for an assembly of disciples and helped Śākyamuni Buddha accomplish the path by leading his disciples to religious conversion. In the Zen tradition we have such examples: Zen Master Muzhou became the primary seat official under Huangbi, and Yunmen under Lingshu, whereby they made the foremost position luminous and clear and thus left lessons for those of later periods. As the name and position are of primary importance, one should not act casually in appointing a person to [this post], should one?

1131a

It is said in the *Collection of Records of the Patriarchal Courtyard (Zutingshiyuan)*:

> The *shouzuo* is the "foremost elder" in the ancient tradition. It is *"sthavira"* in Sanskrit, meaning exactly "the foremost seat holder" here. 1) He must be advanced in ordination age, 2) he must be of noble nature in all conduct of his life, and 3) he must be one who has been fully compliant with the rules and precepts he initially received and has realized the saintly state of transcendence (arhatship) resulting from the practice of the path.

In the Zen tradition today, the person elected as the primary seat official should necessarily be one who has already achieved the Buddhist insight regarding the nature of self, and is able to command his fellow practitioners' respect and obedience in terms of his excellence in both moral virtue and religious training.

2. The Primary Seat Official of the Rear Part of the Practice Hall

Holding a seat on the rear raised platform, the primary seat official of the back part of the hall assists the primary seat official of the front part of the hall in upholding community morale for the pursuit of the goal. His manner of conduct ornaments the rules and regulations as the model for the practitioners. Perhaps this division of the front and rear officials of the practice hall may have resulted from the increase in the number of monastic residents.

Twice a day, at the time of the morning rice gruel and the rice meal at noon, and also at the time of zazen practice, he must enter and depart from the hall through the rear exit. If the position of the primary seat official [of the front part of the hall] is vacated, the abbot must inform the practitioners of this. Ascending the rostrum seat in the Dharma hall on a special day, he invites the official of the rear part of the hall to move to the front part of the hall. The primary seat official should use this proceeding to settle in the designated space at the front part of the hall, and intone a verse of invocation at every meal to symbolize the merit of almsgiving. For zazen practice and for the period of zazen preceding the evening session, he must enter the hall at the time of the third strike of the wooden sounding block located at the practitioners' quarters. It is not necessary to strike the wooden sounding block located at his quarters on each occasion. The rest is identical with the duties of the front hall primary seat official.

3. The Head Secretarial Official

In the *Ancient Regulations* this office was called *"shuzhuang,"* and its function was to be in charge of all literary composition, including nearly all the signboard announcements to be posted at the temple gate, letters of correspondence, and verses of prayers and invocations. In olden days, many renowned practitioners were invited to the imperial court for an audience. Whoever became the abbot of a renowned large temple would have likely been so appointed under the edict of the imperial court, and he had to carry with him a written form of thanks [in response to such an appointment]. Before the time of death, the written form of a will must be prepared. Upon receipt of imperial gifts or enquiries, doctrinal or otherwise, a written form of reply must be composed to express the temple's gratitude or to answer the questions. Yet the abbot must be fully in charge of the great Dharma and cannot divert his attention to literary composition. Originally this particular position was adopted from military headquarters, where generals had a secretarial office in charge of recording the names of soldiers, their duties, and so on. In Zen temples, the secretarial office was especially institutionalized to deal with similar tasks. Besides this secretarial office, there is a position called *"shuzhuang"* in each temple, to which a practitioner is appointed as one of the abbot's assistants in handling more private letters of his correspondence. This is called the private secretarial function (*neiji*) of the abbot's office.

A renowned case of secretarial office activity was exemplified by Huinan (1002–1069) of Mount Huanglong. Again, another known example was Qingyuan (i.e., Zen Master Foyan [1067–1120]), who was appointed to this position under Zen Master Fayan of Mount Dongshan (i.e., Mount Wuzishan). The latter wished to glorify the title of the secretarial position by having Qingyuan, who was well versed in non-Buddhist literature, assist him in disseminating Zen in the religious world. Moreover, Dahui Zonggao (1089–1163) also previously held a similar position. In general, it is satisfactory if the holder of this position tries to follow these three major figures as models of conduct.

4. The Tripiṭaka Hall Official

This official should handle the library of sacred scriptures (i.e., the Tripiṭaka sutra building) and must also be an expert in the scholarship of scriptural interpretation. According to the *Ancient Regulations,* when someone wishes to read a scripture and enters the library hall, he first notifies the hall master, [who is in charge of recording] his intent, and goes with him to the Tripiṭaka office. The Tripiṭaka hall official then escorts him to a desk and seat and greets him with an informal prostration with unopened sitting cloth. Today, however, practitioners read scriptures at the practitioners' quarters, hence no table or chair is set up in the scriptural hall. Nevertheless, when an official is appointed to this office he is obliged to do his best in checking the cases that hold the texts and their catalogues, supplying whatever texts are lost or missing, drying and wiping any item that is moist and wet, and patching and rebinding any item that has a torn and broken binding. If practitioners come to read the scriptures, the Tripiṭaka hall master sets out the catalogue book, looks for the scripture cases corresponding to those titles assigned by the practice hall office, and hands them to the practitioners. When the texts are returned, they must be referred to the record book again to be replaced in the proper stack in order to prevent texts from being misplaced or lost.

Reflecting upon the origins of our Zen tradition, its essence was long since declared as having been transmitted outside verbal or written teachings. So why are some practitioners assigned to be in charge of the scriptural library? The answer is that whatever the Buddha said to his disciples and whatever he prescribed for their conduct became the teachings (sāsana; jiao) and regulations (vinaya; lü). Is any reason whatsoever for us, the members of the Zen community, not to follow his teaching and regulations? Especially because our tradition claims that the ultimate experience, the supreme insight, cannot be trapped by the constraints of language but transcends forms of speech and action. Since such is the mystery of ultimate self-nature handed down [from the Buddha himself], isn't it quite proper for us to comply with the insight he verbally taught and the conduct he prescribed? Again, this has been the patriarchal intention, wishing for us to seek the ultimate insight (theoretical and ethical) in all Buddhist text collections as well as in all non-Buddhist literature and expecting us to be able to face heretic insults and respond to them with greater expediency. This is called the "principle of neither adherence nor rejection" (buji buli). In later periods, as the number of practitioners greatly increased, two Tripiṭaka buildings were required to be built [to serve] as the eastern and western libraries.

5. The Guest Reception Official

This official deals with the reception of high-ranking guests. In general, he initially meets with government officials, patron donors, established senior practitioners, and renowned virtuous personalities who happen to visit the temple, receiving them with the propriety of incense and a serving of tea. He then sends his novice attendant to inform the abbot about such visitors. He escorts each visitor to see the abbot, and when the meeting is over he determines the subsequent schedule for the visitor and escorts him to wherever he is to stay. If a visitor is of lower-ranking status than his own, he meets the visitor at his office, and if the latter wishes to see the abbot or the administrative head as well as various other quarters, he sends an attendant to accompany him to the respective destination.

The transient guest quarters (*danguoliao*), which come under [the jurisdiction of] this office, must be kept neat as to the bed curtains, furnishings, lamp oil, and charcoal for burning. New arrivals (*xindao*) must be treated well so that their stay is comfortable. If the director of practitioners' affairs is temporarily absent, the guest reception official executes some of his duties, checking to see if the morning rice gruel and the noon rice meal are properly set for them in the outer practice hall and ensuring that they are served [without fail]. If he encounters the situation of a death among the guest practitioners, he must take charge of the funeral account with the help of his practitioner assistant. If one of the new arrivals dies, he assumes the role of the director of the funeral rite for the deceased. When Shüehbao stayed at Mount Dayang and when Chanyue stayed at Mount Shishuang, they held this position. It is therefore not to be slighted.

6. The Bath Hall Official

In general, on the day designated for bathing, a signboard should be posted before the noon meal to inform the practitioners. In winter months, bathing should be scheduled once every five days, while during the hot season it should be scheduled every day to wash away sweat. The official of this office oversees the tasks of preparing the bathing room, hanging towels on the racks, setting out trays for washing the face, providing wooden shoes to wear inside the tub and cloths to spread on the wooden floor. He assigns the novice attendant of the ceremonial leader (*cantouhangzhe*) to be in charge of the day. After the noon meal, the bath hall master (*yutou*) notifies the director of practitioners' affairs, the primary seat official, and the abbot of the bathing room's readiness and after striking the drum three times, he bathes the image of the guardian bodhisattva in the practice hall. He should be mindful of inviting the guardian bodhisattva to take a bath while preparing the special wooden bucket for bathing the image of the guardian bodhisattva, pouring a small quantity of bath water, and offering incense and prostrations.

After the wooden sounding blocks are struck three times in succession in various parts of the corridors throughout the temple, a series of drumrolls follows, indicating that the time for the practitioners to bathe has arrived. Next, a second series of drumrolls signals the time for the training faculty officials to bathe. The third series of drumrolls signals the time for the novice attendants to bathe. The abbot may take his bath at this time and, if he so wishes, a screen should be set up in the bathing room to separate the sections. The fourth series of drumrolls signals the time for the lay workers to bathe, and the very last members to bathe are the attendants who supervise the workers (*jianzuohangzhe*) and the administrative officials. As to the boiler, after the bathing has been completed the fire must be suppressed by sprinkling water carefully over the flames and coals, and the hearth cleaned and dried. Leftover embers should be stored at a safe distance.

The order of bathing must be specified on the signboard outside the bathroom.

(Nowadays, it is believed that the abbot is supposed to bathe after the members of the training faculty have all finished, and that the administrative officials are supposed to bathe after the novice attendants have all finished. This is wrong. If the abbot wishes for some reason to take his bath at the same time as the training faculty members, no separating screen is required between them. He does not go into a private room but disrobes at the front section of the dressing room.)

A small wooden sounding board should be hung inside the room, with instructions written on a tablet posted next to it, reading: "One strike: add hot water; two strikes: add cold water; three strikes: stop. This is the standard signal." 1131c

When a donor donates the cost of bathing for the practitioners, a service of sutra chanting should be performed, followed by an invocation of merit transference. If one realizes why the mysterious touch of water is as clear and transparent as it really is, and experiences this fact as having already been abiding in Buddha-nature, then it is not an insignificant donation to bear the cost of the practitioners' bathing, is it?

7. The Shrine Hall Official

The practitioner at this office is in charge of handling the incense burners and candle stands in the various shrine halls, and keeps everything neat and tidy by wiping dust from these items and the desks. When it becomes windy, he must extinguish the incense burners and candles, and tie up the bottom of the banners to prevent them from blowing near the flames of lamps and lights. Diverting money offered by donors for incense for other purposes of the temple is forbidden. On the commemorative day of the Buddha's birthday, he is obliged to prepare the sweet water to be used by the practitioners to bathe the statue of the infant Buddha, and on the four monthly days of religious observance (*siqiri*) he must also open the doors of the shrine halls so that general visitors may pay their respects.

8. The Abbot's Assistant Officials: The Incense Offering Assistant, the Secretarial Record Assistant, and the Guest Reception Assistant

The functions of these practitioner assistants are the closest and most intimate with the daily life of the abbot. Observing [numerous notable examples of] their master's practice of the path and virtue, listening to his teaching and instruction in the morning and evening, and thereby closely guarded from undesirable influence while encouraged by desirable influence, they may aspire to reach the great goal of the Dharma and path [as exemplified by the abbot]. Thus, they should become well disposed to maintain the decorum of respect and reverence [toward the master] at all times. The way Ānanda attended Gautama Buddha or Xianglin attended Yunmen is a matter of great importance for the path of the Buddhas and patriarchs. How can this be slighted?

In general, it is the duty of the assistant official in charge of incense offering to record the words of the abbot whenever he speaks on the occasions of his [official functions], such as the ascent to the rostrum seat at the Dharma hall, the supplementary session, general exhortation (*pushuo*), instruction by individual visitation (*kaishi*), prayer invocation (*niansong*), canceling the evening session (*fangcan*), special serving rites on the four annual festivity days (*juelatewei*), interviewing a guest upon request (*tongfuxiangli*), establishment of residency (*guada*), the rite of offering incense (*shaoxiangxingli*), the word of insight (*fayu*), and so on.

Next, it is the duty of the assistant official in charge of the secretarial record to compose the abbot's correspondence. He must first write a draft for the master's inspection and approval. If the secretarial record official is absent from the temple, this assistant official is in charge of composing the official letters of the temple.

Next, it is the duty of the guest reception assistant to prepare the abbot's invitations and carry out the rite of a special serving [of tea or sweet hot water], whenever the latter receives special guests or renowned senior practitioners, or at the four annual celebration days, such as the first day of the summer retreat, and so on.

When neither the director of practitioners' affairs nor the guest reception official is available [to address] the needs of the practitioners, or if [these officials] are temporarily absent from the temple, the abbot's three assistant officials are obliged to act as their proxies according to the foregoing prescribed conduct.

(Some say that the assistant in charge of the secretarial record and composition has nothing to do with any other areas of work. This [assertion] is wrong, without any basis whatsoever.)

When the abbot is away from the temple for some length of time, these assistant officials return to the general quarters of the resident practitioners and engage themselves in daily practice along with them. If [the abbot's] absence is brief [in duration, however], they do not leave their official positions.

9. The Personal Managerial Assistant

(This position is not part of the official order.)

Many of our predecessors appointed to this position a well-trained person experienced in monastic life. He must be able to command loyalty from others, rescue others from their mistakes, mobilize the capable and talented, and know how things are going within and without. Being expedient and all-embracing, he should be able to harmonize the higher and lower ranks into a good, working unity. There is an episode about Mian, who appointed Qingruo as his personal managing assistant and acquired Songyuan as his Dharma heir through this assistant. After Dongsou appointed the primary seat official Sheng as his managing assistant, his monastic discipline became ever more rigorous in practice. Nowadays, many abbots frequently appoint an inexperienced junior practitioner to this position, and such appointments often result in damaging the virtuous name of an abbot and in serious mismanagement. One must be cautious about this.

10. The Medicinal Care Assistant

(This position is in the official order.)

This practitioner assistant attends the abbot with the duty of prescribing medicine at all times. He assists him also in dealing with things around him and helps the managerial assistant. He should be compassionate in overseeing the novice attendants and workmen in daily matters. If a guest happens to visit in the absence of the other assistant, he is obliged to assume his role in notifying the abbot about the visitor and assisting him with the incense offering. Or if no one is available, he is obliged to refer matters in question to the proper officials, and in this way he should act on behalf of those who are not available, according to the given situation. A mature person, humble and courteous in nature, should be appointed to this position.

11. The Assistant in Charge of the Image of the Guardian Bodhisattva

(This official is not part of the official order, stays behind the practitioners in the practice of the path, and takes meals in the outer hall.)

It is desirable to appoint a person devoted to the path of practice [to this post]. He is obliged to prepare and offer meals twice a day, offering the sublime image morning rice gruel and rice at noon; to strike the octagonal wooden post with the mallet located at the back of the practice hall; to check the seats of the practitioners prior to zazen practice; and to reduce the lighting during the night. In addition, along with the director of practitioners' affairs, he handles the monetary transactions during the auction of items left by the deceased. When the abbot passes away, he keeps the account book of the funeral rite. When the primary seat official preaches as the abbot's proxy, he assists him with the incense offering. Or [on behalf of other officials], he may strike the octagonal wooden post with the mallet and intone the names of the Buddhas. Even after his term is complete he may retain the title of "assistant official" as long as he stays at the temple where he was originally appointed. When the two elder practitioners Tuigeng and Duanqiao were practitioners, they were once appointed to this position. They were able to cultivate good associations with their fellow practitioners and thereby encouraged them to progress in the practice of the path.

III. The Administrative Officials of the East Order

1. The Head Administrative Official

In the *Ancient Regulations,* only the office of administrative head (*jianyuan*) was instituted. Later on, however, due to the fact that the temples, in general, became larger and the number of resident practitioners increased, the present office of head administrative official (*dujiansi*) was added to oversee all aspects of the administration. [He is] in charge of replenishing the incense and lighting materials to be used in the morning and evening, receiving government officials and patron donors, keeping the record of accounts dealing with revenue and expenditure in cash or in kind (i.e., grain crops), and always working to maintain the annual fiscal balance. He respects the master, loves his fellow resident practitioners, and upon meeting with other officials serves for whatever business might be at hand and reports the results to the abbot for approval. He reprimands and instructs the novice attendants and workmen, rather than unreasonably punishing them by whip. Even when they deserve disciplinary action and punishment, he should instead consult with others about the matter, applying due consideration and mercy, and give warnings. Anyone in this position should avoid abusing his power, restrain acts of violence, and prevent the matter from receiving a criminal indictment from the government. He must be impartial when assigning people to the various positions of estate operation and storage, and also must refrain from organizing a group for his personal interest, which would cause vexation or spite among his superiors or subordinates.

In the past, when the monastic institution was at the height of its vitality, there were many instances in which a west hall official, a primary seat official, or a secretarial official was invited to take this position, and in turn, the administrative head was invited to take the primary seat office or the secretarial office. Otherwise, an appointee for this position must be qualified by having a high ordination age, must be well experienced in life and tradition, be clean and capable, public-minded and courteous, not to mention having the practitioners' respect and obedience. Even when someone is no longer required to continue in a public position, if that person's spiritual endowment is rich and distinguished, if he is harmonious with his superiors and subordinates, and even if it is his second consecutive term, he may not be removed from the position. Such a person may even be invited repeatedly to stay on, precisely because no one would feel harmed by his remaining in the position.

Accordingly, in earlier days there were no more than five or six retired officials in each temple who stayed in the private quarters or in the retirees' hall. The treasury official or any other official of the lower ranks did not withdraw to the retirees' hall until after his third term. Nor did the associate administrative official or the head administrative official withdraw to the retirees' hall or to the private quarters, respectively, until their third term was over.

In case of reappointing someone who has retired, it is better to avoid any kind of suspicion by placing him first in the public domain, namely, the practice hall, as a regular practitioner, unbound to any official position. Then one may reappoint him to his former office. If he does not fail to participate in the morning rice gruel and the noon meal in the practice hall, the morale of the novice attendants and lay workers, while serving food to him, will improve by itself or will become firm, just as Yangji assisted Ciming and Shichuang assisted Hongzhi. These examples should be the paradigm of the position in question.

It is said in the *Outline of the History of Zen Practitioners (Seng-shilüe,* by Zanning of the Song dynasty):

> The three qualifications of administrative officials are comparable to the huge ropes that are linked to fishing nets. By controlling these ropes, one can control all the nets so [that they can be] spread well. In Sanskrit it is called *vihāra-svāmin (momodi),* which means the director of a monastic residence, namely, the head administrative official in our case.

Again it is said in the *Great Collection of Sutras of the Mahā-samghika School (Mahāsamnipāta-sūtra; Dajijing)*:

> It is difficult to administer the things that belong to the
> sangha. I (the Buddha himself) should allow only two kinds   1132b
> of people to be in charge of the things that belong to the
> Three Treasures: 1) arhat (*aluohan;* saint) [one who has real-
> ized the final state of transcendence], 2) *srota-āpanna (xutuo-
> xuan;* stream-enterer), one who has reached the initial state
> of transcendence, and this is further twofold: a) one who holds
> fast the moral and religious rules and disciplines (*vinaya* and
> *śīla*) and knows karmic retribution; and b) one who adheres
> to repentance [of all his actions], fearing that he might be
> still subjected to some offense after this life.

2. The Director of Practitioners' Affairs

As the director of a monastic community, this official accommo-
dates himself to all circumstances in order to maintain the harmony of the sangha. He must determine whether or not the ordination certificate that each practitioner presents when applying
for residency is authentic. When discord occurs among the practitioners, or when items have been lost, he is obliged to resolve the
cause of such problems and restore the harmonious flow of community life. There is hardly anything he does not deal with as far
as practitioners' affairs are concerned, within and without the
practice hall; namely, their ordination age, seniority order, monastic career, and the chart of assigned spaces of their residency in
the hall. Through his vocal performance he calls the names of the
sacred scriptures for chanting, leads the rite of prayer, and concludes it with the invocation of merit transference. He must direct
his mind with utmost care toward the sick and the deceased.

The ceremonial conduct of the director of practitioners' affairs
(*weina*) at mealtimes is as follows: Twice each day he goes to the
practice hall for meals. Upon hearing the sound of the bell located
in front of the practice hall, he leaves his seat in the outer hall,

enters the inner hall, offers incense before the altar of the guardian bodhisattva using his left hand, and stepping back two and a half steps, bows toward the altar. He then stands with palms joined to the side of the [octagonal] wooden post equipped with its mallet. First, he looks at the prayer invocation of the day and the names and the localities of the deities to whom it is addressed. When the sound of the bell and drum end, he makes the first strike on the octagonal post with the mallet, whereupon the practitioners open their almsbowls. When the practitioners have completed opening their almsbowls, he makes the second strike, then with palms joined prays toward the deities of the day in silence. Stabilizing the octagonal wooden post with his left hand, he then intones the names of the Buddhas:

> May all the members of the hall intone the ten sacred names in unison: the Luminous Pure Dharma Body Vairocana Buddha, the Buddha with the Perfect Reward Body, and so on.

As each name is intoned, he strikes the post with the mallet with his right hand, which should not be raised more than five inches from the post. Each strike should be made as soon as the sound of the name intoned has totally died out, with an adequate time interval, neither too quickly nor too slowly.

At the moment when the primary seat official finishes reciting the third verse of the "almsgiving prayer" (*shishi*), he turns and goes to stand by the head position of the raised platform at the back of the rear hall. When the first serving is completed throughout the hall, he steps forward and strikes the wooden post with the mallet once again, goes with palms joined before the altar of the guardian bodhisattva, and bows. He then goes out and takes his seat in the outer hall. If the meal has been donated by a patron through a monetary gift, after striking the post with the mallet at the completion of the first serving he turns left, goes around behind the altar, bows before the primary seat official, and once again strikes the post with the mallet, then leaves the hall. This gesture conveys that the sangha has received the alms gift from the donor.

If the director has unavoidable business elsewhere or has to take a temporary leave of absence, he must himself transfer the record book of ordination ages, the record of temporary leaves, and the detailed record of the practice hall to the guest reception office and request them to take charge of these record books.

According to *A Record of the Inner Law Sent Home from the South Seas* (*Nanhaijiguichuan*, by Yijing [635–713]), the term *weina* is explained as a compound of Chinese and Sanskrit terms; *wei* means *gangwei* in Chinese, and *na* in Sanskrit. Both together render the word *jiemotuona* (Sanskrit: *karmadāna*). The abbreviation *weina* is a compound meaning "pleasing the practitioners" (*yuezhong*).

Also, in the *Vinaya in Ten Chapters* (*Sarvāstivāda-vinaya; Shisonglü*), it is said that because no one in the monks' hall knew the time, the practice of indicating the time by striking the wooden sounding board was instituted. And it is further said that the Buddha established the position of *weina* as the director of the monastic residence, since no one prepared or cleaned the lecture and dining halls, nor did anyone cover the floor with cloth, nor did anyone try to subdue discord created by undisciplined monks, and so forth. Also, in the *Treatise on Vocal Sound* (*Shenglun*), [the name of this office] is interpreted as "the order" or "proceedings," namely, one who knows the proceedings of the monastic events.

3. The Treasury Official

In the *Ancient Regulations*, this position was called *kutou*, "kitchen storage master." Today, in many temples it is still called "cupboard master" (*guitou*), while in the northern region it is called "wealth holder" (*caibo*). In actuality, these are all the same position. This position was probably created initially in order to reduce the burden of the administrative head's duties by dividing the areas of administration into two. The treasury official handles the revenue and expenditure of the temple's public money, commodities, properties, stores of rice and wheat, and sometimes compiles the

1132c

almanac. He oversees the novice attendants in their daily calculation of the accounts concerning revenues and expenditures, and has one of them present the day's accounts (*feidan*) to the abbot. This is called the "daily accounts" (*ridan*). There are other accounts, such as an account closed every tenth day (*xundan*), an account closed monthly (*yuedan*), and the annual account, inclusive of all others, that concerns the yearly revenues and expenditures. This last one is called *zhihuangzongbu*. There are other record books concerning rice, flour, and various flavoring materials (*wuwei*). These must be included in the abovementioned account books.

In general, the temple's properties and commodities, no matter how small, have to be shared by all the practitioners in the ten directions (i.e., all regions, everywhere). Therefore, unless an expenditure is required for the reception and send-off of special guests of honor, such as government officials and patron donors, or for those occasions of celebration in which all practitioners participate, one must refrain from expediting the public account or taking advantage of it. The treasury official is obliged to select subordinates, whether senior or junior, who are alert and energetic in mind, skilled in calligraphy and accounting, and who are honest in nature and have integrity. Any items required for the sick must be provided at once. If the stores are damaged by sparrows and mice due to carelessness, or if rice and wheat grain become wet because of negligence, and if there are those who do not comply with the standard service for prompt supply of each of these items as well as for their careful preservation, the abbot is obliged to bring any such unfit personnel under his control and thereby deal with them over the course of time.

4. The Kitchen Official

The duty of this official is to prepare and serve the rice gruel in the morning and the rice at the noon meal every day for the practitioners. In preparation and serving, he must always maintain sanitary standards with utmost care. He must be resourceful in using available quantities of supplies and attentive to his workplace. He must also be thrifty about supplies belonging to the public (i.e., the monastic community) and never waste them through extravagance. Instructing the novice attendants to keep the rules, he must not allow them to become idle and negligent in matters of public action (i.e., serving food to the practitioners [*hangyi*]), or participating in physical labor (*puqing*). The kitchen official must treat farmworkers kindly, and at planting time, [which requires heavy labor], should give them some reward and equal benefit among themselves. At the morning and noon meals, he eats the same food in the kitchen hall as what is served to the practitioners in the practice hall. When the pails of gruel or rice are ready for transport, he must first burn incense and perform prostrations toward the practice hall before they are delivered.

5. The Maintenance and Construction Official

The duty of this official is to handle all kinds of labor [required for maintenance of the temple buildings]. In general, he is obliged to carry out [all necessary] repairs and restoration from yearly damage and deterioration, such as roof leakage, that occur to the temple buildings and various resident quarters. Movable items, whether belonging to the household or otherwise, must always be checked against the inventory. Clerical and construction manpower must be calculated in regard to the degree of progress, so as to prevent idle workers, nonproductive food expenditure, robbing of the public fund, and damage to the temple institution. He must oversee security measures for the estate farms and cottages; the mills for grinding and hulling grain; the cattle, boats, and carts for transportation; and policing against fire, theft, and robbery. By sending messengers, reward and punishment must be properly accorded for the kinds of work done. Honest service and hard work must be especially rewarded. If there is a large-scale construction project, this official must appoint assisting members to help handle the matter.

IV. Miscellaneous Duties

1. The Head Official of the Practitioners' Quarters

The duty of this head official is to manage the scriptures and household items for the practitioners' quarters: to replenish tea, sweet hot water, fuel for their use, and also to oversee the cleaning of the quarters and the washing of the towels for head-shaving. Every day after the morning rice gruel, a novice attendant of the tea master in charge of the tea serving (*zhatou*) strikes the wooden sounding block three times to signal the return of the practitioners to the practice hall. The associate head official of the quarters (*liaochang*) takes his seat symmetrically a little away from the head official in the same line, while the master of the first quarters (*liaozhu*) and the master of the second quarters (*fuliao*) take their seats to the right and left of the room, facing each other. The master of the second quarters steps forward to burn incense and returns to his seat. Thereupon, the tea master in charge of serving announces: "How are you, sir?" The practitioners perform a gesture of greeting in unison. If it is the first day of the month or the mid-month day, the tea master should strike the wooden sounding block to assemble the practitioners for the serving of sweet hot water as prescribed on these days. The manner of burning incense and serving the sweet hot water is the same as for a regular occasion.

1133a

2. The Master of the Quarters and Associate Master of the Quarters

In order to make the daily life of the practitioners comfortable, the head official of the practitioners' quarters should assign their respective seating spaces in accordance with ordination seniority, inviting each member from lower to higher. The names are copied and posted on the tablet for each space. Assigned on a rotation shift every ten days, the master of the quarters assists the head official of the quarters in carrying out these tasks. When the practitioners return to the practice hall in the morning and evening, he is in charge of inspecting the desks for scripture reading, and, if practitioners have left things behind, he collects and examines the items with witnesses present and returns them to the owners. He is obliged to keep the stores of household items in order and to prepare incense, candles, tea, and sweet hot water for the practitioners' use. He must not allow any nonresidents from outside to stay in the quarters overnight or to bring things there for sale. Moreover, a third candidate practitioner should be nominated beforehand as assistant master of the quarters (*wangliao*), and this person will be appointed the next associate master of the quarters. When the master of the quarters has fulfilled his term, he requests to be relieved from duty through the recognition of the director of practitioners' affairs, whereas when the associate master of the quarters has completed his term, he requests to be relieved from duty through the recognition of the head official of the quarters.

3. The Infirmary Official

This official is in charge of nursing the sick. He provides them with hot water, medicine, oil lamps for lighting, charcoal and fire, rice gruel and rice as well as all flavoring items (salt, etc.), making these items available for their use at all times. If the temple's budget does not provide sufficient funds [for these items], and if the infirmary official can afford it, he may purchase whatever is needed from his own funds, or he may invite patron donors to provide it to the office when needed. Even when filth is scattered over the floor, seats, clothing, and bedclothes, he should clean them by washing, rinsing, and so forth, never indulging a sense of disgust. Among the eight kinds of fields of merit (*puṇyakṣetra; futian*), attending to the sick is the foremost.

4. Head of Cleaning

The tasks of sweeping the grounds, cleansing the air with incense, replacing used bamboo scrapers [for the toilet] with new ones, cleaning the lavatories, and boiling and adding water must all be carried out whenever required. Even when things become somewhat messy, the task [of the head of cleaning] is to immediately restore the original cleanliness. He is obliged to inspect washcloths and pails and change them if necessary. This task is invariably beneficial to whoever serves in this position, because it strengthens the mind toward the practice of the path. If the head of cleaning wishes to retire from the post, the practice hall official is obliged to post a note on the bulletin board beforehand, reading:

> The post of head of cleaning has been vacated. To volunteer for this, please put up your name.

Someone wishing to volunteer [for the post] takes the board to the director of practitioners' affairs to express his intent. Thereupon, the official reports it to the abbot for approval and then appoints him to the post.

5. The Fundraising Official

In general, monastic temples where practitioners live always have the problem of being short of funds. Therefore, in order to support the practitioners sufficiently, it is always necessary to rely upon the assistance of patron donors by inviting their donations through the fundraising preacher. His activity of soliciting funds is necessary in order to balance a constant annual deficit. However, too-frequent fundraising activity must be avoided, as it might become oppressive to patron donors.

6. The Head of the Farmyard

Unhesitatingly [the holder of this post] takes the lead in heavy physical labor. He cultivates the soil, sows seeds for vegetable crops, irrigates the fields when necessary, and thereby provides a steady supply of fresh vegetables and so on to the kitchen hall throughout the year.

7. The Head of Mill Operations

[The holder of this post] is in charge of hulling and grinding grain. His function is indispensably related to the supply of rice and noodles for the practitioners. It is the norm to appoint to this post someone whose mind is established on the path of practice and who is well-acquainted with the mechanics and processes of grinding and hulling grain.

8. The Head of the Water Supply

[The holder of this post] is obliged to prepare hot water by 3:00 A.M. to supply the practitioners for face washing and brushing their teeth. He also supplies hand cloths, water trays, lamps, and dental powder so that there is no shortage. In the winter months, it is necessary to dry the washed hand towels. He must get up early in order to prepare these items for the practitioners, taking care not to create any inconvenience to them.

9. The Head of the Charcoal Supply

[The holder of this post] is in charge of securing kindling and charcoal before the [winter] season in order to protect practitioners from severe cold weather. He is obliged to invite patron donors or to request temple funds in order to procure the adequate quantity 1133b needed for each winter season.

10. The Head of Estate Management

[The holder of this post] is obliged to inspect the demarcation of the temple's rice fields, repair the estate cottages, supervise farming, and settle disputes with the farmers. He may handle small or trifling incidents but if the situation is of some magnitude and negatively affects the monastic institution, it must be reported to the temple and the matter taken up with due procedure. In recent times, innumerable evils have been observed to happen in the affairs of many temples, and the most extreme cases have involved estate management. The following three points briefly explain the extent of the problem.

The common characteristic of this evil, first and foremost, in all temples, is the fact that the post of estate management is the object of fierce competition. But how could such a post be open and attainable to anyone and everyone who wants it? Accordingly, some hold grudges against the abbot for not appointing them to the post, and they create discord between superiors and subordinates. Once appointed to this position, however, the appointee often stays on, rarely leaving the temple even for short periods of time, and thereby becomes undeterred in doing practically anything, including creating discord, bringing lawsuits, using up temple funds originally donated for the practitioners, or even creating debts for the temple, thereby resulting in years of ongoing problems. [In such a situation,] it is natural that the temple community's morale and discipline would decline, while the farmers may become contemptuous, slighting their duty of paying dues to the temple. This is the second evil.

Even if a mature and capable person is appointed [to this post], he is obliged to deal with the prefectural and district governments, and will likely have to deal with the clerks of local governments, in the city or village, or neighboring wealthy landowners. If he is unable to meet the customary standard in establishing relationships with these agents, there necessarily develops a detrimental gap. Even when there has been no clear expenditure, by cunning contrivance a deficit may result, and there is no benefit whatsoever in this case to the temple or to the person in regard to his own religious goals. Thus, the expense for running the estate often takes half of the temple's entire budget. This is the third evil.

There is a difference between the way a temple operates such estates and the way a secular private owner operates his holdings.

It is never the case that temples assign members widely in various parts of the estate operation in the way a wealthy family uses its clan members extensively. A temple estate may have a group of farmers at the time of sowing, a group of supervisors (*jiagan*) for farming, and at harvest time the temple sends a practitioner in charge of revenue and his attendants for the task. Although there are other nominal posts, such as transportation (*shuna*), dike repair (*xiuyu*), and grain distribution (*biaoliang*), these tasks are entrusted, only when necessary, to a group of retired officials to do the job as quickly as possible, and who return to the temple as soon as the task is completed. This way not only saves the cost of manpower but also sometimes prevents possible disasters by reducing the expenditure required. Thus, it serves both communal and individual goals simultaneously. Today, many temples have abandoned their estate operations, leaving their facilities like abandoned houses. If the abbot and the retired officials truly wish to restore their temple institution, to save costs, reform evils, and eliminate unnecessary expenses they should start with abolishing the temple estate as the first step. If, however, there is someone who, even facing grave difficulties, is capable of managing such an estate, his appointment may be separately discussed along with the idea of an honorarium.

11. The Head of Collection of Various Estate Revenues

In the *Ancient Regulations,* in the very beginning there was no post such as estate revenue officer under the head of estate management. Only in recent times was this office created. Since this post was established there have occurred innumerable evils. There are cases where, upon becoming abbot, a person secretly appoints someone who has been convicted of a crime, or out of personal interest, he falls into favoritism in appointing someone to such a post. There are also cases when officials and managing practitioners who have just retired [upon the appointment of a new abbot] overreach the latter's authority in appointing someone; or there are some who demand their own appointment due to their power base in the temple community; or those who organize a group in order to obtain the post on the basis of its majority. There are even some who take the post by physical force. There is no end of such examples, which in all cases are harmful both to the temple community and individuals. Even though everyone might wish to rectify this state of affairs and restore the proper form of the temple institution, there is no way to realize this goal. Only if there are retired officials who are honest and assist the abbot may it become possible to select an appropriate person in terms of public election and appoint him over some limited area of responsibility. Or it may also be possible to appoint a person by lottery from among the practitioners.

Anyone who holds this post must be rigorous in his standard of personal conduct and motivated to serve the community of practitioners. One must not impose heavy demands on the farming families. If [the holder of this post] is able not to cause any loss to the temple's economy, it would be equally beneficial to others as to himself.

1133c

V. The Primary Seat Official Elected as Dharma Teacher

1. Electing the Primary Seat Official as Occasional Teacher

Since this is a serious and grave matter, one should not lightly choose the appointee. If the person now serving the temple community as its primary seat official, who, on account of his virtue, once stayed at a renowned temple elsewhere as its west hall guest, and if this person commands the practitioners' respect and obedience, he may be recommended to the abbot to be elected as the occasional teacher. If the abbot agrees, he conducts a special ascent to the Dharma hall to address the practitioners, stating:

> Due to the recent increase in the number of temple members, we must invite a proper person and reach agreement on the doctrinal banners so as to establish a grand occasion of exhortation. Fortunately we have currently such a person residing in this temple, whose insight is high and clear and whose high ordination seniority has endowed him with supreme wisdom. I shall shortly descend this chair and, along with the dual order officials and the practitioners, implore him to consent to opening his room of instruction and give his special exhortation.

The abbot then descends. The attendant of the abbot's office carries two signboards, reading respectively "Individual Instruction" and "General Exhortation" on a crepe-wrapped board, and below the high seat, along with the practitioners, implores the primary seat official, saying:

> All resident practitioners have wished for some time to receive an exhortation from your reverence. We earnestly wish that in your compassion you will grant your consent.

The person thus invited goes to the abbot's office. After offering incense and performing a prostration with unopened sitting cloth, he thanks him, saying:

> So-and-so has fortunately found a waystation here. Though I am afraid that my performance may have been poor, as I have been invited under your cognizance I do not dare refuse it.

The abbot replies:

> The Buddhist teaching is very important for all of us. I request respectfully that you grant us your consent.

After this formality, the novice attendant of the practice hall office rings the practice hall bell, while the practitioners escort the primary seat official as elected teacher to his quarters. The abbot thanks him for his consent with a prostration with unopened sitting cloth and sees him off, and also then bows toward the practitioners who are escorting him.

The director of practitioners' affairs goes to the primary seat official's quarters and requests his assistant to post the signboard indicating "General Exhortation." He sets up a Zen chair, a Zen dusting brush (*fuzu*), a staff, an incense burner, and candle stands in the skylit room (*zhaotang*) adjacent to the back of the practice hall. A series of drumrolls calls the practitioners to assemble in lines in the practice hall, and the elected teacher takes his position. The director of practitioners' affairs, leaving his east order position, burns incense, and through performing protrations in unison with the practitioners, once again requests him to give an exhortation. Thereupon, the elected primary seat official sits cross-legged, while the dual order officials bow toward him and the abbot does likewise. When he completes his exhortation, the director of practitioners' affairs once again performs prostrations in unison with the practitioners to express thanks. Immediately following, the elected teacher, carrying incense in his sleeve, pays a visit to the abbot's office to express his thanks. Performing the formality of two prostrations with opened sitting cloth and three prostrations with unopened sitting cloth, he states:

> I have completed the task with which I was entrusted, with my poor but best effort. May you in your compassion overlook my lack of sophistication.

He then makes rounds at the quarters of the administrative office and the other quarters, bowing to express thanks. The abbot's office is obliged first to prepare a meal of rice mixed with sprouts for the elected teacher and then a serving of sweet hot water and the evening meal. That evening, the abbot's office also schedules a serving of sweet hot water and cake for him, inviting the dual order officials as participants, and including the elected teacher's assistant. Next day, the abbot conducts a special serving of tea at the practice hall for the primary seat official who is now the elected teacher. The abbot's guest reception assistant posts the signboard indicating the serving of tea. (Format given below.) He visits the quarters of the primary seat official as elected teacher and, after burning incense, invites him to the serving of tea. The manner and proceedings are the same as those for serving tea for the newly appointed primary seat official. The primary seat official too is obliged to conduct a special serving of tea for the practitioners. The proceeding is identical with that of a special serving of tea sponsored by the front and rear hall primary seat officials for the practitioners. On the following day, the abbot invites the elected teacher, the primary seat official, to a special dinner reception and the dual order officials are invited to participate.

2. Electing Various Renowned Virtuous Primary Seat Officials as Occasional Lecturer

The abbot is obliged to talk to the prospective primary seat official beforehand [about his possible election as an occasional teacher]. If the latter welcomes the idea, the abbot invites him for tea, with the dual order officials participating. At the signal of drumrolls, the abbot ascends the rostrum seat in the Dharma hall. Without immediately announcing his invitation, he introduces the idea in a polite and earnest manner. Descending the high seat, he then implores the primary seat official in unison with the practitioners to open his room for exhortation. The practice hall bell is rung, and the practitioners escort him to his quarters. The manner and proceeding of the serving of tea, sweet hot water, and the meal reception are identical as before. The appointment and resignation of the primary seat official do not mix with those of the dual order officials, nor is there any ceremonial form of transfer between the old and new officials.

1134a

Format of the Signboard

The Venerable Abbot, master of the temple, will serve tea at the practice hall today after the noon meal. This is especially intended for the newly appointed primary seat official. For expressing congratulations, the administrative officials as well as the practitioners are invited. May you grant your participation.

Date and month

Respectfully stated by So-and-so
Office of the Abbot's Assistants

VI. The Appointment and Resignation of the Dual Order Officials

1. Appointment and Resignation of the Training Faculty

Each member of the training faculty should be selected on account of both his ability and virtue. If one critically characterizes those mediocre officials of the present day, [we see that] they indulge in lengthy entertainment with drink and food as their major function, and thereby compel those who remain in poverty and in the practice of the path to withdraw more and more into the storehouse of the scriptures. Why should such indulgence in a pleasant lifestyle be necessary in the monastic community? The abbot must rectify this kind of evil trend.

In the *Ancient Regulations,* only five official titles were mentioned, namely, the administrative head (*jianyuan*), the director of practitioners' affairs, the kitchen official, the maintenance official, and the treasury official. When his term ended, by striking [the octagonal wooden post] with the mallet at the practice hall the official announced his resignation to the practitioners and thereby rejoined them in the practice hall. In the beginning there were no individual quarters, and the monastic institution flourished. Today, the number of retired officials in many temples, large and small, has often surpassed a hundred, and that of service men and workmen twice as many. On the contrary, the practice hall is vacant with no one residing in it. During the era of Taiding (1324–1328 in the Yuan dynasty), his excellency Grand Minister Tuohuan of the Commission for Buddhist and Tibetan Affairs had his agency classify all Zen temples into three groups of "higher" (*shang*), "middle" (*zhong*), and "lower" (*xia*). This was done in order to limit the number of administrative officials in these different classes of institutions. This practice must be maintained.

When their term is about to end, officials must beforehand convey their resignation from their posts directly to the abbot. When the date of resignation is determined, the abbot has the attendant notify the dual order officials. That evening, when the evening bell is rung, the former administrative officials as a group visit the abbot and, after burning incense, declare their resignations, perform a prostration with unopened sitting cloth, and present the account book (*kuji*) and the keys to the abbot before leaving the office. If the [resigning official] is someone whom the abbot wishes to stay on, he sees him off by escorting him to the administrative office. The abbot's assistant burns incense, serves him sweet hot water, and urges him to stay on.

Next day, as early as the bell indicating the fifth watch of the night (3:00 A.M.), the training faculty officials, carrying incense in their sleeves, visit the abbot's office, and after performing a prostration with unopened sitting cloth, express their intent to resign. If there is someone whom the abbot wishes to stay on, he performs the same propriety as before, and, serving him sweet hot water, encourages him to stay on. The abbot now has the guest reception attendant invite, according to the name list, his new officials together with the west hall guest and residents of the retiree's hall, to meet him at his tea reception after the morning gruel.

In the practice hall, when the first serving of rice gruel is completed, the former administrative officials enter the hall from the rear entrance. The administrative head strikes the octagonal wooden post with its mallet once and announces:

> May I speak to the practitioners. So-and-so and others were assigned through the abbot's compassion to administrative offices during the past term. Because of the declining power of our minds, we have conveyed our resignation to the venerable abbot and we are now returning to the practice hall to join you. Respectfully announced.

After striking the post once again, they proceed toward the seat of the abbot, passing to the left of the altar of the guardian bodhisattva, and perform the propriety of two prostrations with opened sitting cloth and three prostrations with unopened sitting cloth. After the first opening of the sitting cloth, the former administrative head says:

> So-and-so and others were selected to serve during the last term. We fear, however, that our performance may not have fully matched the expectation of your reverence, and cannot help feeling regretful about it, sir.

After the second opening, he enquires about the well-being of the master and the officials conclude their formal greeting with three prostrations with unopened sitting cloth. Stepping back and going around the altar, they line up before the altar, perform three prostrations with fully opened sitting cloth, then turn to make a round of the hall, starting from the primary seat official's raised platform. Returning to mid-hall, they bow to the altar and leave the hall.

After breakfast, the attendant of the abbot's office escorts the new official appointees to the reception hall. When the serving of tea is over, the abbot rises and burns incense, returns to his seat, and announces:

> The former dual order officials conveyed to me their intent to resign. Since these posts cannot be left vacant, I have requested So-and-so and others to take the administrative

1134b

offices, and So-and-so and others to take the offices of the training faculty.

In this manner, he calls all the names [of the new officials] one after another in reference to their respective office titles.

The abbot steps forward and stands before the incense burner. His assistant invites the new appointees to proceed, and then proceeds first toward the master and performs a prostration with unopened sitting cloth. The new administrative officials likewise step forward and perform the propriety of two prostrations with opened sitting cloth and three prostrations with unopened sitting cloth. At the first opening of the sitting cloth, the leader says:

> We, So-and-so and others, have joined this community only recently. Hence we know little about how things should be carried out. We fear that our appointment may have been a mistake and cannot help feeling apprehensive, sir.

With the second opening, he says:

> On this day and at this time, we respectfully wish that all is well and felicitous with your reverence, the master of the temple.

They complete the meeting with three prostrations with unopened sitting cloth. The abbot responds with a single prostration. Next, the new appointees to the offices of the training faculty proceed forward and perform the same propriety of two prostrations with opened sitting cloth and three prostrations with unopened sitting cloth, uttering the same greetings as before. As they change seats, the abbot's office serves sweet hot water to all the officials.

(According to the *Xianshun Regulations,* this morning event, i.e., consisting of "inviting the new appointees to take seats, burn incense, and drink sweet hot water," was still practiced in various temples up to that time [Southern Song dynasty, 1265–1275]. An alternative, it is said, is that if there was a plan to have a special serving in the evening of that day, the morning rite could be omitted. The point is that whether or not this special serving should be conducted depends on the abbot's discretion.)

After the serving of sweet hot water has been completed, both of the dual order officials thank the abbot either by performing a prostration with opened sitting cloth or a prostration with unopened sitting cloth, if the former propriety is excused.

The alms-serving attendant tolls the practice hall bell, and the practitioners return to their respective seats where they take the meal. The abbot enters the hall, first escorting the primary seat official of the front hall, followed by the lower-ranking training officials who reach their seats in proper order. Each official performs a prostration with unopened sitting cloth toward the abbot. Next [the abbot] escorts the primary seat official of the rear hall and receives a prostration with an unopened sitting cloth from that official. The new administrative officials as a group must take their positions beforehand on the raised platform that begins with the west hall ranking official's seat. When the abbot returns to his position, the director of practitioners' affairs proceeds toward him and bows, remaining there by his side.

(If the director of practitioners' affairs has already resigned, the abbot's guest reception assistant takes the role.)

The abbot gives the list of names of the new appointees to the director of practitioners' affairs, who in turn, after bowing, goes behind the altar of the guardian bodhisattva, strikes the wooden post with the mallet, and announces:

On behalf of the abbot, may I speak to the practitioners. The former administrative officials conveyed their wish to resign from their posts. Since these posts cannot be left vacant, the Venerable Master, abbot of this temple, has invited the following resident practitioners to take charge of the following positions: So-and-so is appointed to such-and-such post, and so on. Respectfully announced.

Once again, after striking the post, the abbot's assistant immediately ushers the group of new administrative officials in front of the master. The director of practitioners' affairs performs a prostration with unopened sitting cloth and says:

> The administrative officials are requested to take charge of their respective posts.

Again, he strikes the octagonal wooden post with the mallet. The administrative officials perform in unison the propriety of two prostrations with opened sitting cloth and three prostrations with unopened sitting cloth. The statements are identical as before. The officials step back, go around behind the altar, line up before the altar, and perform three prostrations with fully opened sitting cloth. The director of practitioners' affairs leads them in a round through the hall and returns to mid-hall, where they bow in unison. Immediately he steps aside and moves toward the raised platform of the west hall official, leaving the officials before the altar. The novice attendant of the practice hall office announces:

> May the practitioners congratulate the new administrative officials.

All the practitioners in unison perform a prostration with unopened sitting cloth. The novice attendant then announces:

> May the new administrative officials thank the practitioners.

The administrative officials perform in unison a prostration with unopened sitting cloth. For the third time, the attendant announces:

> May the practitioners escort the new administrative officials back to their offices.

As soon as the alms-serving attendant begins to toll the practice hall bell, the abbot, seeing them off, enters their office, receives their prostration with unopened sitting cloth, and returns to the practice hall. After seeing off the abbot, the new officials exchange the standing positions with those of the former officials, thus completing the rite of the ceremonial transfer of duties. They then exchange a prostration with unopened sitting cloth with them, and see the former officials off. The abbot's assistant expresses congratulations to the new officials. Next, leading the practitioners, the training faculty officials express congratulations to the new administrative officials.

After all this has been completed, the practice hall attendant once again announces:

> May the practitioners escort the new primary seat official to his quarters.

Again, the practice hall bell is tolled and the new primary seat official is escorted to his quarters and is congratulated there, in similar manner. The bell is tolled once again, signaling the end of escorting the official. The attendant once again announces:

> May the fellow practitioners escort the new director of practitioners' affairs to his practice hall office.

Once again, the bell is tolled, the conduct of escorting and offering congratulations takes place, followed by another toll of the bell to signal its completion. In this manner, each new official is announced one by one:

> May the retired dual order officials escort the new rear hall primary seat official, the new secretarial official, the new Tripiṭaka hall official, and the new guest reception official to their respective quarters.

The manner of escorting, offering congratulations, and ceremonial transfer between the old and new officials are all identical as before. There follows another announcement:

> May the practitioners escort the former primary seat official and the former head administrative official to their respective quarters.

Again, the tolling of the bell signals the completion of this propriety, and it is announced again:

> May the retired dual order officials escort the remaining former training faculty officials and the former administrative officials to their respective retirees' halls.

The manner of proprieties are again identical as before. Finally, the practitioners escort the abbot back to his office.

At the practitioners' quarters, prior to the foregoing, the new and former masters of the quarters meet, exchange their positions, and perform mutual prostrations with unopened sitting cloth. Without seeing off the old master, the new master receives congratulations.

All the new officials and the former officials together, carry- 1134c ing incense in their sleeves, visit the abbot's office to express their thanks. The incense offered by the new appointees is prepared by the treasury office. After expressing thanks, they are obliged to make a round through the various quarters. The abbot then invites all appointees to his office for a small mid-morning snack. There will also be a meal reception at the abbot's office, for which a meal of rice mixed with sprouts is prepared, and the west hall ranking official as well as the retired officials are invited to participate. Those functionaries in the lesser posts of miscellaneous duties (*liezhizawu*) visit the office of the practice hall on a different day after the new dual order officials are settled, and express their wish to retire from their respective posts. Upon the selection of appropriate candidates one by one, the transfer of duties must be conducted for the new appointees.

2. Appointment of the Administrative Officials after the Morning Meal

In some cases, the abbot does not speak about new appointments but keeps silent until all selections are completed. He gives the copy of the list of the appointees' names to the attendant of the practice hall office. After the morning gruel, before the time when the practitioners hang up their almsbowls at their respective spaces in the practice hall, the practice hall attendant announces:

> May the practitioners stay awhile at your positions. The new administrative appointees will be introduced.

The director of practitioners' affairs goes before the altar of the guardian bodhisattva, burns incense, makes a round through the hall, returns to the abbot, and, after bowing, stands at his side. The abbot gives him the list of the new appointees' names, and he in turn goes around behind the altar, strikes the wooden post with its mallet once, and announces:

> According to the will of the compassionate abbot, I invite the following members to the respective administrative posts as follows.

The director of practitioners' affairs then reads the names and offices, and the assistant escorts each designated official before the abbot to receive his appointment. The remaining proceedings are identical as before. Later, the new officials are invited to a tea reception at the abbot's office. The manner of appointing the training faculty officials is identical to that of administrative officials.

3. Appointment and Resignation of the Practitioner Assistants

After the appointment of the dual order officials is completed, the abbot's assistants follow him to his office and express their intent to resign:

> We, So-and-so and others, have assisted you, our master, for some time. Now we are obliged to express our intent to resign, wishing to pursue the practice of the path with the practitioners. We earnestly wish that in your compassion you grant us relief, sir.

They burn incense, perform three prostrations with fully opened sitting cloth, and withdraw. The abbot then sends his authorization to the practice hall official to appoint the designated persons as his assistants. The official has his novice attendant identify the appointees in reference to the name list and invite the head of the practitioners' quarters and other appointees to his office for a serving of tea. The director of practitioners' affairs burns incense and serves tea. After they finish drinking tea, he stands, burns incense again, and says:

> Just now, on behalf of the abbot, I have invited you, Venerable So-and-so, to be in charge of the post of the abbot's assistant.

Going through the list of names and positions one by one, the director of practitioners' affairs greets each appointee, steps forward to perform a prostration with unopened sitting cloth toward them as a group, and shifts his position. He conducts the serving of sweet hot water himself, and after burning incense requests the appointees to be seated and drink, then returns to his seat. After the serving of sweet hot water is over, he escorts the appointees to the abbot's office. Upon the abbot's appearance, the director of practitioners' affairs steps forward and says:

> In compliance with the compassion of the Venerable Master of the temple, I have just now led the designated appointees here with me as they have accepted the assistant posts. I shall now request them to burn incense and perform prostrations, sir.

When the abbot takes his seat, the new appointees burn incense and perform in unison three prostrations with fully opened sitting cloth. Thereupon, the director of practitioners' affairs escorts them to their new quarters, where they meet with the former assistants and mutually perform a prostration with unopened sitting cloth. After seeing off the director of practitioners' affairs, the new and old assistants exchange their positions for the transfer of the duties.

The procedure is identical to that of the appointment of the training faculty officials.

(In the *Xianshun Regulations,* a unique case is mentioned, in which the abbot himself escorts the appointed practitioner assistants to their quarters, and they are in turn obliged to see off the master after performing a prostration with unopened sitting cloth. The *Zhida Regulations* gives a variation, in which if a new appointee is a renowned, virtuous person, the abbot himself escorts him to his quarters and exchanges a prostration with unopened sitting cloth, and the director of practitioners' affairs only expresses congratulations. This, however, should not be regarded as a norm.)

The novice attendants of the abbot's office, the office workers of extra-temple affairs (*zhiting*) and the sedan chair bearers come to congratulate the new assistants. The novice attendant of the practice hall office leads both the new and former abbot's assistants on a round through the practitioners' quarters. After this, the new practitioner assistants once again go to the abbot's office, burn incense, and thank him with a prostration. The old members return to the abbot's office early in the evening and together with the new members perform a prostration to thank their master. After three days, the abbot sends a note to the practice hall office to let the former assistants return to the practitioners' quarters. They meet the director of practitioners' affairs, and after mutually performing a prostration with unopened sitting cloth, they see the director off. Next, they exchange a bow with the head official of the quarters. After that, they visit the abbot's office, burn incense, and thank him with a prostration.

1135a

The appointment of the assistant of the guardian bodhisattva is made by the director of practitioners' affairs, who is obliged to select a candidate, meet him, and appoint him to the post. The director of practitioners' affairs then escorts him to the office of the abbot, where the new appointee offers thanks with a prostration. As usual, he is given a reception with tea, sweet hot water, and a small snack.

4. Inventory of the Temple's Public Household Items in Each of the Quarters

The household items for the quarters are supplied from the temple's funds and are not transferable. Quite often, however, some practitioners who resided there in charge of a particular function regarded the quarters as a wayside inn, and when receiving a new appointment elsewhere or resigning from their old post, they carry away household items with the help of those from the same native region, emptying the quarters completely overnight and leaving new residents totally at a loss. Since some items are indispensable, new residents are often unable to find them despite a new request to the administrative office. Thus, there is no peace among the top officials or lowly workmen from reasoning about the cause of such an unsatisfactory state of affairs. Even if the missing items can be resupplied, this necessarily causes an expenditure of the temple's funds.

In order to solve this problem, it is necessary for the treasury office to keep a central inventory book, in which household items and amounts from all the quarters are recorded, and the records must be examined from time to time by the abbot and administrative head. Besides this central book, a smaller record book should be kept at each quarter, so that at the time of a new appointment or that of a transfer of official duties it will be possible to compare recorded items in both books with reference to the designated items that are supposed to be in each quarter. Anything damaged must be repaired, through the temple's funds, but missing items must be compensated for by the [residents of that] quarter.

A few days before the day of the transfer of official duties between new and old officials, the treasury official is obliged to visit each quarter, accompanied by his attendant carrying the central record book, and each item is checked and identified, comparing it with the written record. Thus, it is possible to clarify what is missing. The responsibility for losses lies with the workmen of each quarter. What is lost need not be sought for, however.

If any discovered difference is compensated by them [according to the appropriate monetary value of the item or otherwise,] that is the end of the matter. If there are additional items, these must also be recorded in both books. It is hoped that this matter should be given careful scrutiny.

VII. The Proprieties of Special Servings at Various Quarters

1. The Abbot's Special Serving of Sweet Hot Water for the New and Former Dual Order Officials

The abbot's guest reception assistant instructs the guest reception attendant to prepare the crepe-wrapped board with an incense burner and candle stands, and goes to the primary seat official's quarters to convey the invitation to both the former and new training faculty officials. After burning incense and performing a prostration with unopened sitting cloth, he says:

> The abbot wishes to invite both your reverences for a special serving of sweet hot water at the reception hall.

Next, he visits the administrative office, and after burning incense, conveys the same invitation to both the former and new administrative heads (here, incense is offered but no prostration is required). The statement is identical to the above. The guest reception assistant must visit all the other dual order officials, new and former, to convey the same invitation. He should also extend the invitation to participate in the special serving to the retired officials of the temple.

Curtains should be hung around the interior of the reception hall, and all the seating arrangements must be indicated on the floor. The main participant is seated to the abbot's left, with a space between them. The new training faculty members should be seated in the first section of the hall (i.e., the front right half), while the new administrative officials are to be seated in the second section (i.e., the front left). The former training faculty and administrative officials are seated in the third section (i.e., the middle right of the hall) and in the fourth section (i.e., the middle left of the hall), respectively, facing each other. The rest of the retired officials of the east and west orders who are participating in this special reception are seated at the right and left ends of the main section, respectively. The incense offering assistant sets up the seat name tablets beforehand, and at the appointed time, begins to drum. When the guests assemble, the guest reception assistant leads the propriety of the special serving. (The ceremonial propriety is identical to that of serving sweet hot water for a small number of participants [*xiaozuotang*]).

Late in the evening, sweet hot water and cake will be served. Next day, after the morning rice gruel, the abbot invites the former and new officials for tea, and later the administrative head also invites them for the same. Although the invited individuals may be excused from the latter function, they are obliged to attend the serving of tea at the abbot's office, and afterward to visit the administrative office to offer thanks for the occasion. At mid-morning, the administrative office prepares a snack for them, and thereafter for the next three days the office continues to have rice gruel and rice meals delivered to the former officials at their quarters.

2. The Practice Hall Office's Special Serving of Tea and Sweet Hot Water for the Former and New Practitioner Assistants

After a meal of rice mixed with sprouts (*caofan*) is served at the abbot's office, the director of practitioners' affairs sends his attendant to invite both the former and new practitioner assistants for tea. At the same time, he invites the assistant of the guardian 1135b bodhisattva of the practice hall, before the zazen practice preceding the evening session, to arrange the seats and place the seat name tablets at his quarters, extending the invitation to the head official of the practitioners' quarters. The director of practitioners' affairs now has the wooden sounding block at his quarters struck, receives the guests, and invites them to take their seats. (The manner is identical with that of the administrative office's serving.) It is preferable, however, that this serving of tea be conducted prior to the abbot's special serving of sweet hot water. In general it must be done in a way that does not interfere with the major event that takes place at the abbot's office. Thus, in order to invite the former and new practitioner assistants for the special serving of tea, the practice hall official may have to wait until the abbot's special serving of tea for the new primary seat official is completed. Those who are invited here are obliged to express thanks the next morning.

3. The Head Administrative Official's Special Serving of Sweet Hot Water and an Evening Meal for the Former and New Dual Order Officials

After the serving of an occasional meal (i.e., rice mixed with sprouts, *caofan*) at the abbot's office, the administrative head accompanies the guest reception attendant, carrying a crepe-wrapped tray equipped with an incense burner and candle stand, to visit the former and new primary seat officials as well as the former administrative head. After burning incense, he invites them by saying:

> This evening, after the serving of sweet hot water is completed at the abbot's office, we will conduct a special serving of sweet hot water at the administrative office. I earnestly request you to grant us your honorable presence.

Immediately following this, the guest reception attendant further invites them, saying:

> After the serving of sweet hot water, an evening meal will be served for the guests, sir.

In addition, an invitation is extended to the old and new officials of the major and minor positions, and especially to the west hall ranking official and the retired officials as honorable participants.

The seats and name tablets must be set up in terms of the four divisions. The new training faculty officials' seats are set in the first section (i.e., front right of the hall), the former faculty officials in the second section (front left), the former administrative officials in the third section (middle right), and the estate management official and treasury administrative official in the fourth section (middle left). Additional seats are prepared for the new administrative officials as a group in the main section, but only the new director of practitioners' affairs is supposed to take a seat as participant. The seats of the retired officials who participate in this serving must be arranged in the fashion previously referred to in the serving of sweet hot water at the abbot's office, [namely, the retired officials of the east and west orders should be placed on the right side of the main seat and the left side of the participant's seat, respectively]. As soon as the serving of sweet hot water at the abbot's office is finished, the administrative office strikes the wooden sounding block located there. The guests enter the hall and stand by their designated seats. The head administrative official goes around to each seating section, requesting the guests to take their seats, then burns incense on behalf of the guests of each section and bows, repeating this according to the order of the seating arrangements. Finally, returning to mid-hall, he burns incense on behalf of the special participant and takes his seat, requesting the serving. Thereupon the serving of sweet hot water begins. When the ceremony is completed he stands, proceeds to the incense burner, and thanks the guests for their presence. The guests then take off their robes and settle themselves on their seats for the evening meal.

4. The Practice Hall Official Escorts the Former Primary Seat Official and Head Administrative Official to Their Almsbowl Seats

Three days after the transfer of duties between the former and new dual order officials, and prior to the end of the silent period (i.e., before the dawn zazen is completed), the director of practitioners' affairs sends his attendant, accompanied by a man carrying a crimson lantern, to invite both the former primary seat official and former head administrative official for a serving of sweet hot water at his office. The director of practitioners' affairs duly receives the guests, burns incense, and, after drinking sweet hot water, says to them:

> Your spotless term has been fulfilled. Hence, in accordance with the temple's manner of honoring, I have the honor to escort your reverences to your almsbowl seats in the practice hall.

Ushering them into the practice hall from the rear entrance, he first escorts the former primary seat official and next the former head administrative official to their respective seats on the raised platform. Each exchanges a prostration with unopened sitting cloth, and during the day, both officials return to the hall to place their almsbowls at the assigned seat space.

5. The Abbot's Meal Reception for the Former and New Dual Order Officials

The abbot conducts a special ascent to the Dharma hall and expresses his thanks by referring to the names of the former and new dual order officials one by one. When this is over, the two groups of officials come before the rostrum seat to express their thanks. The guest reception assistant, accompanied by a guest master attendant carrying a crepe-wrapped board with an incense burner, candle stand, and incense case, comes before the former and new training faculty and administrative officials, and, after burning incense, conveys the abbot's invitation to them, saying:

> The venerable abbot, master of the temple, wishes to serve a special meal for your honors at the reception hall at noon, sirs.

The guest master attendant then invites the other associate

officials, old and new, for the same reception, and simultaneously extends the invitation to the retired officials as honorable participants.

The seats are arranged and the name tablets set up in the reception hall. When the guests have assembled, the abbot is notified, and he enters the hall, welcoming the guests' presence. As each guest finds his seat and stands beside it, the abbot's incense offering assistant and the guest reception assistant together go around the hall, requesting the guests to take their seats. When all are seated, they burn incense and bring forward the tables. Thereupon, all the assistants line up before the abbot, bow to him in unison, and take their respective positions, carrying out the serving of sweet hot water and the presentation of each meal. During the meal, the incense offering assistant leaves his seat to burn incense and deliver monetary gifts. When the meal is over, he and the other assistant retrieve the tables. A series of drumrolls signals the beginning of the serving of tea. (The propriety is identical with that of the special serving of sweet hot water.) With three drumbeats, the former and new dual order officials leave their seats and perform the formal propriety of two prostrations with opened sitting cloth and three prostrations with unopened sitting cloth to express their thanks.

6. The Abbot's Special Serving of Tea for the New Primary Seat Official

The morning after the evening special meal reception, the incense offering assistant reminds the abbot that a special serving of tea is due for the new primary seat official. The assistant instructs the guest reception attendant to prepare the crepe-wrapped board with an incense burner, a candle stand, and an incense box. The guest reception assistant draws up the signboard. (The format, previously given, is identical with that of the special serving of tea for a renowned, virtuous primary seat official.) The guest reception assistant visits the primary seat official's quarters, and after burning incense and performing a prostration, says:

1135c

> After the noon meal, the venerable master abbot wishes to hold a special serving of tea at the practice hall in honor of your reverence. Please grant us your honorable presence.

The guest reception master then informs the practitioners by posting the signboard indicating the serving of tea, and also invites the administrative officials and practitioners to participate.

The abbot's assistants set up the name tablets indicating seating and conduct the ceremonial serving.

(The ceremonial proceedings are identical to those of the special serving on the four major days of annual festivity [*sijie*]. The only difference is that no incense table is placed by each head monk at the four raised platforms, nor is the propriety of making a round in the hall for invitation conducted.)

When the serving of tea is over, the teabowls are retrieved from the seats of the abbot and the primary seat official. At once, the latter goes before the abbot and performs the formal propriety of two prostrations with opened sitting cloth and three prostrations with unopened sitting cloth. At the first opening of the sitting cloth he says:

> Today I am honored by this special serving of tea. My gratitude is greater than I can express. I cannot help feeling great regret [for this inability, sir].

At the second opening, he enquires about the well-being of the abbot, and concludes with the propriety of three prostrations with unopened sitting cloth. The primary seat official goes out of the hall, passing behind the altar of the guardian bodhisattva, and turns right to the outer hall. The abbot escorts him and returns to his place to take the teabowl. The practitioner assistant burns incense (signaling the practitioners to participate in the drinking of tea), then takes down the teabowl from the altar. After three drumbeats, the practitioners leave their seats. The primary seat official waits for the abbot at the lower left section of the Dharma hall and thanks him for the serving of tea.

7. The New Primary Seat Official's
Special Serving of Tea for the Rear Hall
Primary Seat Official and the Practitioners

(If there is no rear hall primary seat official, the member of the training faculty next in rank is served.)

The morning after the abbot's special serving of tea, the new primary seat official visits the abbot's office carrying incense in his sleeve and invites the master, saying:

> Today, at the end of the noon meal, a special serving of tea is scheduled [for the rear hall primary seat official as well as the practitioners] at the practice hall. I earnestly appeal to your compassion to grant us your honorable presence.

The new primary seat official then proceeds to the quarters of the rear hall primary seat official, carrying a written invitation (format given below) and a crepe-wrapped board equipped with an incense burner and candle stand. After burning incense, he invites him for the serving of tea:

> Today, at the end of the noon meal, a special serving of tea is scheduled at the practice hall in honor of your reverence and the practitioners. May I request your honorable presence.

Thereupon, he presents the letter of invitation. The rear hall primary seat official, recipient of the special serving of tea, instructs his master of the quarters to give the document to the serving master and request him to post it on the left section of the wall outside the practice hall. The envelope is also attached along with the document. Next, he instructs the attendant of the practice hall office to inform the practitioners about the invitation and post the signboard indicating "tea serving." When the metal gong located at the kitchen hall is struck to signal the serving of tea, the primary seat official of the front hall should make a round through the practice hall, inviting the practitioners for the serving of tea.

The fellow practitioners are called to assemble by the signal of drumrolls and the ceremonial serving begins. The propriety of the serving is identical with any of the other special servings.

Format of the Letter of Invitation

The front hall primary seat official, Bhikṣu So-and-so, has the honor of holding a special serving of tea at the practice hall after the noon meal. This is especially intended for the primary seat official of the rear hall and the practitioners. This invitation is also extended to the administrative officials as honorable participants.

Date and month

Respectfully prepared
by So-and-so

Format of the Envelope

Letter of Invitation for

The Primary Seat Official of the Rear Hall
as well as the Practitioners

Respectfully sealed
by So-and-so

1136a
8. The Abbot's Serving of Tea for the Training Officials by Visiting Their Quarters

After the serving of tea and sweet hot water at his office, the abbot makes his visit individually to the quarters of the training officials and serves tea. Composed and calm, with warmth, he inspects whatever is needed in their quarters and requests the treasury officials to supply it.

9. The Serving of Tea on the Occasion of the Transfer of Duties Between the Former and New Dual Order Officials

While awaiting the completion of the abbot's special serving of tea for the new primary seat official, those who have been newly appointed to the dual order offices visit their respective former officials with due dignity, carrying incense in their sleeves. After burning incense and performing prostrations with unopened sitting cloth, the new appointees invite them with the following words:

> After the noon meal, in honor of your reverences, tea is served at the officials' quarters.

Accordingly, each of the dual order officials instructs the practitioner in charge of tea to extend his invitation to a member of the other order, and in addition two retired officials, one each from the east and west orders, as participants.

(If a west order official extends his invitation to his predecessor, he is obliged to extend his invitation to an administrative official of the east order to the main seat on the same line allocated to his predecessor, and, in addition, to invite a lower-ranking west order official as a participant. If anyone higher in rank is invited, the order of the seating arrangements is disturbed. Again, if an east order official invites his predecessor for tea, he is also obliged to invite a training official to the main seat on the same line allocated to his predecessor, and in addition, invite the treasury official, lower in rank, as a participant.)

In the official quarters, the main guest's seat must be set on the right side of the back of the room. The seats of the officials on the right and left front of the hall are to be placed respectively by the participants from the two orders. After the noon meal, the wooden sounding blocks located by both quarters are struck. The host official first receives the main guest, followed by the other participants, and then requests them to take their seats. First burning incense for the main guest, then for the participants, the host official takes his seat, signaling the serving of tea to commence. After the serving of tea is completed, the main guest stands and, receiving incense from the host, burns it, performs a prostration with unopened sitting cloth, and departs.

The next day, the host official instructs the practice hall attendant to invite the former official for the serving of a snack, so as to complete the proceeding of official transfer between the former and new officials. For this occasion, some notable participant superior to the main guest may be invited as a participant. For instance, when the primary seat official of the front hall invites the former primary seat official as his main guest, one of the two other participants may be the west hall official and a retired administrative official of the east order. If the guests represent all officials of the administration, the host of the proceeding should invite the west hall ranking official, the retired administrative officials, and the present training officials as honorable participants.

In the administrative office, curtains must be hung and the main seat should be set at the rear of the hall, while participants should be seated in the right and left sections of the hall. If a training official is invited as participant, he should be seated to the left of the main guest with a space in between, and if he is in the same order as the main guest, their seating order should reflect the difference in their ranks. On the next day, there should be the serving of a snack. The seating arrangement for the serving of simple food is identical with that of the previous day for the serving of tea. The west order official, however, ends the serving of a snack according to the rank of the guest reception official, whereas, the east order official should end it according to the rank of the director of practitioners' affairs. As to the procedure of ceremonial transfer between the former and new practitioner assistants, the director of practitioners' affairs must always be invited to participate in the serving of tea as well as servings of simple food. (The seating arrangement and conduct of serving are all identical as before.) In recent times, it has become common to invite unrelated guests and locals for the serving of snacks, but this is not proper conduct.

10. The Serving of Tea on the Occasion of Leaving and Joining [Each Official] Quarters

When someone joins the retirees' hall, he must report it to the master of the practitioners' quarters and post a signboard indicating the serving of tea. At the left side of the board he should attach a small note that says:

> So-and-so invites honorable colleagues for tea to be served after the noon meal.

After the meal, he prepares incense and candles, and all bow in unison. Requesting the master of quarters to stay at the main seat, the person who serves tea takes his temporary seat at the guest position. He stands, burns incense, bows to every member, returns to take his seat again, and the serving of tea and retrieval of the teabowls are carried out. The master of the quarters stands and expresses thanks before the incense burner.

When someone is appointed a training official and is to leave the retirees' hall, he is obliged to conduct the propriety of serving tea for the official transfer of duty. The next day, he requests the practitioner in charge of tea to report to the master of the quarters and post the signboard indicating the serving of tea. After the noon meal, striking the small wooden sounding block in the practitioners' quarters, the practitioner in charge of tea stands to the right of the entrance to the quarters, greets the practitioners, and proceeds to the incense burner to bow. The master of the quarters takes the main seat and the practitioner in charge of tea takes a   1136b
seat to the right of the main seat with some space in between. After seating himself in an easy manner, he stands, burns incense, bows, and returns to take his seat again. Thereupon, the serving of tea is carried out. The master of the quarters and the other practitioners rise and give thanks for the tea before the incense burner, see off the person who sponsored the tea reception, and depart.

When someone is appointed to be a training official and leaves the practitioners' quarters, he requests the practitioner in charge of tea beforehand to report it to the master of the quarters and to post the signboard indicating the serving of tea. After the noon meal, when the wooden sounding board is struck, he stands to the right of the entrance to the quarters, greets the practitioners, enters the quarters to stand at his position, and, after a bow, requests them to take their seats. He proceeds to the middle of the room as well as to the right and left sections of the quarters to burn incense, and bows to the center, right, and left sections. Thereupon, he bows toward the central shrine, and the head official of the practitioners' quarters greets him. They are seated face to face across the middle section of the room and the serving of tea is carried out. The head official of the quarters comes before the incense burner to express thanks for the tea and see off the newly appointed training official as he departs.

When someone joins the quarters, he is obliged to sponsor the serving of tea (the ceremonial conduct is identical to that of the present case). However, the head official and associate official of the quarters take the main seat and guest seat, and the sponsor of the serving of tea cannot enter to take his seat by himself.

11. The Training Officials' Serving of Tea at the Practice Hall

After completing the propriety of the serving of tea on the occasion of leaving the practitioners' quarters, the newly appointed training official is obliged to prepare the signboard to indicate the serving of tea (format given below). He requests the practitioner in charge of tea to post it on the left-hand wall of the outer practice hall, and, properly attired, visits the abbot's office and invites him to the serving of tea. The practitioners are further informed of the serving of tea by signboards posted at each of the quarters. The training official requests the alms-serving master beforehand to prepare hot water and arrange the teabowls, while the treasury official provides tea and candles. After the noon meal, while the practitioners remain in their seats, the serving of tea begins.

The new training official enters the hall, burns incense, and performs the serving of tea.

(The remaining propriety is identical with that of the first day of each month and mid-month day.)

Format of the Signboard for the Serving of Tea

Such-and-such quarters have become congested, and it is not possible for all to be seated for the serving. Today, therefore, the serving of tea will be conducted at the practice hall after the noon meal. May all practitioners grant their presence with compassion.

Date and month

Respectfully prepared
by So-and-so

Format of the Envelope

[Addressed with the title "Zen Masters"]

Officials of This Temple
Renowned Elders of the Zen World
Local Practice Associates
Honorable Practice Hall Practitioners

VIII. The Ceremonial Incense Offering by the Dual Order Officials through the Proceeding of Pairs from the East and West Orders

In general, whenever the dual order officials are scheduled to offer incense in successive pairs from both orders, it is signaled by the sound of the cymbals. The director of practitioners' affairs first steps forward from his order to stand before the incense burner, turns around to face the audience, bows to the abbot, and burns incense on his behalf. (The abbot's assistant presents him an incense case.) Next, with a bow, he requests officials of both orders to burn incense. Thereupon, two officials from both groups form a pair by stepping out from their positions, turn toward the abbot, and bow in unison. (This is called "to borrow incense" [*jiexiang*].) The two officials proceed to the incense burner and burn incense.

(If it is in the commemorative occasion of the imperial birth-day or the memorial rites for the Buddha and patriarchs, as well as for the master of the Dharma lineage, there is no need for the bows symbolizing "to borrow incense." If the west-hall ranking official is present in the east order position, he is obliged to offer incense prior to the dual order officials. It is not correct, however, to say that the primary seat official who once held a position of abbot should also burn incense before the dual order officials. He should form a pair with the administrative head of the east order.)

End of Chapter VI: The Dual Order Offices

Chapter VII

The Practitioners of the Zen Community

I. Preface to the Chapter

Just as the bottomless ocean [at the eastern end of the earth] sustains all the water flowing into it, and the vast forest of *deng* trees has evolved [from a single discarded cane], the practitioners' community comes into being through the gathering together of multitudes. Today, the monastic residents gathered together in a large temple have multiplied to as many as hundreds or a thousand in number. [Providing their provisions] exhausts the temple's granary, and burning wood for cooking has stripped the mountainside into a barren wasteland. Such is the result of a large-scale community. Moreover, coming from all directions, they gather together as if returning to [their own homelands,] as if already owning the place. But for what reason?

Presumably, the Buddha's sole reason was to rescue ordinary people who suffer from the cycle of life and death, transmigrating through the three levels of existence, and thus he singlemindedly sought to clarify the way of phenomenal configuration, understand 1136c the true nature of psychophysical elements (*dharmas*), and thus realized the highest state of wondrous enlightenment. Accordingly, the Buddha enabled all sentient beings, human and non-human, to participate in his realization of the highest good and taught them how to become one like himself. Because of this, people have served the Buddha's disciples just as they served the [original] master.

225

Jostling one another with their shoulders and following toe to heel, practitioners quite frequently arrive, yet people continue to serve them, concerned only that their service might not be sufficient. Despite the numbers of resident practitioners, [lay supporters] rarely fall into indolence. If this were not the case, many a legal dispute would have been raised over a square foot of land or a peck of grain. How could it be otherwise, other than foolishness on their part, that [the people] donate plots of land for us to expand our residential quarters, or that they sacrifice their suppers in order to feed more of us? We practitioners are fed here and reside here. But for what reason? Indeed, for what reason?

End of Fascicle Four

Fascicle Five

Chapter VII (*continued*)

II. The Proceedings for the Rite of *Śrāmaṇera* Ordination

1. Ordination Procedure: The Rite of Head-shaving and Receiving the Precepts under Oath

In general, a novice attendant must first obtain his ordination permit (*dudie*). He then takes the certificate and a crepe-wrapped board to the sponsoring master (*upādhyāya; benshi;* here identical with the abbot), and also to the dual order officials for their review. At each office he burns incense and performs three prostrations. After the date of ordination has been set, he prepares [a set of] offerings and prepares himself for the rite of head-shaving (*titou*).

(The ancient Vinaya prescribed that [the ordination place was to be set up in] a seven-foot-square area enclosed with screens, sprinkled with scented water, and where seats were arranged. Today, however, [the ordination place] is usually set up in the Buddha hall facing the Buddha statue, or the seats are arranged to face each other. If the [ordination is to take place] in the Dharma hall, a Buddha image, fragrant flowers, incense, and candles should be placed there in due accordance with the tradition. Now, the following section refers to the case of the event taking place in the practice hall, simply because it is more convenient to accommodate seating space for a larger number of practitioners.)

The candidates for the rite of ordination must first request the director of practitioners' affairs to determine: 1) the ordination master (*jieshi*), 2) the master of ceremonial chanting (*zuofansheli*), and 3) the master of ceremonial instruction (*yinqingsheli*). The evening before the day of ordination, the candidates have their heads shaved; a small knot of hair is left on the top of the head. (This small topknot is called *cūḍā* in Sanskrit and *zhouluo* in Chinese, meaning "a little knot.")

A seat and table for the ordination master should be placed symmetrically a little distance away from the abbot's seat (here the abbot serves as preceptor), and on the table are incense, candles, a portable incense burner, and a pair of sound-making ferrules (*jiechi*). The chair and table of the master of ceremonial chanting should be placed to the right of the guardian bodhisattva's altar, opposite the seat of the ordination master. On this table there should be a stand-set bell (*qing*). The robe (*kaṣāya; jiasha*), the garment (*zhiduo*), and the ordination certificate [of each candidate] are placed on the table before the altar of the guardian bodhisattva.

The master of ceremonial instruction escorts the candidate novices, whose heads have been shaved, from the novice attendants' hall as cymbals are played [to accompany the procession]. The group stops at the shrine of local spirits, the patriarchs' hall, and the Buddha hall to offer incense and perform three prostrations at each place. On coming to the practice hall, they stand in line outside. The hall bell is tolled to assemble the practitioners. The west order training officials and the abbot enter the hall, one after another. Only then do the ordination master and the other two ceremonial masters enter the hall, where they perform three prostrations with fully opened sitting cloth before the altar of the guardian bodhisattva and then take their respective places. At the same time, the practitioners settle themselves in meditation posture. The master of ceremonial instruction steps toward the ordination master and performs three prostrations with fully opened sitting cloth, then kneels with his right knee on the ground and his palms joined together. The ordination master enquires of him, "Have all the practitioners assembled?"

1137a

The ceremonial master replies, "Yes, they have assembled, sir."

The ordination master asks, "Are all the practitioners in accord and harmonious?"

The ceremonial master replies, "Yes, they are, sir."

The ordination master asks, "Being settled in full accord, what do they expect to accomplish?"

The ceremonial master replies, "To participate in the rite of ordination for the candidate novices who have shaved their heads and received the precepts under oath, sir."

The ordination master concludes, "So be it."

Thereupon, the master of ceremonial instruction folds his sitting cloth and escorts the novices who are to receive the rite of head-shaving into the hall, while ringing his hand-bell.

The novices perform three prostrations toward the altar of the guardian bodhisattva, three prostrations before the ordination master, and then kneel. Thereupon, the master of ceremonial chanting rings the large standing bell (*daqing*) and recites:

> Endowed with the fivefold supernatural powers, the divine and immortal person (i.e., the Buddha) restrained those who have no sense of remorse or shame for the sake of those who strived for moral perfection motivated upon remorse and shame. The Perfected One (*rulai*) thus established the rules of injunction and expounded them every half-month in order to explain the benefit of those injunctions. Veneration to all the Buddhas with a deep bow.

Having finished reciting this passage, the master of ceremonial chanting again speaks, asking: "What is Brahmā?"

(What is the meaning of this sacred scripture? The ultimate goal is the yonder shore. May the Buddha open the subtle and secret Way and preach it widely to the people of the world.)

Having completed his recitation, he once again speaks to the ordination master, requesting:

> May your reverence exhort for the sake of those who have shaved their heads and are ready to receive the precepts under oath.

The master rises from his seat and all the practitioners stand in unison after him. He then takes up the portable incense burner and says:

> There is the incense of the moral precepts (*śīla*), the incense of meditative concentration (*samādhi*), the incense of transcendent insight (*prajñā*), the incense of the resulting state of liberation (*vimokṣa*), and the incense of the insight that recognizes the realization of this state of liberation (*vimukti-jñāna-darśana*), all of which, as one, permeate the entire world just as light illuminates from beyond the horizon of the clouds. It is offered to the immeasurable numbers of Buddhas in all directions, to the immeasurable numbers of Dharmas in all directions, and to the immeasurable numbers of Sanghas in all directions. It perfumes the senses of seeing, hearing, and so on and transforms them into ultimate quiescence. May all sentient beings also accomplish this quiescence as well.
>
> Therefore, this morning, at the moment of inaugurating the meritorious rite of head-shaving and the conferment of the precepts, I shall pray, foremost, for the imperial throne to enjoy an everlasting longevity of ten thousand years and that his ministers and subjects live a long life of a thousand years; for the sake of universal peace to prevail throughout the land and for the Dharma wheel to perpetually turn; for the temple buildings and the grounds to increase their majestic influence and protect the Dharma and the residents of the temple by warding off troubles; for the patron donors of all regions to be adorned with fortune and wisdom; for those who have been associated with this temple to be assured of physical and mental health and peace; for the aged teachers and parents to accumulate good karma ever higher in the practice of virtues; for

those who undergo the rite of head-shaving to have no difficult obstacles in their course of practice; for those who suffer in the three hellish realms of existence and in the eight calamitous conditions to be totally liberated from the cycle of suffering; and for those who abide in the nine desirable states of existence and those who are born of the four different modes to without fail reach the far shore.

I now request the practitioners to intone this prayer along with me: "Veneration to the Luminous Pure Dharma Body Vairocana Buddha, and so on."

(The master and practitioners complete the prayer of calling the ten sacred names of the Buddhas.)

When the practitioners take their seats again, the master of ceremonial instruction takes the portable incense burner and instructs the candidate novices, saying:

You should request the master to grant you the rite of ordination in your own words. If you cannot do so, follow along reciting the words as I say them. In general, whenever "So-and-so" appears, you should replace it with your own name.

The master of ceremonial instruction then recites the passage, [as the novices follow it]:

Venerable (name of the ordination master), may you record my request in your mind. I, So-and-so novice, now request you to be the master on my behalf to officiate in the rite of head-shaving and receiving the precepts. Venerable, I pray, as my master, may you officiate in the rite of having my head shaved and receiving the precepts. As I depend on your officiating, I may be able to accomplish the rite of head-shaving and receiving the precepts. May your compassion be with me.

The entire group of candidate novices performs a prostration after the last passage, "May your compassion be with me"; they repeat this passage for a second time and perform a second prostration, and again repeat the passage and perform a third prostration. They then kneel before the master, left knee up and right one down, with palms joined together.

The ordination master then says:

> O novices, sons of good families... (at this, the novice candidates murmur a response), the fountainhead of the mind is totally quiescent and the ocean of *dharmas* is profoundly deep. Whoever is astray in it will forever sink down and be lost, whereas whoever is enlightened of it will realize liberation outright. If one wishes to propagate the supreme path to others, there is no better way than that of renunciation. The path is vast and wide like empty space; it is clean and pure like the moon brightly shining. When one's practice of the path is assisted by proper conditions, such as authorized with the rules of the precepts, the goal of the path is not really far distant because such conditions initially help each one overcome distracting thoughts and eventually realize the state of transcendence. It was for this reason that Śākyamuni Buddha, the Great Sage, renounced his princely status together with his golden wheel, left the palace during the night, took off his precious garment of universal rule, and cut off his hair in the forest. Even as a bird made a nest upon his uncombed hair and a spider built its web between his eyebrows, he [continued to] practice [the state of] quiescence, experienced the everlasting truth, severed obstructive impurity, and thereby realized supreme enlightenment.
>
> No Buddha of the three periods [of past, present, and future] ever has taught or will teach that a layperson can realize the ultimate path. Nor could any of the past patriarchs, were they engaged in an ordinary life of impurity, ever have succeeded in delivering others. Therefore, [the state of ultimate realization] was directly transmitted from one Buddha to another only through their own hands, and the patriarchs transmit it only through patriarchs. Free from

1137b

232

secular entanglements, they have rightly become the vessel of the Dharma transmission. Hence, no heavenly demon could do anything but look on with folded arms and the heretics were eventually converted, and whosoever renounced his secular life and received ordination could discharge the four kinds of indebtedness toward his respective benefactors (i.e., rulers, parents, teachers and associates, and patron donors) and carry out his task of delivering sentient beings from suffering to liberation. Thus, it is said that as one transmigrates through the three worlds, one cannot discard the bond of indebtedness and attachment nor can one enter into the state of transcendence unless he does it through decisively severing himself from indebtedness. Whoever accomplishes this, however, is truly one who pays his indebtedness. After renunciation, one's conduct ought to be beyond the ordinary sense of obligation, subject neither to worshiping kings and rulers nor to worshiping one's parents.

[Now] you may leave this place for a short while to reflect upon your indebtedness to the rulers of the land as well as upon the parental virtue by which you have been brought up. With utmost earnestness, you should worship [your rulers and parents] and convey your farewell to them, as you may not repeat this again after the moment of renunciation.

2. The Rite of Head-shaving and Receiving the Precepts under Oath

The candidate novices perform a prostration to express their thanks. The master of ceremonial instruction signals by ringing his handbell and leads them out of the hall. Facing north, the novices in unison perform three prostrations to express thanks to the ruler of the land and another three prostrations to express thanks to their parents. Immediately, they change into their practitioners' garments, return to the altar of the guardian bodhisattva, and perform three prostrations. They then turn toward the ordination master, perform a prostration and kneel before him, left knee up and right one down, with palms joined together.

The ordination master takes up a pitcher, sprinkles water on the head [of each candidate], moistening the hair with his finger, and shaves it off with a knife. After this he calls for the practitioners to chant the verse in praise of renunciation in unison:

> Well done, men of courage.
> You have thoroughly understood that the world is
>   impermanent.
> Renouncing this secular world, you set your course toward
>   the goal of nirvana;
> It is most extraordinary and inconceivable!

The verse is chanted three times, and the candidates step back and perform a prostration toward the master. Thereupon, the master of instruction leads them to before the sponsoring master (*upādhyāya;* in this case, the abbot) and all kneel before him, left knee up and right one down, with their palms joined together. The master takes up a knife and says:

> The last remaining knot of hair is called *cūḍā* and can be cut off only by the sponsoring master of the candidate novices. I shall now remove the knot of hair on your behalf. Do you allow me to do so?

After the candidate novices answer, "Yes, sir," the master speaks a word of insight to commemorate the event and recites the verse of head-shaving:

> Though his original appearance has changed, he is resolute
>   in upholding his goal.
> Severing himself from attachment and leaving his
>   relations,
> He is intent upon propagation of the holy path.
> May he hold fast his resolution to help all people toward
>   deliverance.

Three times the master chants the verse as the practitioners follow in unison. The candidates perform three prostrations toward the master and kneel before him, left knee up and right one down, with palms joined together. The master, holding up the *kaṣāya* robes in his hand and uttering a word of insight, places a [folded] robe on the head of each candidate, and intones the verses to be recited when donning the robe:

> How great is the robe that embodies liberation,
> The robe that is a formless field of merit!
> Wearing it and upholding the precepts authorized by the
>   Tathāgata,
> I am determined to assist all sentient beings to reach
>   nirvana as widely as I can.

This is repeated three times, with the practitioners following in unison. At the moment the chanting is over, the candidate novices, wearing the robe, perform three prostrations toward the sponsoring master, toward the image of the guardian bodhisattva, and then to the ordination master and immediately kneel before him, left knee up and right one down, with palms joined together.

The ordination master says:

> O sons of good families, the Dharma is like a great ocean: the more you dive into its depths, the deeper it becomes. You have already renounced the secular world; hence, you must first accept the threefold refuge (*sangui*) and the five precepts (*pañcaśīla; wujie*). Qualified by these steps, you may be allowed to approach and join the authentic sangha. Next, you are obliged to accept the ten *śrāmaṇera* precepts (*śrāmaṇera-saṃvara; shamishijie*), fit for the life of novices, through which you are entitled to share in whatever benefit, material or spiritual, belongs to the sangha. The crucial matter is single-minded sincerity and never being of inattentive, lax nature. Now I shall call for the presence of the Three Treasures on your behalf so that they may witness our ceremonial conduct.

The ordination master then takes up the portable incense burner to offer incense and continues:

> I pray with my mind in full concentration and call for the boundless Buddha treasure. May those enlightened ones who have accomplished the ten final stages (*daśabhūmi; shidi*) and the three tenfold preliminary stages of the bodhisattva as prescribed in the sacred scriptures brought back from the ocean storehouse (i.e., the Mahayana sutras, such as the *Flower Ornament Sutra,* etc.), those who have attained the five saintly fruits of discipleship (*pañca-phalāni; wuguo*) and those who are advancing toward each of the four higher saintly states (*catvāraḥ pratipannāḥ; sixiang*), may they all descend to manifest themselves in response to my prayer and witness the conduct of the following rites.

1137c

After repeating this prayer three times, the ordination master then says:

> O sons of good families, if you wish to have the precepts confirmed upon you, you must first repent and be cleansed of your faults and flaws, just as cloth must be washed before it is dyed. Now, you must repent with utmost sincerity by following along with my recitation of the verse of repentance:

> Whatever evil karma I have committed in my past lives,
> Rooted in beginningless forces of desire, hatred, and delusion,
> All a result of my acts of body, speech, and mind,
> I now repent of all of it completely, without remainder.

The master repeats the verse three times as the practitioners follow in unison, and the candidate novices perform three prostrations. They then kneel before the master, left knee up and right one down, with their palms joined together.

The ordination master says:

> O sons of good families, the Dharma has already cleansed your actions (karmas) of body, speech, and mind. You are

now obliged to take refuge in the Buddha, Dharma, and Sangha.

He then immediately calls for the recitation of the set of ceremonial phrases for conversion:

> I take refuge in the Buddha,
> I take refuge in the Dharma,
> I take refuge in the Sangha.
> I take refuge in the Buddha, the most honorable, highest
>   being [among all humans].
> I take refuge in the Dharma, the most honorable [truth]
>   that transcends the profane.
> I take refuge in the Sangha, the most honorable among all
>   human assemblies.

> Now, having already taken refuge in the Buddha, Dharma,
> and Sangha, I declare that the Perfected One (Tathāgata)
> who realized the ultimate truth and supreme enlightenment
> is my master, and I now take refuge in him. From this moment
> onward, I call the Buddha my teacher and will not take refuge
> in any other evil, wrong teachers and heretics. May the
> Buddha's compassion be upon us.

The candidates for ordination silently concentrate on these passages while the practitioners recite them along with the ordination master.

(From the initial passage, "I take refuge in the Buddha," to the last passage, "May the Buddha's compassion be upon us," the entire set of verses must be repeated three times; however, the last passage, "May the Buddha's compassion be upon us," is to be repeated twice at the end of the second recitation of the verses and three times at the end of the third recitation.)

At the end of each recitation, the candidates for ordination perform one, two, and three prostrations, respectively, after which they once again kneel before the master, left knee up and right one down, with palms joined together. The ordination master says:

O sons of good families, you have already forsaken the evil teaching and taken refuge in the right teaching. The efficacy of the [moral and religious] norms of action has already permeated the whole of your being. If you wish to know the rules of the precepts and maintain them, you must vow to keep the set of five rules:

As long as I live (literally, "till the end of my body and life"),
I will not commit an act of killing,
I will not commit an act of stealing,
I will not commit an act of sexual indulgence,
I will not commit an act of lying,
I will not commit an act of becoming intoxicated.

The ordination master then says: "These are the five rules of the [Buddha's] precepts, with which you must comply. Answer me: Will you uphold these rules?"

The candidates answer, "Yes, we will, sir."

The ordination master continues, "The foregoing five member rules of the precepts must not be violated separately or all together. Answer me again: Will you keep these rules of the precepts?"

The candidates again respond, "Yes, we will, sir."

"So be it," completes the master.

Thereupon the candidates for ordination perform three prostrations and again kneel before him, left knee up and right one down, with palms joined together. The ordination master says:

O sons of good families, the foregoing set of five rules is the initial step to enter the path of enlightenment and the foremost cause to escape from the cycle of the threefold evil courses of life. Next, you must accept the ten rules of the precepts prescribed for aspiring novices. Whoever is committed to these rules in external form is called "one who aspires to become a Buddhist disciple" (śrāmaṇera; qince). Whoever observes these rules under his master's guidance and receives the same benefit from the sangha is an authenticated novice worthy of becoming a practitioner. [Therefore,] you are most obliged to accept the ten rules of the precepts:

As long as I live, I will not commit an act of killing,
I will not commit an act of stealing,
I will not commit an act of sexual intercourse,
I will not commit an act of lying,
I will not commit an act of drinking,
I will not rest or sleep on a high and wide bed,
I will not wear hair ornaments, necklaces, anointments, or
    perfume,
I will not watch a performance of theatrical singing and
    dancing,
I will not carry any gold, silver, coins, or precious stones,
I will not partake of food at any unauthorized time.

1138a

The foregoing ten rules of [moral and religious] purity must not be violated individually or communally. Answer me: Will you maintain the rules of the precepts?

The candidates for ordination reply, "Yes, we will."
"So be it," completes the master.
The novices then perform three prostrations and once again kneel, left knee up and right one down, with palms joined together.
The master of ordination again speaks:

O sons of good families, having now committed yourselves to the foregoing precepts under oath, you must uphold them reverentially in practice. Commit no transgression. The precepts and disciplines you have acquired are dedicated to the Three Buddhist Treasures, and they become seeds sown in the rich field of merit. You must act in accordance with the teachings and instructions as guided by your respective masters. You must always keep your mind respectful toward those who rank higher, middle, or lower in their respective places (in the sangha) and exert effort in the practice of the path, so that you may discharge your indebtedness to your parents. Refrain from wearing colorful clothes, as clothes are only for the purpose of covering the body. Do not be indulgent in seeking tasty food, the purpose of which is only to sustain your life. Refrain from wearing hair ornaments, perfume, make-up, and so on. Nor should you watch or listen to anything attractive or seductive in visual or auditory forms. Speak with dignity and correctly. Refrain from speaking of others' faults. If people are in a dispute, you must talk to each party and encourage them to reconcile. There should be a normative distinction between men and women. No vegetation should be destroyed at random. You should not befriend anyone who is unwise, nor should you venerate anyone who is not holy. Keep with you at all times the standard garments and a single almsbowl. You should not take food other than at the prescribed time, nor should you speak unless it is proper and appropriate. Be diligent in finding meaning, and study the past to know new things. When sitting, keep yourself in a state of meditation. When standing, occupy yourself with chanting sacred scriptures. You must close up the three evil paths but open the gate that leads to nirvana. Placing yourself among those engaged in practice, you must enhance your right actions (karma) and your mind of enlightenment (*bodhicitta*) and never retrogress. Observe things through the insight of *prajñā* for the distant future with clarity, help sentient beings in all spheres of existence, and pray for their realization of supreme enlightenment. If you apply your mind in these ways, you are a true disciple of the Buddha.

The novices perform three prostrations to the ordination master and again kneel, left knee up and right one down, with palms joined together. The master stands, burns incense with the portable incense burner, and intones the following invocation of merit transference:

The merit accrued from the foregoing rites of head-shaving

and receiving the precepts under oath is dedicated to the dragon (*nāga*) and heavenly (*deva*) protectors of the Dharma, the supernatural gods presiding over the temple buildings. May their majestic spirits be enhanced, secure the sangha and protect the Dharma. May the abbot of the temple always be the [excellent] ferry or bridge to help people across the ocean of suffering. May the management officials become the pillar and foundation stones of the religious tradition for a long time to come. May the practitioners who have gathered in this hall equally ride the ship of *prajñā* insight. May the ordained novices equally reach the yonder shore of enlightenment, discharge all of the four kinds of indebtedness, and deliver people who transmigrate through the three realms of existence. May all sentient beings of the Dharma world equally realize the ultimate knowledge (i.e., omniscience, *sarvajña*).

Veneration to all Buddhas, bodhisattvas, *mahāsattvas*, and Mahāprajñāpāramitā presiding in the ten directions and the three times. 1138b

On completion of this recitation, the ordination master takes his seat.

The master of ceremonial chanting rings the standing bell and recites the following verses in praise of the Buddha:

> Abiding in this world like pure extended space,
> Like a lotus that is untouched by water;
> Yet the purity of [the Buddha's] mind even surpasses it,
> I salute him with a deep bow, the Highest and Most
>   Honorable One.
>
> I have taken refuge in the Buddha. I am determined to
> realize enlightenment and uphold my mind to strive for
> the path, without ever retrogressing.
>
> I have taken refuge in the Dharma. I am determined to
> realize omniscience and acquire the great gate of transcendent concentration.

I have taken refuge in the sangha. I am determined to resolve disputes so as to enter together with others the ocean of harmonious unity.

The merit accrued from the foregoing rites of head-shaving and receiving the precepts under oath is the limitless, excellent, good cause that we shall dedicate to those innumerable other worlds to venerate those holy beings who preside there.

At the moment when the master of ceremonial chanting begins the verses praising the Buddha, with the line, "Abiding in this world like pure extended space," the master of ceremonial instruction immediately rings his hand-bell to signal the ordained novices to perform three prostrations before the ordination master. They then turn toward the guardian bodhisattva's altar and again perform three prostrations. The master of ceremonial instruction then bows and leads the ordained novices to the outer hall, where they wait at the lower-ranking (left-hand) section. The ordination master and the other two masters perform three prostrations with fully opened sitting cloth before the altar of the guardian bodhisattva and leave the hall. When the practice hall attendant tolls the hall bell three times, the abbot leaves the hall, and the practitioners descend from their sitting platforms.

3. Post-ceremonial Activities

The primary seat official leads the practitioners to the abbot's office in order to express congratulation. If there are a great number of practitioners, the abbot must receive their congratulations at the Dharma hall, where the guest master's attendant has beforehand set up an area with incense, candles, an incense burner, flower vases, a screen, and a chair. First, the ordination master and the other two masters perform the formality of two prostrations with opened sitting cloth and three prostrations with unopened sitting cloth. At the first opening of the sitting cloth, they say:

As assigned, we have completed the rite of ordination, conferring the precepts to the newly ordained novices. Though we tried hard, due to our lack of cultivation in matters of propriety we fear that it may have taken much longer than the venerable expected. We cannot help but feel extremely embarrassed, sir.

The abbot replies:

Since the ceremony was about the young novices' rite of head-shaving, I know how much effort you have exercised to complete it successfully.

At the second opening of the sitting cloth, they enquire after the abbot's well-being, and then complete the three prostrations with unopened sitting cloth. The abbot responds with a single prostration.

Next, the primary seat official and the practitioners step forward to burn incense and perform prostrations, some opening their sitting cloths, some not, and some are excused from either formality. Next, the abbot's official assistant and disciples burn incense and perform three prostrations with fully opened sitting cloth, proceed forward without folding up their sitting cloths, and express congratulation to the master, saying:

The candidate novices have successfully undergone the rite of ordination, witnessed by the participant practitioners. We are all delighted and cannot help rejoicing together in this supreme occasion, sir.

Once again they perform three prostrations and proceed forward to enquire of the abbot's well-being. They then perform another three prostrations and fold up their sitting cloths. Next, the newly ordained novices burn incense and perform three prostrations with fully opened sitting cloth, proceed forward without folding up their sitting cloths, and say:

So-and-so and others have been allowed to fully receive
your reverend's tradition and with good fortune have been
authorized to wear the *kaṣāya* robe. Thus, freed from the toil
of worldly matters, we are able to sever ourselves from the
net of attachment. We cannot help feeling profoundly grateful, sir.

Once again they perform three prostrations, step forward, and
say:

On this day and this auspicious moment, we respectfully wish
that all is well and felicitous with the abbot, master of the
temple, who sponsored our ordination.

Thereupon they perform another three prostrations and fold
up their sitting cloths.

[After this,] the abbot makes a round through the practitioners' quarters to return his thanks, while the newly ordained novices
visit each of the office quarters to express their gratitude. They
settle into the novice quarters and await another occasion when
they will be authorized to ascend the Dharma platform to receive
the precepts of the Mahayana tradition. The word of thanks to be
expressed by the newly ordained novices is as follows:

So-and-so and others have been authorized to receive the initial rules of the precepts, and thereby we have been placed
at the beginning rank of the practitioners despite our meager qualifications. We are most grateful for the protection
and assistance bestowed upon us.

The abbot answers:

In some of your past lives you may have been assured of completing the rite of receiving the precepts, as you have now
accomplished this. By remaining steadfast with them and
holding fast to your vow, you must exert effort in assisting
the teaching of our religion.

4. The Newly Ordained Novices
Join the Practice Hall

After completing the rite of ordination and the conferment of the
śrāmaṇera precepts, the newly ordained novices notify the abbot
of the date on which they wish to take the next step of joining the
life of the practitioners in the practice hall. Next, they report the
date to both the primary seat official and the director of practitioners' affairs. On the appointed day, after the moment when the
director strikes [the octagonal wooden post] with the [mallet] to
signal completion of the first serving of rice gruel at the early
morning meal, the ceremonial leader escorts the newly ordained
novices into the hall, where they line up before the altar of the   1138c
guardian bodhisattva. After a bow and offering incense, they perform three prostrations with fully opened sitting cloth and, without folding up their sitting cloths, step forward and say:

> So-and-so and others have been granted permission to join
> the community of the practice hall. Today, we come to pres-
> ent ourselves here by following the honorable practitioners.
> We cannot help feeling a sense of humble hesitation.

They again perform three prostrations and say:

> On this day and at this auspicious moment, we respectfully
> wish that all is well and felicitous with the abbot, master of
> the temple, who sponsored our ordination, as well as the ven-
> erable primary seat official and all of the Zen masters.

Stepping back, they perform another three prostrations and
fold up their sitting cloths. Lining up before the abbot, they bow
in unison toward him, and turn to proceed on a round through the
hall, starting from the seat of the primary seat official. On reaching the outer hall, they return to mid-hall, bow to the guardian
bodhisattva's altar, and leave the hall. After that, they return to
the hall to conduct the rite of opening their assigned space in the
hall and chant along with the practitioners.

5. Ascent to the Platform to Receive the Mahayana Precepts under Oath

It is said that all the Buddhas of the past, present, and future realized the path through renouncing the secular world. All the patriarchs who transmitted the seal of the Buddha mind (*foxinyin*) through successive generations are, without exception, homeless mendicants (*śramaṇas* or *bhikṣus*). Because they strictly maintained the codes of the Vinaya discipline and prevailed well in the three worlds, it goes without saying that the vow to maintain the precepts and discipline is the prerequisite for the practice of Zen and for the pursuit of the path. Unless one dissociates oneself from transgression and prevents oneself from engaging in unethical conduct, how could anyone become a Buddha or a patriarch?

In order to receive the precepts under oath, a candidate should prepare three kinds of robes, an almsbowl, and new clean garments. If he has nothing new, he may substitute used ones which have been washed thoroughly and cleaned for the occasion of completing the rite of ascending the Dharma platform. Entering the elevated sitting platform area of the Dharma hall, he must concentrate on receiving the precepts under oath and refrain from diverting his attention elsewhere. Wearing the same attire as did the Buddha, upholding the same body of precepts and disciplines as did the Buddha, and enjoying the practical consequences as did the Buddha—all this is not at all a minor matter and must not be taken lightly. If someone uses another's robes and bowl on loan or lets someone else use his own, even though he may ascend the platform and receive the precepts under oath he has not really received them at all, and though he has become a practitioner in external form but has not been endowed with the precepts internally, he is thus like someone who has placed himself at an empty gate and eats up the donor's gifts for nothing. Those who have already received the precepts attributed to the path of *śrāvakas* (disciples of the Hinayana tradition) must receive the Mahayana precepts of the path of bodhisattvas. This is the gradual procedure to enter the religion.

6. Steadfast Adherence to the Precepts

After receiving the [sacramental conferment of] the precepts, one must be determined to uphold the rules at all times—even to the extent of being willing to die for the Dharma rather than live without it. One is obliged to know in detail the types of offenses, the methods of discharging them, and the methods of preventing them from arising. One should learn in detail what rules one ought to comply with and what offenses one ought to avoid through reading the *Vinaya in Four Divisions* (*Dharmaguptaka-vinaya; Sifenlü*) as to its detailed rules and offenses:

1. The four grave offenses or "defeats" (*pārājika; boluoyi*);

2. The thirteen offenses requiring temporary suspension from the sangha (*saṃghāvaśeṣa; sengqieposhisha*);

3. The two indeterminable offenses concerned with encountering the opposite sex (*aniyatau; buding*);

4. The thirty offenses of expiation requiring forfeiture (*naiḥsargikaḥ pāyattikā; nisagi*);

5. The ninety offenses requiring expiation (*pātayantika; boyiti*);

6. The four offenses requiring confession (*pratideśanīyāni; boluotisheni*);

7. The one hundred minor offenses concerned with the rules of training and conduct (*śaikṣakaraṇīya; zhongxue*);

8. The seven offenses concerned with the ways for settling legal disputes (*adhikaraṇaśamathā; miezheng*);

9. The ten grave offenses of the Mahayana precepts prescribed in the *Brahmajāla-sūtra* (*zhongjinjie*); and

10. The forty-eight minor offenses of the Mahayana precepts prescribed in the same sutra (*qingjie*).

In addition, one must read these sources and thereby become well informed about the offenses in detail, so as to know what a given case might be. One should not fall uncritically into mediocre notions but should be cautious by referring to the real words of the Buddha.

One must not partake of improper food (*buyingshi*). (There are three kinds: 1) alcohol, 2) spicy vegetables, and 3) animal flesh. Onions, leeks, garlic, scallions, coriander, and so on, are classified as the second spicy food, whereas various meats are classified as the last one. One should not partake of these kinds of food.)

Nor should one partake of any food at a restricted period of time (*bufeishishi*). (No food is permitted other than rice gruel at breakfast and rice at the midday meal. Practitioners ought not to partake of any food at any other time in compliance with the time restrictions.)

Monetary and sexual matters are a far more serious cause of misfortunes than poisonous snakes. One should most carefully stay away from them. It is important for Buddhist practitioners to think of sentient beings with compassion, just as one might feel about one's infant child, to match one's thought and words and speak truth with honesty, to read the Mahayana scriptures and nurture the strength of the vow of meritorious conduct. When one strives with one's vow to realize a degree of purity in upholding the precepts, the Buddha-Dharma manifests itself in that person of its own accord. If there is no sheepskin in one's possession, how is it possible to think of transmitting beautiful wool to anyone else? Therefore it is said in the sacred scripture that one must make an effort to keep one's precepts spotlessly clean as if protecting a bright pearl with all one's strength.

III. Necessary Articles Required for the Practice of the Path

When one wishes to enter the life of a Zen monastery or temple, he must aquire a set of necessary articles (literally, "tools," *daoju*) for pursuit of the path. It is said in the *Collection of Middle-length Discourses* (Madhyama Āgama; *Zhongahanjing*) that items that must be kept in one's possession or anything that helps in the practice of the path are called "tools for the path" as well as "tools for enhancing the good Dharma." In the *Sutra on the Bodhisattva Precepts* (*Bodhisattva-prātimokṣa-sūtra; Pusajiejing*) such necessary items are defined as "tools to help people and to accord with the Way."

1. Three Kinds of Robes

In general, there are three kinds of robes: 1) the outer robe (*saṃghāṭī; sengqieli*) [namely, the large robe (*dayi*)]; 2) the upper robe (*uttarāsaṃgha; yūduoluoseng*), [namely, the robe made of seven strips of cloth (*qitiao*)]; and 3) the inner robe (*antarvāsaka; antuohui*), [namely, the robe made of five strips of cloth (*wutiao*)]. (These are called "triple robes." Hence, it is wrong to call the robe made of seven strips of cloth, the undergarment (*pianshan*), and the loincloth (*qun*) together the "triple robes." The large robe is again of three kinds: 1) the greater one made of twenty-five, twenty-three, or twenty-one strips of cloth; 2) the medium one made of nineteen, seventeen, or fifteen strips of cloth, and 3) the lesser one made of thirteen, eleven, or nine strips of cloth.)

The origin of the "rice-paddy robe" (*tianyi*) is given in the *Mahāsaṃghika-vinaya* (*Mohesengqilü*). The Buddha is said to have stayed one day in front of Indra's rock cave [near the city of Rājagṛha], and observed that the rice field spread out below was neatly marked by ridges into precise patterns. Thus, he is said to have explained to Ānanda that the robes of the past Buddhas were all like that field, and thereupon suggested to him that his disciples should model their robes after the pattern. The *Record of the Rising Splendor of the Tradition (Zenghuiji)* gives an explanation as follows: The rice field demarcated by ridges holds water and nourishes good rice seedlings, which eventually nurture the human body and life. The Dharma robe as symbolized by the rice field is moistened by water which gives four kinds of benefits (i.e., boundless kindness, compassion, joy, and transcendence) and raises rice seedlings comprising three kinds of good results (i.e., freedom from greed, hatred, and delusion). Thus, the robe symbolized by the rice field supports the life of wisdom which abides in the Dharma body.

2. The Sitting Cloth

This item is called *niṣīdana* (*nishitan*) in Sanskrit and "a cloth on which one takes seat as he wishes" (*suizuoyi*) in Chinese. In the *Mūlasarvāstivāda-vinaya* (*Genbenpinaiye*), it is transliterated as "*nishidanna*" and translated in Tang Chinese as "*zuoju*," or "equipment for seating." According to the *Vinaya in Five Divisions* (*Mahīśāsaka-vinaya; Wufenlü*), it is "equipment" for protecting the body from the ground, keeping the robes as well as the monastic bedsheet from becoming soiled, and hence it is prescribed that "each monk should carry his own cloth for sitting." The *Mahāsaṃghika-vinaya* provides further information about the size of the cloth, as follows: its length should be twice the length of the Buddha's arm, and its width one and a half times [the length of the Buddha's arm]. (Since the length of the Buddha's arm is two feet four inches in our scale, the sitting cloth should be four feet eight inches by three feet six inches.)

3. The Undergarment

As prescribed for monks in the Vinaya discipline (*lüzhi*), there was only an ancient garment, the *saṃkakṣikā* (*sengqizhi*). (This is called, in translation, "a cloth that covers the upper arm and shoulder," and is also called "a cloth that covers the armpit.")

The size of this robe is long enough to cover the left upper arm and right-side armpit. Perhaps it was a custom in ancient India that this garment was overlapped by the other three robes. Zhudaozu said in the *Chronicle of the Wei Dynasty* (*Weilu*) that the court officials of the Wei did not consider it proper for Buddhist monks to keep their right shoulder and arm exposed, and thus a one-shoulder garment, called *piantan* ("one-sided shoulder cover"), was made which was then patched on to the regular *saṃkakṣikā*, [thus covering the whole upper torso]. Accordingly, this was called *pianshan*. (That the garment we have today is open in the back but connected at the collar is a legacy of this Wei court order.)

4. The Loincloth

According to the *Great Tang Dynasty Record of the Western Regions* (*Datangxiyuji*) [by Xuanzang], *nifuxie*[*na*]; (*nivāsana*) (here, *xie* is abbreviated from *sanggeqie*) was called in Tang Chinese *qun*. In other Vinaya translations, it is rendered as *niepanseng* or *nihuanseng*, or, meaning "inner garment" (*neiyi*), as *chuiyi*.

(The term *chui* meant in early times a boat or a round vessel in which to keep rice. It was called *chui* because the loincloth looks like such a vessel without its lid.)

5. The One-piece Garment

According to oral tradition, the priests of long ago felt that it was inconvenient that some predecessors had an undergarment but no loincloth while others had a loincloth but no undergarment. They were innovative in bringing about the present-day form of the one-piece garment by combining both into one. There was an episode in which Puhua, [a contemporary of Linji (d. 867)] begged for a one-piece garment made of wood [before he died]. Dayang (941–1027) left a pair of leather shoes and a one-piece garment [as an innovation for his disciples]. Hence, the garment in question was already in use [as long ago as the Tang].

6. The Almsbowl

This is called *boduoluo* (*pātra*) in Sanskrit and *yingliangqi* in Chinese, [meaning a vessel that can be used according to an individual's need as to quantity]. Here, *bo* is its shortened alternative. It is also called *boyu*, which is a compound of Chinese and Sanskrit syllables (i.e., *bo* for *pātra* and *yu*, which means "bowl" in Chinese]. The *Sutra of the Collection of the Original Acts of the Buddha* (*Buddhacaritasaṃgraha-sūtra; Fobenxingjijing*) tells of two merchants in northern India, Dilifu[suo] (Trapuṣa) and Balijia (Bhal- 1139b lika) by name, who one day offered the World-honored One almsfood made of wheat flour, butter, and honey. The World-honored

One recollected that the Buddhas of the past all invariably carried their respective bowls to receive alms, and wondered to himself what kind of receptacle he should use now in order to receive alms from the two merchants. At that moment, the four guardian gods of the heaven at once brought four golden vessels before him. The World-honored One, however, did not accept them, because no person who had renounced the world could keep such precious items. Thereupon, the guardian kings of the heavens tried to cause him to accept their gifts of four bowls, each set made of silver, glass, lapis lazuli, ruby, agate, and *juqu,* but the Buddha would not accept any of these.

In the meantime, Vaiśravaṇa, the guardian king of the northern heaven, spoke to the other three, saying: "As I recollect, a long time ago, the guardian generals of the blue sky brought us four stone-carved vessels that can be used to receive food. At that moment, a god, Vairocana by name, reminded them that they should not use these stone-carved bowls for receiving food but exclusively for offering alms to the Perfectly Enlightened One. In this period of ours, a perfected being (Tathāgata), Śākyamuni by name, has appeared in this world. It should be best that these four stone-carved vessels should be presented to that Tathāgata." As instructed, the guardian kings of the four corners of heaven presented the four stone-carved bowls to the Buddha. The World-honored One thought to himself that since these kings had given him the four bowls with genuine devotion, if he had accepted only one without accepting the other three, a sense of unfairness might result in the minds of the other three kings, creating an impression of partiality on his part. Thus he decided to accept all four and make a single bowl out of them by merging them into one. He stacked them one upon another on his left palm and compressed them from above with his right hand, thereby producing a single bowl with four corners for touching the mouth. Then, the World-honored One exhorted the listeners in the following verse:

> Meritorious conduct of my past lives produced many
> results,

Whereby the mind of compassion and purity has arisen
within me.
Because of this, the four guardian kings of the heavens,
Immaculate and steadfast, had come to offer me the bowl
I need.

7. The Staff Topped by Pewter Rings

This item is called *khakkhara* in Sanskrit and *xizhang,* or "a pewter-topped staff," in Chinese. According to the *Pewter Staff Sutra (De-daotichengxizhangjing),* the Buddha is said to have told his disciples that they should keep a staff topped by pewter because all the Buddhas of the past, present, and future have kept and will keep [such a staff]. The staff in question is also called a "wisdom staff" or "staff of virtue," because it symbolizes the source of insight and practice and their merit. Mahākāśyapa asked the Buddha, "Why does the cane have pewter rings on top?" The Buddha replied, "*Xi* ("pewter-top") symbolizes lightness. Relying on this staff, its holder can remove his defilements and escape from this triple world. *Xi* symbolizes insight. Because it helps its holder to realize wisdom and insight, *xi* symbolizes awakening. Because it awakens its holder to the ultimate nature of the triple world as suffering and empty, *xi* symbolizes separation. That is to say, its holder is to be freed from the five kinds of desires."

The pewter-topped staff equipped with two edges, each holding three rings, is said to have been produced by Kāśyapa Buddha, while a staff equipped with four edges holding twelve rings is said to have been innovated by Śākyamuni Buddha.

8. The Walking Stick

According to the *Vinaya in Ten Chapters,* the Buddha is said to have permitted his disciples to keep a walking stick (*zhuzhang*). The tip of this stick is protected by an iron point in order to make it durable. The same Vinaya scripture also says that the Buddha permitted the use of the stick for two reasons: 1) it aids the elderly of little physical strength; and 2) it helps the sick with a frail body.

9. The (Zen) Dusting Brush

According to the Vinaya scriptures, the disciples (*bhikṣus*) suffered from insects and hence were allowed to make dusting brushes (*fuzi*). According to the *Mahāsaṃghika-vinaya*, the Buddha is said to have permitted his disciples to make brushes out of thread, torn cloth, grass, and bark. But they were prohibited to use any brush made of animal hide, such as that of a cat, cow, or horse, as well as one decorated with a gold or silver handle.

10. The Prayer Beads

In the *Sage Mandala Sutra* (*Munimaṇḍala-sūtra**; *Mounimantuoluojing*) the prayer beads are called *bosaimo,* or *shuzhu* in the Liang Chinese dialect. They are "a tool that assists the concentration of the mind and the discipline of practice." In the *Soapberry Tree Sutra* (*Ariṣṭaka-sūtra**; *Muhuanzijing*), the following story is related:

> Once upon a time there was a ruler named Boliuli. He said to the Buddha, "Since my country is small and located in a remote region, I have always felt insecure. The Dharma storehouse is so deep and wide that it is impossible for a person to practice everything. Please, teach me the essentials of the Dharma."
>
> The Buddha replied, "If you want to annihilate your mental defilements, make a set of prayer beads by piercing a hole through one hundred and eight soapberry tree seeds, string them together with a thread, and carry this with you at all times. Recollect the names of the Three Treasures: '*Namo Buddha, Namo Dharma, Namo Sangha,*' and upon completing each repetition of this phrase, move one of the beads from one side of your finger to the other, and in this way you will

gradually reach one thousand times and even ten thousand times. And if you feel no mental and bodily disturbance, then you will be able to leave your life and be reborn in the Yāma Heaven, [which is filled with supreme light]. When you reach the number of one million times, you should be able to remove the one hundred and eight delusion-bound karmas and thereby realize the fruit of eternal bliss."

The king replied that he would practice as instructed.

11. The Water Jar

This is called *kuṇḍikā* (*junzhijia*) in Sanskrit, and *ping* ("jar" or "bottle") in Chinese. One ought to always keep a clean jar filled with water wherever one goes, to use for washing one's hands. According to Yijing's travelogue, *A Record of the Inner Law Sent Home from the South Seas,* two kinds of water pitchers (*kuṇḍi*) are recorded: one of earthenware, which holds drinking water, and a second made of either copper or iron, which holds water for washing.

12. The Water Filter

In the *Record of the Rising Splendor of the Tradition* it is said that although this is a small tool, the benefit it provides is exceedingly great because it protects lives. In China, however, Buddhist practitioners seldom carry such an item. The frequent use of this is also attested to in the Vinaya literature. According to the *Mūla-sarvāstivāda-vinaya,* the *One Hundred and One Formal Acts of Resolution* (*Genbenbaiyijiemo*) mentions five kinds of water filters (*lüshuinang*):

1. A square filter (*fangluo*). (This is made of silk cloth three by three feet or three by two feet, and usable in flexible sizes, smaller or larger, in different circumstances. The cloth must be made of the finest silk threads closely woven, so that it does not [let through] tiny insects. A [less closely] woven silk cloth or coarse hempcloth, if used, does not serve the purpose of protecting life.)

2. A jar for mendicancy, *faping* (i.e., *yinyangping,* "magic bottle").

3. A jar filter (*junchi*). (The mouth of this jar is covered with silk cloth, and one uses it by immersing it into flowing water with a rope and retrieving it when it is filled.)

4. A dipper filter (*zhuoshuiluo*).

5. A cloth filter (*yijiaoluo*). (*Yijiao* here does not mean a corner of the *kaṣāya* robe but simply a thickly woven silk cloth that is picked up by its corner. It is used by placing it over the mouth of a jar or over a bowl into which water is poured, thereby filtering the water.)

The Venerable Zongze, Cijiao Dashi (author of the *Monastic Regulations of the Zen Garden*) collected the sources about water filters from sutras and Vinaya texts and composed thirty-one verses on the subject. Because of the abundance of descriptions he did not record them all, but in the end concluded that the so-called filter cloth (*lüluo*) could not [produce an ample enough quantity of filtered water] for the use of a multitude of people.

In the first year of Chongning (1102), the Venerable Zongze built a large washbasin by the side of the well in front of the kitchen hall of Hongjiyuan Monastery. Above this basin, close to its upper edge, was set another smaller basin, from which water was made to drop through a passage on its corner through a filter cloth placed beneath. Even when [a large quantity of] water was poured into the upper basin [from buckets dipped in the well], no overflow occurred, and as many as five practitioners could easily wash their feet [at the same time]. A similar system was built for the rear room of the bath hall. It is essential for all monastic residents, practitioners as well as novice attendants, to use filtered water [in order to avoid injuring living beings], by setting up a filtering system in the lavatory. When the Venerable Zongze later on resided at Changlusi, he installed a similar water-filtering system at the side of each well in that temple, in more than twenty places.

Unless water is filtered at a temple at all times, the transgression [of "killing tiny insects" by the resident practitioners] comes to be the responsibility of the head of the temple. Therefore, it is earnestly hoped that effort be exercised toward the installation of water-filtering systems as widely as necessary.

13. The Precept Knife

In the *Outline of the History of Zen Practitioners,* it is said that a small knife, called a "moral preservation knife" (*jiedao*), is also a tool necessary for the practice of the path, because it symbolizes the severance of all evils.

1140a

IV. Traveling for Zen Practice and Training

1. The Traveling Pack

In earlier days, practitioners wore hats when traveling and carried within them scriptures, a tea set, and so on. Robes and garments were packed in two parcels, one carried in front and the other on the back. The certificate container (*zibutong*) and the precept knife were inserted in the parcels. Today, however, we use two pieces of indigo-colored cloth to pack the parcels. First, we use one of the cloth pieces to wrap garments and so on into a parcel and [this bundle] is then wrapped in oil paper. Next, the other piece is used to rewrap the parcel into a square package, then a small chain is placed around it, and a hook attached to the top. The ordination certificate is placed in a sack which is carried hanging around the neck in the front. The *kaṣāya* robe is tightly wrapped in a handkerchief and placed in a hip parcel which is carried on the lower torso, while socks and shoes are placed in a sack that is carried on the back. A walking stick is carried in the right hand, and when we meet other practitioners on the road, we hold our hands together, the right hand over the left [held at chest level] (*chashou*) to greet each other as we pass by. If one intends to stop over at a temple or monastery, upon reaching the gate he must take off his pack and hold it in his hands and enter the transients' quarters. At the resting place (*anxieju*), he unties the pack, removes his socks and shoes, washes his feet, changes his garment, and dons his *kaṣāya* robe before meeting the guest reception official.

2. Traveling for Zen Practice and Training

Bidding farewell to one's master and teacher, a Zen practitioner should travel afar in search of a renowned Zen master endowed with insight and practice [to ask for his instruction]. Upon finding such a master, the practitioner requests the temple to grant him residency.

(According to the Vinaya texts, *bhikṣu*s may stay wherever there is Dharma and food. They may also stay where there is Dharma but no food. They ought not, however, to stay where there is no Dharma even if there is food.)

According to the *Ancient Regulations,* when a practitioner arrived at a monastic temple, he first met with the guest reception official, and then visited the practice hall office to complete a ceremonial proceeding, thereby establishing his residency and securing an assigned space [in the practice hall] and a desk space for reading scriptures [in the practitioners' quarters]. Only after completing these procedures did he visit the office of the abbot's assistant to register his residency and pay his respects to the abbot through the propriety of veneration.

Today, however, when practitioners reach a certain monastery where they intend to visit the abbot or establish residency, they first go to the transient quarters. Choosing someone capable and well experienced in the Zen tradition as their ceremonial leader and donning proper attire, they visit the guest reception office as a group, wait to the right of the office entrance, and the cermonial leader conveys their interview request, announcing: "We, new arrivals, request an interview."

Thereupon, the guest reception official invites them into his office. The leader says:

On this day, we respectfully wish that the venerable Zen master and guest reception official enjoy every blessing in daily life. We have been aware for some time of your religious accomplishments, and now, having this opportunity to meet you, we are most grateful, sir.

The guest reception official replies:

It is very fortunate for this temple to receive each of the venerables coming from such a long distance.

The official bows, bids the visitors to sit, burns incense, serves tea, and briefly enquires about their careers in the tradition. After this, the visitors stand, give thanks for the tea, and return to the transient quarters, while the guest reception official pays a return visit to them. The ceremonial leader receives him, and when all in unison greet him, the guest reception official says:

Though this is a belated return, I wish that the venerables, honorable Zen masters, enjoy every blessing in daily life. I am especially obliged to thank you for the visit you made just a short while ago. I am most grateful, sirs.

The reply is:

The manner of decorum was already expressed at the time of our meeting. It was not necessary for the venerable to take the trouble to come down here.

The ceremonial leader sees the official off at the gateway as he leaves.

(i) The Visit to Honor and Venerate the Abbot

If the new arrivals wish to pay respect to and venerate the abbot, they must visit the office of the abbot's assistants after the evening session is completed to meet with the official assistant, where they exchange the same propriety as before. Rising after performing a prostration, the ceremonial leader says:

I, So-and-so, and others have come to pay our respect to and venerate the venerable master. We humbly request you to be of assistance in conveying our wish to the master.

The assistant official invites them to sit and enquires in detail about the purpose of their visit. [Through this questioning, he ascertains] whether the guests are from the same province as the abbot, whether they are related to him in the lineage of Dharma transmission, or whether they have held subordinate offices in other temples. He then says:

May the venerables withdraw for a time to your resting quarters and wait till I report to you, sirs.

At once, the assistant goes to the abbot and informs him of the guests' wish. If the request is granted, the assistant dispatches the guest master of the abbot's office to visit the practitioners the next morning, while the early morning bell is being tolled, to report to them that their meeting with the abbot will be arranged. If the abbot has no immediately available time to grant [their request for a meeting], the assistant must go by himself carrying a lantern to the guests at their resting place [that night], to return [the abbot's] greeting to them. He should assuage them with a reassuring word about their wish to meet the abbot.

(ii) The Propriety of the Interview Meeting

1140b The propriety of the meeting is to be held after the morning gruel at the reception hall. With the ceremonial leader as head, the guest practitioners assemble to wait for the abbot. When he is escorted by his assistant into the hall, the ceremonial leader steps forward and says:

May your reverence sit cross-legged.

He turns to the incense burner, offering incense with his left hand, and then steps back to perform the formal greeting [of two prostrations with opened sitting cloth and three prostrations with

unopened sitting cloth] in unison with the others. At the first opening [of the sitting cloth], he says:

> I, So-and-so, and the others have for some time heard that
> your reverence maintains high standards in the practice of
> the Way. We are most grateful today to have an opportunity
> to see your countenance.

At the second opening [of the sitting cloth], he says:

> Today, at the time of reverence, we wish that the venerable,
> master of the temple and great teacher enjoy every blessing
> in daily life.

The group then completes the greeting with three prostrations
with unopened sitting cloth. If anyone [among the guest prac-
tioners] has received his patriarchal succession from the abbot, he
must first say:

> I, So-and-so, and others have taken refuge in your compas-
> sion for a long time.

Burning incense and performing prostrations may be conducted
respectively. When all [the guest practitioners] take their seats, the
assistant official burns incense and serves tea, while the abbot
enquires of their home regions, their previous names, and the temples where they were in residence for the last summer retreat. Each
question must be answered with reference to actual facts, and one
should refrain from speaking too much. Rising from their seats, [the
guest practitioners] proceed to burn incense and express their thanks:

> It has been an important reception that the venerable has
> granted us. We are most grateful for it, sir.

The abbot sees them off. The ceremonial leader says:

> Our reverence to you, sir.

Subsequently, they visit the abbot's assistant's office to express
their thanks:

Arranging the meeting must have taken much effort, for which we are especially grateful.

When [the guest practitioners] return to the transient quarters, they line up outside the entrance on the lower-ranking side (i.e., the left of the entrance when facing it) to await the abbot's return visit. After greeting him with a bow in unison, they follow him into the quarters and greet him, saying:

Though it is a different moment, we respectfully wish once again that the venerable master, head of the temple, enjoy every blessing in daily life. No sooner have myself, So-and-so, and the others returned from greeting and venerating you as a group and individually than we have [already] received your courtesy return. We are most grateful for your presence once again.

The abbot replies:

Though the resting quarters may not be very convenient, I hope that you will be able to continue your stay.

The guest practitioners see the abbot off. The ceremonial leader moves to the higher-ranking side (i.e., the right side of the entrance when facing it) to receive and escort the abbot's assistant into the quarters. After greeting him in unison with the others, he says:

Though it is a different moment, we wish that the venerable assistant official, Zen master, enjoys every blessing in daily life. Though it was our duty to come together to venerate you at your quarters, on the contrary we are [now] receiving your second visit. We are most grateful for your courtesy.

The assistant official replies:

It is fortunate for this temple to have received your visit as honorable guests traveling from such a long distance. We only regret very much that we have not been able to express our thankfulness earlier to you, sirs.

Nowadays, many of those who travel for training and learning do not stay in the transient quarters (*danguo*[*liao*]). Wherever they go they try to stay at the resident quarters of a temple official by finding someone who comes from the same native province as them. The standard of conduct of earlier days is no longer followed. When the abbot receives a renowned guest visitor, he should escort him afterward to the guest quarters to express his thanks. When a senior practitioner visits the abbot, he is obliged to wait at the lower left part of the Dharma hall for the abbot's arrival, so that the abbot may be excused from returning the propriety to the guest. Moreover, the abbots of the five major monastic establishments are not required to make a return visit to express such propriety.

Between breakfast and the noon meal, the guests are invited to [partake of] refreshments, and that evening to a special serving of sweet hot water; the guests must wear their robes on this occasion. The abbot receives them and escorts them into [the reception hall]. After burning incense and expressing a general greeting concerning the weather, they take their seats, and the practitioner assistant invites them to drink sweet hot water. After drinking, they rise from their seats, proceed to the incense burner, and give thanks for the serving of sweet hot water. They must perform the formality of two prostrations with opened sitting cloth and three prostrations with unopened sitting cloth. They then [immediately] take off their robes and take their seats at the evening meal table. If the abbot has no free time, he must ask a training official to take his place in sharing the meal with [the guests]. When the abbot is in attendance he must burn incense, and if he participates in the serving of sweet hot water, he must perform the utmost propriety for the occasion. Next morning, after the morning gruel, the guests are invited to a tea reception. With the ceremonial leader at the head, they stand in line before the reception hall to wait for the abbot's arrival. When he approaches, they step forward, bow in unison, and say:

> After the duration of an overnight stay, we respectfully wish that the venerable master, head of the temple, enjoy every

blessing in his daily life. I, So-and-so, and the others have been given a favorable reception and we are most grateful.

The guests then take their seats, the abbot's assistant burns incense, and they drink tea. After [the tea reception] is over, the guests stand and go before the incense burner to perform the formality of two prostrations with opened sitting cloth and three prostrations with unopened sitting cloth. At the first opening [of the sitting cloth], they say:

I, So-and-so, and others have enjoyed the warm tea serving. We especially express our appreciation for this occasion, and we are most grateful.

At the second opening [of the sitting cloth], they say:

On this day and at this respectful moment, we wish that the venerable master, head of the temple, enjoy every blessing in daily life.

Then, stepping back, they perform three prostrations with unopened sitting cloth. The abbot sees them off, following after them for two or three steps.

(iii) Establishing Residency

In the case of visiting practitioners wishing to establish residency, the ceremonial leader, representing the group, approaches the abbot and says:

I, So-and-so, and the others, consider the matter of life and death to be of prime importance and are concerned with the nature of impermanence and the swiftness of change. Because we have heard of for some time the high standards the venerable holds in the practice of the path, we have come to join your community. We earnestly entreat the venerable master to accept our request with compassion.

After saying this, without waiting for an answer of "Yes" or "No," [the guest practitioners] immediately perform a prostration with unopened sitting cloth and say:

We thank you for accepting our request for residency.

The abbot is obliged to grant residency to the ceremonial leader at once. The remaining guest practitioners, however, may directly petition the abbot to obtain his permission, approaching him at any time or place, morning or evening, wherever he might be. Those accompanying the abbot should not block them from doing so. When their request is granted, they perform a prostration with unopened sitting cloth and obtain from [the abbot] a note of his approval. The practitioner then takes the document to the office of the abbot's assistants to register his name, saying: 1140c

Just now, I have received the abbot's compassionate approval and would like to register my name at the office of your quarters.

The assistant official in due order dispatches a note marked with the guest's name to the practice hall office. The director of practitioners' affairs sends his attendant to invite the new arrival for tea and, after serving tea, examines the new practitioner's ordination certificate in order to register it in the "Record of Practice Hall Residency." (This is explained in detail below, part V, section 1.)

The new resident, however, must wait to be escorted to the practice hall. If, for some reason, he has to go in and out of the hall beforehand, he must follow the rules of the practice hall.

To obtain a permit for temporary absence from the monastery, one must wait until half a month has passed. In the *Ancient Regulations,* the duration of the application for a temporary travel permit was always limited to a period of half a month, and beyond this period one had to follow the same procedure again to reestablish one's residency and [was obliged] to abide by the rules of the practice hall. In case of the sickness or death of one's parents or religious teachers, the duration of a practitioner's absence is not bound by the above rule.

In general, it is customary to show one's reverence for the path of his teacher to place a chair [for the teacher] in the reception hall. When interviewing new arrivals, the abbot must take his seat in a mid-position and request them to burn incense and perform prostrations with opened sitting cloth [toward the chair]. While sitting near the chair, he bids the new arrivals to drink tea. This is not against propriety. Even today, this is still practiced in the northern regions (i.e., north of the Yangzi River).

In recent times, some newly ordained novices, soon after obtaining residency, dare to share seats of the same ranking as those of senior monks who held residency in major monasteries, and dare to exchange mutual veneration with them as equals. Mistaking certain wrong examples as standard, they regard them as ancient tradition and perpetuate them, thus creating the wrong effect. If one tries to usurp a rank equal [to that of his superior] by surpassing his own rank, he likely invites ridicule by outsiders. The path of reverence toward one's teacher has been in total jeopardy. Being respectful toward one's teacher is identical to being respectful to the Dharma. When the Dharma is respected, the standard of the monastic institution improves. In the western countries (i.e., Central Asia, Tibet, and India), the way students attend their teachers is comparable to the way they respect their rulers and parents. I am simply afraid that our [manners] are no match for this standard, and we must learn from them.

3. The Group Interview

In the major monastic temples, where numerous practitioners reside and where senior practitioners are strict and rigorous [about the rules of practice], there is no form of propriety for frequent and continual interviews. New arrivals are obliged to wait for more new arrivals, while each visits the assistant's office to register his name, until a group of twenty or thirty new arrivals has formed, so that a group interview may be held. The assistant official counts the number of the group and notifies the abbot. Either at the beginning of the ninth month, before the winter months, or in the new year season, the group of new members choose someone known for administrative skill or well experienced in monastic affairs as their ceremonial leader. On the scheduled day, with the appointed member as their leader, they go to the reception hall and line up in front of it. The assistant official notifies the abbot and escorts him into the hall. The ceremonial leader steps forward and says:

May we request your venerable to take a seat cross-legged.

The abbot utters an instructive word, and the ceremonial leader replies. Next, the ceremonial leader steps back to perform a bow in unison with the others, offers incense, and expresses thanks. Next they thank the assistant official. The following morning they attend a tea reception at the abbot's office and thereafter formally request his permission for residency. Waiting while the document of approval (format given below) is sent to the practice hall office, they will be escorted to join the members of the practice hall. The procedure of joining or returning to the hall is as mentioned above, and the abbot returns his propriety when they come to thank him for granting their residency.

(iv) Format for the Approval Document

The following are the names of those who have established residency as approved by the abbot's compassion:

Senior practitioner So-and-so
Senior practitioner So-and-so
[and so on]

Date

Reported by So-and-so
Office of the Assistants

V. Establishment of Monastic Residency

1. The Full Procedure for Establishing Group Residency in the Practice Hall

Upon receiving the document of approval from the abbot's assistant's office, the practice hall official sends his novice attendant to invite the new arrivals for a tea reception. Each invited person carries with him his ordination certificate, and the ceremonial leader carries a small incense case to perform his ceremonial role for establishing residency. Led by the ceremonial leader, all the invited new arrivals meet the official, perform a prostration with unopened sitting cloth, and greet him with an enquiry about the weather and his well-being. They are then invited to take their seats and finish drinking tea. Rising from his seat along with the rest, the ceremonial leader speaks to the director of practitioners' affairs, saying:

> I, So-and-so, and the others have received approval from the abbot. All of us have brought our certificates and we earnestly request the venerable to examine and record them.

The director of practitioners' affairs replies:

> It is fortunate and a pleasure for us to secure the path of quiescence and solitude together with the venerables as residents.

The ceremonial leader collects all the certificates from the members and gives them to the director. After performing a prostration with unopened sitting cloth, [the director of practitioners' affairs] copies the necessary information [from each certificate] into the "Record of Practice Hall Residency." When this is completed he returns the members' certificates to them but keeps the ceremonial leader's certificate.

The attendant of the practice hall office announces:

May the venerables request your leader to head the ceremony
to return to the practice hall.

Thereupon, the ceremonial leader leads the group of practitioners into the practice hall from the right side of the front entrance,
where they line up in front of the altar of the guardian bodhisattva.
[The ceremonial leader] burns incense and, in unison with the group,
performs three prostrations with fully opened sitting cloth. He
makes a round through the hall from the higher section through
the lower section of the hall, returns to the front of the altar, and
bows [together with the others]. They then move back, making the
member at the end of the line lead as far as the board edge of the
altar. The director of practitioners' affairs enters the hall and, after
burning incense, proceeds to take a position in the higher section
of the hall. An attendant carries the [ceremonial leader's] certificate
on a crepe-wrapped board, and the director instructs the attendant
to return the certificate [to the ceremonial leader]. Having received
it, the ceremonial leader performs together with his group members a prostration with unopened sitting cloth toward the director
of practitioners' affairs and sees him off as he leaves the hall. (If it
is before the noon meal, the director leaves from the rear entrance;
if after the noon meal, he departs from the front entrance.)

The ceremonial leader does not go beyond the threshold of the
hall. The director of practitioners' affairs distributes the document
of residency confirmation to the various quarters of the temple
(format given below). The same attendant ushers the new residents to the practitioners' quarters and strikes the wooden sounding block located within the quarters three times. The master of
the quarters receives them as they enter the quarters and
exchanges a prostration with unopened sitting cloth and an enquiry
about the weather and their well-being. When this is over, the ceremonial leader takes his seat at the side of the master of the quarters and offers an empty bowl to him. Thereupon, the ceremonial
leader stands, burns incense, and with a bow, expresses his thanks
[on behalf of the new residents], saying:

I, So-and-so, and the others have been directed by the director of practitioners' affairs to request you to assign our space units in this quarters, of which you are in charge. May you in your compassion help us in this matter.

The master of the quarters replies:

Welcome to the venerables who have arrived here. It is a pleasure, moreover, to secure the path of quiescence and solitude together with the venerables.

Immediately the new residents perform a prostration with unopened sitting cloth and move toward the east [side of the quarters] while the master of the quarters moves toward the west [side]. Once again they exchange a prostration with unopened sitting cloth. The master of the quarters leads the new residents to line up before the altar of Guanyin (Avalokiteśvara Bodhisattva) to bow. He then makes a round through the aisles of the quarters, returns to before the altar, and, after a bow, withdraws. The attendant of the practice hall office escorts the new members to meet the head official of the practitioners' quarters. They exchange a prostration with unopened sitting cloth with the head official, and the ceremonial leader then says:

On this day, we respectfully wish that the venerable Zen master of the quarters enjoys every blessing in daily life. By the abbot's compassion, I, So-and-so, and the others have been directed to be close to the various offices and we earnestly request your assistance. We are most grateful.

Next, they visit the quarters of various training officials [of the west order] and the administrative offices [of the east order] and, at each quarters, they exchange a prostration with unopened sitting cloth and an enquiry into the weather and the others' well-being. The officials are obliged to see them off. Nowadays, in many cases this kind of meeting does not occur and only a message is sent, or it is said that the propriety of prostration should only be conducted at the quarters of the primary seat official. However, all this is wrong; the dual order officials should pay a return visit to the new residents when they express thanks to them by performing a prostration in return.

Format for Reporting a New Residency

Residency has been established for the following:

1. Senior Monk So-and-so, Surname and Province, and Ordination
2. Senior Monk So-and-so, Surname and Province, and Ordination
3. And so on.

Day and month

Reported by So-and-so,
Practice Hall Official

(The report sent to the assistant's office is in actuality the same report received by the abbot's office; the abbot's name is omitted to show reverence. The report sent to the offices of the front hall primary seat official, the office of the abbot's assistants, and the practitioners' quarters should provide information concerning the year of ordination and the native province [of each new member], but this is not the case with the report that is sent to the other offices.)

2. Simplified Procedure for Establishing Residency

As soon as the abbot has granted residency, the assistant official sends the document of approval to the practice hall office. The director of practitioners' affairs invites the new arrivals to a tea reception, records their ordination certificates in the "Record of Practice Hall Residency," and directs them to the practitioners' quarters. The director of practitioners' affairs first stands in the higher section of the quarters to exchange a prostration with 1141b unopened sitting cloth and then moves to the lower section of the quarters to again exchange a prostration with unopened sitting cloth. The ceremonial leader says in greeting

> We are fortunate to be once again received by the venerable, sir. We are most grateful.

The director replies:

> The quarters may not be convenient. It would be fortunate, however, if I could obtain your pardon for any of its short-comings.

The ceremonial leader accompanies the director of practitioners' affairs outside the quarters and stands to the right of the entrance to see him off. The practice hall attendant strikes the small wooden sounding block inside the quarters three times. The master of the quarters receives the new residents. The propriety is the same as before.

3. Establishing Residency by the West Hall Primary Seat Official

If a renowned practitioner from one of the major monastic establishments wishes to obtain residency, he is obliged to express his intent clearly along with the formal statement. The abbot must consider whether individual quarters are available for him, or if there is a vacant seat to practice zazen in the practice hall appropriate for his rank and agreeable with the higher- and lower-ranking members. If these matters are evaluated and resolved affirmatively, [the abbot] accepts the request in question.

The following day, the ranking practitioner attends a tea reception and says:

> I, So-and-so, have come here especially to take refuge, because the matter of life and death is of prime importance.

Immediately he performs a prostration with unopened sitting

cloth. He will be invited on that day or another day to a tea reception to meet with the dual order officials and the retired officials. The abbot rises to burn incense, returns to his seat, and says:

> The west hall primary seat official of Such-and-such Temple has not abandoned us and has come to stay with us in order to guard the path of quiescence and solitude. May the dual order officials and the retired officials kindly escort him to his resident quarters.

The new guest resident steps forward and says:

> As I came here to seek refuge, I am most grateful that the heavy burden that I represent has been well received.

The abbot, along with the dual order officials and the retired officials, escorts him to his quarters. After exchanging a prostration with unopened sitting cloth, the new ranking resident sees the abbot off. He then takes his main seat, invites the abbot's assistant into the quarters to exchange a bow, and then sees him off. He again invites the dual order officials as well as the retired officials into the quarters and, after a bow, sees them off. As soon as this propriety is completed, he proceeds to the abbot's office, carrying an incense case, to express his thanks. Escorted in by the practice hall attendant, he visits the offices of the dual orders and the retired officials in order to return his thanks to them. On the following day, the abbot invites him to a special meal and tea reception. Moreover, this high-ranking resident is to be invited to tea on every first and mid-month day as an equal of the retired officials.

4. Establishing Residency by Renowned Officials of Major Temples

In general, when such a high-ranking official seeks to obtain residency, he is obliged to attend the morning tea reception on the second day, and afterward he should say:

> I, So-and-so, have come here especially to take refuge, because the matter of life and death is of prime importance. I earnestly wish that my request be included in the residency record.

He immediately performs a prostration with unopened sitting cloth. If the abbot accepts the request, he immediately invites the new member as well as the primary seat official, the administrative official, and the director of practitioners' affairs to a tea reception in order to introduce them to each other. When the serving of tea is over, the abbot rises to burn incense and escort the guest to his quarters. The guest steps forward and says:

> I am most grateful for your acceptance of my request to be included in the residency record. I am simply happy to join the practitioners in the practice hall and follow the rules of their life.

The abbot, however, replies:

> We shall follow the standard propriety of this temple in escorting you to your quarters, sir.

In accordance with the name and rank of his previous position, he is escorted to either the retirees' hall or to the hall of the retired subfunctionaries. After performing a prostration with unopened sitting cloth, he sees the abbot off.

At the quarters, the escorted guest exchanges a bow with the master of the quarters and says:

> Benefited by good relations in my past lives, I have fortunately relied on the venerables of these quarters.

The master of the quarters replies:

> We are delighted to witness the maturation of such past relations and happy to share this residence with you, sir.

The new resident moves to the main seat. He receives the abbot's assistant into the quarters and, after exchanging a bow, sees him off. When the exchange of a bow with the dual order officials has been completed, he pays a visit to the abbot's office, carrying an incense case in his sleeve, and expresses his thanks to him for the individual quarters to which he has been assigned. The practice hall office attendant escorts him on making rounds through the administrative offices and the various quarters of the training officials to express his thanks.

As an alternative procedure, if the abbot's office dispatches an official note to the primary seat official, requesting him to act on his behalf to escort the guest resident to his quarters, the primary seat official immediately sends a practice hall attendant to invite an official representing the administration, the director of practitioners' affairs, the abbot's assistant official, as well as the guest resident to come to his quarters. The primary seat official burns incense and serves tea for these officials. [In the meantime,] the abbot sends a message to the guest resident, saying that the temple community as a whole will escort him to his quarters. When they enter the gate of the guest resident's quarters, the primary seat official takes the main seat on behalf of the abbot and exchanges a prostration with unopened sitting cloth with the guest. The guest then moves to the main position, while the primary seat official moves to the guest position, and they exchange a bow in unison with the administrative official and the director of practitioners' affairs. The remainder of the procedure is identical to the above.

5. Establishing Residency by a Relation in the Dharma Lineage or a Former Subfunctionary

Regardless of the time of year, someone who is related in the abbot's Dharma lineage or someone who formerly served as a subfunctionary under the abbot [at another temple] can come directly to the office of the assistant official, explain the purpose of his visit, and request the official to convey his intent to the abbot. The person burns incense and performs prostrations with opened sitting

1141c

cloth. If he is of lower rank than the abbot, if he formerly attended him as his assistant, and so on, he is obliged to receive the propriety prescribed for such relations. The procedure of assigning residential quarters, however, is the same as before, namely, in accordance with the person's previous rank and position.

6. Establishing Residency through an Interview Requested by Casting Incense

When a new arrival is unable to present himself at the proper time, either because of certain unavoidable conditions or due to not having received a message to forego his intended visit, he is allowed to approach the abbot whenever possible. Upon seeing the abbot, he casts an incense case to the floor and says:

Allow this new arrival to pay veneration to you, sir.

He then performs a prostration with unopened sitting cloth. Picking up the incense case, he requests permission for residency. If the abbot grants permission, the assistant official sends the document of approval to the practice hall office. The following procedure is identical as before. If the residency chart (*tuzhang*) is already finalized, he is obliged to request the practice hall office to place his name in the chart. Or if there are numerous residents, he is to be placed at the end of the ordination order.

7. The Propriety of Giving Thanks for the Granting of Residency

In the *Ancient Regulations*, those who were permitted to join the practice hall were obliged to conduct the propriety of giving thanks at once for the residency granted to them. [Otherwise,] they would have to wait till either one of three later occasions to do so, namely, before the winter solstice, before the new year, and before the summer retreat.

[An episode relates:] Zen Master Fozhao (ca. twelfth century) moved from Yuwang (Ayuwangsi) to Jingshan (Xingshengwan-shousi), accompanied by Quanguyun as his assistant at his inauguration as abbot. At that time, the master was troubled by so much bowing in thanks for granting permission for residency, he instituted a rule that the propriety of giving thanks had to be accomplished altogether and at once before the summer retreat. There was a tendency at the time, however, for the new practitioners who had just joined, before staying long enough in the seats assigned upon their arrival, to move to other seats in the eastern and western sections of the hall, and thus many of them neglected the propriety of giving thanks for receiving permission for residency through the winter or even the following summer. Fozhao, therefore, settled the case by ruling that the propriety of giving thanks for permission for residency should be accomplished before either the summer or winter season of each year.

Prior to the time of the propriety, the assistant official examines the "Record of the Ordination Year" of the practice hall office, and assigns one of the eldest in ordination seniority among the new arrivals to be the ceremonial leader and another as co-leader.

(In earlier days, a person who was once the assistant to the abbot of a major temple was customarily chosen as the ceremonial leader. Often, however, the sense of harmony was disturbed by competition and disputing which temple was of higher or lower status. According to the original regulations, even an assistant official of the abbot, having returned to the practitioners' quarters, was obliged to follow the rules of the quarters as one of its residents. Therefore, it is proper to assign ceremonial leadership on the basis of ordination seniority. Since reliance on ordination seniority was the norm set forth by the Buddha, how and why could the order of various charts of seats or positions or ordination tablets in the practitioners' quarters be determined in terms of temple status? Such determination must be made to comply with seniority based on ordination dates, because, first, it was the Buddha's own ruling in his Vinaya rules and discipline; second, it eliminates the possibility of competition and dispute; and third, it brings harmony to the members so as to encourage sharing residency. It is probably best for the abbot to endeavor to follow the system of ordination seniority.)

The ceremonial leader must learn various proprieties by obtaining the small chart. Grouping the practitioners in several subgroups consisting of three members, and assigning one in each group as the sub-leader, he instructs them in detail to memorize set statements and to learn the manner of conduct to precisely execute their movements foward and backward, turning and bending, so that no embarrassing gap would result in the actual performance [of these movements]. The attendant of the practice hall office makes a copy of the name list of the new residents and draws up an announcement (format below) as a small notice that says:

> Those newly approved residents are each requested to contribute money for the purchase of incense and to be ready for the performance of the propriety of giving thanks for the approval of their residency.

> Reported by So-and-so Attendant
> Practice Hall Office

The practice hall attendant posts this notice in front of the practitioners' quarters, collects the incense money, and delivers it to the abbot's office through his assistant. The assistant official consults with the abbot to determine the date of the occasion. This is to be reported by posting a notice on a bulletin board:

> Those newly returned brethren (seniors and juniors) are requested tomorrow after breakfast to visit the abbot's office to express thanks for the granting of their request for residency.

> Day and month

> Reported by So-and-so
> Office of the Assistants

On the appointed day, the abbot's seat should be placed either in the reception hall or in the Dharma hall, together with tables, incense burners, flower vases, and candle stands. The assistant official hands over a pack of large-grain incense to the ceremonial leader, who in turn hands it to his co-leader to hold. The ceremonial leader leads the new residents to their positions as indicated by the chart. He accompanies the assistant official to escort the abbot into the hall and, returning to his position, bows in unison with the others. Thereupon, he steps forward and says to the abbot:

> May I request you to sit cross-legged.   1142a

Stepping back with his left foot, he turns and passes to the right of the incense table, returns to his place, and bows in unison with the others. The co-leader then takes the pack of incense out of his sleeve and hands it to the leader. The ceremonial leader receives it in his sleeve with a small bow; with his hands clasped over his chest, he steps toward the incense table, burns incense with his left hand, returns by the same route as before, and bows in unison with the others. Leading the first three members, he and the others open their sitting cloths; the abbot stretches out his hand, signaling [by this gesture that they are] excused from [performing the] full propriety. The three immediately stand and fold up their sitting cloths. The ceremonial leader steps forward and says:

> So-and-so and the others, due to good fortune from past lives, have been permitted to reside under your protection. We are most grateful.

As before, he steps back, goes around the right end of the incense table, returns to his place, and, after a bow, again opens his sitting cloth. The abbot once again excuses him from the full propriety. The ceremonial leader stands, folding his sitting cloth, steps forward again and says:

> On this day at this respectful moment, may the venerable master of the temple enjoy every blessing in daily life.

Once again he returns to his position and, after a bow, performs three prostrations with unopened sitting cloth. The abbot responds with a prostration. The first three practitioners bow, turn to the left, and go around to the end of the line. Thereupon the next three step forward to take the place of the first group. Their statements and manner of conduct are identical to the preceding. The ceremonial leader remains in place next to the assistant official and watches each group as they complete the propriety. When his co-leader reaches his former position, he joins him and, leading all the members, they bow in unison and withdraw.

The ceremonial co-leader heads the procession, while the ceremonial leader brings up the rear. When the procession arrives outside the entrance of the practitioners' quarters, the co-leader stands outside at the lower side of the entrance. He enters the quarters from the right-hand side of the entrance, turns around toward the lower-ranking section of the quarters, and directs the members to form lines, as many as are needed according to their number. He steps forward and stands next to the ceremonial leader to await the arrival of the master, and they receive him with a bow in unison with the other residents. He then turns to enter the quarters, escorting the abbot. All members step forward or back, maintaining their lines and adequate distance between themselves with due attention to each other. The ceremonial leader turns toward the incense burner, performs a prostration with unopened sitting cloth, and says:

> Though this is another moment, we respectfully wish that the venerable master, head of the temple, enjoys every blessing in daily life. We, So-and-so, and the others, are obliged to express our thanks through veneration to you for the residency you have granted us. We have now received your gracious visit. We are most grateful, sir.

All members see the abbot off as he leaves.

The ceremonial leader moves to the higher-ranking side outside the entrance and remains there, while the co-leader leads the members by turning around toward the higher-ranking section of the quarters. Bidding the members to remain there, the co-leader goes to stand next to the ceremonial leader, and together they escort the abbot's assistant official into the quarters. The ceremonial leader says:

> We, So-and-so, and the others, are fortunate that we have acquired our residency with your assistance. We have now received your gracious visit, for which we are most grateful.

The ceremonial leader alone sees him off. Next, the dual order officials are escorted into the quarters. After performing a prostration with unopened sitting cloth, the ceremonial leader says:

> At this moment, we respectfully wish that the primary seat official, the administrative official, and all the other Zen masters enjoy every blessing in daily life. We have not only been granted residency but have also received your visit. We are most grateful.

The ceremonial leader sees the dual order officials off, and then returns to stand in the higher-ranking section of the hall. The co-leader leads the group members, turning behind the altar of Guanyin Bodhisattva, to stand before the incense burner. He calls the group to attention by looking back toward the end of the line and, stationing himself upright facing toward the ceremonial leader, he performs a prostration with unopened sitting cloth and says:

> We, So-and-so, and the others, are very much obliged to you for your thoughtful guidance, and hence express here our special thanks.

The members must be instructed in the performance of this propriety beforehand. On the appointed day, it is necessary for the guest reception master of the abbot's office and the attendants of the practice hall office to rise early and prepare the notice of return propriety by copying the originals and posting them in front of the practitioners' quarters. The abbot's notice is posted in the higher-ranking section, while that of the dual order officials is posted in the lower-ranking section (format given below).

Format of the Notice of Return Propriety

The Venerable Abbot, master of the temple, will visit the leader of those practitioners who acquired their current residency for the sake of the return propriety after the morning rice gruel.

Day and month

Message upon instruction
So-and-so, Attendant of the
Guest Reception Master

The Venerable Primary Seat Official and the Administrative Official will visit the leader of those practitioners who acquired their current residency for the sake of the return propriety after the morning rice gruel.

Day and month

Message delivered
So-and-so, Attendant of the
Practice Hall Office

8. The Abbot's Special Tea Reception for New Residents

(See also the similar reception given by the dual order officials, chapter VI, part VII, section 1.)

The guest reception assistant prepares the invitation for the tea reception by copying the list of the ordination dates, ranking, and names of the new residents (format given below). On the appointed day, as early as the time of morning bathing, a table, brushes, and an inkslab should be set up in the sky-lit hall (*zhao-tang*), [the room adjacent to the practice hall]. The new residents are requested to line up and inscribe under their respective names, "So-and-so has respectfully received the invitation."

As to those renowned senior practitioners who once held positions in other temples, the day before the guest reception master must deliver to them letters of invitation prepared according to their ordination dates and request them to place their signatures on the sheets with their names.

The assistant official instructs the guest reception master to draw up copies of the name tablets marked "special serving" for each guest, according to their ordination seniority, either in terms of the quadruple seating arrangement (*sichu*) or that of the sextuple seating arrangement (*liuchu*). The primary seat official is invited as an honorable participant, while a renowned practitioner from a major monastic temple must necessarily be requested to take a seat directly facing the abbot. If there is any disagreement, the eldest in ordination age among the renowned practitioners from a major temple must be recommended to take that seat. The ceremonial leader should be seated directly facing the main participant. In general, even though some members have already been escorted to their individual quarters and performed the return propriety of thanks to the abbot for their residency, they are, without exception, also obliged to attend this reception.

On the appointed day, after the noon meal, the new residents are called to assemble by the signal of drumming. The assistant official, escorting them in, enters the reception hall with a bow, and the abbot receives them with a bow. Next the abbot exchanges a bow with the main guest, while the other guests, finding their positions according to the name tablets indicating their respective seats, stand before their assigned seats. The incense offering and guest reception assistants conduct the proceedings of the reception for the left- and right-side sections of the seated guests, respectively, greeting the guests one by one and bidding them to take their seats. Incense is burned to signal the invitation for the guests to offer incense, to signal the drinking of tea, and to signal the presence of the main guest. Then both assistant officials perform drumming and withdraw from the hall. This is identical with the propriety of the small reception to serve sweet hot water held on the four annual celebration days. The main guest of the reception leads his colleagues in expressing thanks for the reception [by performing the formal propriety of two prostrations with opened sitting cloth and three prostrations with unopened sitting cloth]. On the first opening [of the sitting cloth], he says:

> We, So-and-so, and the others, are obliged to express our thanks for today's reception especially served for us. We are most grateful, sir.

On the second opening [of the sitting cloth], he says:

> On this day at this respectful moment, may the venerable master of the temple enjoy every blessing in daily life.

Returning to the line of his colleagues, he performs three prostrations with unopened sitting cloth in unison with the others and withdraws.

The next day, the administrative official instructs the attendant of the guest reception master to prepare the letters of invitation for tea, according to the ordination dates and names but without titles or ranks, and waits for the invitees in front of the practitioners' quarters to obtain their signatures indicating acceptance of the invitation, "So-and-so has respectfully accepted the invitation."

The invitees assemble at the administrative reception hall, where the primary seat official is the main participant. The wooden sounding block located in the hall is struck to signal commencement of the reception. The proceedings are conducted by the head administrative official and the director of practitioners' affairs.

Again, on the following day, the primary seat official and the other training faculty officials obtain the signatures of the invitees in the same manner as before. The new residents assemble at the skylit hall where the head administrative official is the main participant. The wooden sounding block located in the skylit hall is struck to signal commencement of the reception. All members of the training faculty conduct the proceedings. In the case of four or six training officials, divided into two groups, they conduct the proceedings in making rounds to bow; in the case of three or five training officials, the primary seat official burns incense and takes a position in the center, standing. In the *Ancient Regulations,* this propriety continued for three days, but today it is completed within a day in most Zen temples. The seating tablets and the drum may be borrowed from the abbot's office. The training faculty and administrative head, keeping a seat vacant for the abbot, mutually serve as the main participants. The seating position and the proceedings are the same as before. (The only difference is that when the invitees express their thanks, they are, without fail, obliged to move away from their seats, turn toward the host and bow, and then offer the word of thanks. Nowadays, it is customary to [speak the word of thanks] while remaining seated, but this is not a proper observance of the propriety.)

Format for the Letter of Invitation for the Tea Reception

Invitation by the abbot:

The new residents, So-and-so senior practitioner, and the other senior practitioners whose names are listed below.

[Names listed here]

The abbot, master of the temple, invites the above venerables to a tea reception to be held today after the noon meal at the reception hall. It is earnestly wished that all the venerables attend this special reception.   1142c

Day and month

Respectfully requested by So-and-so
Office of the Abbot's Assistants

Invitation by administrative and training faculty officials:

The new residents, So-and-so senior practitioner, and the other senior practitioners whose names are listed below.

[Names listed here]

The administrative head and the training faculty officials invite the venerables listed above to a tea reception to be held today after the noon meal at the administrative office. It is earnestly wished that all the venerables compassionately attend this special reception.

> Day and month
>
> Respectfully requested by
> Bhikṣu So-and-so and Others
> Administrative Office

In the case of the reception given by the training officials, the list of sponsors' names ends after the guest reception official. The propriety to be conducted at the skylit hall is the same.

VI. Zen Practice and Training

1. Zazen Practice

Every day after the morning rice gruel, the attendant of the practice hall office reports the zazen practice schedule to the primary seat official. He also posts a tablet indicating the zazen practice in front of the practice hall and at the practitioners' quarters to inform the practitioners. The alms-serving master is obliged to set up incense and light candles within the practice hall. The wooden sounding block located outside the practice hall is struck once to call the practitioners to return to the hall and sit cross-legged facing the wall. As the practitioners gradually assemble in the hall, the wooden sounding block is struck a second time to inform the training officials who participate in zazen practice. At the moment when they all enter the hall, the wooden sounding block is struck a third time, somewhat softly. Thereupon, the second master of the quarters (*fuliao*) closes the entrance to the quarters and strikes the wooden sounding block located in front of the primary seat official's quarters three times. The first strike is made when the abbot leaves his quarters, the second when he reaches midway, and the third when the abbot enters the practice hall. The primary seat official burns incense in front of the altar of the guardian bodhisattva and makes a round through the hall, from the lower-ranking section to that of higher ranks, and then takes his place, sitting cross-legged. Next, after notifying the abbot, three strikes are made in a similar manner as before on the wooden sounding block located at the abbot's quarters. The abbot enters the hall, burns incense, and makes a round of the hall from the higher-ranking section to the lower ranks, and sits cross-legged at his place.

After zazen practice, the practitioners gradually arise from their places in order to rest. They must pay attention to the [position of] their immediate neighbors in both directions, so as to coordinate [their movements] with the others, whether arising or sitting, swift or slow. In this way, one will not be [embarrassingly left behind] by a neighboring practitioner. Some [practitioners] may leave their quilts (*liubei*) in the hall and do not act as the others do. Or some may return to their seats after a while and leave their *kaṣāya* robes [at their places] as the others do, yet do not participate in the zazen session but remain outside the hall. In either case, such people must be caught and reprimanded.

The practice training officials and the practitioners are equally obliged to restrict their entering and leaving the raised sitting platform. Only the primary seat official is allowed to come or go from his seat by passing in front of the abbot.

The attendant of the practice hall office, having observed the time of the noon meal, duly notifies the primary seat official, saying, "The release from zazen practice is in order, sir." Going behind the altar of the guardian bodhisattva and passing to its right, he reaches the entrance, rolls up the hanging screen, takes the tablet down, and in a low voice announces the end of zazen practice. The abbot and the training officials leave the hall, while the practice hall attendant stands to the extreme right near the entrance and bows toward them [as they leave].

There is no daytime zazen practice on days when the temple is scheduled to receive a renowned guest, to conduct a ceremonial prayer, to perform labor tasks, sutra chanting, or a funeral rite, or on the day of head-shaving and laundry at the practitioners' quarters. Nor is there the regular Zen discourse but zazen practice scheduled on a regular day after the Zen discourse should be held as usual. The abbot and the primary seat official make a round through the hall.

At the practice hall is a tablet indicating practice hall guard duty, inscribed with the following:

> Practice hall guard duty must be carried out by rotating shifts. Once a practitioner has completed a rotation shift, he starts again from the beginning. Inscribed on both sides by Abbot So-and-so with his signature.

Following the order of the space units assigned according to ordination dates, the tablet must be transferred every day to the next person lower in line, after the bell of the fifth watch of the night (*wugeng;* 3:00–5:00 A.M.). The practitioner in charge must guard the practice hall throughout the day. Whenever a practitioner wants to open his wardrobe, post his nameplate over his space unit, take down his almsbowl, or pull out his quilt, he is obliged to notify the person in charge. The guard of the day may be relieved of his duty temporarily when the bell is rung to signal the end of each zazen practice by placing the tablet in the custody of the assistant of the guardian bodhisattva and requesting him to look after the hall. At nightfall, every member stays in his own space unit. The tablet is to be passed to the next person early the next morning. Recently, the number of practitioners in charge of the hall has increased so that they form large groups. They chew 1143a fruit seeds and gather for idle talk and laughter, perpetuating such behavior and making it an evil custom, and they disturb the quiet of Zen practice. The abbot as well as the primary seat official must especially strive to prohibit such behavior and reprimand anyone who acts otherwise.

2. The Manual of Zazen Practice

Generally speaking, a bodhisattva who seeks the insight of *prajñā* should raise the mind of great compassion, issue forth the universal vow [of liberation], engage himself in the ardent practice of *samādhi,* and resolve to liberate sentient beings. He does not seek liberation merely for himself but renounces all causes of trouble and brings myriads of thoughts to rest, so as to unify body and mind and make no distinction between motion and stillness. He must measure each meal as to its adequacy and regulate hours of sleep and rest, prepare a thick seat cushion in a quiet environment and sit in the full cross-legged (lotus) position or in the half-lotus position. The left hand is placed on the right hand and the thumbs of both hands touch. The body is held straight in sitting, with [the ears balanced in line with the shoulders] and the nose and abdomen vertically aligned. The tongue rests on the upper palate, the lips and teeth are firmly closed, and the eyes remain slightly open so as to avoid falling asleep.

When a practitioner realizes the state of concentration, he acquires the utmost superior power. In ancient times, those practitioners who were well trained in the practice of zazen always kept their eyes open while abiding in deep concentration. Zen Master Yuantong of Fayunshan is said to have scolded his students who sat with eyes closed. There is a deep meaning, therefore, in the expression, "Wherever there is a dark hill there lies a [dark] cave where devils abide." One must not delve into thoughts that arise, whether good or bad. As soon as a thought arises, he must become aware of it. He must always be aware of what arises in the sphere of consciousness without losing clear discrimination, and without becoming dull or scattered. A myriad of years is nothing but one moment of thought, which is neither discontinuous nor continuous. This is the essential Way (or method) of Zen practice.

Zazen is in itself the doctrinal gateway of "comfort and ease." People, however, frequently hate it but this is no doubt because they have not realized its essence. Once one realizes it, one experiences all the elements of natural configuration [of the four kinds of coarse elements] becoming light and peaceful, and all the mental elements becoming refreshed and sharp. The taste of insight into the Dharma nourishes one's spirituality, a quiescent state of everlasting illumination. Waking and sleeping are, as it were, identical, and life and death are as one. One must singularly manage one's mind to have cognizance of this experience (*kenxin*), and never be blind to it. Nevertheless, it is often the case that when the path is lofty, one's wayfaring is more likely to be even more intensely disturbed by devils in thousands of situations.

If once, however, you can manage to bring right mindfulness (*zhengnian*) into your present consciousness, no obstacle can disturb or delay anything, just as it is explained in the *Śūraṃgamasūtra,* in the *Tiantai Practice of Śamatha and Vipaśyanā (Tiantaizhiguanfamen)* by Zhiyi (538–597), and in the *Manual of Practice and Realization (Xiuzhengyi)* by Guifeng (Zongmi, 780–841). If one analyzes devilish disturbance in detail, one becomes aware that everything arises from one's own mind and not from outside [of it]. When the power of *samādhi* and *prajñā* becomes superior, devilish obstruction disappears of its own accord.

When you are ready to emerge from *dhyāna,* you should move your body slowly and arise from your seat with ease and grace, never abruptly and roughly. After coming out of a state of *dhyāna,* you should try to retain the power of concentration, contriving various means skillfully.

Among all forms of practice, *samādhi* (meditative concentration, absorption) is regarded as the best. If one does not engage in meditation (*dhyāna*) and concentration (*samādhi*), one is bound to become totally lost in the triple world of existence, dallying in external causes. There is thus an instruction: If you want to gather pearls, you must first calm the waves. When the water is moving, it is difficult to look for pearls. The water of *samādhi* is clean and transparent and reveals the pearl of the mind of its own accord. Thus, it is said in the *Sutra of Perfect Enlightenment (Yuanjue-jing)* that the insight of *prajñā,* free from obstruction and spotlessly clean, arises on the basis of Zen concentration (*samādhi; chanding*). The *Lotus Sutra* also says that one should practice "mind concentration" in a tranquil environment and settle himself at ease, immovable like Mount Sumeru.

This means that it is always on the basis of the condition of quiescence (*jingyuan*) that you may transcend the state of an ordinary person as well as that of a holy person. In the past, those who passed away while sitting cross-legged or while standing must have been firm in the power of concentration. Even as you strive to attain this state of concentration, it is feared that you might still stumble [and not realize it]. If you postpone or procrastinate in realizing it, how much less of a chance will you have to overcome the force of karma! My respected Zen colleagues, it would be my pleasure if you would repeat the foregoing passages three times 1143b and thereby strive for realization of supreme enlightenment, equally benefiting yourself and others.

End of Fascicle Five

Fascicle Six

Chapter VII (*continued*)

3. Zazen Practice
[Prior to the Evening Zen Session]

After the noon meal, the practice hall attendant reports to the primary seat official the time of late afternoon zazen practice. He also posts a tablet indicating the zazen practice [to be held before the evening Zen session] in front of the practice hall and the practitioners' quarters. At dusk, incense is burned and candles are lit in the practice hall. The wooden sounding block located in front of the practitioners' quarters is struck to signal [the practitioners to assemble]. After the first strike, the practitioners enter the hall; at the second strike, the training officials enter; and at the third strike, the primary seat official enters.

(On this occasion, it is not required to strike the wooden sounding block located in front of the primary seat official's quarters; however, the block must be struck three times before the evening Zen session [or an evening lecture session].)

This procedure is much the same as the case of reporting to the abbot and striking the wooden sounding block of the abbot's office to announce the time of zazen practice. In some temples, it is against the regulations to not wear the *kaṣāya* robe for the occasion of Zen sessions.

When the cooking of the evening rice gruel has been completed, the practice hall attendant notifies the primary seat official:

The release from Zen practice is in order, sir.

He passes behind the altar of the guardian bodhisattva and to its right, reaches the front entrance, takes down the tablet, and strikes the practice hall bell three times, at which time all practitioners bow in unison while remaining in their seats. The abbot leaves the hall, followed by the training officials. Thereupon the practitioners descend from the raised sitting platform and pull out their bedding to a half-open position. Previously the abbot and the training officials had all come to the practitioners' quarters for the evening meal. Perhaps, in ancient times, practitioners used to approach the abbot every evening for instruction and exposition as a general practice. Because of that, the abbot led all the members of the temple to assemble for the Zen session. At the drum signal, they proceeded to approach the abbot. The term "evening session" (*zuosan*) came from this practice. [There is an episode related to this.] Because the region of Fenzhou was very cold, the honorable Shanzhao canceled this type of evening session [on severe wintry days], and the phrase, "the release from the Zen (dialogue) session" (*fangsan*), derived from it.

4. The Evening Zen Session

Today, in monastic institutions where numerous practitioners reside, the "evening Zen session" (*wansan*) is still practiced with the original meaning. This is called the "great Zen practice session" (*dazuosan*) and it is nearly identical to a regular Zen session. The only difference, however, is that the primary seat official does not burn incense after entering the practice hall but proceeds directly to his place and waits for the abbot to enter and sit cross-legged at his seat. The practice hall attendant strikes the wooden sounding block at the primary seat official's quarters three times, and the practitioners turn around to face each other while sitting cross-legged on their seats. The primary seat official descends from his seat, leaves the hall through the rear entrance, reenters the hall through the front entrance, burns incense before the altar of the guardian bodhisattva, makes a round through the hall as usual, and then returns to his place and sits cross-legged.

1143c   If the abbot conducts the evening session, the practice hall bell is not rung; the guest reception master of the abbot's office makes three drumbeats, signaling the abbot to leave the hall. The primary seat official, leading the practitioners, follows him to the Dharma hall or to the abbot's reception hall. When he takes his seat on the chair, the assistant official, the dual order officials, and the east and west hall [high-ranking guest] officials each step out individually from their regular positions and bow [to the abbot] (prior to the beginning of his exhortation). After the exhortation is over, the practitioners withdraw to their quarters for an evening meal.

If there is no evening session, the practice hall attendant goes before the primary seat official and, after a bow, says:

> The master of the temple (literally, "the master of the practice hall," *tangtouheshang*) has canceled the evening session, sir.

Passing behind the altar and reaching the midpoint near the front entrance, the practice hall attendant bids the attendant in charge of meal proceedings (*heshi*) to announce, in a drawn-out voice:

> The Zen session has been canceled.

When the practice hall bell is rung three times, the practitioners descend [from the raised sitting platform] and bow in unison. The primary seat official leaves the hall first, followed by the abbot and the training officials. The practitioners then pull out their bedding in full and go to the practitioners' quarters for the evening meal.

During a period when a series of Zen sessions is conducted, it is better to alternate days with a session with days having no session, so that the junior members can learn the proceedings. If, due to a variety of reasons, the evening session is repeatedly canceled, the alms-serving master, acting in place of the primary seat official, is obliged to pull open his bedding halfway, along with the practitioners. In the evening, when the wooden sounding block in front of the practitioners' quarters is struck three times, they leave their quarters and return to the practice hall. When the evening bell is tolled (or, if the temple is in a city, at the signal of drumbeats), the training officials enter the hall. The primary seat official also enters the hall at the sound of the bell, burns incense, and makes a round through the aisles of the hall. Next, the abbot enters, burns incense, and makes a round.

When the timekeeping bell (*dingzhong*) signals the first watch of the night and fifth point (i.e., 8:40 P.M.), the abbot leaves the hall, followed by the training officials. When an extended session of zazen is requested (*zaiqingchan*), the abbot reenters the hall from the rear entrance and settles on his seat without making a round through the hall. The training officials follow the practitioners, and those who are taking a rest return immediately to their bed spaces. The abbot leaves the hall during the late-night watch.

When the sound of the primary seat official opening his pillow is heard, the practitioners make ready to take their nightly rest. Those who wish to continue practicing zazen are not required to follow. Next morning, the practitioners are awakened by three strikes of the wooden sounding block. The practitioner assistant for the guardian bodhisattva pulls around the hall towel rack to surprise late risers. When the practitioners finish washing and return to the hall, the primary seat official enters first, burns incense, and makes a round through the hall. Next, the abbot enters, burns incense, and makes a round in the same way. At the signal of four drumbeats (i.e., the fourth watch of the night and the fifth point, 2:40 A.M.), the abbot leaves the hall. At the sound of the hall bell, the primary seat official leaves. The rest of the training officials and the practitioners leave the hall a moment later through the rear entrance, change their garments and hats, and, after a rest, return and wait on their bed spaces. Sometimes the primary seat official returns to the hall and once again makes a round through the aisles of the hall. When the hall bell has ceased ringing, the metal gong located at the kitchen hall is sounded to signal the time to fold up the bedding [and put it away in the storage rack]. The alms-serving master is obliged to fold up the primary seat official's bedding. The practitioners may then leave the hall as they wish. Contemplation of the Buddhas or scriptures should be simultaneously practiced [along with zazen].

5. Individual Request
for Special Instruction

In general, a practitioner who wishes to have special instruction from the abbot must first speak to the assistant official, who will convey his wish to the master, "So-and-so practitioner wishes to visit the abbot's office (*fangzhang*) for special instruction this evening." If [the abbot] grants the request, the practitioner comes to the assistant's office after evening meditation and waits for the the assistant monk to prepare incense and candlelight and escort him to the abbot. With a bow, the practitioner burns incense, performs nine prostrations with fully opened sitting cloth (*dazhanji-ubai*), and folding up the sitting cloth, steps forward and says:

> As I, So-and-so, regard the matter of life and death of primary importance and am concerned with the swiftness of transformation, I earnestly request the venerable master in his compassion to grant me special instruction with words of expediency.

The practitioner is obliged to stand with solemn respect at the master's side and listen to his words intently. When it is over, he steps forward to burn incense and once again performs nine prostrations with fully opened sitting cloth. This is called the propriety of "giving thanks for causes and conditions" (*xieyinyuan*). If the full formality is excused, he should perform prostrations with unopened sitting cloth. The practitioner is also obliged to drop in at the assistant official's office to thank him.

1144a

6. The Propriety of Partaking of the
Morning Rice Gruel and the Noon Meal

In the early morning, after the metal gong located at the kitchen hall has been struck to signal the release from morning silence, and later, at mealtime while awaiting the sound of the kitchen hall metal gong, the practitioners go to their respective places in the practice hall where their almsbowls are kept and take them down. They then enter the practice hall, bow before the altar of the guardian bodhisattva, and proceed, with palms joined together, to their respective seats. At the moment of ascending the raised sitting platform, they are obliged to greet their neighbors [on each side and across the aisle with a bow]. With your back to the raised sitting platform, first use your right hand to pull up your left sleeve and hold it by the left armpit, and then use your left hand to pull up the right sleeve and hold it by the right armpit. Then, supporting your weight on both hands placed on the board behind you, shove your sandals below the board [with your foot] and then first bend in your left foot and pull in the right foot next, proceeding to carry your whole body backward a foot or so across the wooden board. Then sit cross-legged, spread the *kaṣāya* robe to cover the knees, neither revealing the undergarment nor letting it hang down over the platform. (Details of this process are given below in section VII, part 3.)

The administrative head, the director of practitioners' affairs, the maintenance official, the assistant official, and so on have their seats on the raised sitting platform of the higher section of the outer hall, whereas the training officials of guest reception, of the bath hall, of the Buddha hall, of the fundraising preacher, of the infirmary, and so on have their seats on the raised sitting platform of the lower section of the outer hall. In the *Ancient Regulations,* the abbot came to the practice hall every day. At breakfast, he first sits in the outer hall, and when the practice hall bell is rung, he enters the hall. All the practitioners at once descend from the raised sitting platform and greet him with a bow in unison before taking their seats again. Nowadays, the abbots of many monastic temples enter the hall to take their seats while the large bell is still being tolled, and when the practice hall bell is rung, they descend from their seats in order to bow in unison with the practitioners. By simply encountering the ceremonial acts of the first day of the month or of the mid-month day, or of the Zen lecture session of every fifth day of the month, it would be difficult for new arrivals at the monastic temples to know anything about ceremonial protocol in their early training. Before our time, our predecessors discussed why all must descend to the floor to bow in unison, and concluded that it was meant to be the time of each day when the officials of various quarters and the practitioners all exchange bows in unison. On the basis of this interpretation, it follows that wherever Zen practitioners live together, it is necessarily the norm that each day early in the morning all members descend from the raised sitting platform to exchange greetings with a bow in unison.

7. Attending the Special Tea and Sweet Hot Water Reception

The propriety involved in the tea and sweet hot water reception by the abbot and the dual order officials is a rather serious matter for a number of reasons. One must not be negligent about it. Once invited, one must be on time to attend the event. First, you must observe the tablet indicating the seating places carefully and memorize the seating order so as to avoid the possibility of embarrassing confusion. If you are sick or pressed by nature and unable to attend such a reception, you must convey through a colleague your apology and reason to the hosting official. It is, however, inexcusable to not attend a reception hosted by the abbot. Anyone who does not attend [such a reception] due to negligence is certainly not entitled to live under the same roof.

8. The Request for Universal Participation in Tasks of Labor

The rule of "universal participation in the task of labor" is meant to equalize the work contribution of individuals, whether higher or lower in rank. In general, wherever a number of people live together, there should necessarily be things accomplished on the basis of all members' cooperative effort. Should such a necessity arise, the administrative head must first notify the abbot, then send an attendant to report the matter to the primary seat official and the director of practitioners' affairs, and assign the practice hall attendants to distribute the tasks among all the practitioners and post the tablet that indicates "all-out work for all members." A small piece of paper [indicating the time and place] should be posted on this board. At the sound of the wooden fish-shaped gong (*muyu*) or the drumbeat, every member tucks up his sleeves with a strip of cloth over his arms and assembles at the designated place for the task of labor. Except for the guard of the practitioners' quarters, the practice hall guard, and the sick and aged, every practitioner is equally required to participate in such tasks. In this connection, the maxim of the ancient master [Baizhang] should be recollected: "A day of no work is a day of no eating."

VII. The Rules and Regulations of Daily Conduct

1. Introduction

Zen Master Wuliangshou said [in the introduction to his *Daily Regulations*],

> Escaping from worldly dust and leaving human convention, shaving the head and wearing the *kaṣāya* robe, and pursuing the path by sojourning in various monastic institutions, one must clearly know the rules and disciplines of these institutions.

Unless you know the rules by heart in the act of lifting up or putting down things, and also unless you are in accord with the normative disciplines in the act of moving or stopping, even if you have good teachers and colleagues, how would you be able to penetrate deeply into and intensely experience the subject of your pursuit? Since wrong behavior easily becomes an established custom through repetition and learning, it is very difficult to reform. Such wrong customs will devastate the seats of the monastic centers, and affect through chain reaction practitioners' minds, causing them to become negligent in their religious pursuits. Because such fault and sickness are so frequently observed in everyday life, it has finally led to the compilation of those paradigmatic rules of Baizhang as models.

If one seeks the origin and goal of these [paradigmatic] rules, one must spend days from morning to night [studying them]. In order to escape from the [mind's lack of understanding] about these rules, it is necessary to put each of these rules into practice immediately, and only after strict adherence to each [rule] can one claim that one has pursued the nature of the self, clarified the forms of the mind, understood the problem of life, and grasped the nature of death. The rules of the secular world are [essentially] identical with those of the sacred. The practitioners who renounce [secular life] and are constantly traveling can bequeath their rules to those who have not renounced [secular life]. For many householders are not inferior physically or mentally to those who have left the householder life, and they are equally obliged to discharge their indebtedness to the Buddhas and patriarchs. The model rules of daily life will be respectfully enumerated in the following.

2. The Rules for Morning Proceedings

As to the rules of conduct among the practitioners, you should not go to sleep before others do, nor should you get up after others have. Before the timekeeping bell signals three o'clock in the morning, you must arise energetically and put your pillow at the foot of the bed space. It is not yet necessary to fold up the bedding, as this may disturb your immediate neighbors who are still asleep. Pull yourself together and sit straight with the whole body, so as not to create wind which may disturb your neighbors. If you feel fatigue, push the quilt off your feet, pick up your towel with the left hand, and intone the following verse:

> From three o'clock in the morning until dusk, every sentient being must reflect upon himself with the following prayer:

"Even if my life should end at this very moment, may I immediately be reborn in the Pure Land."

Then, go out to the washstand, lifting the hanging screen [of the practice hall] softly. You must not make noise by dragging your sandals or gargling loudly. It is said in the *Ancient Regulations:*

> When one lifts the hanging screen to go out of the entrance of the hall, one should not let his hand drop until it is all the way down. After coming out of the hall, one should never drag one's sandals.

The water tray for washing one's face must be gently handled, and one should not use too much hot water. Dip the right fingers in dentifrice and rub the left side of the mouth, then dip the left fingers in dentifrice and rub the right side of the mouth. Do not dip your fingers in the dentifrice again; it should be cautioned that one's mouth odor may be transmitted to others [in this way]. When rinsing the mouth, lean forward with your head down and after taking the water, spit it out with both hands downward; it is cautioned that [if you spit water while standing upright,] it may splash over nearby buckets that are being used by others.

You must not wash the head. There are four disadvantages for yourself and others [in doing so]: 1) it stains the washtray, 2) it soils the towel with oil, 3) it withers the hair, and 4) it injures the eyes.

Do not make noise by blowing your nose, splashing water onto your face, loudly [expelling water from the mouth], or defiling the washing trays by spitting. The *Ancient Regulations* set forth the [general] rule as follows:

> Washing the face at three o'clock in the morning is for the primary purpose of religious practice. [Expelling water from the mouth] and stamping with the sandals are most annoying to the practitioners who are seriously engaged in practice.

While washing your face do not fight others for towels, nor should you use the towel to wash your head. After washing your face, hang up the towel or place it to dry over a fire.

When entering the practice hall through the higher-ranking section, step into the hall with the left foot first; conversely, when entering from the lower-ranking section, step into the hall with the right foot first. Then ascend the raised sitting platform, fold up your bedding halfway, and sit upon it cross-legged. When changing your garment, you must put the new one on over the old one, keeping yourself covered while taking the old one off. You must not expose any part of your body while changing clothes, nor should you create a breeze by moving hurriedly.

1144c

If you wish to burn incense and venerate the Buddha, you should do so while the timekeeping bell is being rung. Carry the *kaṣāya* robe in your sleeve, leave the hall by the rear entrance, and don the robe outside. Regardless of whether you are at your seat or away from it, when you are about to put on the *kaṣāya* robe, with palms together, [raise the robe] to your forehead and intone the following verse:

> How great is the robe of liberation;
> Formless yet the field of every merit.
> Wearing this robe now with veneration,
> I am determined to wear this robe in all my lives to come.
> *Oṃ siddhāya svāhā* (*anxituoyesuohe*).

To fold up the *kaṣāya* robe, first pull the grip portion and untie the ring. You should not hold the robe in your mouth or use your chin to pull the robe. After folding up the robe, you must bow again before leaving the area.

When venerating the Buddha at the shrine hall (*diantang*), you must not occupy the central part of the floor lest you obstruct the abbot's entrance into [the hall] for the rite of veneration. Nor should you call the names of the Buddhas out loud, nor should you walk beside someone who is performing the rite of veneration. You must take a place in the empty rear part of the hall. When the bell signals three o'clock, recollect in your mind this verse:

> May the sound of this bell go beyond this Dharma world.
> May it be heard by all those who abide in the dark, ghostly world of iron prisons.
> May those who suffer in the three deplorable realms of existence be freed from it,
> Ending the perpetual warfare of sword-wheels.
> May all sentient beings establish supreme enlightenment.

When the abbot and the primary seat official are practicing zazen in the practice hall, no one can enter or exit the hall through the front entrance. [At the end of morning zazen practice, at the time of "minor release of silence" (*kaixiaojing*), everyone must fold up their bedding and place the pillow within it. The way to fold the bedding is to first find the two front corners and stretch the quilt by hand straight in front. Then fold that one half into half, and next fold the other half which is closer to you into half. You must not extend the quilt into the neighboring space by folding it sideways, nor should you let any sounds escape when pulling the quilt, nor should you create any air movement by shaking it. You may either go to the practitioners' quarters to have an herbal medicine drink, or engage in the practice of a "meditational stroll" (*jingxing*) in the hall, eventually returning to your almsbowl position by turning [left] toward your upper shoulder (i.e., the left shoulder). When entering the hall from the front entrance, you must step in from its southern [left-hand side] corner; you are not allowed to approach from the northern corner or from the center. This is perhaps out of reverence for the abbot.

3. The Rules for Meal Proceedings

As to meal proceedings, when the wooden fish-shaped gong is sounded signaling mealtime, no one is allowed to enter the hall. You may request a meal attendant to fetch your bowl and sit in the outer hall. Or, returning to the practitioners' quarters, you may join the serving team. When you enter the hall and reach your assigned position to take meals (*bowei*, literally, "almsbowl position"), keep your head slightly lowered and bow toward your neighbors on both the higher and lower sides as well as across the aisle. If you have already been seated, when your neighbors come to their seats, you are obliged to join your palms together. The *Ancient Regulations* has the following:

> Unless one greets with respect the practitioners of the higher and lower seats as well as those across the aisle, there is no difference between a Buddhist gathering and [a gathering] of brahmans.

After the sound of the wooden fish-shaped instrument, the metal gong in the kitchen hall is sounded to signal practitioners to take their almsbowls down. Rise and stand straight for a moment, then turn again toward your upper shoulder (i.e., to the left), with both palms together, ready to take the bowl down. First, with your right hand release it from the hook, then with your left hand support it while turning around and bending down to place it on the floor. In this way, you can avoid colliding with your neighbor with your back hip. When the hall bell rings, everyone must descend to the floor to greet the abbot, who is entering the hall, and all bow in unison. No one, however, should move their hands to the right or left. When descending to the floor, move close to the wooden board-edge and bow and, after descending, you must not let your *kaṣāya* robe hang over the board [while standing in front of it]. After the greeting, all once again ascend the raised platform in a careful manner, not abruptly tossing your body onto it.

Set the almsbowl on the board-edge, and upon hearing the sound of the mallet [striking the octagonal wooden post], you are obliged to intone the following verse from memory:

> The Buddha was born in Kapilavastu,
> Enlightened in Magadha,

First preached in Vārāṇasī,
Entered nirvana at Kuśinagara.

As to the manner of "opening the bowl," first recite, with palms joined together, the following verse mindfully:

Now I have opened the Tathāgata's almsbowl
That spontaneously measures the quantity of need.
I wish, along with all sentient beings, to realize the
insight that
The donor, the recipient, and the alms received are all
of the nature of emptiness.

1145a Thereupon, untie the knot of the wrapping cloth [around the almsbowl] and take out the clean handkerchief to cover your lap and knees. The wrapping cloth must be folded into a triangular form, so that it may be placed on the board-edge without hanging over.

First, unfold the tray sheet (*bodan*), pick up the bowl with your left hand, palm upward, and set it on the tray-sheet. Then using the thumbs of both hands, take out the [three] nested bowls (*fenzi*). Lay them out [from right to left], smaller to larger, and do not make a clattering noise while handling them, nor should your fourth and fifth fingers touch the bowls. Fold the drying cloth of the bowl into a small size, and place it together with the sack holding the spoon and chopsticks, laying these horizontally nearest your place (literally, "to the body"). When placing the utensils into the sack, you should put the spoon into the sack first [and then the chopsticks], but when removing them from the sack, take out the chopsticks first, [then the spoon]. The utensils are to be laid out horizontally, with the handle of the utensil regarded as clean facing toward the upper (i.e., left) shoulder. The bowl-cleaning spatula (*boshua*) must be laid vertically to the side of the second bowl, with its tip extending half an inch out from the tray sheet, so that alms [for the sake of the hungry ghosts] may be placed on it. Neither the spoon nor the chopsticks should be used for this offering, and it ought to be no more than seven grains of rice. If [the offering] consists of less than this amount, it is regarded as showing greed for food. Whenever food is received [in the almsbowl,] it is a general rule to make such an offering, but when food has not been received, it is not permissible to make an offering directly from the serving ladle.

While the director of practitioners' affairs intones the names of Buddhas, the practitioners hold both palms together, with the fingers held evenly. Join your palms together [and let your hands] lightly graze your chest; do not let your fingertips reach the mouth. The following statement is found in the *Ancient Regulations:*

> There are those who hold both palms together but do not [rest] the hands on their chest. Both hands cross each other at the fingers, with the fingertips almost sticking into their nostrils. In dragging the sandals and lifting up the entrance screen, there is no refined cordiality whatsoever. Uttering sounds like [expelling water] and leaking breath, they look like [battlefield] heroes.

When receiving food, you are obliged to hold the bowl with both hands and intone the following verse from memory:

> When one receives almsfood, one must wish that
> All may have the Zen experience of delight as their food,
> And be filled with the sense of rejoicing in the Dharma.

In order to request more or less [food from the server], signal by keeping your right hand still or raising it slightly [to indicate that you have received enough].

When the octagonal wooden post is struck with the mallet [to signal the completion of the first serving], you must observe your neighbors [so as to be in tandem with them], lift the [main bowl] straight up in front of your forehead, and make a slight bow. Do not shake [the bowl] to the right or left. After bowing, you must intone the "Verse of Fivefold Reflection" on almsfood:

> First, reflect upon the many labors [made by other people in order for this food to be served to you] and for what reason [has this food been served to you].

Second, reflect upon whether your virtue and practice have been perfected or are far from satisfactory, and [renew your resolution before] partaking of the almsfood.

Third, reflect upon whether your mind is prevented [from evil thoughts] and freed from wrongdoing, because such [actions] are caused by desire, and so forth.

Fourth, reflect upon whether you regard food as good medicine and use it properly to treat illness and prevent emaciation of the physical form and [to maintain] strength.

Fifth, reflect upon whether you are aware that it is for the sake of realizing the ultimate goal of the path that you receive this almsfood.

Next, you must produce some alms and intone the following verse from memory:

O host of hungry ghosts, I now make an offering of food
    for you;
This food is offered widely in all ten directions, for all the
    hungry ghosts.

As to the manner of eating, you must not bring your mouth to the bowl, nor bring the bowl to the mouth. Whether taking up the bowl or putting it down, you must not make noise either with the spoon or chopsticks. You should not cough or sneeze. If this naturally occurs, you should cover your nose with your sleeve. You must not scratch your head, because dandruff may fly and fall into the bowls of neighboring practitioners, nor should you [put your finger in your] ear, nor make noise when chewing rice and drinking soup. You should not collect rice in the center of the bowl, nor should you take a large amount [of food] into the mouth [in one bite], nor should you open your mouth in anticipation of the food, nor should you let food drop from your mouth, nor should you pick up and eat food with your fingers. If there remains any vegetable sediment, leave it below the edge of the bowl. Do not create [malodorous] wind which might affect neighboring seats. If you are afraid of doing so, you may take a seat in the outer hall after obtaining permission from the director of practitioners' affairs. Do not rest your hands on your knees. Request only as much food as you need. Do not leave food after eating a part of it. Wet food (i.e., soup, side dishes, etc.) should not be placed in the primary bowl. Do not eat by pouring soup into the primary bowl and sifting rice from it. Do not eat rice by mixing it with side dishes in the primary bowl. While eating, pay attention always to your neighbors on each side, so as not to be too far [ahead or] behind in the proceedings. You must not start cleaning the bowl with the spatula before the second serving has been completed, nor should you make noise by sucking the tip of the spatula. Before the food is served, you should refrain from creating mental defilement. The *Ancient Regulations* has enumerated these misbehaviors as follows:

> Foolishly looking around in all directions, becoming
>   depressed or angry;
> Thinking of food, swallowing saliva and thus coughing
>   frequently;
> Pouring rice gruel, slurping soup, and stuffing food into
>   the mouth;
> Opening the seat and spreading the bowl set, making
>   noise everywhere toward all neighbors.

1145b

As to the manner of washing the bowl, water is placed in the primary bowl and the smaller bowls are washed in due order in the [main] bowl, but [do not wash] the spoon and chopsticks in it. [Wash the bowls using only the thumbs and first two fingers, keeping the fourth and fifth fingers extended;] after the bowl washing is done you may bend your fourth and fifth fingers. Do not gargle, as it makes noise, or spit water into the bowl. You must not wash the bowl while [the water] is boiling hot. Before the remaining water has been discarded, no one is allowed to remove the cloth used to cover the lap. Do not use this cloth to wipe sweat [from your face] The residue water must not be thrown onto the floor; [before it is discarded in the bucket], you must intone the following verse from memory:

> This water with which I have cleansed the bowls
> Tastes like ambrosia.
> I offer it to all the hungry ghosts,
> Wishing that they all be gratified by it.
> *Oṃ mahorase svāhā (anmoxiuloxisuopohe)*.

As for the manner of placing the smaller bowls back into the primary bowl, use the thumbs of both hands to pick up each bowl in due order and place them [gently] one after another into [the main bowl]. After this has been completed, hold your palms together and recollect the verse that is recited at the end of each meal:

> Having finished the food, I feel the strength of my
>   physical body,
> Whose majesty shakes the heroes in all directions and in
>   the three times.
> Neither abiding here nor remaining yonder, nor holding on
>   to a moment of thought,
> I wish that all sentient beings acquire supernatural
>   powers.

At the signal of the striking of the wooden sounding block in the practitioners' quarters, the practitioners return to their quarters and bow. If someone does not return to his assigned position, it is regarded as being rude to the fellow practitioners. Entering the quarters as well as coming to your seat is performed exactly as is done in the practice hall. Remaining in position, wait for the moment when the master of the quarters finishes burning incense, then bow to your neighbors, both higher and lower in rank.

4. Drinking Tea and Reading Sutras at the Practitioners' Quarters

When practitioners take their seats to have tea in the practitioners' quarters, they must be careful not to allow their robes to hang down. Nor should they talk and laugh with others with their heads close together. Do not greet others by a single raised hand, nor collect leftover (powdered) tea. Thus, the *Ancient Regulations* has this to say:

> When ascending the raised sitting platform, you must not
>   let your robe hang overboard.
> Some greet others with a single hand, but for what reason?
> Some secretly collect powdered tea, thus becoming the
>   laughingstock of bystanders.
> Detestable is the wasting of time by neighboring
>   pathseekers who [talk idly] with their heads close
>   together.

After drinking tea, if you want to read sutras do not unfold the text scroll too widely but limit it to [a two-page length]. You must not walk about in the quarters carrying the sutra in your hand, nor should you let its binding cord hang down, nor should you read it aloud, nor should you lean against the wallboard. The *Ancient Regulations* thus has these words:

> Reading sutras aloud irritates neighboring practitioners,
> Leaning back on the wallboard is a slight to the fellow
>   practitioners.

It is advisable to leave the quarters early for zazen practice. Do not wait until you hear the signal of the wooden sounding block.

5. Using the Lavatory

When going to the lavatory, according to the *Ancient Regulations,* you must change into the robe made of five strips of cloth (*wutiaoyi;* namely, a simplified robe). Take a clean handkerchief and hang it over the left arm. Untie the string belt and hang it upon the bamboo rack, and take off the simplified robe and one-piece garment. Neatly fold them up and put them together with the handkerchief, marking the place. You must not engage in laughter and conversation, nor should you urge others in the lavatory to hurry across the doorway. Enter the lavatory carrying a water bucket in your right hand. When changing sandals, do not leave them in disarray. Place the bucket of water in front, and snap your fingers three times in order to warn the hungry ghosts who feed upon feces. Squat down and maintain the right posture, do not groan nor spit saliva or nasal mucus, nor should you make conversation with another through the wall. The *Ancient Regulations* says:

> At the doorway, snap your fingers lightly.
> If someone still remains within, why is it necessary to
>   speak aloud?
> Using bamboo spatulas in the lavatory, you must distin-
>   guish an unused one from used ones.
> When coming out of the lavatory, you must not leave the
>   shoes in disarray.

Do not pour water on both hands for cleansing. When the left hand is used for cleaning, cover the thumb and the two adjacent fingers, and do not use many bamboo spatulas. The *Ancient Regulations* says:

> You may use warm water but not too much.
> Stop fooling around with the bamboo spatulas.

After using the spatulas, wash them with water and leave them in the space near the lavatory. When there are many practitioners in line, do not stay too long because it inconveniences others. Leave the water bucket where it was before. Using your dry hand, fix your underwear and put on the under-robe. Open the door with your dry hand and come out, carrying the bucket with the left hand. You must not touch the door panel or the side of the door with your wet hand. Pick up a pinch of ash and then dirt with your right hand, not with your wet hand. You must not spit saliva to mix with the dirt. Wash the left hand and then use [soap] to wash the hand [and forearm] up to the elbow. You must intone a mantra at each act of cleansing (mantras given below).

1145c

According to the Mahayana Tripiṭaka text, the *Sutra of the Garland of the Bodhisattva (Yinglojing)*, it is said:

312

In general, whosoever goes to the lavatory and does not intone the prescribed mantras will never be able to cleanse his defilement, even upon reaching the subterranean depth of the golden layer by using as much as ten times the [amount of] water in the Ganges River to wash his defilement away. No matter how often he presents himself in the shrine hall to worship the Buddha, it is said to be of no use. Therefore, one must maintain the mantras steadfastly and intone them seven times each on every occasion. Because of this practice, the ghosts and spirits always accompany him and protect anyone who intones them accordingly.

When going into the lavatory, intone the charm: *Oṃ krodhāya svāhā* (*Angenlutuoyesuohe*).

When washing: *Oṃ hanāmṛte svāhā* (*Anhenangmilidisuohe*).

When washing the hands: *Oṃ śuklāya svāhā* (*Anzhuqieluoyesuohe*).

When purifying the body: *Oṃ śrīye sahe svāhā* (*Anshiliyisuoxisuohe*).

When purifying defilement: *Oṃ vajrodaka ṭha svāhā* (*Anfeizheluonangjiazha*).

Finally, cleanse your mouth with fresh water. Some Vinaya rules prescribe the method of cleansing after urination.

6. Miscellaneous Rules for Daily Conduct

[After visiting the lavatory], one may chew a toothpick and return to the practice hall and zazen practice. As long as no signal is heard from the kitchen hall metal gong, you should not return to the practitioners' quarters. Nor should you wash your clothing before the morning gruel. Nor should you open your storage box before the morning rice gruel, before the noon meal, or after the signal canceling the evening session. If it is an unavoidable situation, you must speak to the person responsible for the respective matter of concern. For instance, in the case of the practitioners' quarters, you must speak to the master of the quarters. In the case of the practice hall, you must talk to the assistant official of the guardian bodhisattva. After the noon meal is over, no one is allowed in the practice hall in order to put their heads together for idle talk. Nor should you read sutras or any kind of text in the practice hall. While engaged in a meditational stroll between the higher- and lower-ranking sections, you must not take a direct passage [from one side to another] through the hall. Do not count coins by displaying them on your seat, nor hang your feet over the board-edge while sitting on the raised platform. The one-foot-wide board-edge is regarded as a clean space for three reasons: First, it is the space where the almsbowl is used; second, it is the space where the *kaṣāya* robe is placed; and third, it is the space toward where one's head is directed during sleep at night. You must not walk on the raised platform across neighboring space units. Nor should anyone open their storage box by squatting down on the floor. Nor should you descend from the raised platform by stepping on the board-edge.

After going around outside the temple wearing grass sandals and the simplified robe made of five strips of cloth, no one is allowed to step into and walk about in the Buddha's shrine hall or the Dharma hall [without first changing their clothes]. The *Ancient Regulations* says:

> After entering into the lavatory with a shoulder exposed
> Or walking in the field outside wearing grass sandals,
> No one should step into the Dharma hall,
> Nor encounter any senior practitioner (i.e., without first
>   changing into the proper clothing).

You should not wear the practitioner's sandals with bare feet. Nor should you walk hand in hand with another while explaining the secular truth as to its rightness and wrongness. The *Ancient Regulations* has the following words:

> Separating oneself from one's parents and leaving one's
>   original teacher,
> What would one intend to accomplish by traveling afar to
>   seek knowledge?

Whoever has not settled with the matter of the religion of
    the Zen tradition,
May not accomplish anything, even until they become
    white-haired. Whose fault is this?

At the Buddha's shrine hall, you must not lean on the railings
of the building, nor should you suddenly move quickly like a crazy
person. The *Ancient Regulations* says:

Movement must be conducted with gentle walking,
For which one must learn Assaji's majestic demeanor,
Words must be spoken in a low voice,
For which one must learn Upāli's manner.

Do not stay in the shrine hall just to pass time. The *Ancient
Regulations* says:

One must not go to the shrine hall for no purpose,
Nor should one step into the stupa compound to waste time.
Unless one visits [these places] to sweep the ground or
    sprinkle scented water,
No matter how often [one visits, as numerous as] the sands
    of the Ganges River, the benefit would diminish to
    nothing.

When washing your clothing after the noon meal, you must
keep one shoulder covered. Nor should you soak the garment by
pouring hot water directly from a jar. After using the bamboo poles
and drying racks, they must be returned to their place. When the
wooden sounding block is struck to signal the time for washing
the feet, [indicating the end of laundry work,] you must not compete with others to obtain a washbucket. If you have boils or sores
that itch, you must wash your feet after the others finish, or go
somewhere not directly within sight to do so. Each practitioner
must act expediently to avoid any occasion that might incur disturbance in the minds of his fellow practitioners. You should return
to the practice hall without waiting for the signal of the wooden
sounding block when your work is done.

When evening zazen practice is over, each practitioner opens his bedding to one-half size and descends to the floor. If the evening Zen session has been canceled, when the wooden sounding block located at the primary seat official's quarters is struck, everyone turns around to face each other across the aisle. Whenever the wooden sounding block is struck as a signal, everyone is obliged to return to the practice hall. Once the signal has been completed, no one is allowed to enter the hall. No one should remain standing outside the hall. When the abbot and primary seat official leave the hall, the practitioners can open their bedding and descend from the raised platform, and after a bow, proceed to the practitioners' quarters for the evening meal. When each one has settled in his position, he should not, however, get up or immediately stand up to fetch his meal. Nor should anyone shout aloud or compete to obtain items such as gruel, rice, salt, vinegar, and so on. After the evening meal, one must leave the quarters but not go beyond the

1146a　main gate or to any of the smaller quarters. No one is allowed to return to the practice hall or walk through the corridors without wearing the regular robe. Nor should anyone wait for the signal of the wooden sounding block to leave the practitioners' quarters.

When the evening bell is tolled, each practitioner, with palms together, silently and mindfully recites this verse:

> Listening to the sound of the evening bell, we feel that
>   defilement is reduced,
> It increases far-reaching insight, inducing enlightenment,
> It helps us out of hell and the fiery pit.
> Let us aspire to realize Buddhahood and help sentient
>   beings.

Everyone must first return to his floor space to practice zazen. You must not scratch your head on the raised meditation platform, nor should you make noise by manipulating your prayer beads on the raised platform, nor should you exchange conversation with your immediate neighbors. If the practitioner next to you is not yet well cultivated, you must help him improve himself by way of skillful words, and never hold a sense of dislike toward him. After the bell [is rung] to signal the end of zazen practice or the time to sleep, no one may use the front entrance for going or coming. Awaiting the moment when the primary seat official prepares his pillow, those who feel extremely tired go right to sleep. While sleeping, lie on your right side, not [on your back] facing straight upward, because this is called the dead man's sleep. Sleeping [with your face down] is called indulgent sleep because it creates bad dreams. Wrap the kaṣāya robe in the handkerchief, and place it above your head (i.e., on the board-edge). Today many practitioners place it below their feet, but logically this is not a convenient practice.

7. The Rules for Bathing

On bath day, carry your toiletries in the right hand, enter the bath hall from the lower-ranking section, and, after a bow, go to an empty space. After greeting your fellow practitioners to the right and left, hang the sash of the robe made of five strips of cloth over the bamboo rack, spread the bathing garment (yufu) on the floor, place the toiletries to the side, and disrobe. Before taking off the one-piece robe, remove your underwear and wrap the loincloth around your body to prevent the bathing trousers (yuqun) from becoming loose. Then untie your underwear [above and below] and place it in the wrapping cloth. Next, take off the one-piece robe and tie it together with the sash and the robe made of of five strips of cloth. The *Ancient Regulations* says:

> When you hear the three drumbeats and enter the bath hall,
> Separate those clothes that directly "touched" the body
>   from those that are "clean."

Wrap all your clothing into one bundle, turning it front and back, and then change into the wooden footwear. Do not enter the bathwater with bare feet. You should wait your turn to bathe at an empty spot in the lower-ranking section and must not occupy the space reserved for the training officials and senior-ranking practitioners (called the higher-ranking section).

Be careful not to pour hot water over another's body. Do not dip your foot inside the bucket, nor urinate inside the bathing room, nor prop your feet up on the bucket, nor exchange laughter and conversation with others. Do not rest your feet over the trough, nor bail water out. Do not pour water over your body with a bucket while standing. If there are other practitioners nearby, you must prevent any water from splashing upon them. Do not let the loincloth drop from your body. Do not dip your feet into the water bucket to wash them, nor use too much hot water. Those who have wounds should wash the wound with moxa cautery or use medicinal materials. Those with itching sores must bathe last and not try to enter into the bath any earlier by hassling [others]. Do not use the public washcloths for cleaning your head or face, because these are used for hand-cleaning after wearing the undergarment, and thereby you put the robe made of five strips of cloth on over it. After coming out of the bath, greet those on the right and left, ascend the raised platform, and sit cross-legged for a while facing the wall. Then, first donning the robe and the one-piece robe, descend to the ground, take down your bathing trousers while bundling up the loincloth into it. This is because the wrapping cloth may have become wet. Holding the handkerchief in your left hand, greet [those on] the right and left, then leave the hall. Find the names of the donors and chant sutras or intone mantras as you wish, concluding with an invocation of merit transference.

8. The Rules for Being at the Fireside

During the winter months, when approaching the fireside, you must first sit on the fireside board, then turn around to the back, and, sitting properly, greet [those on] the right and left. You must not play with the fire shovels and pokers, nor should you blow on the fire or let ashes fly up. Do not exchange conversation by putting your head together [with others], and neither should food items be placed in the embers. Do not dry your sandals to the point

1146b

of scorching, nor burn your shins or clothing. Do not expose your underwear by rolling up the one-piece robe. Do not spit or toss filth into the fire.

9. Conclusion of the Daily Rules of Conduct

The rules of daily conduct as previously collected are concerned with the major events that take place in the lives of practitioners and are not intended to be heard by established senior practitioners. It is hoped that these rules may be helpful to those who are junior in their religious careers. There are many more intricate and detailed rules concerned with the major categories of monastic events, such as the ascent to the Dharma hall, admission to the instructional room, the supplementary session, sutra chanting, prayer invocation, making rounds through the practitioners' quarters, the commencement and completion of retreats, interpersonal proprieties, packing and traveling, and funeral rites and auctions. These regulations have already been introduced [elsewhere] in detail. Since renowned senior masters have written their respective elucidations in great number concerning the rules and regulations, I shall refrain from bringing up their words here again in order to avoid unnecessary excess.

VIII. *An Exposition on the Model Zen Principles of Conduct (Guijingwen)*

The following was written by Great Master Cijiao, the honorable Zongze (ca. twelfth century):

> Representing the fragrant dual trees (i.e., Bodhidharma and his master Prajñātara), Bodhidharma transmitted the [benevolent] shade to the eastern land and produced a single flower as its auspicious manifestation. Ever since the coming of the patriarch from the west, the facility of the Zen monastic institution was destined to evolve fundamentally for the community of practitioners.

[1. The Normative Principles for the Community of Practitioners]

Thus came to be the position of senior head official (abbot) to teach the community of practitioners in the Zen religion.

So did the position of primary seat official to provide model leadership for the community of practitioners.

So did the position of the head administrative official to support the community of practitioners.

So did the position of the director of practitioners' affairs to harmonize the community of practitioners.

So did the position of kitchen official to prepare daily provision for the community of practitioners.

So did the position of maintenance official to engage himself in various tasks for the community of practitioners.

So did the position of treasury official to keep accounts of revenues and expenditures on behalf of the community of practitioners.

So did the position of secretarial official to deal with recording and correspondence for the community of practitioners.

So did the position of Tripiṭaka hall official to preserve the sacred scriptures for the community of practitioners.

So did the position of guest reception official to receive and attend patron donors on behalf of the community of practitioners.

So did the position of [abbot's] assistant to communicate requests and invitations between the abbot and the community of practitioners.

So did the position of the master of the quarters to guard the personal possessions, clothing, and almsbowls for the community of practitioners.

So did the position of infirmary master to provide care and medicine for the community of practitioners.

So did the positions of bath master and water supply chief

to provide sanitary bathing and laundry for the community of practitioners.

So did the positions of charcoal supply chief and fireplace chief to shield the community of practitioners from cold weather.

So did the positions of alms campaign leader and fundraising master to make appeals for monetary and alms donation for the community of practitioners.

So did the positions of farmyard chief, mill operator chief, and estate management master to devote themselves to the tasks of labor for the community of practitioners.

So did the position of cleaning task chief to sweep and scrub on behalf of the practitioners.

So did the position of meal servers to wait upon the community of practitioners in serving them food.

As given before, the practitioners' career of pursuit of the path is perfectly equipped with all kinds of assistance in every dimension, and the provision that supports their physical health is manifest in all varieties of realization. The community of practitioners has no worry whatsoever and can devote themselves singlemindedly to the pursuit of the path. The community of practitioners is honorable and precious to human society and enjoys leisurely freedom from the work of [securing one's] material needs. Thus, the community of practitioners, which is immaculate and transcendent, is the highest. Reflecting upon the assisting works of the multitude, shouldn't we know and discharge our indebtedness?

[2. The Practitioners' Adherence to the Normative Principles]

From morning zazen to the evening Zen session, the practitioners should exert effort in the pursuit of the path, without losing one moment. This is the way to discharge one's indebtedness to the senior head of the monastic community.

The practitioner should learn the propriety of the order of high and low, and be firmly in command of the decorum whether in movement or stationary. This is the way to discharge one's indebtedness to the primary seat official.

The practitioner should respect the external regulations and adhere to the inner rules. This is the way to discharge one's indebtedness to the head administrative official.

The practitioner should be harmonious, like milk and water, with the other practitioners in six ways (i.e., physical harmony, in sharing the same residence; verbal harmony, in the absence of disputation; volitional harmony, in sharing the same action; disciplinary harmony, in sharing the same practice; harmony of thought, in sharing the same understanding; and harmony of receiving benefit, in sharing equal amounts). This is the way to discharge one's indebtedness to the director of practitioners' affairs.

The practitioner should receive the food that is offered for the sake of realizing the goal of the practice. This is the way to discharge one's indebtedness to the kitchen official.

The practitioner should carefully use and look after the household items of his current quarters. This is the way to discharge one's indebtedness to the maintenance official.

The practitioner should refrain from misusing public items (i.e., things belonging to the monastic temple). This is the way to discharge one's indebtedness to the treasury official.

The practitioner should refrain from taking and carrying pens (i.e., so as to engage in writing and intellectual abstraction) but diligently exert effort in the practice, as if putting out a fire burning on top of their head. This is the way to discharge one's indebtedness to the secretarial official.

The practitioner should examine his mind of understanding in reference to the ancient teachings under bright windows and on a clean desk. This is the way to discharge one's indebtedness to the Tripiṭaka hall official.

The practitioner should [be humble about] his accomplishments, [not brag of] his career, and speak no adulation. This is the way to discharge one's indebtedness to the guest reception official.

The practitioner should always be available and punctual in presenting himself prior to the appointed time when requested. This is the way to discharge one's indebtedness to the abbot's assistant.

In dealings with his colleagues, the practitioner should be firm, like a mountain, regardless of whether it is a vase (i.e., a minor item) or a bowl (i.e., an important item) that is missing. This is the way to discharge one's indebtedness to the master of the quarters.

The practitioner should keep his mind calm as to his sickness and suffering, and willingly take the [prescribed] rice gruel and medicine. This is the way to discharge one's indebtedness to the infirmary hall master.

The practitioner should maintain gentleness and quietude while taking a bath and not be unmindful of the various labors that have gone into the preparation of the bathwater. This is the way to discharge one's indebtedness to the bath hall master and the water supply chief.

The practitioner should keep his mouth shut, his hands together, and withdraw from the fireside in order to let others have a chance [to warm themselves]. This is the way to discharge one's indebtedness to the charcoal supply chief and the fireplace chief.

The practitioner should reflect upon whether his virtue and practice are deserving when receiving almsfood. This is the way to discharge one's indebtedness to the alms campaign leader and the fundraising master.

The practitioner should realize the innumerable labors and benevolent conduct that have brought food to him. This is the way to discharge one's indebtedness to the farmyard chief, the mill operator chief, and the estate management master.

The practitioner should bail water, carry used bamboo spatulas, and have a sense of shame and repentance. This is the way to discharge one's indebtedness to the cleaning task chief.

The practitioner should be easy to follow and simple to serve. This is the way to discharge one' indebtedness to the meal-serving personnel.

If these normative principles are well understood, there will be a perpetual renewal of life in the Zen monastic institution. Those who are endowed [with superior qualities] may realize the goal within one lifetime. Those who are endowed [with mediocre qualities] will nourish and develop Buddha-nature in themselves [for future realization]. There are those who, though not yet possessing insight into the mind's origin, are nevertheless determined not to discard the foregoing principles in vain. The community consisting of these practitioners indeed constitutes the true treasure and most worthy field of merit in this world. It is [like] a ferry or a bridge that immediately leads to the goal of our religion during the current latter-day period, and, at last, one will experience the twofold ultimate fruit of wisdom and blessedness attributed to the Buddha.

[3. The Officials' Failure to Follow the Normative Principles]

If the monastic institution is not reformed and if the wheel of the Dharma does not turn well, this is not the way for the senior master (abbot) to teach the religion to the practitioners.

If the three forms of karma (i.e., acts of body, speech, and mind) are not well regulated, and if the four manners of conduct (i.e., walking, standing, sitting, and lying down) are not respectfully accomplished, this is not the way for the primary seat official to provide model leadership for the practitioners.

If the head administrative official is not broadminded enough to accept every practitioner and does not possess a generous heart with love toward each one, this is not the way for the administrative head to support the practitioners' careers.

If the practitioners feel no peace nor any sense of security, and if those who are demoralized do not leave, this is not the way for the director of practitioners' affairs to please [the community of] practitioners.

If the food lacks the six kinds of tastes (i.e., sweet, hot, salty, bitter, sour, and mild), and if it is not served with the three qualities (i.e., plain, clean, and consistent), this is not the way for the kitchen official to prepare food for the practitioners.

If the buildings and quarters are not well maintained, and if there is a lack of various kinds of household items, this is not the way for the maintenance official to provide the practitioners with secure accommodation.

If the practitioners' basic needs are insufficiently provided for while public property increases, this is not the way for the treasury official to look after the practitioners' well-being.

If the secretarial official is poor in his art of composition and clumsy in calligraphy, this is not the way for the secretarial official to enhance the status of the practitioners.

If the desks and chairs are not well kept and if noises are not contained, this is not the way for the Tripiṭaka hall official to help and wait upon the practitioners.

If the guest reception official disdains the poor, favors the rich, and entertains the laity while slighting his fellow practitioners, this is not the way for the guest reception official to assist the practitioners.

If decorum and respectful appearance are absent and if the order of high and low is [not followed], this is not the way for the abbot's assistant to help the practitioners communicate [with the abbot].

If household items are not diligently looked after and personal possessions are not diligently guarded, this is not the way for the master of the quarters to perform his duty to help the practitioners abide in peace.

If the infirmary hall master does not learn how to care for and serve and if he disturbs the sick, this is not the way for the infirmary master to [care for] the practitioners.

If sufficient hot water is not available and if hot and cold water is not supplied in good balance, this is not the way for the bath hall master and the water supply chief to help the practitioners cleanse their bodies.

1147a

If charcoal and firewood are not sufficiently reserved beforehand and if an inadequately maintained room temperature disturbs the practitioners, this is not the way for the fireplace chief and charcoal chief to serve the practitioners.

If the alms campaign leader and the fundraising master are not public-minded toward donations or have not done [their best to secure funds], this is not the way for them to serve the practitioners.

If the land, despite being sufficiently profitable, and the applied manpower do not fully make ends meet, this is not the way for the farmyard chief, the mill operating chief, and the estate management master to perform their tasks on behalf of the practitioners.

If the cleaning task chief is not diligent in cleaning the lavatory and so forth, and if all necessary items are not fully provided, this is not the way for him to perform his duty to serve the practitioners.

If the meal-serving personnel do not heed even when prohibited nor act for what is in order, this is not the way for them to attend the practitioners at mealtimes.

[4. The Practitioners' Failure to Follow the Normative Principles]

If the practitioners slight the senior master, the abbot of the monastery, ignore the Dharma, and follow their own natural

326

inclinations in various circumstances, this is not the way for them to discharge their indebtedness to the abbot.

If the practitioners have no unified manner of action, whether in sitting or lying down, and if their comings and goings are obtrusive, this is not the way for them to discharge their indebtedness to the primary seat official.

If the practitioners ignore the secular laws and are not concerned with the monastic regulations, this is not the way for them to discharge their indebtedness to the head administrative official.

If the practitioners are not harmonious with each other, whether higher or lower in rank, and if they obstinately dispute with one another, this is not the way for them to discharge their indebtedness to the director of practitioners' affairs.

If the practitioners covet fancy meals and [complain about] humble dishes, this is not the way for them to discharge their indebtedness to the kitchen official.

If the practitioners misuse their current quarters, without caring about those who will reside there after them, this is not the way for them to discharge their indebtedness to the maintenance official.

If the practitioners abuse benefits they have gained from public property (i.e., items owned by the temple) and if they [are wasteful] in using public goods, this is not the way for them to discharge their indebtedness to the treasury official.

If the practitioners misuse writing brushes and inkslabs and show off their writing talent, this is not the way for them to discharge their indebtedness to the secretarial official.

If the practitioners treat the scriptures lightly and look into non-Buddhist books, this is not the way for them to discharge their indebtedness to the Tripiṭaka hall official.

If the practitioners speak flatteringly to lay notables and try to associate themselves with members of the nobility [to gain favor], this is not the way for them to discharge their indebtedness to the guest reception official.

If the practitioners forget invitations or requests and thereby cause others to wait for their delayed appearance, this is not the way for them to discharge their indebtedness to the abbot's assistant.

If the practitioners hoard things and if [they accuse others of theft], this is not the way for them to discharge their indebtedness to the master of the quarters.

If the practitioners anger easily and are difficult to please, and if they do not [patiently] follow the [prescribed treatment] for their illness, this is not the way for them to discharge their indebtedness to the infirmary hall master.

If the practitioners make noise when using ladles and use water with no consideration for others whatsoever, this is not the way for them to discharge their indebtedness to the bath hall master and the water supply chief.

If the practitioners [selfishly sit at the fireside] to warm themselves and refuse others the opportunity to do so, this is not the way for them to discharge their indebtedness to the charcoal supply chief and the fireplace chief.

If the practitioners have little intent toward practicing the path but receive almsfood with no ill conscience, this is not the way for them to discharge their indebtedness to the alms campaign leader and the fundraising master.

If the practitioners eat for no purpose all day long and make no effort toward [practice], this is not the way for them to discharge their indebtedness to the farmyard chief, the mill operating chief, and the estate management master.

If the practitioners spit on walls and mess up the lavatory, this is not the way for them to discharge their indebtedness to the cleaning task chief.

If the practitioners, while advocating for themselves the importance of demeanor, yet do not offer good instruction to the meal-serving personnel over past faults, this is not the way for them to discharge their indebtedness to the meal-serving personnel.

[5. The Prime Importance
of the Practitioners]

In general, no matter how fast one may run about like a whirl-wind thousands of times, there are always some cases in which it is just never enough. Therefore, one must simply know how to discard what is deficient and follow what is advantageous and must deal with the matter of practitioners in similar ways. It is hoped that whoever is reared in the lion's den will become a lion, and whatever grows under a forest of sandal-wood trees may become another member of that forest. Five hundred years from now (i.e., at the beginning of the latter-day period), let there be seen another grand gathering like that once held on Vulture Peak (Mount Gṛdhrakūṭa in Rājagṛha, India). As has been indicated, what will determine the rise and fall of the Zen school lies in the hands of the prac-titioners. The practitioners are the field of merit [in which laypeople find fortune by cultivating] and must be the object of people's respect. When the practitioners are well respected, the Dharma is also well respected, but when they are slighted, the Dharma is also slighted. When a person's commitment to his inner rules is rigorous, he is also respectful toward the external rules. Regardless of whether an abbot or a provider of rice gruel and [rice] meal (i.e., a lay donor) is engaged in the role of religious conversion during his lifetime, or whether an administrative official of a temple happens to be put in charge of such an authoritative position, one must always treat with respect those who wear the same robe, and must not indiscriminately behave arrogantly [toward anyone]. If again, one insists on his superior ego, makes his private inter-ests a public affair, and is inconsistent in all his dealings, how could such a person hold his position for long? Once he returns to the status of a practitioner, how could he then face his fel-low practitioners as their colleague? There is no exception in the law of cause and effect, from which no one can escape.

1147b

[6. The Way and Principles
of Practitioners]

Practitioners are the sons of the Buddha and [fundamentally] no different from the saintly being, the Arhat (i.e., Śākyamuni), hence they are worthy of reverence from heavenly as well as human beings. The morning rice gruel and the noon meal of rice must be prepared to meet all dietary needs. The four kinds of alms and requisites [of a monk] (i.e., food and drink, clothing, bedding, and medicine) must always be provided without a shortage ever occurring. From the time of Śākyamuni, after two thousand years, the inherited shade [of refuge] still covers all his descendants. Of the world-illuminating light emitted from his forehead, not even a portion of its merit is ever exhausted despite all of our usages. You must simply learn how to serve your fellow practitioners and not worry about poverty. There is no difference between holiness and worldliness in the status of a Buddhist practitioner, which is universally accepted in all regions. We already have the term "four regions" (*caturdiśaḥ*) indicating the same meaning. It is true that this world is made up of all kinds of divisions, and yet how could it be right to discriminate against practitioners from different regions or treat them with disdain on account of such differences? The transient quarters are supposed to receive [guest practitioners] and be open to any traveling practitioner for three days. Serve them with due propriety. If someone requests a noon meal temporarily in front of the practice hall, serve him the meal with equanimity. We receive lay visitors after examining their background, so how could we not receive other practitioners like ourselves? If one can transcend the mind of limitedness, there will be no limit to the reward of merit. Within the Zen school, the high and low harmonize their minds and try to put aside mutual deficiencies, if any. One must not expose family scandals. Even though their exposure may not harm anyone, such conduct reduces people's trust and respect in the end. Such an action is comparable to parasitic worms infesting the body of a lion and consuming its flesh from within. Indeed, neither non-human devils nor non-Buddhists could accomplish such destructiveness.

If one wishes to prevent the decline of the [Buddhist] path, to hold up the Buddhist sun for a long time, to increase the majestic luster of the tradition left to us by the patriarchs, and to assist the sacred tasks of the imperial court, one must make the foregoing rules of conduct one's normative principles.

IX. The Prayer for Ailing Practitioners

Should a practitioner become [seriously] ill, those from the same native province and his religious colleagues gather at his bedside, set up incense, candles, and a Buddha image, and conduct a prayer of veneration for the Buddha with the following invocation:

> When [the surface of the] water becomes [still and] transparent, there appears the autumnal moon.
> When an earnest prayer is applied, the meritorious field of fortune manifests itself.
> Indeed, the true foundation of our refuge is the Buddha and his enlightenment.
> This morning, we have gathered for the sake of Venerable Bhikṣu So-and-so
> To clear up the wrongs he has suffered through many past lives
> And repent for the transgressions accumulated through innumerable transmigrations.
> Devoting our utmost sincerity to this end, we now request the holy assembly
> To venerate the Buddhas by calling the sacred names and thereby accomplish a thorough purification.
> May the honorable assembly recite the ten supreme names:
> The Luminous Pure Dharma Body Vairocana Buddha, and so on.

The following invocation of merit transference is then said:

We earnestly wish that the primordial mind may be
    purified,
That the four material principles may become light and easy,
Extending natural life as well as wisdom,
That the physical body may become as firm as that of the
    Dharma body.
Once again, may the honorable assembly conduct a prayer:
Veneration to the Buddhas in the ten directions and the
    three times, and so on.

If the illness is very serious, a prayer directed toward Amitābha
Buddha should be recited ten times. Before this prayer, however,
one is obliged to speak the following word of adoration:

The Buddha Amitābha shines in golden luster,
The sublimity of his features is beyond comparison.
The white ūrṇa, curly hair sweetly rolling, appears on his
    forehead like Mount Sumeru,
His blue eyes are transparent and clear like the four
    surrounding great oceans.
In the illumination shed from his ūrṇa appear
    immeasurable myriads of Buddhas,
And innumerable bodhisattvas also appear within this
    illumination everywhere.
With his forty-eight vows, Amitābha Buddha helps all
    beings toward salvation,
Enabling all, regardless of their nine different
    endowments, to reach the other shore.
This morning, we have gathered for the sake of Venerable
    Bhikṣu So-and-so,
To clear up the wrongs he has suffered through many past
    lives
And to repent the transgressions accumulated through
    innumerable transmigrations.

Devoting our utmost sincerity to this end, we now request
the holy assembly
To venerate the Buddhas by calling the sacred names and
thereby accomplish a thorough purification.
May the honorable assembly call the name of Amitābha
one hundred times,
The names of Bodhisattva Avalokiteśvara and Bodhisattva
Mahāsthāma[prapta] each ten times
As well as the innumerable bodhisattvas abiding in the
great ocean of purity.

The invocation of merit transference is:

It is earnestly wished that Venerable So-and-so regain his
health, as he has not lost the various supporting causes for
his existence. If, however, it is unavoidable for him to come
to the end of his life, may he swiftly realize the goal of rebirth
in the Pure Land. Veneration to the Buddhas in the ten directions and the three times.

While chanting this prayer and the sacred names, practitioners must maintain their minds in purity and refrain from becoming entangled in worldly thoughts.

The Word of the Will

Venerable So-and-so, native of such-and-such province, 1147c
became a Zen practitioner by receiving the ordination
certificate in such-and-such year at such-and-such place. He
came to establish his residency at So-and-so Temple in such-
and-such year and date. Having been struck with an ailment
these past days, it is feared that there is no certainty as to
whether or not he will survive it. Hence he requests that
[after his death] the content of the parcel that he has kept
in his possession be distributed through due official procedure, and that his funeral rite be conducted as prescribed by
the Zen monastic regulations.

Day, month, and year

Orally conveyed by
Practitioner So-and-so, who is ailing

X. The Death of a Resident Practitioner

1. Collecting the Possessions
Left by the Deceased

When a practitioner dies due to illness, the nursing attendant reports this to the infirmary hall master and also to the director of practitioners' affairs, and requests permission to seal the parcel belonging to the deceased. The attendant of the practice hall office reports the [practitioner's death] to the primary seat official, the training and administrative officials, and the abbot's assistant. He then visits the infirmary hall for the departed in order to copy the document of the orally transmitted will. Along with the practitioner in charge of public proceedings, the practitioner who attended the ill person collects the contents of the sutra cabinet [located in the practitioners' quarters], the storage box [located in the practice hall], and all personal possessions, and prepares a record of them, numbering and sealing each item. He then places them on the space unit belonging to the deceased. Excluded from this, however, is the clothing that the deceased's body will be dressed in [for cremation] and other items. (These include the one-piece garment, simplified robe, under- and outergarments, prayer beads, an incense case, a pair of gaiters, a pair of traveling shoes, a handkerchief for shaving the head, a cloth for collecting ashes, and so on.)

These necessary items are gathered together and retained. This procedure must be handled jointly by the infirmary hall master and the practitioner who attended the deceased. If, however, these two cannot leave the side of [other] ailing practitioners, the director of practitioners' affairs and the primary seat official must carry out this task instead.

Even when the deceased has no bamboo case [or other such container] for his personal possessions, an equally dedicated funeral rite should be conducted for him. The record of the revenue from the auction [of the deceased's personal goods] as well as the account of expenditures must be presented to the primary seat official after sealing the documents. The items in the bamboo case, such as those previously collected and sealed, are to be carried to the practice hall office by lay workers who belong to the quarters of the primary seat official, the director of practitioners' affairs, the guest reception official, and the assistant official. In the case that an administrative retiree who resided in the private quarters left behind many bamboo cases after his death, the deceased's possessions, once sealed off, may be placed in that particular quarters but must be guarded by a practitioner assigned by the treasury office. Unless the recently deceased practitioner had previously informed the abbot, the dual order officials, or the retirees about the manner in which he wished his possessions to be distributed, or unless he left a written will in regard to the matter, no one can arbitrarily distribute his possessions to anyone or any place.

(Zen Master Dachuan, while residing at Jingcisi, discovered that the primary seat official and the director of practitioners' affairs had made forgeries concerning certain items that were entrusted by a deceased practitioner, and hence subsequently expelled them.)

When an ailing practitioner closes his eyes (i.e., passes away), the infirmary hall master at once notifies the director of practitioners' affairs and requests the attendants of his office to prepare hot water. The attendants also notify the primary seat official, the guest reception official, the abbot's assistant, and the administrative official of the matter, and arrange for the delivery of a portable funeral shrine and a special bathtub to the hall so that the deceased may be given a final bathing. Bathing the body, they shave the head cleanly. The cloth used for drying the bathed corpse is to be distributed to those who bathed it, and the handkerchief used for shaving is to be given to the person who shaved the head. The director of practitioners' affairs is obliged to supervise them in clothing the corpse, placing it in the portable shrine, and enshrining it within the infirmary hall by setting up the name tablet on the table, with the following words written on it:

> The Enlightened Spirit of Venerable So-and-so,
> Having Newly Entered Perfect Quiescence

If the deceased is the distinguished west hall official, it may be written as:

> The Spirit of the Previous Abbot of Such-and-such Temple,
> So-and-so Title, Zen Master So-and-so

In other cases, the title is given according to the office held by the deceased.

Offering incense, candles, and various food provisions, the sacred assembly of practitioners chant the *Mahākaruṇā-dhāraṇī* before the shrine and thereby settle the deceased spirit through the invocation of merit transference. During the night, the candles are kept lit all night. The practice hall attendants prepare beforehand artificial funeral flowers made of white paper, while the attendant of the deceased offers morning gruel and a noon meal every day. The administrative official serves tea and sweet hot water three times a day and burns incense. The rice gruel and rice meals are to be offered after the regular chanting held at the Buddha hall and also after the release from the evening session. As the practice hall office attendant rings his hand bell and walks

1148a ahead, the primary seat official leads the practitioners before the funeral shrine. As the abbot burns incense, the director of practitioners' affairs calls for chanting the *Mahākāruṇikacitta-dhāraṇī*s and concludes with the following invocation of merit transference:

> From the foregoing chanting of the sutra, we dedicate the merit thereby accrued to Venerable So-and-so who newly entered ultimate quiescence and was enshrined in the transcendent abode of his realization. Veneration to the Buddhas in the ten directions and the three times, and so on.

Next, those practitioners from the same native province [as the deceased] call for chanting the *dhāraṇī*s, and their senior representative steps forward to burn incense. This same rite is to be conducted three times a day. The only difference in the rite officially held by the temple is that the invocation of merit transference refers to the deceased practitioner by the two characters of his name, whereas in the rite held by the private group, the invocation refers to the deceased by the [second] single character, [perhaps adding an honorific post-positional character such as *gong*.] (E.g., Qiumoluoshi [Kumārajīva] is referred to as "Honorable Shi" [Shi Gong]). The invocation is identical.

If the occasion coincides with the first day of the month or midmonth days or with the imperial coronation day, the public conduct of the rite is excused and the funeral proceeding must also be postponed.

2. Requesting Buddhist Funeral Rites

Without fail, the abbot must be requested to conduct the rite of applying fire [to the funeral pyre]. All other [funeral] rites, such as closing the shrine door (*suokan*), lifting the shrine (*qikan*), lifting the remains (*qigu*), depositing the remains (*ruta*), and so on, can be done by inviting the various officials in rotation, upon consultation with the director of practitioners' affairs and the primary seat official, and taking into consideration ordination seniority. On a small white sheet of paper, the document must be written as follows:

> For Venerable Bhikṣu So-and-so, native of such-and-such province, having just accomplished ultimate quiescence. The funeral rite of applying fire [to the funeral pyre] is to be officiated by the venerable master, abbot of this temple, as respectfully requested by the practice hall official, Bhikṣu So-and-so. The other funeral rites will be officiated as acknowledged in this note.

If the deceased is the west hall guest official or a retired administrative official who resided in the individual quarters and left sizable personal possessions, the following additional rites may be conducted: serving tea and sweet hot water (*dianchatang*), turning around the portable shrine (*zhuankan*), turning around the remains (*zhuangu*), and so on. For these rites, an invitation may be sent on the basis of the rotation system to the retired west hall official and primary seat official residing in the individual quarters, and to renowned personalities of the Zen world. The director of practitioners' affairs, accompanied by his attendant carrying a crepe-wrapped board with an incense burner, candle, and incense, visits the abbot's office, burns incense, and, after a bow, says:

> Since Venerable So-and-so entered ultimate quiescence, the rite of cremation has been scheduled on such-and-such date, for which I respectfully request the venerable to conduct the rite of "touching fire."

The director of practitioners' affairs then presents the note of request before withdrawing. The same propriety is used for making the same request to the various training officials. The director prepares a record book of the funeral rites, as a reference to be consulted before making new requests of ritual conduct on the basis of the rotation system.

3. Appraising the Price of Used Items

The director of practitioners' affairs sends the attendants of his office to request the abbot, the dual order officials, and the assistant officials to be present either at the practice hall office or in the adjacent skylit hall. Before [an assembly of] the practitioners, the seal [on the deceased's parcel of personal items] is opened and one by one the items are taken out of the bamboo case and placed either on the ground or on the raised platform. Each item is shown to the director of practitioners' affairs and priced. While the primary seat official settles the price of each item, adjusting [the price when necessary,] the guest reception official and the assistant official write the names of the items on the board and list the prices below each item in accordance with [the prices thus established]. A marker is made by copying the number of each item, which is then affixed onto the item, and the item is then returned to the bamboo case. After that, another sheet listing all items according to their number and price should be prepared for the occasion of "robe auctioning." No one, whether the abbot, the dual order officials, or the residents of various quarters, is allowed to take away any items for public usage. If there is any item that would be useful for the temple, it may be obtained by paying the due price from the overhead (*choufenqian;* i.e., the three-tenths of the entire transaction that belongs to the temple). If there are numerous possessions, the prices of items may be reduced as a whole so as to benefit more practitioners and thereby advance the fortune of the departed.

4. Prayer Chanting the Night Before the Cremation

The afternoon of the day before the funeral procession for the cremation is scheduled, the attendant of the practice hall office must directly report to the abbot and the dual order officials about the schedule and notify the practitioners by posting the signboard indicating "prayer chanting." The treasury office must also be requested beforehand to prepare a food offering and send workmen to set up the area for the funeral rite. Those practitioners from the same province as well as those related in Dharma lineage [to the deceased] compose a word of tribute for the occasion and pay the treasury office for a food offering. Three pieces of incense must be prepared for the funeral offering. If the deceased was a renowned senior practitioner from a large monastic temple, or one of the west hall residents, or a resident of the individual quarters, and if he accomplished a significant contribution to the status and affairs of the temple, the abbot as well as the dual order officials all conduct the rite of offering, while the director of practitioners' affairs 1148b
reads the words of tribute.

After the cancelation of the evening session has been announced, the practice hall bell is rung to assemble the practitioners for the rite of prayer chanting before the funeral shrine. The administrative official burns incense and offers tea and sweet hot water to the shrine beforehand. The abbot burns incense upon arrival and takes his place at the higher main position of the east order. The director of practitioners' affairs steps forward to burn incense and invites a previously designated training official to conduct the rite of closing the portable shrine door. The designated official steps forward from his order to burn incense and, upon returning, bows. Next he bows before the abbot and, turning toward the east order officials, bows and makes a round, passing in front of each of the east order officials down to the last one, then bows [again]. Next, he turns to the west order officials and bows, and after that, bows together with the practitioners. Making a round, he passes in front of each of the west order officials down to the last one, and, if he is an incumbent official, passes through his vacated position, proceeds to the right of the funeral shrine, and stands there. The attendant of the practice hall office carries a chain on a crepe-wrapped board to the official, and, after completing the rite of closing the door, places the chain over the doors of the shrine.

As the abbot returns to his [central] position, the director of practitioners' affairs steps forward to the left of the table, makes a gesture of greeting [to him] and then to the dual order officials, and completes his offering of incense. The director of practitioners' affairs [now] faces the portable funeral shrine and utters the words of prayer:

> We earnestly reflect that life and death alternate, just as hot and cold change one after another. When it comes, it is as swift as the lightning that strikes across the entire sky, and when it departs is like the waves that cease to exist over the entire ocean. On this day, Venerable So-and-so, who has just entered ultimate quiescence, totally exhausted the causes of life and

abruptly departed from a lifelong dream, [having reached the] understanding that every psychophysical element (*saṃskāra*) is transitory and ultimately quiescent, and hence felicitous. The venerable practitioners have assembled at this place to pay tribute to the shrine and call the sacred names of the Buddhas, so as to help the deceased's spirit advance swiftly toward the Pure Land. May I respectfully request practitioners to intone the sacred names: The Luminous Pure Dharma Body Vairocana Buddha, and so on.

Next, the director of practitioners' affairs calls for chanting the *Mahākaruṇā-dhāraṇī* and intones the invocation of merit transference:

> With this prayer and sutra chanting, we dedicate the merit thereby accrued to the venerable practitioner So-and-so, who has just entered ultimate quiescence. We humbly wish that his spirit surpasses the pure sanctuary, that his karmas be free of worldly defilement, that the lotus bloom opens its noblest blossom, and that the Buddha grant him the certificate of supreme destiny. I humbly request the practitioners once again to intone the prayer: Veneration to the Buddhas in the ten directions and the three times, and so on.

The guest-reception official calls for the chanting of the *Śūraṃgama-dhāraṇī*s and intones the invocation of merit transference:

> With this chanting, we dedicate the merit thereby accrued to the venerable practitioner So-and-so, who has just entered ultimate quiescence. We wish that this will enshrine the transcendent abode of his realization: Veneration to the Buddhas in the ten directions and the three times.

When this is done, the abbot returns to his position at the higher end of the east order line and remains standing there. The practitioners of the Zen world, the colleagues, practitioners from the same native province, and those related in Dharma lineage conduct the funeral rite of offerings in due order. Finally, the chanting of the *Mahākaruṇā-dhāraṇī* is called for. The invocation of merit transference is the same as before.

5. The Funeral Procession

[Before] the procession to the funeral site begins, it is a general rule that the treasury official instructs the attendants in charge of the workmen to prepare firewood for the cremation and mobilize various workmen. After all preparations for the funeral procession have been completed, including [gathering] musical instruments such as cymbals and drums, streamers, artificial flowers to scatter, incense and candles, a portable shrine carriage, and so on, the night before [the funeral] the practice hall office attendant reports that everything is ready to the abbot and the dual order officials and also posts a signboard indicating the schedule for the funeral procession. The next morning, after the [octagonal post] is struck with the mallet to signal that the first serving of rice gruel has been completed, the director of practitioners' affairs makes an additional strike and announces:

> This announcement is for all practitioners. After breakfast, you are requested to participate in the procession to accompany the deceased to the cremation site. Except for those who are on duty at the practitioners' quarters and in charge of guarding the practice hall, everyone is equally required to participate. Respectfully stated.

Then the director of practitioners' affairs once again strikes the [octagonal wooden post] with the mallet to signal the end of his announcement, and, with a bow to the altar of the guardian bodhisattva, turns toward the abbot and bows. Straightening his posture by the board-edge of the primary seat official, he proceeds to make a round through the aisles of the hall up to the outer hall, and once again returns to the inner hall to bow toward the altar before going out. If the event coincides with the day of the imperial birthday, the [post should not be struck] and the practice hall office attendant must at once report this to the abbot and the dual order officials.

When breakfast is over, it is announced at the hall:

> May I request the primary seat official and all practitioners to attend the service of sutra chanting at the infirmary hall, scheduled to begin at the sound of the bell.

At the sound of the practice hall bell, the practitioners assemble and the director of practitioners' affairs intones a prayer. When this is over, the director must announce concisely and mindfully:

> We are about to raise the shrine of the departed spirit and proceed to the place where the memorable rite of cremation will take place. May practitioners intone the sacred names of the Buddhas and thereby express the ascending path and assist the spirit in its passage. Veneration to the Luminous Pure Dharma Body Vairocana Buddha, and so on.

Thereupon, the abbot moves to the higher position of the east order, while the director of practitioners' affairs steps forward to burn incense and invites the training official, as prearranged, to take charge of the rite of lifting the portable shrine. When this is done, the attendants play cymbals, lift the shrine, and carry it out to the temple gate. If the rites of serving tea and sweet hot water and turning the shrine around are scheduled, [the shrine at this point] should be turned around toward the temple buildings, and an incense table placed before it. The primary seat official stands before the shrine, while the practitioners line up in two parallel lines [with the shrine at the center]. The director of practitioners' affairs burns incense and requests another training official to take charge of the rite at the gate. When this is done, the procession continues.

If there is no rite of turning around the shrine, the director of practitioners' affairs steps through the gate, stands facing the temple with palms joined together, and calls for the practitioners

1148c

to intone in unison the *Dhāraṇī for Rebirth in the Pure Land* (*Wangshengzhou*). Both lines then proceed in order, the practitioners holding their palms together, and they pick up some artificial wicker leaves [to scatter along the way]. The attendants stand outside the gate, greeting the practitioners with heads down and palms together, and then fall in behind the procession when all have passed by. The director of practitioners' affairs follows immediately behind the shrine, whereas the head administrative official follows at the end of the two lines of practitioners as the rear guard.

6. Cremation

When the procession reaches the "nirvana platform" (*niepantai;* i.e., the cremation site), the head administrative official burns incense and offers tea. Next, the abbot offers incense, then returns to his position. Thereupon, the director of practitioners' affairs steps forward and, after burning incense, invites the abbot to conduct the rite of applying fire [to the funeral pyre]. The maintenance official bows to the abbot and hands him a lit torch, and waits for the completion of the rite. When the rite is over, the director of practitioners' affairs begins a prayer invocation toward the shrine as follows:

> On this day, the venerable practitioner So-and-so, who has entered ultimate quiescence, though once existing by following the change of causal conditions, has now ceased to exist. Thus, the body is about to be cremated according to the tradition. It is wished that by burning the body which was instrumental to his propagation of the Dharma for a hundred years, his passage to reach the goal of nirvana will be helped unfailingly. It is respectfully requested of the honorable practitioners to help the enlightened spirit by intoning the ten sacred names: Veneration to the Western Paradise, to Amitābha Buddha of Great Compassion and Commiseration, and so on.

[The following invocation of merit transference is intoned] after ten repetitions of the prayer:

> In the foregoing prayer, we called upon the ten sacred names in order to help the deceased be reborn in the Pure Land. We earnestly hope that the wisdom mirror distributes its brilliance, the wind of truth disperses variegated colors, and the flower of the enlightened mind will bloom in the *bodhi* garden and help the mind become cleansed of defilement in the ocean of the Dharma-nature. Having offered three servings of tea and having burned incense over a single burner, we shall send its smoke on a cloud-journey. Veneration to the honorable practitioners.

The head administrative official, at the moment when the prayer refers to "servings of tea" and "burning of incense," steps forward to serve tea and burn incense, whereby he expresses the propriety of the temple community as a whole. In this regard, it is improper for the director of practitioners' affairs to do so (i.e., serve tea and burn incense) while intoning the prayer. The director then calls for chanting the *Mahākaruṇā-dhāraṇī* and concludes with the following invocation of merit transference:

> We dedicate the merit accrued by this prayer and chanting for the sake of the venerable practitioner So-and-so, who has entered ultimate quiescence in order to enshrine the transcendental state of his realization after cremation. Veneration to the Buddhas in the ten directions and the three times.

The guest reception official then calls for chanting the *Śūraṃgama-dhāraṇī*s and concludes with the same invocation of merit transference. (Here, however, the word "prayer" [*niansong*] is omitted.)

The practitioners from the same native province and Dharma lineage also chant sutras and conclude with the same invocation of merit transference.

7. The Auction of the
Deceased's Personal Possessions

After the cremation rite, the practice hall office attendant reports
to the abbot, the dual order officials, and the assistant officials that
the auction of the deceased's personal possessions will be held after
the noon meal in front of the practice hall. A signboard indicating
this event is posted to notify the practitioners. Preparation [for
the auction] in the outer hall should be completed by the time the
practitioners descend from their seats after the noon meal. The
abbot and the primary seat official are seated side by side [with
an arm-length's distance in between] in the rear, while the dual
order officials are seated in two parallel lines facing each other.
Just inside the hallway, a table is placed facing the rear of the
hall, equipped with calligraphy brushes, an inkslab, a standing
bell, scissors, and a simplified robe, as well as other necessary items.
[The auction items will be placed] directly on the floor. The practice hall office attendants report to the abbot, the dual order officials,
and the practitioner assistants when these preparations have been
completed. The practice hall bell is rung to assemble the practitioners. The director of practitioners' affairs, the guest reception
official, and the assistant official simultaneously enter the hall and,
on reaching their respective positions, sit facing the rear, while
the practice hall, alms-offering, and meal proceeding novice attendants line up to bow toward the abbot and the dual order officials.
Then the attendants turn toward the director of practitioners'
affairs, the guest reception official, and the abbot's assistant and
greet them with a bow. They place the bamboo basket [contain-
ing the items to be auctioned] before the abbot and the dual order
officials in turn, so that each may inspect the seal. They then receive
the key from the primary seat official, open the basket, take out
the items one by one in numerical order, place them on the floor
display area, and set the empty basket to the side, facing the rear.

The director of practitioners' affairs rises, rings the standing
bell once, and intones a prayer:

The floating cloud has dispersed, and there remains no sight of it whatsoever. The last remnant of a candle has been exhausted in extinguishing its own flame. The possessions of the deceased are hereby auctioned to express this impermanence. May the practitioners now intone [the ten sacred names 1149a of the Buddhas] for the sake of the venerable practitioner So-and-so and assist his enlightened spirit to be reborn in the Pure Land. Veneration to the Luminous Pure Dharma Body Vairocana Buddha, and so on.

After the prayer of the ten sacred names, the director of practitioners' affairs once again rings the bell and says:

The rules of the auction are based on the normative regulations. Everyone is obliged to examine the items with regard to their being old or new, long or short, and so on, for after the sound of the bell ceases, no dispute is allowed. Respectfully stated.

The director of practitioners' affairs once again rings the bell, then holds up the deceased's ordination certificate and cuts it horizontally across the name characters with the scissors, saying:

It is demonstrated to the practitioners that the ordination certificate of the deceased is now torn asunder.

Ringing the bell once again, he hands the certificate to the attendant, who in turn presents it to the dual order officials. The director of practitioners' affairs takes off his *kaṣāya* robe and places it inside the bell, and dons the simplified robe.

The attendants of the practice hall office pick up the items one by one, in numerical order, and hand them to the director of practitioners' affairs who, in turn, presents each item to the participants and calls out its number, description, and price. If an item is estimated to be worth one thousand in cash (i.e., one *guan*), the beginning price to be announced should start at one hundred. The attendants of the practice hall inform all the participants of the price by relaying the announcement. As participants respond [by calling out prices], the amount gradually increases and when it reaches the originally set amount of one thousand, the director of practitioners' affairs rings the bell and announces: "This item is sold for one *guan*." The remaining items are all treated in the same manner. When two people simultaneously respond with a call, the attendant announces: "Both calls are nullified, sir." In this case, the items must be auctioned once again from the beginning until the bell is rung; this is the normative method. The attendant of the practice hall office determines the name of the person who has made the winning bid. The guest reception official copies the name down and places it on the bulletin board, and the abbot's assistant, referring to the name, issues a card and has the attendant in charge of meal proceedings give it to the person. The attendant then puts the item back into the basket. Completing the bidding on each item with the sound of the bell, the director of practitioners' affairs concludes the rite of the auction with the following invocation of merit transference:

> The merit hereby accrued from this auction and prayer is dedicated for the sake of the venerable practitioner So-and-so, who has just entered ultimate quiescence, toward the enshrinement of the transcendental abode of his realization. May I once again request the practitioners to intone the prayer: Veneration to the Buddhas in the ten directions and the three times, and so on.

In recent times, in order to stop disputes and disorder, the lottery method has often been used. (For details on this, see Chapter V, part VI, section 15). Items that are not picked up by the bidders within a three-day period are priced appropriately for subsequent sale, and a record book, the "Funeral Revenue and Expenditure Account Book" (*banzhangshi*), must be prepared. It is said in the *Record of the Rising Splendor of the Tradition*:

> According to the Buddha's own regulations, the meaning of distributing the robes is to create in the mind of the living

the following thought: "It has become like this with him, and it will be like this with me as well."

Such a thought is expected to reduce one's desire and attachment. Today, however, it seems to work to the contrary, for many compete and dispute over the prices bid [for the items of the deceased] and do not reflect upon the [transitory] nature of their own existence. This is the height of stupidity.

8. Depositing the Remains

After cremation, the practitioner in charge of the funeral proceedings, those who come from the same province, and those who are related in Dharma lineage together collect the remains, wrap them in cotton, and cover the bundle with a square cloth. They place the remains in a wooden box, seal it, and carry it back to the infirmary hall.

(The word "new" (*xin*) must be deleted from the name tablet.)

Sutra chanting should be performed three times a day. On the afternoon of the third day, the account book is to be displayed in front of the practice hall, making everything accountable to the practitioners.

(If the formula used differs from the standard format, or if there is some point in question, it should be pardoned with due propriety and notice given above as well as below, and [the issue] rectified on the strict basis of fact. If, on the other hand, there is no factual basis for dispute, one must not involve oneself in causing trouble. Anyone who committed a transgression should be subject to the punishment of expulsion. The abbot as well as the official in charge of the funeral proceedings must remain impartial, fair, and equal-minded. It would be best if he could persuade others through the example of his own behavior.)

Thereupon, the display of the account record ends.

The practice hall office notifies the practitioners beforehand and posts a signboard indicating the rite of sending the ashes to the tower. At the appointed time, the practitioners assembled at the sound of the practice hall bell, and the rite of "lifting the ashes" (*qigu*) is requested at the infirmary hall. Escorting the ashes from the infirmary hall to the memorial tower, they conduct the rite of "depositing the ashes" in the tower. After depositing the ashes, the administrative official seals the tower. The director of practitioners' affairs calls for chanting the *Mahākaruṇā-dhāraṇī* and concludes with the following invocation of merit transference:

> The merit hereby accrued is intended for the sake of Venerable So-and-so, who entered ultimate quiescence, and, on depositing his ashes in the tower, to enshrine the transcendental abode of his realization. Veneration to the Buddhas in the ten directions and the three times, and so on.

The guest reception official calls for chanting the *Śūraṃgama-dhāraṇī*s and practitioners from the same province also conduct a service of chanting. The invocation of merit transference in each case is the same.

End of Fascicle Six

Fascicle Seven

Chapter VII (*continued*)

9. Format for the Accounting Record
Inscribed on a Wooden Board

The following is the record of the auction revenue and its expenditure regarding the late Venerable So-and-so's possessions:

A revenue of one thousand *guanwen* (i.e., one *guan* = one thousand *wen*). (This is the total revenue from the auction. If there are any other items of revenue, they must be detailed in a serial list.)

An expenditure of ninety-one *guanwen*. (The items to be recorded on the wooden board.)

Itemized in detail:

Fifteen *guanwen:* The funeral shrine.
Three *guanwen:* Procurement of funeral offerings.
Three *guanwen:* The rice gruel offering.
One *guanwen:* The shrine lamp oil.
Ten *guanwen:* Paper, brushes, and so on for records; flags, artificial flowers, and wicker leaves.
One *guanwen:* For shaving the head of the deceased.
Two *guan* and five hundred *wen:* For the rite of lifting the shrine and transport of the deceased.
Five hundred *wen:* For preparing hot water for bathing the deceased.
Two *guanwen:* For bathing and cleaning the corpse.
One *guanwen:* For the shrine attendant to serve rice gruel and rice.

Five hundred *wen:* For treasury office attendants to report and prepare the funeral offering.

Five hundred *wen:* For setting the area of the funeral rite with curtains, floormats, and so on.

Five hundred *wen:* For the work of accounting the revenue and expenditure in detail.

Five hundred *wen:* For funeral offerings prepared and delivered from the treasury office to the shrine attendant.

Five hundred *wen:* For a kitchen subfunctionary to cook food provisions.

Five hundred *wen:* For a treasury office tea serving attendant to offer tea and sweet hot water.

Five hundred *wen:* For a ceremonial leader to assist the attendants' activities.

Two *guanwen:* To the practice hall attendants to help provide information.

Five hundred *wen:* For the foreman to arrange manpower for various work and activities.

Five hundred *wen:* For the abbot's attendant to convey the master's commands and carry his incense case.

Ten *guanwen:* For the novice attendants to participate in various prayers and sutra chanting.

One *guanwen:* For practice hall attendants to display the monetary gift records and strike the wooden sounding block.

Two *guanwen:* For attendants of the four offices to serve tea.

Fifteen *guanwen:* For manpower required to lift and carry the portable funeral shrine.

One *guanwen:* For attendants to play cymbals for ceremonies.

Three *guanwen:* For attendants to play drums for ceremonies.

Three *guanwen:* For six workmen to carry the incense table, flags, candles, and so on.

Five hundred *wen:* For novice attendants to create and distribute paper flowers and branches for the funeral procession.

One *guanwen:* For a workman to help with the cremation.

Three *guanwen:* For workmen to assist the abbot's group for the procession.

One *guanwen:* For workmen of the four offices to transport the bamboo cases to auction.

Five hundred *wen:* For the attendant at the auction to affix   1149c
an identity tag on each item to be auctioned.

Five hundred *wen:* For attendants to show each item at the auction.

Five hundred *wen:* For an alms-serving attendant to give each successful bidder a tally.

Five hundred *wen:* For an alms-serving attendant to place auctioned items back into the basket at the auction.

Five hundred *wen:* For the meal-proceeding attendant to deliver the lottery tray to bidders at the auction.

Five hundred *wen:* For a workman to collect the remains after cremation.

One *guanwen:* For a workman to lift the box of ashes when depositing the remains in the tower.

One *guanwen:* For workmen to attend the tower at the time of depositing the remains.

The foregoing are the items included in the expenditure of ninety-one *guanwen.*

An expenditure of two hundred and seventy *guanwen.* (An amount totaling three-tenths of what remains after the foregoing expenditures recorded on the wooden board is to be added to the temple's annual revenue.)

An expenditure of one hundred and thirty-five *guanwen* for Buddhist funeral rites.

Itemized as follows:

Twenty *guanwen:* For the material cost of the cremation rite.

Ten *guanwen:* For a monetary gift at the rite of applying fire to the pyre.

Forty *guanwen:* For the rites of closing and lifting the shrine and lifting and depositing the remains.

Twenty *guanwen:* For monetary gifts at the four ceremonial rites of the foregoing events.

Thirty *guanwen:* For the prayer rite at the funeral site by the director of practitioners' affairs, auction records by the guest reception official and the attendant of the guardian bodhisattva.

Fifteen *guanwen:* For three monetary gifts for the foregoing events.

An expenditure of fifteen *guanwen:* five *guanwen* each for the funeral procession headed by the primary seat official, rear-guarded by the head administrative official, and the chanting led by the director of practitioners' affairs with the hand bell. These are itemized for the above total.

An expenditure of nine *guanwen:* three *guanwen* each for the chanting led by the guest reception official and the abbot's assistant who carried the incense case; two *guanwen* for the attendant of the guardian bodhisattva who handled the auction revenues; and one *guanwen* for the maintenance official who provided the torch. These are itemized for the above total.

An expenditure of fifteen *guanwen* for the attendants of the abbot, the dual order officials, and the practice hall official who served at the auction proceedings and made the records of itemized objects and prices; incidental food provisions three times for their work, of which the cost is received by the abbot's office. These are itemized for the above total.

An expenditure of twenty *guanwen* for the inspection and sanction by the abbot and the dual order officials of the contents of auction, of which the cost of two is received by the abbot's office. These are itemized for the above total.

An expenditure of four hundred and forty-four guan and five hundred *wen* for the service of sutra chanting by the practitioners, of which Guanyin, (Avalokiteśvara) Bodhisattva, the guardian bodhisattva (*shengseng*), and the abbot each receive the amount of two *guanwen;* approximately four hundred regular practitioners each receive one *guanwen;* the practice hall attendants who participate in the chanting, the practitioners-in-absentia, and the recent arrivals, together numbering seventy-five, each receive one half, five hundred *wen.* These are itemized for the above total.

Excluding the foregoing expenditures, an expenditure of five hundred *wen* (diverted for public use by the practice hall office).

The foregoing report is prepared as before [the venerables' inspection]

Date and year	Prepared by So-and-so attendant
	The practice hall office

Records kept by:	Assistant of the guardian bodhisattva,
	So-and-so (signed)
	Guest reception official, So-and-so (signed)

The maintenance official	The Buddha hall master
The kitchen hall official	The bath hall master
The treasury official	The Tripiṭaka hall master
The director of practitioners' affairs	The Tripiṭaka hall master
The treasury official	The secretarial official
The administrative official	The rear practice hall official
The head administrative official	The primary seat official

Signed by all dual order officials

The abbot, signed   1150a

The institution of the wooden board account record (*banzhangshi*) perhaps derived from the custom of earlier times to record whatever information was necessary for accomplishing ritual conduct on a wooden board, whereby it was shown that no arbitrary changes [to the record] were allowed. This has become the practice of preparing a wooden board accounting record on the death of a practitioner of the Zen monastic community. Whenever a practitioner dies, his personal items are distributed at auction for the sake of the other practitioners, by pricing these items before the practitioners' very eyes as a disciplinary measure to counter the greedy accumulation of personal possessions. At the auction, such possessions are assigned a monetary value, necessarily requiring a record of reference inscribed on a wooden board. Other than the amount expended for an event, the remaining money must be divided into three parts and seven parts, with the former amount of three-tenths given to the temple's general fund as overhead.

(For example, in the case of one hundred *guanwen*, thirty *guanwen* would be turned over to the temple's revenues. In the case of there being less than a hundred *guan*, no three-tenths overhead should be considered.)

The remaining amount must be equally distributed to the practitioners. If remuneration for the practitioners' service of chanting sutras is one hundred *wen*, one *guan* must be due for conducting a religious rite, and twice that amount is due to the abbot. Using a revenue of one thousand *guan* as a standard, the distribution of expenditures has been shown in the format above. If a given auction brings a higher amount, a proportional increase should be made as to each expenditure; if it brings in less revenue, a proportional decrease in expenditure should be made. Taking into account the actual circumstances and also taking into consideration the number of practitioners, adequate and expedient changes should be made.

(If a recently deceased retiree official left behind personal possessions such as a rice field, rice crops, cottages, bedding, furniture, and so on, all these must be turned over to the temple. In accordance with the amount acquired from the auction, if it is more than what is necessary, more days of services for chanting sutras may be prescribed to dispense with the excess money as a gift to the practitioners, and by scheduling additional rites and services, such as servings of tea and sweet hot water, turning the funeral shrine around, and so on.)

End of Chapter VII: The Practitioners
of the Zen Community

Chapter VIII

The Annual Celebration Days
and Calendar

I. Preface to the Chapter

Practitioners do not follow the order of their chronological age but that of ordination age, so that [the religious] world is distinguished from the secular one. In the western regions (i.e., the Central Asian Buddhist countries including India), there are three seasons, one of which is established as the period of retreat, during which no one may leave or come to the monastery. The system of order is based on seniority determined by whether one's learning of the Zen texts by heart (*chansong*), practice of cross-legged seated meditation (*xingzuo*) and year of ordination (*shoujie*) [were accomplished] earlier or later than another's. For the duration of ninety days [each year], practitioners [remain in their respective residences] in order to achieve some definite degree of merit in the practice of the path. In the thirty days [prior to the retreat period], each acquires the basic needs of life (i.e., clothing, food, and so on), enabling them to develop Zen insight internally and nurture their physical well-being externally, so that they can sustain peace of mind and body [through the subsequent period of concentration]. Every practitioner is obliged to commit himself to that full period and carry out disciplined training without wasting a moment, and to spare every living thing and be motivated by compassion and patience. What a wonderful institution this is, which has been followed for ten thousand generations!

The five regions of the Indian continent are so vast that the weather in these regions varies between hot, cold, rainy, and dry and is never the same everywhere. Thus, the period of retreat begins in the fourth month in some provinces, in the fifth month in others, and even in the twelfth month elsewhere, although it always begins on the sixteenth day of the month. The so-called rainy season retreat(*yuanju*) has been institutionalized according to the various geographical regions and their seasonal changes. It is sometimes called the "summer retreat" (*zuoxia*) and at other times the "winter retreat (*zuola*), and it was on the basis of this retreat [period] that the meaning of "ordination age" (*jiela*) began to be used to refer to the years of a practitioner's career. It is, however, a kind of baseless vulgar saying that [the expression, "so-and-so many years of winter retreat," originally referring to the determination of a practitioner's career in reference to his ordination age], was distorted to mean that examining the quality of a wax-made statue buried in the ice is to verify the impeccability of a person's practice in terms of clean ice, and that burying a wax-made human form in the ground is the way to examine whether his practice has accomplished the goal or not. How could such distorted ideas have come from our traditional transmission? Moreover, what is practiced and experienced in our tradition cannot be fathomed even by a holy man [such as Laozi]. How much less could such an external object be a measurement of the state of religious transcendence or immanence?

Today, in the Zen monastic institution, the inauguration of the summer retreat is set for the mid-month (i.e., fifteenth) day of the fourth lunar month, and it ends on the mid-month day of the seventh lunar month. If the retreat is set to begin one day earlier, by performing a special ceremony, every retreat participant is enabled to fully concentrate on their intent, the fulfillment of their practice within the retreat period. Thus, omitting or abridging troublesome literary statements is not necessarily discordant with the spirit of the Vinaya discipline. [Some argue that] this is not in accordance with the Vinaya, but they do not realize or understand the intended meaning of the rule hidden outside it. In China, winter begins at the beginning of the year and is regarded as being the start of the four seasons. Everything, whether material or temporal, is regarded as being new and is celebrated by all in their hearts.

1150b

It is important to coordinate the seasonal proprieties [of monastic life] with those of secular society. Since it is the best method of conversion to follow such expediency, the beginning and end of the summer retreat, the winter solstice, and the new year have been institutionalized as the four major festival days [in Zen monastic communities]. The manner of the practitioners in their circling and turning movement is so regulated that the entire session appears to be a grand gathering of supernatural beings, and the vocal exchange of question and answer between host and guest is comparable to that of a lion's roar. Their ceremonial proprieties are well ordered; how glorious it is to regard them!

II. The Inauguration of the Annual Summer Retreat

1. The Presentation of the Residency Chart Draft Prior to the Summer Retreat

On the first day of the third month, it is customary for a Zen monastic temple to issue a residency chart draft (format given below), after which the abbot no longer accepts new residents. The practice hall office copies the number [and names] of practitioners from the residents' "Ordination Record Book" (*jielapai*) and instructs an attendant to present this to the primary seat official, then to the abbot and the dual order officials [for inspection]. [He then] posts it in front of the practice hall and sets up a table below it, equipped with an inkslab and brushes. For approximately three days, after the noon meal practitioners are advised to check the residency chart draft and correct any mistakes or wrong information about themselves. The reason that the chart draft is not immediately finalized as to the record of the units of floor space (*chuangli*) is simply because it is feared that temporary confusion may result from such mistakes, and also because when there are a great number of residents omissions may occasionally occur. Therefore, in order to prepare the residency chart (*tuzhang*), a draft is first made, and each member must examine whether his name and rank appear in it in the proper order of seniority. In recent years, those who like to dispute and create disturbances, based on their strength and motivated by private interests, compete for superiority with others [in regard to their respective Dharma lineages], thereby placing blame on each other and engaging in quarrels, with the result of greater disturbance among the resident practitioners. Such transgressors must be censured and expelled altogether. If, in effect, some do derogate others' names and transgress the norms of the precepts, it is obvious that the director of practitioners' affairs must deal with them by informing the primary seat official about the matter in detail and also by reporting it to the abbot.

Format of the Residency Chart Draft

(The ordination rank is to be written in red ink, while the name is to be written in black ink.)

The Ordination Ages of Practitioners

Name and Title
Ordination Year of Regnal Era

The Original Ordination [authorized by the Tathāgata Bhīṣmagarjitaghoṣasvararāja (Buddha Weiyinwang)]
The Immemorial Past [referred to in the *Lotus Sutra*]

The Venerable Eldest Senior Practitioner Ājñātakauṇḍinya
Ordination [authorized by Śākyamuni Buddha]

The Venerable Master Abbot

So-and-so Senior Practitioner
Ordination, Such-and-such Year of the Zhiyuan Era

So-and-so Senior Practitioner
Ordination, Such-and-such Year of the Yuanzhen Era

So-and-so Senior Practitioner
Ordination, Such-and-such Year of the Dade Era

So-and-so Senior Practitioner
Ordination, Such-and-such Year of the Zhida Era

[and so on]

The foregoing chart is prepared as presented to [the practitioners]. It is feared that there might be some errors; should there be any, each of the venerable practitioners is advised to correct them. May all the venerable practitioners examine, without fail, their respective records given on this chart.

Date and Year

Prepared by So-and-so Official
The Practice Hall Office

2. The Serving of Tea by the New Residents on Joining the Practitioners' Quarters

After establishing membership in the practitioners' quarters, based on the preceding examples, the new residents donate funds to the quarters for the cost of a tea reception. They ask the head official of the quarters which day they should be in charge of the tea serving according to the rotation assignment system, and post a signboard for the tea serving to inform the practitioners. The signboard reads as follows:

Today, immediately after the noon meal, So-and-so senior practitioner and others (three, six, or nine, listed by name) will be in charge [of the tea serving].

Each member must carry a small incense case and be properly attired. They line up beforehand to the right of the quarters' entrance and wait for the practitioners to leave the practice hall. The tea master of the quarters strikes the wooden sounding block in front of the quarters, and when the practitioners have all arrived, he receives them with a gesture of greeting, then returns to his position and stands there.

Those who are serving tea stand in line and, after giving greetings, request the practitioners to take their seats. When everyone is seated, they proceed in two or three groups to the mid-hall incense burner, located between the higher- and lower-ranking sections of the hall. No more than nine practitioners should offer incense. Three practitioners [at a time] step forward [to offer incense, and then] step back and turn around, mutually coordinating their movements [with the other practitioners] in a precise and smooth manner. Forming a line, they bow, and proceed, dividing themselves into separate groups, toward the incense burner and bow. [After offering incense] they return to [the end of their line], bow in unison, and remain standing. This is called "offering incense on behalf of the practitioners." The small wooden sounding block in the hall is struck twice to signal that the serving of tea has been extended to every member in the hall. The jars of tea [for the second serving] are now brought into the hall through the rear hall entrance. Once again, the practitioners step forward in groups of three as before, bow before the incense burner, return [to their places], forming a single line, and bow in unison. This is called the "commendation to drink tea" (*yicha*). When the wooden sounding block is struck once, the teabowls are retrieved and the practitioners all rise from their seats. The head official of the quarters steps forward to the incense burner and on behalf of all the practitioners thanks the practitioners who served the tea. At the same time the practitioners, from their respective positions, [show their thanks] by joining their palms in a gesture of respect. Thereupon, the head official of the quarters returns to his place.

The serving practitioners once again line up and bow. Again they proceed in groups toward the incense burner and bow before it [after offering incense]. This is called "giving thanks for the guests' presence." As before, they step back, form a line, and bow [toward the altar]. The wooden sounding block located in front of the quarters is struck three times, signaling the practitioners to give greetings harmoniously and leave the hall. The head official of the quarters instructs the tea master to invite those who served tea at the reception and serves tea for them. When all the new residents have completed their serving of tea on the occasion of joining the quarters, the head official invites them to the tea reception each day, designating their names on the basis of ordination seniority. The propriety of this tea reception is identical to the above.

3. The Issuance of Various Charts before the Summer Retreat

Once the draft of the ordination chart is finalized, the practice hall official draws up the *Śūraṃgama-dhāraṇī*s ceremonial chart, the prayer chanting and practice hall rounds chart, the bed quilt space unit chart, the almsbowl seating position chart (formats given previosly as well as below), and the ordination age tablet, all on the basis of ordination seniority. The chart showing where each individual keeps his bowl, practices zazen, and sleeps must be divided into sixteen sections. (The remaining charts are not affected by the size of the practice hall.) Excluding those head officials who have individual quarters, the west hall guest official, the primary seat official, and the retired officials who should be assigned to the head position of each section, the remaining practitioners are assigned to the seats of the sixteen sections according to ordination seniority. In the *Ancient Regulations,* one of the officials of the retiree's hall was assigned to a seat which was shared by another practitioner. Later, however, this double assignment was abolished because it created dispute and competition.

The [foregoing] charts, all of which ought to be formulated according to ordination seniority, both original and corrected, must be presented together for inspection, first to the primary seat official and then to the abbot. These charts, when finalized, must be recopied and presented along with the originals. Only the almsbowl seating chart must be presented to all the officials who have individual quarters. On the day of the ceremonial bathing of Śākyamuni, all the charts must be displayed in front of the Buddha hall. The quilt and almsbowl (i.e., zazen and meal position) seating chart (*beibowei*) must be displayed beforehand, with a small bulletin board on which is written:

> After the morning rice gruel, the quilt and almsbowl seats will be assigned. May every practitioner know of this matter. Respectfully stated by the practice hall official on such-and-such day of such-and-such month.

Chart of the Initial Head Seats of the Sixteen Raised Meditation Platforms and Almsbowl Positions

head seats not specified		sleeping positions identical
	inner hall	
(8)	(4) Rs E — D Rs (3)	(7)
Rs	(12) Rs — (11) Rs	Rs
Rs	Rs (16) — guardian bodhisattva shrine — (15) Rs	Rs
Rs	(14) Rs — (13) Rs	Rs
Rs	Rs (10) — (9) Rs	Rs
Rs	B Rs (2) — A — (1) Rs I G C	Rs
(6)	skylit hall — skylit hall	(5)
	S P O N M L K J — outer hall — F H Q Q Q Q Q	
	wooden rack — wooden rack	
	ss ss ss — ss ss ss	

front entrance

Key

A. Abbot

B. West Hall Official

C. Primary Seat Official

D. Rear Primary Seat Official

E. Trainee Primary Seat Official

F. Administrative Head

G. Secretarial Official

H. Director of the Practice Hall

I. Scripture Hall Official

J. Guest Reception Official

K. Master of the Bath House

L. Master of Ceremonial Affairs

M. Master of the Practitioners' Quarters

N. Master of Hermitages

O. Master of Ceremonial Proceedings

P. Master of the Memorial Towers

Q. Assistants to the Abbot's Office

R. Practitioners

S. Recent Arrivals

4. Special Serving of Sweet Hot Water for the Quarters' Residents at the Beginning and End of the Summer Retreat

(Including the *Śūraṃgama-dhāraṇī*s Prayer Service at Its Inauguration and Completion)

At the beginning of the fourth month, or when the practitioners visit the abbot's office to express thanks for having been granted residency, the practice hall official should have already finalized the ordination chart and the head official of the quarters must have completed the following items on the basis of ordination seniority:

1. The sutra cabinet assignment chart.

2. The tea and sweet hot water propriety seat chart.

3. The ordination seniority name list tablet.

4. The seniority of joining the quarters name tablet.

5. The calendar of regular shaving days.

6. The chart of the positions of jars and bowls for serving tea and sweet hot water during the summer retreat.

Whoever wishes to volunteer to be a member of the serving team should note his name down in reference to these positions.

After these charts have been completed, they are displayed together in the rear section of the quarters at the time when the quarters' residents exchange the morning greeting.

On the afternoon of the twelfth day, the practice hall office attendants report to the abbot and the dual order officials that the service of sutra chanting will be held at the practitioners' quarters. A tablet announcing "sutra chanting" is posted at each quarters to inform the practitioners of the event. The head official of the quarters sweeps and cleans the hall. Having prepared beforehand the invitation for a special reception of sweet hot water (format given below) to all the quarters' residents, he posts it in the outer hall lower section of the quarters. The preparation consists of setting up the tablets indicating seating, arranging alms offerings on the altar of the enshrined Guanyin image, placing incense burners and candle stands in both the higher and lower sections of the hall, and heating up the sweet hot water beforehand. The head official of the quarters personally delivers a portion of the sweet hot water to the abbot's office and instructs the tea master of the quarters to distribute it to the quarters of the dual order officials.

1151a11   After these two deliveries of sweet hot water have been completed, the small wooden sounding block located within the quarters is struck. First, the minor propriety of serving sweet hot water is conducted, for which the seating tablets must be reset. This reception is conducted especially for the first master of the quarters, the second master of the quarters, and the *Śūraṃgama-dhāraṇī*s ceremonial leader [of the quarters], who are assigned to carry the jars and cups [for serving the major reception]. The associate head official (*liaozhang*) is invited as main participant. They take their seats when the head official of the quarters, with a gesture of greeting, offers incense, and [they drink a cup of sweet hot water] when he offers incense and makes a gesture of greeting [a second time]. The associate head official then returns to his seat and the minor reception is completed.

The wooden sounding block located outside the quarters is struck to signal the associate head official and the practitioners to enter the hall and stand at their respective seat positions. The assistant to the director of practitioners' affairs, invited as main participant, is seated symmetrically to the head official in the rear section, separated by an arm's length. The associate head official is seated in the front section directly opposite from and facing the head official, while the practitioners take their positions at the fourth seat board according to ordination seniority. Dividing the serving area into two, the first and second masters of the quarters conduct the propriety of the serving. They greet the practitioners one by one with a bow. Upon returning to their places, they make a gesture of greeting to request the practitioners to sit, and burn incense with another gesture. At the signal of two strikes on the quarters' small wooden sounding block, they serve the sweet hot water, and when [all have been served] they make a gesture of greeting to request the practitioners to drink. At the signal of another strike of the quarter's wooden sounding block, they retrieve the serving cups. The associate head official of the quarters steps forward to the incense burner and expresses thanks for the sweet hot water. At the signal of three strikes of the wooden sounding block outside the quarters, all withdraw from their seats.

When the dual order officials enter the quarters, the primary seat official and the head administrative official offer incense, return to their respective positions, and remain standing. The head official of the quarters stands outside to the right of the entrance, waiting for the abbot's arrival. He receives the abbot and follows him into the hall, then burns incense and returns to his position at the end of the west order. As the head official of the quarters steps forward to burn incense, the *Śūraṃgama-dhāraṇī*s ceremonial leader intones the sacred verses and offers the invocation of merit transference. He sees the abbot off. The propriety of the twelfth day of the seventh month (i.e., the last day of the summer retreat) is identical.

Format of the Written Invitation

So-and-so, the Guarding Bhikṣu of the practitioners' quarters, respectfully conducts a serving of sweet hot water this evening at this quarters' hall, especially in honor of the residents of the quarters as a whole as part of the propriety of the inauguration (or completion) of the summer retreat. We earnestly request your honorable presence at this occasion with due compassion.

Day and month

Respectfully written by
So-and-so, Guarding Bhikṣu
The Practitioners' Quarters

Format of the Envelope

Letters of Invitation

To
The Honorable Zen Masters, Resident Members
of the Practitioners' Quarters

From
So-and-so, Guarding Bhikṣu
of the Practitioners' Quarters

1151b11

**5. Inauguration of the *Śūraṃgama-dhāraṇīs*
Prayer Service**

This ceremonial session must be inaugurated on the thirteenth day of the fourth lunar month. The practice hall official copies the ceremonial chart (format given below) beforehand, referring to the records of the practitioners' ordination seniority. He posts this chart along with all other charts in front of the Buddha hall on the day of bathing the statue of the infant Śākyamuni (i.e., the day of the Buddha's birthday celebration), and requests the secretarial official to compose a word of tribute. The director of practitioners' affairs appoints beforehand someone endowed with a good voice to be the ceremonial leader of the *Śūraṃgama-dhāraṇīs* prayer service and accompanies him to the abbot's office and the administrative office to introduce him. Both offices invite the ceremonial leader for a snack, with the director of practitioners' affairs as a participant.

On the appointed day, the director of practitioners' affairs copies [a special] sacred verse to include in the universal invocation of merit transference directed toward all beings. (The verse, composed by Zen Master Zhenxie Qingliao [ca. eleventh to twelfth century], is given below.) The verse is posted on the right and left pillars of the Buddha hall. In some monastic temples, a tablet on which the verse has been inscribed is hung on the pillars. The evening before the day [of the ceremony], the practice hall office attendants notify the practitioners:

> After breakfast tomorrow morning, the *Śūraṃgama-dhāraṇī*s prayer service is scheduled to be inaugurated at the Buddha hall. Every one, properly attired, is requested to attend the service of chanting sutras.

1151c

A tablet announcing the sutra chanting is posted at each quarters of the temple.

The next day, after the morning rice gruel, the dual order officials and the abbot are informed when the preparations have been completed in the Buddha hall. Starting from the practitioners' quarters, the wooden sounding block is sounded to relay the signal to the wooden sounding blocks of all corridors of the temple, ending with that of the abbot's office. When the abbot comes out of his office, this is signaled by three strikes of the metal gong at the kitchen hall, followed by the sound of the large bell, the practice hall bell, and the Buddha hall bell all at once. Arriving at the altar of the Buddha hall, the abbot burns incense, offers tea and sweet hot water to the Buddha, and takes his place mid-hall. Thereupon, the attendants play the cymbals, and the director of practitioners' affairs greets the abbot and the dual order officials, signaling them to offer incense in successive pairs from each order.

(According to the *Ancient Regulations,* there is no performance of prostrations by the practitioners [at this moment in the ceremony]; however, recently it has become customary for practitioners to perform three prostrations. During this time, the abbot kneels, left knee up and right knee on the ground, before the incense burner and makes the respectful gesture of joining his palms together. This same propriety is performed in the ceremonial proceeding for the prayer of imperial longevity and the commemoration of the Buddha's birthday. It is not known for certain which patriarch may have started this tradition. In tracing the origin of this propriety, it may be said that the practitioners' act of prostration and the abbot's kneeling down, as well as the reading of the word of tribute, clearly point to the sense of celebration for imperial longevity and to the sense of gratitude and discharging of indebtedness to Śākyamuni Buddha. These meanings must really be emphasized by strict adherence to the proprieties. On the other hand, the *Śūraṃgama-dhāraṇī*s prayer service is essentially meant to be a prayer on the part of the practitioners for the successful completion of the summer retreat. Hence, the proprieties in question must be inappropriate for this kind of ceremony, and it is best to omit them here and follow the *Ancient Regulations*.)

After the *Verses of Adoration for the Buddha* is recited and the word of tribute is read, the ceremonial leader invokes the presence of the Buddhas and bodhisattvas to the place of the *Śūraṃgama-dhāraṇī*s prayer service, with the practitioners' accord. The ceremonial leader then recites the Sanskrit verse and continues to recite the introductory passage of the *Śūraṃgama-dhāraṇī*s. He initiates the prayer service by intoning the esoteric verses, and upon completion utters the phrase *"Mo-he"* ("Hurrah to the Great Vehicle!"), with which the practitioners again accord in unison. Thereupon, the director of practitioners' affairs gives the following invocation of merit transference:

> The merit accrued from chanting the sutra is dedicated to the goal of absolute truth (*bhūta-tathatā; zhenruo*) and absolute reality (*bhūta-koṭi; shiji*), and also thereby to enshrine the state of supreme enlightenment (*bodhi; puti*) that follows the realization of Buddha-nature (*buddha-phala; foguo*). May this deed help us discharge our obligation resulting from the four kinds of indebtedness, help those who abide in the three worlds to equally realize enlightenment, and

together with all sentient beings of the Dharma world, reach the perfect realization of omniscient knowledge (*sarvathā-jñāna; zhongzhi*). Veneration to the Buddhas in the ten directions and the three periods [of time], and so on.

Each day, the practitioners take a short recess after the morning rice gruel. When the practitioners have changed into ceremonial robes, the practice hall office attendant notifies the dual order officials and then the abbot. After that, the attendants begin striking each of the wooden sounding blocks located throughout the corridors of the temple three times. The kitchen metal gong is sounded three times when the abbot comes out [of his office]. If [the abbot does not come out], the metal gong and the large bell should not be sounded; however, the practice hall bell and the Buddha hall bell should be tolled every day in any case. When the practitioners have gathered in the hall and the chanting of the *Śūraṃgama-dhāraṇīs* has been completed, the ceremonial leader intones the verses of universal invocation of merit transference, chanted by the practitioners in unison. If this ceremonial session coincides with the first day of the month or the mid-month day, the director of practitioners' affairs should express celebration of imperial longevity in his invocation of merit transference. On the thirteenth day of the seventh lunar month, the ceremonial fulfillment of the *Śūraṃgama-dhāraṇīs* prayer service should be conducted (this propriety is identical as before). The only difference is that the ceremonial leader is required to intone the ending passage that comes after the sacred prayer verses, followed by the invocation of merit transference by the director of practitioners' affairs, after which all leave the hall.

The Universal Invocation
of Merit Transference

The foregoing chanting of the sacred *Śūraṃgama-dhāraṇīs*   1152a
has been intoned by the sacred assembly of *bhikṣus*. The merit thereby accrued is dedicated to the *deva* and *nāga* guardians of the Dharma, to the local earth spirits and the gods of the

temple building, the creators of things. May those suffering in the three worlds of existence and of the eight kinds of difficulties be freed. May the four kinds of benefactors and the three worlds of existence be fully rewarded. May the state be in peace while armed revolts are quelled. May the wind and rain be properly ordered so that people have well-being and ease. May this assembly, well disciplined, wish to accomplish an advantageous advance. May everyone traverse through the ten bodhisattva stages with no difficulty. May the temple maintain its serenity, transcending all unexpected disasters. May the patron devotees uphold their devotion and increase in fortune and wisdom. Veneration to the Buddhas in the ten directions and the three times, and to all bodhisattvas, *mahāsattva*s, and Mahāprajñāpāramitā.

1. The Word of Tribute for the Inauguration of the *Śūraṃgama-dhāraṇī*s Prayer Service

Because iron is the essence of tempering and grinding, its edge can never become dull; and because the mirror borrows the luster of a well-polished gem, its reflection can never become darkened. Therefore, our preceding sages (i.e., patriarchs) manifested their capacities, sometimes suppressing and other times enhancing such qualities in order to shatter even the tiniest speck of delusion for the sake of sentient beings. The episode of Mātaṅgī and Ānanda tells how marvelously an illicit magical power was intimidated, and Śākyamuni and Mañjuśrī especially revealed the esoteric means of conversion. From analytical study of the forms of teaching and the method of introspection taught by the Buddha throughout his lifetime career, one may find the doctrines and practices; and yet from the point of view of the esoteric revelation of practice and realization, there is neither realization distinct from practice, nor is there practice separate from realization. It reveals the absolute insight (*zhenjian*) and terminates multiple illusions (*zhuchen*). An empty flower has no stem. Abiding in right concentration, one restrains every inner movement. Still water creates no waves. In reflecting upon the descendants, it may be asked: How many of us understand this? Chanting the words left by our predecessors, we admonish ourselves. May we earnestly wish to reduce myriads of *kalpa*s, as many as the sands of the Ganges River, into a single moment of thought, for there is no distance between now and then. May we also wish to identify all the lands of the ten directions as a single abode of existence, so that all may universally attain supreme enlightenment.

2. The Word of Tribute for the Fulfillment of the *Śūraṃgama-dhāraṇī*s Prayer Service

Glancing back at this monastic community, we see it as if it were the Jetavana Monastery, where innumerable *bhikṣu*s assembled like an ocean. At the great assembly of the disciples, where all in stern dignity gathered at Vulture Peak, the grand universe of three thousand great universes was embraced within a speck of dust, and the three different dimensions of time dissolved into a single moment of thought.

Having reposed upon the voluntary self-reflection at the end of the summer retreat, one neither restrains oneself not to transgress, nor does one exert one's effort; rather, one is totally harmonious and interdependent with the myriads of phenomena as a whole. Irrespective of whether one is mundane or transmundane, [there being no distinction,] each individual's wondrous enlightenment, reflecting each moment of great illumination, manifests myriads and myriads of bodies and surpasses all the fifty-seven stages of realization.

The use of a finger is meant to exemplify the truth that it is not the finger [but what it points to], and thus this finger also ceases to be [merely a finger] simultaneously with its being [that which it points to]. While it resembles emptiness (*śūnyatā*) and contains it within, it is yet juxtaposed with emptiness, and thus emptiness [and form] are reciprocal.

Thus, out of his compassion for those of limited understanding, the Buddha especially encouraged those whose minds
are slow and dull. We have steadfastly adhered to this teaching bequeathed by the Buddha during the period of the summer retreat. Since there has been no obstacle throughout the
period of the retreat, may we earnestly hope that our practice of concentration and insight (*samatha* and *vipaśyanā*)
prevails over the gates of all senses and intellect, and that
the transcendent faculty (*dayong*) arises as often as it may
[within phenomenal faculties] and thereby lead them equally
to enter into the ultimate state of the *śūraṃgama samādhi*.

The *Śūraṃgama-dhāraṇīs* Prayer Service
Seating Chart

				Buddha Altar					
candle	incense burner	candle	candle	incense burner	candle	candle	incense burner	candle	

45—44	43	42	41	40		39	38	37	36	35	34
46										
47	23	24	25	26	27	28	29	30	31	32	33
48										
49	22	21	20	19	18	17	16	15	14	13	12
50	*Śūraṃgama* ceremonial master					director of practitioners' affairs				
51										
52	1	2	3	4	5	6	7	8	9	10	11
53										
54	practi-tioners	training officials	primary seat official	abbot	head admin. official	head assistant	practi-tioners			
55										
56—57	58	59	60	61	62	63	64	65	66	67	68	69

Front

6. The Tablet of Ordination Ages

Officials of the practice hall office, the assistant office, and the practitioners' quarters get together beforehand to draw up the tablet of ordination ages by copying [the ordination record book]. In the afternoon of the fourteenth day, these tablets must be placed in the higher-ranking section of the outer practice hall, in the lower-ranking section of the Dharma hall, and in the practitioners' quarters. Each office sets up a table equipped with an incense burner and candle stands as well as various alms offerings. The practitioners each burn incense, perform prostrations with opened sitting cloth, and then take down their respective tablets in order to place them at their assigned seats.

III. Various Proprieties for the Sweet Hot Water Reception

1152b

1. The Minor Propriety of Serving Sweet Hot Water at the Abbot's Office

At the occasions of the four annual celebration days, according to ancient custom, traditionally three kinds of reception are held at the abbot's office for serving hot sweet water. The first reception prescribes the "dual division seating arrangement" (*fenerchu*). This reception is held for the east and west hall high-ranking officials, with the primary seat official as a participant. The second reception consists of the "quadruple division seating arrangement" (*fensichu*). There are four sections with this seating arrangement: 1) the training officials (the west order) are to take their seats at the first section (i.e., front right) [in the abbot's reception hall; 2) the administrative officials (the east order) take their seats at the second section (front left); 3) the retired west order officials are seated at the third section (middle right end); 4) the retired east order officials are seated at the fourth section (middle left end). The west hall official is invited as a participant.

The third reception consists of the "sextuple division seating arrangement" (*liuchu*). This arrangement requires the subfunctionaries of the head temple as well as all the other various temples to be assigned to the six divided sections according to rank. At the same time, whoever holds a similar position should be seated consecutively within the same section. The primary seat official is invited as main participant for this reception. The office of assistant officials prepares a draft chart beforehand for each occasion and presents it to the abbot before establishing the final seating arrangements.

On the appointed day, seat name tablets must be prepared by inscribing the guest names on each of them. In the afternoon, three crepe-wrapped tables are placed in a line in the reception hall (i.e., the one adjacent to the abbot's office), and the three formal seat arrangements, drawn up as No. 1, No. 2, and No. 3, are displayed in the lower section of the reception hall. It is the duty of the guest reception assistant to handle the reception for the high-ranking officials, such as the east and west hall residents, the front hall primary seat official, and the head administrative official. He is obliged to visit each of their quarters and, after performing a prostration with unopened sitting cloth, makes the following request:

> The abbot requests the venerable's presence at a special serving of sweet hot water this evening at the reception hall, sir.

For those other training officials and subfunctionaries, as well as some renowned practitioners, the attendant of the guest reception master at the abbot's office is sent to invite them respectively with the following words:

> The abbot wishes the venerable to be present at a special reception for serving sweet hot water to be held at the reception hall before the evening session, sir.

Curtains are hung in the reception hall, the seat name tablets placed, the candles lit, incense burned, and after all this is done, the guest reception master's attendant notifies the assistant official and then the abbot, before drumming.

When the guests assemble for the first type of reception, they are greeted by the assistant official. They are led before the abbot, exchange bows with him, go to their respective seat positions designated by the seating tablets, and remain standing. Both the incense offering assistant and the guest reception assistant, dividing the two areas of serving, proceed to stand before each of the guests, greet each one with a bow, and, after requesting them to take their seats, return to their places. The incense offering assistant steps forward to offer incense, and upon returning to his place once again, he and the guest reception assistant go around to each of the guests to bow and burn incense on their behalf. Thereupon, the abbot's office wooden sounding block is struck twice to signal the completion of the serving of sweet hot water. Then the guest reception official goes around [once again], commending each of the guests individually to drink, and thus the reception is accomplished. Next, the incense offering assistant steps forward to burn incense on behalf of the participant. With the signal of a strike on the wooden sounding block the cups are retrieved, and at the signal of five drumbeats the guests are obliged to leave. The proprieties of the three types of reception are identical.

The proprieties of the serving of tea and sweet hot water were the major and most common tradition in Zen monastic temples. But because disruptive quarrels, concerning whether the seats are too high or too low and so on, frequently occurred among guests in recent years, [this tradition] has mostly been abandoned. However, each abbot must try to revive this propriety and established practitioners of the Zen world must urge others to do the same. This propriety is said to be regarded as a practice that should be widely encouraged in the future.

Minor Propriety Seating Arrangements
(symbols ↓, ↑, →, ← show the direction each person faces)

1. The Dual Division Seating Arrangement

Participant (↓)   (↓) Host

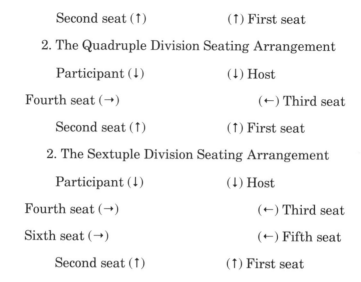

Second seat (↑)   (↑) First seat

2. The Quadruple Division Seating Arrangement

Participant (↓)   (↓) Host

Fourth seat (→)   (←) Third seat

Second seat (↑)   (↑) First seat

2. The Sextuple Division Seating Arrangement

Participant (↓)   (↓) Host

Fourth seat (→)   (←) Third seat

Sixth seat (→)   (←) Fifth seat

Second seat (↑)   (↑) First seat

2. Prayers Given at the Shrine of the Local Spirits on the Four Annual Celebration Days

In general, on the afternoon of the day before [each of the four] annual celebration days, various alms offerings are solemnly set out at the shrine of the local spirits, and incense, candles, a table, incense burner, and water jar are arranged there. The practice hall office attendants post a wooden tablet announcing the scheduled prayer chanting to notify the practitioners. The manner of striking the wooden sounding blocks located throughout the corridors of the temple is identical with that of the three monthly days ending in eight (i.e., the eighth, eighteenth, and twenty-eighth day of each month). The practitioners assemble and stand facing each other at the practice hall. The abbot first visits the patriarchal shrine hall and then the Buddha hall to burn incense and perform three prostrations, at which time the kitchen hall metal gong is sounded three times and the large bell is tolled. When the abbot arrives [at the practice hall] he offers incense and returns to his place. (At the abbot's arrival, the practitioners stand

1152c

with palms together and heads slightly down; the assistant official follows after the abbot with his hands clasped over his chest [*chashou*].) The novice attendants play the cymbals. Thereupon, the director of practitioners' affairs steps forward to greet the dual order officials and burn incense. He leads the prayer chanting and concludes with the appropriate invocation of merit transference (given below).

Invocations of Merit Transference for the Prayer Chanting of the Four Celebration Days

On the Inauguration Day of the Summer Retreat

> We earnestly reflect that a fragrant wind blows over the field, while the blazing sun commands the entire world, and we have today arrived at the first day, as prescribed by the Lord of our religion (i.e., the Buddha), of the summer retreat period, that of restraint from activities. As this is the first day for Buddhist followers to shelter and protect all living creatures, we have respectfully gathered at this shrine of the local spirits to intone steadfastly the sacred names endowed with innumerable virtues and to dedicate the merit thereby accrued to all the spirits enshrined in this hall. We humbly pray for their protection, so that the present retreat may be fulfilled without interruption. May the practitioners intone the prayer, and so on.

On the Fulfillment Day of the Summer Retreat

> We earnestly reflect that a golden wind blows over the field, while the bright sun commands the entire world, and that we have arrived today at the last day of the summer retreat as prescribed by the Lord of Enlightenment. As this day begins the fulfillment of another year of Buddhist ordination, we rejoice that there has been no problem throughout the ninety-day period, and peace and ease have prevailed

with us. By intoning the sacred names endowed with innumerable virtues, we wish to respond to the spirits of this hall to express our thanks. May the practitioners intone the prayer, and so on.

On the Winter Solstice Day

We earnestly reflect that the time of the year's end approaches, while the chapter [of the year] has arrived at the day of the winter solstice (i.e., the page of fortune-telling [*shuyun*]). As this is the day when the sun begins its return course, it is the beginning of the birth of ten thousand classes of beings. Having respectfully assembled the practitioners at the shrine of the local spirits, we intend to intone the sacred names endowed with innumerable virtues and to dedicate the merit thereby accrued to the spirits enshrined in this hall. May the practitioners intone the prayer, and so on.

On New Year's Day

We earnestly reflect that the workings of nature have invisibly carried out their course, while the calendar year once again has renewed itself, and we pray that the four kinds of order be secured in peace, and celebrate New Year's Day. Having respectfully assembled the practitioners at this shrine, we intend to intone the sacred names endowed with innumerable virtues and dedicate the merit thereby accrued to the spirits enshrined in this hall. May the practitioners intone the prayer, and so on.

The Invocation of Merit Transference
Common to All Four Days

We dedicate the merit accrued by the foregoing prayer to the local spirits of the temple environs and the guardian gods of the temple buildings, all enshrined in this hall. We earnestly wish that their supernatural power be well accorded in manifesting advantageous assistance, that the monastic institution become ever more prosperous as granted with everlasting impartial blessing. Once again, may the practitioners intone the prayer: Veneration to the Buddhas of the ten directions and the three periods, and so on.

3. The Administrative Office's Special Serving of Sweet Hot Water for the Primary Seat Official and the Practitioners on the Four Annual Celebration Days

When the prayer chanting has concluded, a special serving of sweet hot water should be conducted at the practice hall. The head administrative official must prepare a note of invitation for this reception beforehand (format given below), and after the noon meal he visits the front hall primary seat official, accompanied by the guest reception attendant carrying a crepe-wrapped board equipped with an incense burner and candle stand. Burning incense and performing a prostration with unopened sitting cloth, the official says:

> We are pleased to announce that a special reception for a serving of sweet hot water will be conducted in honor of the venerable primary seat official and the practitioners at the practice hall this evening. May the venerable, with due compassion, be present at this reception.

The head administrative official presents the written invitation to the primary seat official, who, in turn, instructs the tea master of the practitioners' quarters to give it to the alms-serving master, to be posted on the wall of the lower-ranking section of the outer practice hall. Following the notice of this special serving, the guest reception master of the administrative office announces:

> After the sweet hot water reception, an evening meal will be served.

Next, the head administrative official, with an incense case in his sleeve, visits the abbot's office and, after performing a prostration with unopened sitting cloth, invites the abbot:

> We are prepared to serve this evening at the practice hall especially in honor of the primary seat official and the resident practitioners. I earnestly wish that the venerable master, with due compassion, be present at this occasion.

Thereupon, the guest reception master of the administrative office is instructed to extend the same invitation to the retired officials of both orders as well as all the other quarters, all of whom respectively post a tablet indicating the event at their quarters. When each official has been individually invited, the seat assignment tablets are displayed in front of the outer practice hall. The seat of the primary seat official must face the abbot, while the seats of the practitioners are arranged in both the higher- and lower-ranking sections, and an attendant is specially assigned to the person for whom the serving is being conducted.

1153a

When the prayer chanting is over, a series of drumrolls (identical to the noon meal signal) takes place. The practitioners proceed to take their seats at their respective meal positions, while all of the training officials take their seats on the front hall raised sitting platform. The head administrative official enters the hall immediately after them. He greets the primary seat official, inviting him to move from his seat, and requests the other training officials to move up one seat, then guides the primary seat official to his specially prepared place [directly facing the abbot across the hall]. The official then goes out of the hall, passing to the right of the altar of the guardian bodhisattva, receives the abbot, and escorts him into the hall. As the alms-serving master gently strikes the bell located in the outer hall seven times, the head administrative official escorts the abbot to his seat, and, stepping toward the primary seat official, greets him and bids him to take his seat. Thereupon, the head administrative official, beginning from the primary seat official's seat, makes a round through the inner hall, the outer hall, and the higher- and lower-ranking sections, then returns to in front of the altar and bows. The practitioners then take their seats.

The head administrative official burns incense, proceeds to the outer hall in both sections, returns to the altar, and places his incense case on it. Immediately he approaches the main guest, the primary seat official, and bows, then, moving back to the right of the altar, goes before the abbot and bows. He makes another round through the hall with his head down, goes to the outer hall, and then returns to the mid-inner hall, bows [before the altar], and remains standing there. When the practice hall bell is struck twice, he makes the first serving of sweet hot water to the abbot and the primary seat official, and then commences the serving for the practitioners throughout the hall. When [the first serving] is completed and when all the tea jars have been retrieved from the hall, he goes before the primary seat official (i.e., the main guest) and bows. Then turning back to the right of the altar, he proceeds to the altar of the guardian bodhisattva and performs three prostrations with fully opened sitting cloth.

Thereupon, the head administrative official makes another round through the inner [and outer] halls. He then leads the other administrative officials before the abbot and all perform in unison the formality of two prostrations with opened sitting cloth and three prostrations with unopened sitting cloth. On the first opening of the sitting cloth, he says:

> Despite the humble quality of this serving, the venerable has granted us his compassionate presence on this day. This is most gratifying to us, sir.

On the second opening, he says:

> On this day and at this respectful moment, we wish that the venerable master of the temple may enjoy every blessing in daily life.

Stepping back, he and the east order officials complete the formal greeting with three prostrations with unopened sitting cloth.

They then immediately turn around and withdraw by passing behind the right side of the altar, go out to the outer hall, and take their places in line. The primary seat official comes out after them and expresses his thanks to the head administrative official by performing a full prostration with unopened sitting cloth, and once again returns to his special seat from the side of the higher-ranking section.

The head administrative official once again enters the hall to burn incense and withdraws. The practice hall office attendant announces: "May the practitioners take their bowls down."

An attendant carries in the evening meal set on a table for the abbot and the primary seat official respectively, while the practitioners open their almsbowls.

(The west order officials, however, do not take their bowls down; they will be provided with a meal by the kitchen office.)

When the evening meal has been served and is completed, the practitioners withdraw at the signal of three drumbeats.

[Prior to this special serving,] the abbot issues an announcement on the bulletin board to excuse the formal propriety, as follows:

> On such-and-such celebration day and on the following day, the propriety will be received at the Dharma hall, so there is no need to come to the abbot's office. It is respectfully wished that this must be made known to every resident practitioner. So stated for consideration by So-and-so, abbot of this temple.

This announcement is posted on the higher-ranking section of the practice hall, and the practice hall bell will not be struck to cancel the evening session.

(According to the notices put up by various groups, each member visits the meeting sponsored by each regional group.)

There is no difference in these proceedings for any of the four annual celebration days, the only exception being that on the winter solstice day, after the serving of sweet hot water, some fruit and an evening meal will be served.

Format of the Announcement of the
Special Serving of Sweet Hot Water

This evening at the practice hall, the administrative office will conduct a special serving of sweet hot water in honor of the primary seat official and the practitioners in order to express the propriety of such-and-such celebration day. It is earnestly wished that all practitioners, with due compassion, be present at this occasion.

Date and month

Respectfully stated by So-and-so
Bhikṣu of the Administrative Office

4. The Propriety for the Inauguration
of the Summer Retreat

At 3:00 A.M. on the appointed day, the propriety of burning incense and prostrations with opened sitting cloth should be conducted before the abbot at his office by all the resident practitioners of the temple, namely, the dual order officials, the retired officials of higher and lower ranks, those from the Zen world, the sub-functionaries, those who come from the same province, and the direct disciples of the abbot. [This propriety is not required] if an announcement excusing it is posted on the bulletin board in the outer practice hall. The assistant official notifies the abbot that his ascent to the Dharma hall is in order, instructs the attendants to inform the practitioners, and posts the tablet with the notice.   1153b

After the morning rice gruel, when the abbot has completed preaching, he explains the entire process of the required proprieties in thorough detail:

After his descent, the abbot is obliged to first exchange: 1) a propriety with the west hall official of a prostration with unopened sitting cloth;

2) Next, a propriety to respond to the head administrative

official for the propriety of two prostrations with opened sitting cloth and three prostrations with unopened sitting cloth;

3) Next, a propriety to respond to the primary seat official and the practitioners for their performance of two prostrations with opened sitting cloth and three prostrations with unopened sitting cloth;

4) The head administrative official who has returned to his office receives the primary seat official accompanied by the practitioners, and exchanges the propriety of three prostrations with unopened sitting cloth with the primary seat official and the practitioners;

5) The primary seat official returns to the practice hall, waiting at the higher-ranking section of the outer hall, and receives the rear hall primary seat official's visit accompanied by the practitioners, who arrive at the lower-ranking section of the outer hall, and exchange the propriety of three prostrations with unopened sitting cloth;

6) After this is done, all members take their places as prescribed by the chart of prayer chanting service in the outer hall. The primary seat official leads the practitioners into the hall and, while making a round through the hall, each takes his place at his prescribed position. The primary seat official then leaves his place, burns incense before the altar, performs three prostrations with fully opened sitting cloth, and makes a round through the inner and outer halls before returning to his place. When [the primary seat official] has returned to his position, the attendant in charge of proceedings announces:

> The primary seat official's return greeting to the practitioners, and the propriety of three prostrations with unopened sitting cloth is in order.

The practitioners then perform three prostrations with unopened sitting cloth;

7) Next, the head administrative official enters the hall, burns incense before the altar, performs three prostrations with fully

opened sitting cloth, immediately makes a round through the hall, and then stands at his place by the altar's board-edge. The attendant announces:

> The head administrative official's return greeting to the practitioners and the propriety of three prostrations with unopened sitting cloth is in order.

After exchanging three prostrations with unopened sitting cloth, the head administrative official remains and waits for the arrival of the abbot.

8) [Finally,] the abbot enters the practice hall, burns incense, performs three prostrations with fully opened sitting cloth, then immediately makes a round through the hall and returns to his place. The attendant announces:

> The abbot's exchange of greeting with the practitioners and the propriety of three prostrations with unopened sitting cloth is in order.

Again the attendant announces:

> The practitioners are required to perform in unison the propriety of three prostrations with unopened sitting cloth.

Following this, the abbot is scheduled to make a round through the various quarters of the temple.

When the abbot descends from the rostrum seat, the attendants promptly bring incense, candles, tables, incense burners, and water vases into the Dharma hall and finish setting up the tables in a straight line. The west hall ranking official steps forward to perform prostrations. Next, the head administrative official steps forward to burn incense and perform the propriety of two prostrations with opened sitting cloth and three prostrations with unopened sitting cloth. On the first opening [of the sitting cloth] he says:

> Having been granted an opportunity to serve the venerable during this year's retreat, I am obliged to pray for nothing

but the safe fulfillment of my duty with the assisting power of the Dharma, sir.

On the second opening he says:

On this severe summer day and at this respectful moment, I reverentially wish that the venerable master of this temple may enjoy every blessing in daily life.

Stepping back, he completes his greeting with three prostrations with unopened sitting cloth, to which the abbot responds with a single prostration. Next, the primary seat official, leading the practitioners, burns incense, and the retired officials and residents of the various quarters all follow the primary seat official and burn incense in due order. The propriety of two prostrations with opened sitting cloth and three prostrations with unopened sitting cloth and both wordings of the greeting are all identical.

When the officials step back, the abbot sits down cross-legged and the assistant officials and his disciples burn incense and perform [the same set of] prostrations. Next, the ceremonial leader, representing the group of novice attendants, burns incense and performs prostrations. Next, the lay carpentry leader, leading the foremen, clerical workers, sedan chair bearers, various workmen, and so on all pay homage to the abbot.

The primary seat official, leading the practitioners, visits the administrative office and exchanges with the head administrative official the propriety of three prostrations with unopened sitting cloth. The rear hall primary seat official, leading the practitioners, returns to the lower-ranking section of the practice hall and takes his place, while the front hall primary seat official takes his place in the higher-ranking section. The practice hall office attendant announces:

The fellow practitioners' exchange of the propriety with the primary seat official is in order.

They perform three prostrations with unopened sitting cloth

and immediately take their places at their respective positions as prescribed in the prayer chanting seating chart. The primary seat official enters the inner hall, leading the practitioners in a partial round, then stops at his place and remains standing there; [the practitioners also stop and stand at their respective places]. The assistant official and the newly arrived practitioners make a half-round of the hall, while the assistant takes his place behind the altar and the new arrivals take their places [before the rear entrance,] facing each other. The primary seat official goes before the altar, burns incense, performs three prostrations with fully opened sitting cloth, and immediately makes a round through the hall before returning to his place. The attendant announces:

> The primary seat official returns the propriety to the practitioners.

The practitioners then perform three prostrations with unopened sitting cloth.

[Next,] the head administrative official enters the hall, burns incense, performs prostrations with fully opened sitting cloth, immediately makes a round through the hall, and stands at his place by the altar's board-edge. The attendant announces:

> The head administrative official returns the propriety to the practitioners.

The practitioners once again perform three prostrations with unopened sitting cloth in unison. After this is done, however, the official does not leave the hall. The abbot enters the hall, burns incense before the altar, and performs three prostrations with opened sitting cloth, then proceeds to make a round through the hall and returns to his seat.

(The direct disciples of the abbot must leave the hall from the rear entrance without fail to avoid congestion. When all the proprieties have completed, they return to their places for tea.)

The attendant announces again:

The venerable master abbot's exchange of the propriety with the practitioners is in order.

All the practitioners perform three prostrations with unopened sitting cloth in unison. Another announcement follows:

The return propriety of the practitioners in unison is in order.

Then all again perform three prostrations with unopened sitting cloth.

(In the *Ancient Regulations,* it is said that if the administrative official leaves before the abbot enters the hall, the latter has no opportunity to make a return greeting to the former. Perhaps, the rule that "whoever makes a propriety of greeting ought to receive a return propriety" has been instituted recently, since the time of the Venerable Xiyu [i.e., Shaotan, ca. thirteenth century] and the Venerable Yishan [i.e., Lewan, ca. thirteenth–fourteeth centuries]. Those who are well versed regard this rule as correct.)

The head administrative official shifts his position and goes out of the hall, followed by the assistant official and the new arrivals.

The assistant official returns to the inner hall and with the gesture of a bow bids the practitioners to sit, and the practitioners take their seats. The assistant official proceeds to the incense burners in mid-hall, burns incense in the higher- and lower-ranking sections of the inner hall as well as in the outer hall, returns the incense case to its place, and, stepping back a little, makes a bow toward mid-hall, toward the higher- and lower- ranking sections, and toward the outer hall, then returns to stand mid-hall. With the signal of two strikes of the practice hall bell, the serving of tea is completed. After the jars have been carried out of the hall, the assistant official stands at mid-hall as before. With the signal of one strike of the bell, the teabowls are retrieved, and with the signal of three strikes, the assistant official goes out of the hall and the practitioners leave the hall as well.

The abbot proceeds to make his rounds at the various quarters in due order. At each quarters, a chair and an incense table

1153c

should be set up, and the resident practitioners should receive him outside the entrance. The abbot begins his rounds at the first quarters located in the eastern corridor and proceeds to the incense table set at each quarters. Along with the member residents, the master of the quarters burns incense and says:

> On this day, although it is our duty to make a congratulatory visit to the venerable, we have instead received your gracious visit.

After placing incense [in the burner], he further says:

> Receiving the venerable's gracious blessing, we are extremely gratified, sir.

Following a few steps behind the abbot, he returns to the incense table and stands at its right side with palms together, bowing until the procession completely ends. He then brings up the rear of the procession making rounds through the quarters. In this way, the residents of each quarters follow in the procession, and all finally arrive at the Dharma hall. The abbot stands in the middle of the space between the incense tables while the practitioners, in groups of three, come to stand before him and, after a bow, proceed through the quarters. Thus, making a round through the various quarters and reaching their own quarters, the resident members stand to the side of the incense table with palms joined together, in order of seniority [letting the following groups pass]. When the rounds are completed at the last quarters, the propriety of the congratulatory procession ends. The proceedings are identical for all four annual celebration days.

5. Appointed Discourse or Holding a Zen Dusting Brush on the Four Annual Celebration Days

At the supplementary session, the abbot announces:

> Tomorrow, after the noon meal, the head administrative official, the director of practitioners' affairs, and the assistant official

are requested to take the tablet of "appointed preaching" and a Zen dusting brush to the primary seat official and other training officials and invite them to give an exhortation for the sake of the practitioners.

The next day, after the noon meal, the incense offering assistant instructs an attendant of the guest reception master to carry a walking cane, a tablet, and a Zen dusting brush, and a workman to carry a crepe-wrapped board equipped with an incense burner and a candle stand. They accompany the head administrative official and the director of practitioners' affairs to visit each of the training officials' quarters. The two officials respectively visit each training official, burn incense, and say:

> Due to his compassionate wish, the abbot instructed us, So-and-so and others, to respectfully forward the tablet of "appointment of preaching" and a Zen dusting brush to the venerable here and invite the venerable to preach for the sake of the practitioners this evening.

After the invitation is extended individually to each of the training officials, the primary seat official and the others who have accepted it visit the abbot's office together, accompanied by their attendants carrying the tablet, Zen dusting brush, and walking cane, and report to him their acceptance [of the invitation to preach]. The abbot is especially obliged to encourage them before they leave. The primary seat official turns to his place and says:

> Since I cannot refuse your gracious appointment, may I earnestly hope for the venerable's compassion to have the Dharma seat available for my use on this occasion, sir.

In ancient days, different seats were set up for such an occasion but today it is more customary to use the [abbot's preaching] seat. We no longer hear today about the ancient practice.

Next, the appointed preachers visit the assistants' office to request the use of the drum for the evening, and instruct the tea attendant to invite the guardian bodhisattva's assistant and some well-versed Zen specialists to their tea reception. After burning incense, they make this request:

> This evening, we are scheduled to give an exhortation and shall be in need of an assistant to burn incense on our behalf and also some Zen conversants to exchange dialogue with us.

Again they instruct the attendant to post the tablet indicating "appointed preaching" at the practice hall. Although the abbot has invited the appointed preachers for an evening meal, he should excuse them if they decline to attend and have the meal delivered to them instead.

The practice hall office attendants set up a screen and seat for the abbot on the left side of the Dharma seat. While the evening bell is being tolled, an attendant notifies the appointed preachers and the abbot, and at once starts to drum to assemble the practitioners for the session. The propriety is identical to that of the supplementary session. The abbot enters [the Dharma hall] and immediately goes to stand at his prepared seat. The head administrative official, the director of practitioners' affairs, and the assistant official simultaneously proceed to the appointed preacher and bow to him in unison. The appointed preacher then steps toward the abbot and bows; next, he bows to the head administrative official and continues to bow to each member of the order. Next, he goes to stand before his own order and bows to each member. Immediately after this, he lifts both hands above his head before the practitioners, bows in unison with them, ascends the rostrum seat, and sits cross-legged. 1154a

The assistant of the appointed preacher, along with the abbot's assistant, comes to the foot of the high seat and bows [to the preacher]; the officials of both orders and the west hall official one after another bow [toward the appointed preacher]. Finally, the abbot bows [toward him], at which moment the preacher rises and, standing by the seat, says:

> May the practitioner assistant request the abbot to sit cross-legged.

The appointed preacher's assistant proceeds to the abbot and bows to him, immediately turns around to ascend the rostrum seat, burns incense, lifts the Zen dusting brush to hand to the lecturer [along with the sitting cloth] and bows, then stands at his place at the [appointed preacher's] side with hands clasped over his chest. The preacher gives his instructive words and completes his talk with a dialogue exchange. He presents the essentials of his Zen understanding and a [short] word of thanks to the abbot, the dual order officials, the retired officials, and the practitioners of all quarters. [Finally,] raising a particular Zen problem (i.e., *kōan*), which the abbot had presented at his supplementary session the previous night, the preacher gives his own commenatry on it or expresses its hidden meaning in a poetic verse. He then descends the high seat, goes before the abbot to bow, and returns to his [usual] place. The next appointed preacher follows the same proceedings and propriety.

When all of the appointed discourses have been completed, the guest reception master of the abbot's office announces an invitation to the preachers to a serving of sweet hot water and fruit, just as after a supplementary session. The appointed preachers, carrying incense cases in their sleeves, visit the abbot's office together to give thanks for the opportunity, and receive the serving of sweet hot water. The next day, the abbot invites them for tea. If the head administrative official prepares the noon meal and simultaneously invites [the appointed preachers] for tea and a snack in mid-afternoon, the abbot is obliged to ascend the Dharma seat some other day to express his thanks and invite them to a special serving. An alternative is that the west hall official is invited to preach on the second evening. During the supplementary session the abbot may request him to preach with due praise for his capacity. The west hall official raises his own doctrinal issue, presents a Zen problem, gives commentary, or explains its hidden meaning in a poetic verse, so as to arouse the practitioners' interest in the path. In recent days, the propriety of giving thanks has become so conventional and overburdened with too many niceties that it is rather detestable to hear, and invites ridicule from knowledgeable practitioners. Generally, the appointed preaching is meant to be a gift of the Dharma. If one is obliged to speak on matters of time and propriety, it should be enough just to mention names as a whole or to give brief accounts.

6. The Abbot's Special Serving of Tea for the Primary Seat Official and the Practitioners on the Four Annual Celebration Days

On the appointed day, after breakfast, the guest reception assistant copies the invitation for tea reception (format given below), and visits the primary seat official's quarters, accompanied by his attendant carrying a crepe-wrapped board equipped with an incense burner and candle stand. After burning incense and performing a prostration with unopened sitting cloth, he says:

> After the noon meal today, the abbot has scheduled us to conduct a special tea reception at the practice hall, especially for the sake of the primary seat official and the practitioners. He earnestly requests the venerable's presence at this occasion.

He presents the notice of invitation to the official and posts it in the higher-ranking section of the outer hall, while his attendant extends the invitation to all other training officials and the other quarters, and requests the head administrative official as the main participant. The tablet indicating "tea serving" is posted [in the practice hall].

At the signal of the kitchen hall metal gong, the guest reception assistant enters the practice hall, burns incense before the altar of the guardian bodhisattva, and performs three prostrations with fully opened sitting cloth. He makes a round through the hall, stops at mid-hall to bow, and leaves the hall. This is called "the invitation for tea by making a round through the practice hall" (*xuntangqingcha*). The seating position tablets must be arranged in the outer hall.

The primary seat official is seated opposite the abbot [across the hall], while the head administrative official is seated symmetrically to the right of the abbot, at a distance of an arm's length. The seat of the director of practitioners' affairs is next in the line, while the lower administrative officials are seated symmetrically to the right of the main guest of honor, separated by a distance of an arm's length. At the signal of drumming, the practitioners assemble and the incense offering assistant conducts the propriety. (The propriety is identical with that of the special serving of sweet hot water by the administrative office.)

The primary seat official approaches the abbot and expresses his thanks for tea through the formality of two prostrations with opened sitting cloth and three prostrations with unopened sitting cloth. At the first opening of the sitting cloth, he says:

> I am most grateful for the honor of such a special reception of tea conducted at this hall on my behalf.

At the second opening, he says:

> On this day and at this moment, I respectfully wish that the venerable master of this temple may enjoy every blessing in daily life.

Stepping back, he begins to perform [the propriety of] three prostrations with unopened sitting cloth; however, the abbot is supposed to excuse him [of the remaining prostrations after the first one], to which he duly responds with a single prostration with unopened sitting cloth. The primary seat official turns around, passes behind the altar to its right, and leaves the hall. The abbot follows him to the entrance and then returns to his place. The assistant official burns incense to give thanks for the presence of the participants. The [practice hall] bell is tolled, the cups are retrieved, and, as before, drumming signals a recess. The primary seat official first goes to the Dharma hall and waits for the abbot's arrival to express his thanks. If the formality is excused, he simply bows.

1154b

Format of the Reception Notice of Tea Serving

The Venerable Abbot, master of the temple, will conduct a special serving of tea at the practice hall today after the noon meal, especially for the sake of the primary seat official and the practitioners, to express the propriety of Such-and-such celebration day. Moreover, the invitation is extended to the administrative officials to be present as main participants.

> Date and month
>
> Respectfully stated by So-and-so
> Office of the Abbot's Assistants

7. The Administrative Office's Special Serving of Tea for the Primary Seat Official and the Practitioners on the Four Annual Celebration Days

On the second day of the annual celebration, after breakfast, the administrative official prepares a notice of tea reception (identical to the notice of the serving of sweet hot water), to inform the practitioners of this event, and posts the tablet announcing the tea reception at the practice hall. At the signal of the kitchen hall metal gong, the head administrative official enters the practice hall to make a round, inviting the practitioners for tea just as the abbot's assistant official did previously for the sweet hot water reception. After the noon meal, the seating placement tablets must be set up. The practitioners assemble at the signal of drumming. The official requests them to take their seats by making a gesture of greeting, burns incense on their behalf, requests them to drink tea, and makes a round through the hall, stopping to bow at mid-hall. He proceeds before the abbot and performs the propriety of two prostrations with opened sitting cloth and three prostrations with unopened sitting cloth and the two sets of the word of greeting, which are identical to those of the occasion of sweet hot water reception.

8. The Front Hall Primary Seat Official's Reception of Tea for the Rear Hall Primary Seat Official and the Practitioners

On the third day of the annual celebration, the primary seat official prepares a notice of invitation (format given below), and visits the quarters of the rear hall primary seat official and the abbot's office in order to convey his invitation for a tea reception. The proceedings of serving tea and the propriety of ceremonial conduct are identical with those of the special tea serving by the administrative office. The only difference is that the seats of the administrative officials must be placed.

Format for the Invitation for Tea

The front hall primary seat official, So-and-so Bhikṣu, has respectfully scheduled the tea reception at the practice hall today after the noon meal, especially for the sake of the rear hall primary seat official and the practitioners, to express the propriety of the celebration day. This invitation is extended to the administrative officials to be present at this occasion as main participants.

Date and month

Respectfully prepared
by So-and-so

Format of the Envelope

Letter of Invitation
To
The Venerable Rear Hall Primary Seat Official
and the Practitioners

Respectfully sealed
by So-and-so

9. Serving Tea on the First Day of the Month and the Mid-month Day after Making a Round through the Practice Hall

When the abbot finishes the ascent to the Dharma hall and preaching, he says:

> Upon descending this high seat, we shall make a round through the practice hall and have a cup of tea.

When the practitioners reach the front hall, they stand at their positions as prescribed in the prayer chanting chart, and then enter the practice hall in a line in due order. The new arrivals and the assistant official follow the line of the practitioners in the procession, and upon reaching the back of the guardian bodhisattva's altar, the new arrivals stand at their positions facing the back of the altar and the assistant official. The practitioners proceed through the hall and take their respective positions. The practice hall bell is rung seven times and the abbot enters the hall, burns incense, and makes a round through the hall before returning to his place. The administrative officials enter the hall and line up in front of the altar to bow, then turn toward the abbot and bow before him. They then make their round beginning from the raised sitting platform of the primary seat official. The new arrivals and the assistant official, following the administrative officials, leave the hall.

The incense offering assistant then returns to mid-hall and bows, requesting the practitioners to take their seats. When the practitioners have settled in meditation posture, he proceeds to burn incense [on the respective incense burners set] at both the higher- and lower-ranking sections of the inner hall and in the outer hall, first at its lower section and then its higher section. Returning to the mid-inner hall, he places the incense case on the altar and bows toward all the sections of the practice hall before their respective incense burners. This completes the offering of incense for invitation. He then returns to the mid-hall position, and the practice hall bell is struck twice to signal the serving of

1154c

tea. [When the tea has been served and] the jars are carried out of the hall, he once again burns incense and makes bows as before, requesting the assembly to drink tea, and again returns to the mid-hall position. A single sound of the bell signals the retrieving of the cups, and three sounds of the bell signal the abbot's departure from the hall. The primary seat official and the practitioners leave the hall in due order. If the abbot cannot make the evening tea serving for some unavoidable reason, or if he has been away from the practitioners for some time, he will have tea with the practitioners after the morning rice gruel. The assistant official's ceremonial conduct is the same as before.

10. The Abbot's Tea Reception at the Novice Attendants' Hall

After the serving of tea at the practice hall on one of the four annual celebration days, the assistant official and guest reception master together visit the novice attendants' hall to serve tea. The guest reception master has beforehand requested the ceremonial master to post a tablet announcing the tea serving, and to inform the residents of the attendants' hall. Prior to the occasion the abbot's office sends tea to the kitchen hall, water is boiled and cups set out, and the kitchen official is invited to participate. The kitchen official receives the assistant official on his arrival at the administrative office, and the ceremonial master and the infirmary master, leading the novice attendants, receive the two officials at the hall gate. The assistant official takes his seat at the main position, because he is conducting the serving of tea on behalf of the abbot, while the kitchen official sits to his right, separated by an arm's length. The assistant official goes to mid-hall and burns incense, and, returning to his seat, requests the resident novice attendants to take their seats. When the drinking of tea is completed, the kitchen official sees the assistant official off, while the ceremonial master and the infirmary master together see off the kitchen official outside the hall entrance. Immediately afterward, both officials visit the abbot's office to express their thanks for the tea.

11. The Serving of Tea by the Head Administrative Official and the Training Official at the Attendants' Hall

When the abbot's tea reception ends, the administrative official visits the attendants' hall to serve tea. The official sits at the main position, while the kitchen official is seated to his right, separated by an arm's length. The conduct of this propriety is identical to that of the assistant official. The novice attendants see off the two officials, and the ceremonial master greets them:

> The ceremonial master and the resident attendants shall visit the administrative office to express thanks for this tea reception, sir.

The guest reception master of the administrative office conveys the message:

> The administrative official has excused the return propriety.

When the practice hall tea is finished (for details, see chapter VI, part VII, section 11) the training officials instruct an attendant of the practice hall office to notify the ceremonial master that they are ready to conduct a serving of tea and request him to post the signboard to inform the residents [of the novice attendants' hall]. The kitchen official is invited as a participant.

(The propriety is identical with that of the administrative official. The ceremonial master's promise of a return visit as a gesture of thanks when seeing off the administrative official, as well as the latter's message excusing the return propriety is also identical.)

IV. Monthly Calendar of Events During the Year

First Lunar Month

First Day (in some temples this also occurs in the fourth

month): a ceremonial procession, sutra chanting, prayers for peace and security by the resident practitioners.

New Year's greeting messages to government officials, patron donors, and the major monastic temples.

Seventeenth Day: The Memorial Day of Baizhang.

Second Lunar Month

First Day: Closing of the hearth in the inner practice hall; this is not done if it is a mountain temple and if the weather is still very severe.

Fifteenth Day: The Memorial (Nirvana) Day of Śākyamuni Buddha.

Third Lunar Month

First Day: The practice hall office issues the draft of the "Record Book."

The Spring Memorial Day or "Clear and Bright Day" (*qing-mingri*): The administrative office instructs the practitioners to clean the patriarchal hall, the patriarchal commemorative towers, and the patron donors' family shrines; to solemnly arrange due offerings; and to conduct the service of sutra chanting.

1155a

A signboard is posted, prohibiting any act of harvesting from the temple's hills and forests and its tea and bamboo fields.

Fourth Lunar Month

First Day: Closing of the transient quarters.

Fourth through Fifth Day: The rite of incense offering as request for general exhortation.

Eighth Day: The Birthday of Śākyamuni Buddha and the ceremonial bathing of the statue of the infant Buddha.

The administrative office prepares a special offering of rice cooked with plant leaves prior to the day of this event.

The abbot's office invites the practitioners for light refreshments prior to the summer retreat.

Thirteenth Day: Setting up the area for the *Śūraṃgama-dhāraṇī*s prayer service.

Fifteenth Day: The inauguration of the summer retreat.

Depending on the weather conditions, this is the time to take down the heavy warm screen at the hall entrance and put up the light cool one.

Fifth Lunar Month

Fifth Day: The Duanwu Festival Day. Early in the morning, the administrative official burns incense in the practice hall and serves sweet flag tea.

The abbot's ascent to the Dharma hall and inauguration of the prayer session for the growth of rice seedlings in the field.

The practice hall office issues the list of sutras to be chanted at the various quarters.

The maintenance official checks the building compounds to repair roof leakage, clean the buildings, and clear the sewage and ditch drainage systems.

The abbot visits the quarters, hermitages, and commemorative towers, and each of these offices conducts a tea reception throughout the day.

Mosquito nets are set up in the practice hall.

Sixth Lunar Month

First Day: The rising of heat; the primary seat official excuses the striking of the wooden sounding block located at the outer practice hall to signal zazen practice.

Entering the hottest time of summer, the practice hall official airs out and arranges the hall mats.

The charcoal supply master or the managing treasury official prepares charcoal balls.

Seventh Lunar Month

First Ten Days: The practice hall official issues the list of sutras to be chanted at the various quarters on Ullambana (Memorial) Day.

Donations are collected from the practitioners prior to the day and a box of cooked rice for offering is prepared.

Thirteenth Day: Completion of the *Śuraṃgama-dhāraṇī*s prayer service.

Fifteenth Day: Commencement of the summer retreat, the Ullambana Day service, sutra chanting, and alms-serving.

Eighth Lunar Month

First Day: Opening the transient quarters (the guest reception official has had the mats of the quarters aired out beforehand).

Practitioners of deep intent and practice are not yet prepared to leave their space units.

The practice hall mosquito nets are taken down.

Ninth Lunar Month

First Day: The primary seat official again begins to strike the wooden sounding block to signal zazen practice at the practice hall.

The practice hall official arranges for repair of the window screens of the practice hall with glue and paper. The cool summer screen at the hall entrance is taken down and the warm winter screen is put up.

Ninth Day: The administrative official burns incense in the early morning and serves herb tea (dogwood-leaf tea) for the practitioners.

The abbot ascends to the Dharma hall and conducts interviews with practitioners coming from all directions with the intent of establishing residency at the temple.

Tenth Lunar Month

First Day: The opening of the hearth in the practice hall and granting of the group interview.

Fifth Day: The Memorial Day of Bodhidharma.

Eleventh Lunar Month

Twenty-second Day: The Imperial Councilor's Memorial Day.

Winter Solstice Day: The administrative office beforehand purchases fruit to be served to the practitioners.

Appointments to and resignations of official positions should be completed during this month; this may be conducted on New Year's Day.

The abbot's office serves light refreshments for the residents prior to the winter season.

Twelfth Lunar Month

Eighth Day: The Commemorative Day of the Buddha's Enlightenment. The administrative office beforehand prepares special rice gruel cooked with red beans.

Thirty-first Day: Closure of all record books.

End of Chapter VIII: The Annual Celebration Days and Calendar

End of Fascicle Seven

Fascicle Eight

Chapter IX

The Monastic Sound Instruments

1. Preface to the Chapter

In ancient times, conversion [to Buddhism] was spontaneous and there was no need of [external] teaching. Only when conversion became less than perfect did the discipline of interpersonal propriety and of musical harmony become necessary. Even a peasant's spontaneous singing accompanied by rhythmic striking of the ground is better than the most skilled performance of musical instruments, and better also is the taste of a wine fermented in a simple cask than those of wine products fermented in five different stages. Hence, a word born of spontaneous inner conversion is most valuable, because it has derived from that essential conversion.

The founding father of our religion in India initially revealed such spontaneous conversion in which, insofar as it is concerned with the wondrous enlightenment originally within each person, there is no difference whether one is saintly or worldly. Since actual things that are equally real rather have purity and defilement, the insight of nondifference does not depend on [the depth or shallowness of an individual's] practice and realization, nor does it refer to [the superiority or inferiority of his] efficacy and usage. And yet those who have no insight are dazed and stupefied like someone who is deaf and dumb. Because of this, the Buddha set forth his teaching in compliance with the different capacities of individual

409

disciples and introduced various sound signals to assemble them. His teaching became the literature of the three baskets (i.e., the Tripiṭaka: Sutra-*piṭaka,* Vinaya-*piṭaka,* and Abhidharma-*piṭaka*), and his [principal] practice was meditation and concentration (*dhyāna* and *samādhi*). His career promoting the method of conversion continued for forty-nine years before [his *parinirvāṇa*).

The Sanskrit term *ghaṇṭā* (*jianzhu*) means a bell, [an object,] whether made of clay, wood, copper, or iron, that when struck creates a sound—a metallic bell, a stone bell, a cymbal, a drum, a wooden post and mallet, a wooden sounding block, or a conch shell. Following the practice of the sound instruments used in Indian monastic temples, the Zen institution has continued to use various sound instruments after their fashion even today for the purpose of warning against confusion and idleness, encouraging compliance with the teachings and regulations, giving guidance for those who abide in dark subhuman states, and pleasing gods and humans.

If great concentration (*dading*) is always maintained and if transcendent function (*dayong*) always remains quiescent, while hearing one does not hear, and while being aware one has no awareness. Thinking thus, one strikes a sound object and the mysterious wind [of religion] should suddenly arise (i.e., spontaneous transformation). There is neither thinking (*wusi*), nor is there any orientaion toward achieving a goal (*wuwei*), the Buddha's spontaneous conversion in itself shines forth forever, and the world of his benevolent longevity opens limitlessly. Is this not the veritable capital city of purity and peace?

2. The Large Bell

The large bell (*dazhong*) has its origin in assisting commands in monastic temples. When tolled in the early morning, it breaks the long night and warns those who linger in sleep. When tolled in the evening, it creates awareness of dark ignorance and reveals the state of delusion. It is better to draw its wooden striker leisurely rather than hurriedly, because the longer the sound lasts the more desirable it is. When [the large bell is] tolled, there should be three cycles, each consisting of thirty-six tolls, altogether making one hundred and eight. In addition, there should be three rather rapid tolls to signal the beginning and ending.

When a novice attendant tolls the bell, he should mentally intone the following verse:

> May the sound of this bell reach beyond the Dharma world,
> so that it may be heard by all those who suffer,
> imprisoned in gloomy darkness.
> May their hearing and the sound be purified and may they
> realize total comprehension.
> May all sentient beings thus realize perfect enlightenment.

After chanting this, he should call the name of Guanyin Bodhisattva (Avalokiteśvara). If he calls the name before each time he tolls the bell, the benefit will be very great.

The large bell should be tolled eighteen times on other occasions: 1) on the day of the imperial birthday festivity, sutra chanting, and assembly at the Buddha hall and recess from it; 2) on the three days of each month ending in eight (the eighth, eighteenth, and twenty-eighth) to conduct the prayer chanting (*sanbaniansong*); 3) on the commemorative days of the Buddha's birthday, enlightenment, and nirvana; 4) on the inauguration and fulfillment days of the   1155c
*Śuraṃgama-dhāraṇī*s prayer session and chanting; 5) during the proceeding of the morning rice gruel and noon meal at the practice hall and also during evening zazen practice before opening the bedding; and 6) on the day the temple will receive government officials, [a new] abbot, or renowned guest officials, and also when these people depart the temple and are seen off. In the last case, however, the tolling of the bell is not confined to the specific number cited above; the administrative official is in charge of this matter.

3. The Practice Hall Bell

Whenever the practitioners are to assemble [at the practice hall], the practice hall bell (*sengtangzhong*) is tolled. This bell is tolled seven times to signal the abbot's entrance into the practice hall to meet with practitioners. The following occasions are signaled by tolling the bell three times: the abbot's departure from the hall after the breakfast and the noon meal; to announce the cancelation of the evening session; when the abbot makes a round through the hall on the first day of the month and the mid-month day; and when the abbot leaves the hall after drinking tea. (If the abbot does not leave the hall, or if he is away from the temple at the time, there is no tolling of the practice hall bell.)

During the time of prayer chanting in the outer practice hall, a gentle tolling of the bell is required for each instance of calling the sacred names of the Buddhas; at the last calling of the name, another toll is added to signal the end. The practice hall official is in charge of this.

4. The Buddha Hall Bell

The Buddha hall bell (*dianzhong*) is tolled when the abbot comes to offer incense at the morning and evening service. The bell is tolled seven times to call the practitioners to assemble at the Buddha hall, but the tolling of this bell must be coordinated with the tolling of the practice hall bell without fail. The hall master is in charge of this matter.

According to the *Records on All Things Concerned* (*Gantong-chuan,* by Vinaya Master Daoxuan), it is said that the Buddha Krakucchanda made a bell out of a granite rock at the Temple of Sutras in India. At sunrise, many Buddhas manifested themselves along with it and esoterically exhorted and revealed the twelve categories of sutras. Thus, it was impossible to count the number of those who had realized arhatship after listening to the teachings of those Buddhas [that were revealed through the sound of the bell]. The *Ekottara Āgama* (i.e., *Aṅguttara Nikāya*) has the following passage: "Whenever a bell is tolled, all evil paths and all suffering cease to be." Again, in the *Chronicle of Jinling* (*Jinlingzhi*) [written in the Yuan period (in the southern capital city of Jinling), it is said that there was a man who died a sudden, violent death and went down to the place of the underworld ruler. There he saw a man totally imprisoned and fettered by a wooden [torture] rack. This man told him that he was formerly the ruler of the Southern Tang but because Song Jiqiu mistakenly killed those of Hezhou who had surrendered, this suffering had been imposed upon him. When he listened to the sound of bells, his suffering ceased temporarily. Therefore, he requested the man to convey to the present ruler who had succeeded him his desire that a large bell be put up on behalf of his well-being. The man, thus instructed, returned to this world and reported the matter to the ruler. Thus the grand bell was built and dedicated to Qingliangsi. Engraved on this bell was the phrase: "This is presented to the eminent ancestor ruler, Emperor Xiaogao, so as to help him be liberated from darkness and suffering."

5. The Large Metal Gong

The large metal gong (*daban*) is struck for three long rounds on two occasions during the day, as part of the breakfast and noon meal proceedings. After the fish-shaped wooden gong (*muyu*) is sounded, the metal gong is struck three times to signal the beginning of the meal and then struck continuously in diminishing intervals. This is called "the long metal gong" (*changban*). On occasions of prayer chanting and the *Śūraṃgama-dhāraṇī* prayer session, the metal gong should be sounded three times for each occasion, to warn against fire and candle flames. When used to announce night watches, it is to be struck according to their respective numbers.

6. The Small [Wooden] Blocks

The abbot's office, the administrative office, the quarters of the primary seat official, and the other quarters each keep their own small wooden sounding blocks (*xiaoban*), and at the time of the release from silence in the early morning, all these blocks are struck simultaneously for one long round. When used to signal an event to a small group of people, each block is struck three times. The practitioners' quarters have small wooden sounding blocks in both the inner and outer areas. The wooden sounding block located outside should be struck three times at the time of the practitioners' greeting each day, and at the time of regular zazen practice as well as zazen practice prior to the evening session. It is also sounded before the practitioners' return to their quarters. On the occasions of servings of tea and sweet hot water, the small wooden sounding blocks are also struck for a long round [at diminishing intervals]. The block located inside the quarters is struck three times on the occasion of the establishment of residency, two times when cups are delivered to the hall for tea or sweet hot water, once when the cups are retrieved, and three times when the practitioners leave the practice hall. In case of the minor propriety of serving sweet hot water, it is sounded for one longer round.

7. The Fish-shaped Wooden Gong

On the occasions of breakfast and the noon meal, the fish-shaped wooden gong (*muyu*) is struck for two long rounds with diminishing intervals. For all-out mobilization of the practitioners to perform a task requiring physical labor, it is struck for a single long round; for a similar mobilization of the novice attendants, it is struck for two long rounds.

Tradition holds that the fish is always awake, day and night, and therefore carving a fish form out of wood and striking it every day is intended to warn against human ignorance and indolence.

8. The Mallet [and Octagonal Wooden Post]

During the two occasions of breakfast and the noon meal at the practice hall, prior to opening the almsbowl sets, the mallet is used to make a [sharp] sound by striking it against [the octagonal wooden post], which signals the prayer of intoning the names of the Buddhas. It is also used to signal the intoning of the almsgiving verse and the completion of the first serving, as well as to signal the occasion of almsgiving [by lay donors], and for any public announcement.

The director of practitioners' affairs is responsible for executing these signals. The assistant of the the guardian bodhisattva signals the practitioners to leave the practice hall by making a single sound [with the mallet and post]. This [instrument] is also used by the head administrative official to announce his resignation from office as well as to announce a new official's appointment. [Finally,] it is used by the representative official of the neighboring temples before announcing the new abbot's inauguration preaching. This is called "the mallet signal for public announcement."

Śākyamuni Buddha one day ascended the rostrum seat before an assembly of all his disciples. Bodhisattva Mañjuśrī signaled an announcement with a mallet, saying: "We have clearly understood the Dharma of the Dharma King. That Dharma of the Dharma King is indeed like this." Śākyamuni Buddha then descended the rostrum seat. [This shows another use of this instrument.]

9. The [Stand-set] Bell and Small Hand Bell

The stand-set bell (*qing*) is used during the morning and evening incense offering at the Buddha hall by the abbot or the head administrative official, as well as during the practitioners' religious service of chanting the sacred scriptures or intoning esoteric prayers. [Sounding this instrument] is the responsibility of those who are in charge of the Buddha's shrine hall. It is also used by the director of practitioners' affairs during the auction of the possessions of a deceased practitioner, and by the master of ceremonial chanting when the novice attendants undergo the rite of head-shaving. The small hand bell (*xiaoshouqing*) is always carried by the practice hall office attendant and is used to punctuate the beginning and ending of chanting or intoning by the practitioners.

10. The Cymbals

The cymbals (*maobo*) are played by the novice attendant when the director of practitioners' affairs requests the abbot and the dual order officials to conduct the ceremonial rite of successive offering of incense by the abbot and both dual order officials; and at the first day and mid-month day prayer celebrations held at the Tripiṭaka hall as well as during the ceremonial rite of circumambulation of the hall. They are also played at the welcome reception for guests, at the time of sending the dead to the funeral site, at the time of the novice attendants' head-shaving, at the time of the ceremonial circumambulation, and at the reception for the new abbot on the day of his inauguration at the temple.

11. The Drum

In general, the drum (*gu*) is played to signal the abbot's ascent to the Dharma hall, his supplementary session, his general exhortation, and his individual instruction for a visitor to his office. For the ascent to the Dharma hall, the drum should be sounded for three consecutive rounds.

(First, three light beats are made to signal the beginning; next, with a stick in each hand, beat the drum so as to gradually shorten the intervals between strikes, reciprocating heavy and light beats, so that the sound is harmoniously lengthened, arising and receding repeatedly, tremulous and reverberant like the resounding of spring thunder. The first round consists of striking with a long interval and lengthened reverberation; the second round is begun with a short and halting stroke, a little faster but with a level continuity in its sounding; the third round is a somewhat muffled sounding throughout and ends at the moment the abbot ascends the rostrum seat. The end signal is three beats made with both sticks simultaneously.)

One round of drumbeats signals the supplementary session, a series of five beats signals the general exhortation, and three beats signals the practioners' visit for individual instruction; these drumrolls are done with somewhat longer intervals between strikes.

The tea reception is signaled by a long round of drumming; the assistant official is in charge of this. The noon meal is signaled by three rounds of drumbeats identical to the manner of announcing · the abbot's ascent to the Dharma hall, but this can be shortened and abruptly ended [by a single round]. A long roll of drumbeats [with increasingly shorter intervals] signals the mobilization of all members for a task of labor. The drum signal for night watches is three equal beats in the early evening, the number increasing according to the number of the hour. Timekeeping is the responsibility of the administrative official. The drum signal for bathing is communicated by four different rounds, reflecting the different groups of bathers, and each round gradually culminates in accordance with the number of practitioners who have already bathed. The bath hall official is in charge of this matter. (For details, see chapter VI, part II, section 6.) The foregoing methods of drumming must be maintained consistently regarding the forms and occasions. One should never let these [viable] methods of communication lapse. At the time when a new abbot inaugurates his appointment at the temple, all the instruments should be played together.

1156b

It is said in the *Sutra of Golden Splendor* that Bodhisattva Ruciraketu (Xinxiangpusa) dreamed of a golden drum during the night. Its form was elegant and great, and it emitted brightness in all directions like the sun. Within this illumination, he saw all the Buddhas of the ten directions, on seats of lapis lazuli under a tree bearing numerous jewels, surrounded by hundreds of thousands of disciples listening to their preaching. A man who looked like a brahman struck the drum with a piece of aspen wood and uttered in a loud voice some verses that conveyed the meaning of repentance. When Bodhisattva Ruciraketu awakened from the dream, he went to the Tathāgata and told of the golden drum and the verses of repentance of which he had dreamed. Also, in the *Śūraṃgama-sūtra,* the Buddha is said to have asked Ānanda, "Ānanda, moreover, do you hear in this Jetavana Monastery the sound of the drum that conveys the time of meals, and the sound of the bells that call the monks to assemble? As the drums and bells resound from one preceding moment to another subsequent moment in continuity, what do you understand [with these sounds]? Do the sounds come to your ears, or do your ears go to the origin of the sounds?"

End of Chapter IX: The Monastic Sound Instruments

Glossary

Amitābha ("Immeasurable Light"): A transcendental Buddha associated with great compassion, who resides over a blissful realm, or Pure Land, into which believers in his salvific power will be reborn. *See also* Pure Land.

Ānanda ("Joy"): The name of Śākyamuni's cousin, close disciple, and personal attendant.

anuttarā samyaksaṃbodhi: Unsurpassed, ultimate awakening or *bodhi*. *See also bodhi*.

arhat ("worthy one"): A saint who has completely eradicated the passions and attained liberation from the cycle of birth and death (samsara); the highest stage of spiritual achievement in the Hinayana. *See also* Hinayana.

Avalokiteśvara: A great bodhisattva who represents great compassion.

birth and death: The cycle of transmigration or rebirth in samsara, the world of suffering, to which sentient beings are subject as a result of their actions (karma). *See also* karma.

bodhi: Enlightenment; a state in which one is awakened to the inherent enlightened nature, or Buddha-nature, of all reality; a direct experience of ultimate truth or ultimate reality. *See also* Buddha-nature.

bodhicitta ("enlightenment mind"): The aspiration to achieve enlightenment.

Bodhidharma (470–543?): An Indian monk who came to China and became the First Patriarch of the Chan/Zen school. He is said to have spent nine years facing a wall in zazen at Shaolinsi. *See also* Zen school; zazen.

bodhisattva ("enlightenment being"): One who has given rise to the profound aspiration (*bodhicitta*) to achieve enlightenment in order to help liberate all sentient beings from samsara (birth and death); the spiritual ideal of the Mahayana. Bodhisattvas undertake a course of practice of the *pāramitā*s (perfections) and attain various stages (*bhūmi*s) on the way to Buddhahood. *See also* Mahayana; *pāramitā*s.

Buddhahood: The state of being or becoming a Buddha; the goal of the bodhisattva path.

Buddha-nature: The basic enlightened nature of sentient beings, which is chronically obscured by their ignorance and attachment to dualistic views. According to the Zen school, enlightenment is nothing other than the complete unfolding of one's inherent Buddha-nature. *See also* Zen school.

Buddhas of the ten directions and the three periods of time: Buddhist cosmology postulated that there existed and will exist an innumerable number of worlds in the universe throughout past, present, and future, and hence, believed that innumerable numbers of Buddhas appeared, are appearing, and will appear in these worlds. Ten directions refers to the four cardinal directions (north, east, south, west), the four intermediate directions (northeast, southeast, northwest, southwest) and the zenith and nadir, thus meaning all directions, everywhere.

Chan school. *See* Zen school.

dhāraṇī: A mystic or incantatory phrase or formula, particularly emphasized in the rituals of Esoteric Buddhism. *See also* esoteric.

dharma: A phenomenon, thing, or element; the elements that make up the perceived phenomenal world.

Dharma: The Buddhist teachings; part of the Three Treasures. *See also* Three Treasures.

Dharma body. *See* three bodies.

Dharma-nature: The essential nature of all that exists, synonymous with ultimate reality.

Dharma world (*dharmadhātu*): The realm (*dhātu*) or world of Dharma, ultimate reality.

dhyāna (Ch.: *chan;* Jp.: *zen*): Meditation, a state of meditative concentration and absorption. The primary practice of the Chan/Zen school. *See also* zazen; Zen school.

esoteric: A reference to teachings and practices of the Esoteric Buddhist tradition, which emphasize the recitation of mystical phrases called *dhāraṇī*s or mantras. *See also dhāraṇī*.

First Turning of the Great Wheel: A reference to the Buddha's first teaching, or "turning of the wheel of Dharma," in which he taught the Four Noble Truths. *See also* Four Noble Truths.

four groups of followers: The four main classes of Buddhist followers: monks (*bhikṣu*s), nuns (*bhikṣunī*s), laymen (*upasāka*s), and laywomen (*upāsikā*s).

four modes of birth: According to Buddhism, the four ways that sentient beings may be born—1) from a womb (viviparous), as with mammals; 2) from an egg (oviparous); 3) from moisture or water born; and 4) through metamorphosis.

Four Noble Truths: The fundamental Buddhist teaching, given by the Buddha in the First Turning of the Great Wheel—1) the truth of suffering; 2) the truth of the cause of suffering; 3) the truth of the cessation of suffering; and 4) the truth of the eightfold path that leads to the cessation of suffering, i.e., right view, right thought, right speech, right action, right livelihood, right effort, right mindfulness, and right meditation. *See also* First Turning of the Great Wheel.

Great Vehicle. *See* Mahayana.

Hinayana ("Small Vehicle"): A term used by Mahayana Buddhists to describe the teachings of early Buddhism, which had as its spiritual ideal the arhat. The two paths of Hinayana practice are the *śrāvakayāna* and the *pratyekabuddhayāna*. *See also* arhat; *pratyekabuddha; śrāvaka;* Mahayana.

incarnate body. *See* three bodies.

kalpa: An eon, an enormously long period of time.

karma: Lit., "action," any act of body, speech, or mind, which leads to rebirth in samsara according to whether it is morally good, evil, or neutral. *See also* birth and death.

kaṣāya: A monk's robe. In the Zen tradition, it embodies faith in the Dharma.

Kaundinya: One of the five original disciples of the Buddha.

kōan: A conundrum or paradoxical phrase, story, or episode from the life of an ancient master used as an object of meditation, which cannot be grasped or solved by reason, thus forcing the practitioner to break through to a deeper level of comprehension. Though not exclusive to it, *kōan* practice is especially emphasized in the Linji (Rinzai) sect of Chan/Zen. *See also* Linji sect; Zen school.

Linji sect (Jp.: Rinzai): Along with the Sōtō sect, one of the two main branches of Chan/Zen. Originating with the ninth-century Chinese master Linji, it was brought to Japan at the end of the twelfth century by Eisai and emphasizes the study and practice of *kōan*s. *See also kōan;* Sōtō sect; Zen school.

Mahākāśyapa: The disciple whom the Buddha designated as his successor, according to the Chan/Zen school. Also called Kāśyapa.

mahāsattva ("great being"): An epithet for a great bodhisattva. *See also* bodhisattva.

Mahayana ("Great Vehicle"): A form of Buddhism that developed in India around 100 B.C.E. and which exalts as its religious ideal the bodhisattva, great beings who aspire to enlightenment on behalf of all sentient beings. *See also* bodhisattva.

Mañjuśrī: A great bodhisattva who exemplifies transcendent wisdom.

Māra: In Buddhist texts, the personification of death or evil; a symbol of the afflictions that hinder progress on the path to Buddhahood.

nāga: In Indian mythology, a type of supernatural being in the form of a dragon or serpent; one of eight such supernatural beings that serve as protectors of the Dharma.

nirvana: Liberation from the cycle of birth and death (samsara), a state in which all passions are extinguished and the highest wisdom (*prajñā*) attained; *bodhi*, enlightenment. *See also* birth and death; *bodhi; prajñā.*

*pāramitā*s: Six practices, or qualities, perfected by bodhisattvas on the path to Buddhahood—1) generosity (*dāna*), 2) morality or precepts (*śīla*), 3) patience (*kṣānti*), 4) energy (*vīrya*), 5) meditation (*dhyāna*), and 6) wisdom (*prajñā*). *See also dhyāna;* bodhisattva; Buddhahood; *prajñā; śīla.*

parinirvāṇa: Complete nirvana, commonly used to describe the nirvana of the Buddha. *See also* nirvana.

patriarchs: The lineage of masters in the Chan/Zen school, beginning with the First Patriarch, Bodhidharma, an Indian monk who, according to tradition, established the Chan teaching in China in the fifth century. *See also* Bodhidharma; Zen school.

prajñā: Nondiscriminating or transcendental wisdom, the understanding of the emptiness (*śūnyatā*) of all phenomena in their actual realities. One of the *pāramitā*s of a bodhisattva. *See also* bodhisattva; *pāramitā*s; *śūnyatā.*

prātimokṣa: A part of the Vinaya which contains the disciplinary rules for monastics. *See also* Vinaya.

pratītyasamutpāda: A basic Buddhist doctrine that all phenomena come into being only in dependence on causes and conditions and exist only as long as those causes and conditions prevail. Also called the chain of causation.

pratyekabuddha ("solitary enlightened one"): One who has attained enlightenment through direct observation and understanding of the principle of dependent origination (*pratītyasamutpāda*) without the guidance of a teacher, and who does not teach others. One of the two Hinayana paths. *See also pratītyasamutpāda;* Hinayana.

precepts: Vows concerning moral conduct (*śīla*) taken by lay Buddhists and monastics. The five basic precepts are: 1) not to kill, 2) not to steal, 3) not to commit adultery, 4) not to lie, and 5) not to take intoxicants. In addition, there are two hundred fifty monastic rules for monks and three hundred forty-eight for nuns. *See also śīla.*

Pure Land: A blissful, transcendent Buddha land or realm presided over by Amitābha Buddha, in which believers in his salvific power will be reborn. Also the name of a major East Asian Buddhist school which emphasizes the practice of worshiping Amitābha. *See also* Amitābha.

reward body. *See* three bodies.

Śākyamuni: The historical Buddha who lived in India in the fifth century B.C.E., and whose life and teachings form the basis of Buddhism.

samādhi: A meditative state of concentration, focusing the mind on one point; also a transcendent mental state attained by the repeated practice of meditative concentration.

śāmatha and *vipaśyanā:* Meditative practices which entail calming the mind (*śāmatha*), stilling discursive thought, in order to prepare a stable base for the practice of meditative insight (*vipaśyanā*).

samsara. *See* birth and death.

sangha: The community of Buddhist monastics. Capitalized, it is part of the Three Treasures of Buddha, Dharma, and Sangha. *See also* Three Treasures.

Śāriputra: One of the original disciples of the Buddha, called "foremost of the wise."

śīla: Moral conduct or the practice of the precepts; one of the six *pāramitā*s. *See also pāramitā*s.

śīla, samādhi, and prajñā: The practices of morality, meditation, and wisdom, which are also part of the *pāramitā*s. *See also pāramitā*s.

Sōtō sect (Ch.: Caodong): One of the two main branches of Chan/Zen Buddhism, along with the Linji (Rinzai) sect; founded in China during the Tang dynasty and brought to Japan in the early thirteenth century by Eihei Dōgen. *See also* Linji sect; Zen school.

śramaṇa: Mendicant; another name for a Buddhist monk, originally applied to those who maintained an ascetic practice.

śrāmaṇera: A male Buddhist novice.

śrāvaka ("word-hearer"): Originally, a disciple of the Buddha, one of those who heard him expound the teachings directly; later, the term came to refer to one of the two kinds of Hinayana followers, along with *pratyekabuddha*s, to distinguish them from followers of the Mahayana. *See also* Hinayana; Mahayana; *pratyekabuddha*.

srota-āpanna ("stream-enterer"): The first of four stages of spiritual attainment in the Hinayana; one who has entered the stream of the Dharma. *See also* Hinayana.

śūnyatā: "Emptiness," a central and fundamental Buddhist teaching that all phenomena arise only in dependence on causes and conditions (*pratītyasamutpāda*) and thus are "empty" of self-existence or inherent nature; nothing, therefore, has "real," independent, permanent existence. *See also pratītyasamutpāda*.

Tathāgata: An epithet for a Buddha, meaning one who has gone to (*gata*) and come from (*āgata*) suchness (*tathā*), or ultimate reality.

three bodies: The three bodies in which a Buddha may appear—1) the Dharma body (*dharmakāya*), synonymous with ultimate truth or ultimate reality; 2) the merit body (*saṃbhogakāya*), which a Buddha receives as a reward for eons of practice and in order to expound the Dharma to bodhisattvas and others; and 3) the incarnate body (*nirmāṇakāya*), the physical form of a historical Buddha, such as Śākyamuni. *See also* Śākyamuni.

Three Treasures: The Buddha, the Dharma (the Buddhist teachings), and the Sangha (the community of Buddhist followers).

three vehicles: The Buddhist paths followed by *śrāvaka*s, *pratyekabuddha*s, and bodhisattvas respectively. *See also* bodhisattva; *pratyekabuddha*; *śrāvaka*.

Tripiṭaka: The three divisions or "baskets" (*piṭaka*s) of the Buddhist canon: the Sutras, discourses and teachings of the Buddha; the Vinaya, codes of monastic discipline; and the Abhidharma, scholastic treatises on the Buddhist teachings.

universal ruler (*cakravartin*): The ideal king, as conceived of in Indian philosophy. Also called wheel-turning king.

Vaipulya sutras: "Extensive" sutras, another name for the Mahayana sutras. *See also* Mahayana.

vinaya: Moral conduct or precepts, as practiced within the monastic community. Individual moral conduct is referred to as *śīla. See also śīla.*

Vinaya: Texts containing precepts and rules of conduct for monastics; along with the Abhidharma and the Sutras, one of the three divisions of the Tripiṭaka. *See also* Tripiṭaka.

Way (Ch.: Dao): The Buddhist path; the ultimate state of enlightenment, *bodhi. See also bodhi.*

yin and *yang*: A Chinese Daoist concept of the balance of negative and positive principles, or energies, of the universe.

zazen: Seated (*za*) meditation (*zen,* from *dhyāna*), the practice of sitting meditation emphasized in Zen Buddhism. *See also dhyāna;* Zen school.

Zen school: A major school of East Asian Buddhism that developed in China (where it was known as Chan) in the sixth and seventh centuries, and was subsequently transmitted to Japan. The Chan/Zen school evolved new approaches to religious practice based on a lineal succession of Buddhas and patriarchs through direct transmission from master to disciple, and emphasizes the practice of meditation (Skt.: *dhyāna;* Ch.: *chan;* Jp.: *zen*) as the best means to a direct experience of enlightenment (*bodhi*) and realization of one's own Buddha-nature. *See also bodhi;* Buddha-nature; patriarchs.

Bibliography

Contemporary Studies and Translations

Buswell, Robert E., Jr. *The Zen Monastic Experience*. Princeton, NJ: Princeton University Press, 1993.

Foulk, Griffith: "The 'Ch'an School' and Its Place in the Buddhist Monastic Tradition." Ph.D. dissertation, University of Michigan, 1987.

—. "Myth, Ritual, and Monastic Practice in Sung Ch'an Buddhism," in *Religion and Society in T'ang and Sung China*, Chapter 3, pp. 147–208. Patricia Buckley Ebrey and Peter N. Gregory, eds. Honolulu: University of Hawai'i Press, 1993.

Ichimura, Shohei, trans. and ed. *Zen Master Dogen's Monastic Regulations* (Institute Series 1). Daihonzan Eiheiji (Japan) and North American Institute of Zen and Buddhist Studies. Tokyo: Tōkō Printing Co., 1993.

—. *Zen Master Keizan's Monastic Regulations* (Institute Series 2). Daihonzan Sojiji (Japan) and North American Institute of Zen and Buddhist Studies. Tokyo: Tōkō Printing Co., 1994.

Kagamishima, Genryū, et al., eds. *The Monastic Regulations of the Zen Garden with Translation and Notes (Yakuchū Zennen Shingi)*. Tokyo: Sōtō Shū Shūmuchō, 1972.

Leighton, Taigen D., and Shohaku Okumura, trans. *Dōgen's Pure Standards for the Zen Community: A Translation of Eihei Shingi*. Albany, NY: State University of New York Press, 1995.

Miyata, Hishido, trans. "A Japanese Translation of the Ch'ih-hsiu Pai-chang Ch'ing-kuei (Choku-shu Hyakujo Shingi) with an introduction and subnotes." *Kokuyaku-issai-kyo,* Shoshubu 9, pp. 191–369.

Nishimura, Eshin. *The Thought and Method of Self-Enquiry (Koji-kyūmei-shisō-to-hōhō)*. Kyoto: Hōzōkan, 1993.

Yokoi, Yuhō, trans. *Regulations for Monastic Life by Eihei Dōgen—Eihei-Genzenji-Shingi*. Tokyo: Sankibō Buddhist Bookstore, 1973.

Bibliography

Editions of the Text (listed chronologically)

Baizhang Zen Monastic Regulations (Revised under the Yuan Imperial Edict) (*Chixiubaizhangqinggui*), eight fascicles. Compiled by Dongyang Dehui and edited by Xiaoyin Dasu, China, 1336.

Five Monasteries (Gozanban) edition, Japan, 1356; Chōroku reprint edition, 1462; Kannei edition, 1629; Manji edition, 1661.

Zhengtong Ming edition, China, 1442 (Ming Tripiṭaka 204, 1–2).

Kyōho Edition, Japan, 1720, edited by Mujaku Dōchū; Meiwa reprint edition, 1768.

Qing edition, China, 1871.

Taishō Shinshū Daizōkyō edition, Japan, 1924–36, Taishō Vol. 48, No. 2025.

Commentaries (listed chronologically)

Yangyi: "A Summary of the Baizhang Ancient (Original) Regulations" (*Baizhanggugui*) in his epilogue to the "Chapter of Baizhang," in "Codes of Monastic Regulations of the Zen Tradition," fascicle six of the *Jingde Records of the Transmission of the Flame of Dharma (Jingdechuandenglü)*, thirty fascicles, compiled by Yongan Daoyuan. China, 1004.

Unshō and Tōgen: *A Commentary on the Baizhang Monastic Regulations* (*Hyakujōshingishō*), twelve fascicles. Japan, 1462.

Mujaku Dōchū: *A Commentary on the Baizhang Monastic Regulations with Left-side Notes (Hyakujōshingisakei)*, twenty fascicles, Japan, 1718. A contemporary edition of this commentary was published as the eighth title in the Zen Studies Series (Zengaku Sōsho), two volumes (Kyoto: Chubun Shuppansha, 1977; second edition, 1986).

Yuanguang Yirun: *Record of Testimony and Meaning of the Baizhang Zen Monastic Regulations (Baizhangconglinqingguizhengyiji)*, nine fascicles. China, 1823.

Sources on Zen Monastic Regulations (listed chronologically)

Monastic Regulations of the Zen Garden (Chanyuanqingui), ten fascicles. Zhanglu Zongze, China, 1103. Also known as the *Chongning Monastic Regulations*.

Daily Monastic Regulations for Entering the Zen Community (Ruzhongriyongqinggui). Chongshou, China, 1209.

428

Eihei Zen Monastic Regulations (Eiheishingi), two fascicles. Eihei Dōgen, Japan, 1237–1249.

Monastic Regulations Indispensable for Entering the Zen Community (Ruzhongxujiqinggui). Author unknown, China, 1263.

Collected Essentials of the Revised Zen Monastic Regulations (Conglinjiaotingqingguizongyao), two fascicles. Weimian, China, 1274. Also known as the *Xianshun Regulations*.

Zen Monastic Regulations Ready for Use (Chanlinbeiyunqinggui), ten fascicles. Yixian, China, 1311. Also known as the *Zhida Regulations*.

Huanzhuan Monastic Regulations (Huanzhuanqinggui), one fascicle. Mingben, China, 1317.

Enichisan Ancient Monastic Regulations (Tōfukujishingi). Enni, Japan, 1318.

Keizan Monastic Regulations (Keizanshingi). Jōkin Keizan, Japan, 1324.

Daikan Monastic Regulations (Dajianqinggui), one fascicle. Qingzhuo Zhengdeng, Japan, 1332.

Monastic Regulations for Village Temples (Cunsiqinggui), two fascicles. Danliao Jihong, China, 1341.

Indispensable Knowledge on Zen Monastic Dual Order Offices (Conglinliangxuxuzhi), one fascicle. Feiyin Tongrong, China, 1639.

Ōbaku Monastic Regulations (Huangpiqinggui), one fascicle. Yinyuan Longqi, Japan, 1670.

Documents of Zen Monastic Symbols and Implements (Zenrin Shōkisen), twenty-one fascicles. Mujaku Dōchū, Japan, 1741. An encyclopedic volume on the codes, proceedings, systems, and various implements of Zen monastic temples; for monastic regulations, see the "List of Transmitted Codes of Regulations" (*Jushomokurokushingi*).

Texts Mentioned or Cited in the *Baizhang Zen Monastic Regulations*

Amitābha-dhāraṇī (Wuliangshouzhou; Immeasurable Life Dhāraṇī) in *Sukhāvatīvyūha (Amituojing; Smaller Sutra on Amitāyus)*, Taishō Vol. 12, No. 366, 348a29–348b18. English translation by Hisao Inagaki, in *The Three Pure Land Sutras*, Revised Second Edition (Numata Center, 2003). Also in the *Ritual of Meditative Practice and Worship Dedicated to the Tathāgata Amitāyus (Wuliangshourulaiguanxinggogyangyigui)*, Taishō Vol. 19, No. 930, 71b–71c.

An Exposition on the Model Zen Principles of Conduct (Guijingwen). Zongze, twelfth century.

A Record of the Inner Law Sent Home from the South Seas (Nanhaijigui-neifachuan), four fascicles. Yijing (635–713). Taishō Vol. 54, No. 2125. English translation by Li Rongxi, *Buddhist Monastic Traditions of Southern Asia* (Numata Center, 2000).

Book of Regulations (Qingguai). No specific book.

Brahmajāla-sūtra. (Fanwangjing), two fascicles. Translated by Kumārajīva. Taishō Vol. 24, No. 1484.

Chronicle of Jinling (Jinlingzhi). Probably refers to the *Zhida Jinlingxinzhi* by Zhang Xuan, fourteenth century.

Chronicle of the Wei Dynasty (Weilu, refers to the lost *Weishilu),* compiled by Shi Daoliu and completed by Zhu Daozu, ca. 419. See Paul Pelliot in *T'oung Pao* XXII, 1923, p. 102.

Collection of Middle-length Discourses (Madhyama Āgama; Pāli: *Majjhima Nikāya; Zhongahanjing),* sixty fascicles. Translated by Saṅghadeva, 397–398. Taishō Vol. 1, No. 26.

Collection of Records of the Patriarchal Courtyard (Zutingshiyuan), eight fascicles. Compiled by Muan Shanqing, 1098–1100.

Dhāraṇī for Changing Disaster to Fortune (Xiaozaijixiangtuoluoni), two fascicles. Translated by Amoghavajra. Taishō Vol. 19, No. 963.

Dhāraṇī for Inviting Great Rain (Dayunzhou), two fascicles. Translated by Amoghavajra. Taishō Vol. 19, Nos. 991–993.

Dhāraṇī for Rebirth in the Pure Land (Wangshengzhou). Translated by Kumārajīva. Appears at the end of the *Sukhāvatīvyūha (Amituojing; Smaller Sutra on Amitāyus),* Taishō Vol. 12, No. 366. Also in *Bayiqie-yezhanggenbendeshengjingtushenzhou,* translated by Guṇabhadra, Taishō Vol. 12, No. 368.

Diamond Sutra (Vajracchedikāprajñāpāramitā-sūtra; Dachengjingangban-ruoboluomijing), one fascicle. Translated by Kumārajīva. Taishō Vol. 8, No. 235. (Translations by Bodhiruci and Paramārtha also extant).

Ekottara Āgama. (Pāli: Aṅguttara Nikāya), fifty-one fascicles. Translated by Gautama Saṅghadeva. Taishō Vol. 2, No. 125.

Flower Ornament Sutra (Avataṃsaka-sūtra; Huayanjing), eighty fascicles. Taishō Vol. 10, No. 278.

Great Collection of Sutras of the Mahāsaṃghika School (Mahāsaṃnipāta-sūtra; Dajijing), sixty fascicles. Translated by Dharmakṣema, et al. Taishō Vol. 13, No. 397.

Great Perfection of Wisdom Sutra (Mahāprajñāpāramitā-sūtra; Banruo-poluomituojing), twenty-seven fascicles. Also simplified to *Perfection of Wisdom Sutra (Prajñāpāramitā-sūtra; Banruojing)*. Translated by Kumārajīva. Taishō Vol. 8, No. 223.

Great Tang Dynasty Record of the Western Regions (Datangxiyuji), twelve fascicles. Xuanzang. Taishō Vol. 51, No. 2087. English translation by Li Rongxi (Numata Center, 1996).

Lotus Sutra (Saddharmapuṇḍarīka-sūtra; Dachengmiaofalianhuajing), seven fascicles. Translated by Kumārajīva, 406. Taishō Vol. 9, No. 262. English translation by Tsugunari Kubo and Akira Yuyama (Numata Center, 1993).

Mahākāruṇikacitta-dhāraṇīs (Dabeixinuoluoni; Esoteric Prayer Verses Praising Great Compassion), one fascicle. Translated by Bhagavaddharma. Taishō Vol. 20, No. 1060.

Mahāsāṃghika-vinaya (Mohesengqilü), sixty fascicles. Translated by Buddhabhadra and Faxian. Taishō Vol. 22, No. 1425.

Manual of Practice and Realization (Xiuzhengyi), eighteen fascicles. Zongmi (780–841).

Mūlasarvāstivāda-vinaya (Genbenpinaiyea), fourteen fascicles. Translated by Yijing. Taishō Vol. 24, No. 1458.

Nirvana Sutra (Mahāparinirvāṇa-sūtra; Dabanniepanjing), forty fascicles. Translated by Dharmakṣema (385–433). Taishō Vol. 12, No. 374.

One Hundred and One Formal Acts of Resolution (Genbenbaiyijiemo), ten fascicles. Translated by Yijing. Taishō Vol. 24, No. 1453.

Outline of the History of Zen Practitioners (Sengshilüe), three fascicles. Zanning, 978–999. Taishō Vol. 54, No. 2126.

Pewter Staff Sutra (Dedaotichengxizhnagjing), one fascicle. Translator unknown. Taishō Vol. 17, No. 785.

Precious Mirror of Human and Heavenly Worlds (*Rentianbaojian*), two fascicles. Tanxiu, 1230.

Record of the Rising Splendor of the Tradition (*Zenghuiji*). Probably refers to the *Tiantai Sijiaoyijizhu zenghuiji* (*Tendai shikyō gishucchū zōkiki*) by Hōtan Sōshun (1654–1738).

Records on All Things Considered (*Gantongchuan*). Daoxuan (596–667).

Regulatory Rules of the Patriarchal Hall (*Zutanggangji*). Haihui Shouduan (1025–1071).

Sage Mandala Sutra (*Munimaṇḍala-sūtra**; *Mounimantuoluojing*). Perhaps lost.

Soapberry Tree Sutra (*Ariṣṭaka-sūtra**; *Muhuanzijing*), one fascicle. Translator unknown. Taishō Vol. 17, No. 786.

*Śūraṃgama-dhāraṇī*s and *Śūraṃgama-sūtra* (*Dafodingwanxingshoulengyenjing; Sutra on the Buddha's Omnipotent Valiant March*), ten fascicles. Taishō Vol. 19, No. 945.

Sutra of Golden Splendor (*Suvarṇaprabhāsottama-sūtra; Dachengjinguangmingjing*), four fascicles. Translated by Dharmakṣema (385–433). Taishō Vol. 16, No. 663.

Sutra of Perfect Enlightenment (*Yuanjuejing*), one fascicle. Taishō Vol. 17, No. 842. English translation by Peter N. Gregory, in the volume *Apocryphal Texts* (Numata Center, 2004).

Sutra of the Benevolent King (*Renwangbanruoboluomijing*). Taishō Vol. 8, No. 245.

Sutra of the Collection of the Original Acts of the Buddha (*Buddhacaritasaṃgraha; Fobenxingjijing*), sixty fascicles. Taishō Vol. 3, No. 190.

Sutra of the Garland of the Bodhisattva (*Yingluojing*), two fascicles. Translated by Jufonian. Taishō Vol. 24, No. 1485.

Sutra of the Heap of Jewels (*Mahāratnakūṭa-sūtra; Dabaojijing*), one hundred and twenty fascicles. Translated by Bodhiruci. Taishō Vol. 11, No. 310.

Sutra on the Bodhisattva Precepts (*Bodhisattva-prātimokṣa-sūtra; Pusajiejing*), one fascicle. Translated by Dharmakṣema. Taishō Vol. 24, No. 1500. This is the earliest translation of several similar texts, such as No. 1501, 1579, 1581, and 1583.

Tiantai Practice of Śamatha and Vipaśyanā (Tiantaizhiguanfamen), twenty fascicles. Zhiyi (538–597). Taishō Vol. 46, No. 1911.

Treatise on Vocal Sound (Shenglun) refers to the *Vyākaraṇa* or *Śabdavidyā-śāstra,* a treatise on Sanskrit sounds and structure.

Verses of Adoration for the Buddha. Not specific; perhaps refers to the *Vandana.*

Vimalakīrtinirdeśa-sūtra (Weimojiesuoshuojing), three fascicles. Translated by Kumārajīva. Taishō Vol. 14, No. 475. English translation by John R. McRae, *The Vimalakīrti Sutra* (Numata Center, 2004).

Vinaya in Five Divisions (Mahīśāsaka-vinaya; Wufenlü), thirty fascicles. Translated by Buddhajīva. Taishō Vol. 22, No. 1421.

Vinaya in Four Divisions (Dharmaguptaka-vinaya; Sifenlü), sixty fascicles. Translated by Buddhayaśas with Zhufonian, 405. Taishō Vol. 22, No. 1428.

Vinaya in Ten Chapters (Sarvāstivāda-vinaya; Shisonglü), sixty-one fascicles. Translated by Puṇyatara in collaboration with Kumārajīva. Taishō 23, No. 1435.

Index

A List of the Volumes of
the BDK English Tripiṭaka
(First Series)

Abbreviations

Ch.:	Chinese
Skt.:	Sanskrit
Jp.:	Japanese
Eng.:	Published title
T.:	Taishō Tripiṭaka

Vol. No.	Title		T. No.
1, 2	*Ch.*	Ch'ang-a-han-ching （長阿含經）	1
	Skt.	Dīrghāgama	
3–8	*Ch.*	Chung-a-han-ching （中阿含經）	26
	Skt.	Madhyamāgama	
9-I	*Ch.*	Ta-ch'eng-pên-shêng-hsin-ti-kuan-ching （大乘本生心地觀經）	159
9-II	*Ch.*	Fo-so-hsing-tsan （佛所行讚）	192
	Skt.	Buddhacarita	
10-I	*Ch.*	Tsa-pao-ts'ang-ching （雜寶藏經）	203
	Eng.	The Storehouse of Sundry Valuables	
10-II	*Ch.*	Fa-chü-p'i-yü-ching （法句譬喻經）	211
	Eng.	The Scriptural Text: Verses of the Doctrine, with Parables	
11-I	*Ch.*	Hsiao-p'in-pan-jo-po-lo-mi-ching （小品般若波羅蜜經）	227
	Skt.	Aṣṭasāhasrikā-prajñāpāramitā-sūtra	

Vol. No.		Title	T. No.
25-V	*Ch.*	Yü-lan-p'ên-ching （盂蘭盆經）	685
	Skt.	Ullambana-sūtra (?)	
	Eng.	The Ullambana Sutra	
		(In Apocryphal Scriptures)	
25-VI	*Ch.*	Ssŭ-shih-êrh-chang-ching （四十二章經）	784
	Eng.	The Sutra of Forty-two Sections	
		(In Apocryphal Scriptures)	
26-I	*Ch.*	Wei-mo-chieh-so-shuo-ching （維摩詰所説經）	475
	Skt.	Vimalakīrtinirdeśa-sūtra	
	Eng.	The Vimalakīrti Sutra	
26-II	*Ch.*	Yüeh-shang-nü-ching （月上女經）	480
	Skt.	Candrottarādārikāparipṛcchā	
26-III	*Ch.*	Tso-ch'an-san-mei-ching （坐禪三昧經）	614
26-IV	*Ch.*	Ta-mo-to-lo-ch'an-ching （達磨多羅禪經）	618
	Skt.	Yogācārabhūmi-sūtra (?)	
27	*Ch.*	Yüeh-têng-san-mei-ching （月燈三昧經）	639
	Skt.	Samādhirājacandrapradīpa-sūtra	
28	*Ch.*	Ju-lêng-ch'ieh-ching （入楞伽經）	671
	Skt.	Laṅkāvatāra-sūtra	
29-I	*Ch.*	Ta-fang-kuang-yüan-chio-hsiu-to-lo-liao-i-ching （大方廣圓覺修多羅了義經）	842
	Eng.	The Sutra of Perfect Enlightenment	
		(In Apocryphal Scriptures)	
29-II	*Ch.*	Su-hsi-ti-chieh-lo-ching （蘇悉地羯囉經）	893
	Skt.	Susiddhikaramahātantrasādhanopāyika-paṭala	
	Eng.	The Susiddhikara Sutra (In Two Esoteric Sutras)	
29-III	*Ch.*	Mo-têng-ch'ieh-ching （摩登伽經）	1300
	Skt.	Mātaṅgī-sūtra (?)	
30-I	*Ch.*	Ta-p'i-lu-chê-na-chêng-fo-shên-pien-chia-ch'ih-ching （大毘盧遮那成佛神變加持經）	848
	Skt.	Mahāvairocanābhisambodhivikurvitādhiṣṭhāna-vaipulyasūtrendrarāja-nāma-dharmaparyāya	
	Eng.	The Vairocanābhisaṃbodhi Sutra	

Vol. No.		Title	T. No.
63-IV	*Ch.*	Ta-ch'eng-ch'i-hsin-lun （大乘起信論）	1666
	Skt.	Mahāyānaśraddhotpāda-śāstra (?)	
	Eng.	The Awakening of Faith	
63-V	*Ch.*	Na-hsien-pi-ch'iu-ching （那先比丘經）	1670
	Pāli	Milindapañhā	
64	*Ch.*	Ta-ch'eng-chi-p'u-sa-hsüeh-lun （大乘集菩薩學論）	1636
	Skt.	Śikṣāsamuccaya	
65	*Ch.*	Shih-mo-ho-yen-lun （釋摩訶衍論）	1688
66-I	*Ch.*	Pan-jo-po-lo-mi-to-hsin-ching-yu-tsan （般若波羅蜜多心經幽賛）	1710
	Eng.	A Comprehensive Commentary on the Heart Sutra (Prajñāpāramitā-hṛdaya-sūtra)	
66-II	*Ch.*	Kuan-wu-liang-shou-fo-ching-shu （觀無量壽佛經疏）	1753
66-III	*Ch.*	San-lun-hsüan-i （三論玄義）	1852
66-IV	*Ch.*	Chao-lun （肇論）	1858
67, 68	*Ch.*	Miao-fa-lien-hua-ching-hsüan-i （妙法蓮華經玄義）	1716
69	*Ch.*	Ta-ch'eng-hsüan-lun （大乘玄論）	1853
70-I	*Ch.*	Hua-yen-i-ch'eng-chiao-i-fên-ch'i-chang （華嚴一乘教義分齊章）	1866
70-II	*Ch.*	Yüan-jên-lun （原人論）	1886
70-III	*Ch.*	Hsiu-hsi-chih-kuan-tso-ch'an-fa-yao （修習止觀坐禪法要）	1915
70-IV	*Ch.*	T'ien-t'ai-ssŭ-chiao-i （天台四教儀）	1931
71, 72	*Ch.*	Mo-ho-chih-kuan （摩訶止觀）	1911
73-I	*Ch.*	Kuo-ch'ing-pai-lu （國清百録）	1934
73-II	*Ch.*	Liu-tsu-ta-shih-fa-pao-t'an-ching （六祖大師法寶壇經）	2008
	Eng.	The Platform Sutra of the Sixth Patriarch	

Vol. No.		Title	T. No.
73-III	*Ch.*	Huang-po-shan-tuan-chi-ch'an-shih-ch'uan-hsin-fa-yao （黃檗山斷際禪師傳心法要）	2012A
	Eng.	Essentials of the Transmission of Mind (In Zen Texts)	
73-IV	*Ch.*	Yung-chia-chêng-tao-ko （永嘉證道歌）	2014
74-I	*Ch.*	Chên-chou-lin-chi-hui-chao-ch'an-shih-wu-lu （鎮州臨濟慧照禪師語録）	1985
	Eng.	The Recorded Sayings of Linji (In Three Chan Classics)	
74-II	*Ch.*	Wu-mên-kuan （無門關）	2005
	Eng.	Wumen's Gate (In Three Chan Classics)	
74-III	*Ch.*	Hsin-hsin-ming （信心銘）	2010
	Eng.	The Faith-Mind Maxim (In Three Chan Classics)	
74-IV	*Ch.*	Ch'ih-hsiu-pai-chang-ch'ing-kuei （勅修百丈清規）	2025
	Eng.	The Baizhang Zen Monastic Regulations	
75	*Ch.*	Fo-kuo-yüan-wu-ch'an-shih-pi-yen-lu （佛果圜悟禪師碧巖録）	2003
	Eng.	The Blue Cliff Record	
76-I	*Ch.*	I-pu-tsung-lun-lun （異部宗輪論）	2031
	Skt.	Samayabhedoparacanacakra	
	Eng.	The Cycle of the Formation of the Schismatic Doctrines	
76-II	*Ch.*	A-yü-wang-ching （阿育王經）	2043
	Skt.	Aśokarāja-sūtra (?)	
	Eng.	The Biographical Scripture of King Aśoka	
76-III	*Ch.*	Ma-ming-p'u-sa-ch'uan （馬鳴菩薩傳）	2046
	Eng.	The Life of Aśvaghoṣa Bodhisattva (In Lives of Great Monks and Nuns)	
76-IV	*Ch.*	Lung-shu-p'u-sa-ch'uan （龍樹菩薩傳）	2047
	Eng.	The Life of Nāgārjuna Bodhisattva (In Lives of Great Monks and Nuns)	

Vol. No.		Title	T. No.
76-V	*Ch.*	Pʻo-sou-pʻan-tou-fa-shih-chʻuan (婆藪槃豆法師傳)	2049
	Eng.	Biography of Dharma Master Vasubandhu (In Lives of Great Monks and Nuns)	
76-VI	*Ch.*	Pi-chʻiu-ni-chʻuan　(比丘尼傳)	2063
	Eng.	Biographies of Buddhist Nuns (In Lives of Great Monks and Nuns)	
76-VII	*Ch.*	Kao-sêng-fa-hsien-chʻuan　(高僧法顯傳)	2085
	Eng.	The Journey of the Eminent Monk Faxian (In Lives of Great Monks and Nuns)	
76-VIII	*Ch.*	Yu-fang-chi-chʼao: Tʻang-ta-ho-shang-tung chêng-chʻuan (遊方記抄: 唐大和上東征傳)	2089-(7)
77	*Ch.*	Ta-tʻang-ta-tzʻŭ-ên-ssŭ-san-tsʻang-fa-shih-chʻuan　(大唐大慈恩寺三藏法師傳)	2053
	Eng.	A Biography of the Tripiṭaka Master of the Great Ciʼen Monastery of the Great Tang Dynasty	
78	*Ch.*	Kao-sêng-chʻuan　(高僧傳)	2059
79	*Ch.*	Ta-tʻang-hsi-yü-chi　(大唐西域記)	2087
	Eng.	The Great Tang Dynasty Record of the Western Regions	
80	*Ch.*	Hung-ming-chi　(弘明集)	2102
81–92	*Ch.*	Fa-yüan-chu-lin　(法苑珠林)	2122
93-I	*Ch.*	Nan-hai-chi-kuei-nei-fa-chʻuan (南海寄歸内法傳)	2125
	Eng.	Buddhist Monastic Traditions of Southern Asia	
93-II	*Ch.*	Fan-yü-tsa-ming　(梵語雑名)	2135
94-I	*Jp.*	Shō-man-gyō-gi-sho　(勝鬘經義疏)	2185
94-II	*Jp.*	Yui-ma-kyō-gi-sho　(維摩經義疏)	2186
95	*Jp.*	Hok-ke-gi-sho　(法華義疏)	2187
96-I	*Jp.*	Han-nya-shin-gyō-hi-ken　(般若心經秘鍵)	2203

Vol. No.		Title	T. No.
96-II	*Jp.*	Dai-jō-hos-sō-ken-jin-shō　(大乘法相研神章)	2309
96-III	*Jp.*	Kan-jin-kaku-mu-shō　(觀心覺夢鈔)	2312
97-I	*Jp.*	Ris-shū-kō-yō　(律宗綱要)	2348
	Eng.	The Essentials of the Vinaya Tradition	
97-II	*Jp.*	Ten-dai-hok-ke-shū-gi-shū　(天台法華宗義集)	2366
	Eng.	The Collected Teachings of the Tendai Lotus School	
97-III	*Jp.*	Ken-kai-ron　(顯戒論)	2376
97-IV	*Jp.*	San-ge-gaku-shō-shiki　(山家學生式)	2377
98-I	*Jp.*	Hi-zō-hō-yaku　(秘藏寶鑰)	2426
	Eng.	The Precious Key to the Secret Treasury (In Shingon Texts)	
98-II	*Jp.*	Ben-ken-mitsu-ni-kyō-ron　(辨顯密二教論)	2427
	Eng.	On the Differences between the Exoteric and Esoteric Teachings (In Shingon Texts)	
98-III	*Jp.*	Soku-shin-jō-butsu-gi　(即身成佛義)	2428
	Eng.	The Meaning of Becoming a Buddha in This Very Body (In Shingon Texts)	
98-IV	*Jp.*	Shō-ji-jis-sō-gi　(聲字實相義)	2429
	Eng.	The Meanings of Sound, Sign, and Reality (In Shingon Texts)	
98-V	*Jp.*	Un-ji-gi　(吽字義)	2430
	Eng.	The Meanings of the Word Hūṃ (In Shingon Texts)	
98-VI	*Jp.*	Go-rin-ku-ji-myō-hi-mitsu-shaku (五輪九字明秘密釋)	2514
	Eng.	The Illuminating Secret Commentary on the Five Cakras and the Nine Syllables (In Shingon Texts)	
98-VII	*Jp.*	Mitsu-gon-in-hotsu-ro-san-ge-mon (密嚴院發露懺悔文)	2527
	Eng.	The Mitsugonin Confession (In Shingon Texts)	